Charles James Fox

1 Charles James Fox *Portrait by K. A. Hickel*

John W. Derry

Lecturer in History,
University of Newcastle upon Tyne

Charles James Fox

B. T. Batsford Ltd, London

First published 1972
© John W. Derry

Text printed in Great Britain by
Northumberland Press Ltd, Gateshead
Plates printed and book bound by
Richard Clay (The Chaucer Press) Ltd,
Bungay, Suffolk
for the publishers B. T. Batsford Ltd
4 Fitzhardinge Street, London W1

ISBNO 7134 1118 x

Contents

Illustrations

*The Author and Publishers wish to thank the following for permission
to reproduce the illustrations: the Trustees of the British Museum for
figs 2, 3, 12, 13 and 15-17; the National Gallery for fig 9; the National
Portrait Gallery for the jacket illustration and figs 1, 5-8, 10, 11 and 14;
the Royal Society for fig 4.*

Preface

In writing this study of Charles James Fox, I have sought to direct
attention as much as possible to what Fox himself said, wrote and did. In
this way I have tried to keep him at the centre of the picture, without
submerging him in too great a mass of general background or of detail.
I have not attempted to give a complete narrative of Fox's life and times;
rather I have presented an interpretation which sets him firmly in the
context of eighteenth-century politics, and which seeks to explain his
behaviour as the response of an able, ambitious and frequently unscrupulous politician to the challenges presented by the constitutional framework
in which he reached maturity and which, in some respects, he so
desperately wished to change. I have, therefore, deliberately limited the
amount of personal, domestic, and circumstantial detail provided for the
reader, preferring to concentrate on the principal themes of Fox's career
as a parliamentarian. If I have been more critical than many biographers
I hope I have not been guilty of mere denigration. But it is time that Fox
was portrayed for what he was, and not for what later apologists wanted
him to be. I do not see that his stature is necessarily diminished by placing
him in context, or by recognising that contemporary assessments of him
were not so far from the truth at various stages of his career.

I should like to thank the staff of the Students' Room at the British
Museum for the courtesy and efficiency which they showed to me during
my visits, over a period of years, to work on the Fox Papers and the
Holland House Papers. My debt to the many scholars who have worked
on the late eighteenth century will be obvious to the informed reader;
without the detailed researches which have been so marked a feature of
work on the eighteenth century in recent years it would have been impossible to have attempted a work of this nature. I have, nevertheless,
sought to keep references to a minimum, since I believe that the reader
is often allergic to foot and note disease.

John W. Derry

I *The Young Tory*

Charles Fox was born for politics and for power. His family had been active in public life for a century, and from his earliest years politics were a consuming passion. When he came of age everything pointed to a political career. It was as inevitable as Eton and Oxford and the Grand Tour; as exciting as games of chance and as intoxicating as any of the sensual pleasures which had so thrilled his precocious adolescence.

His father, Henry Fox, was one of the most able, and one of the most notorious, of eighteenth-century political managers, a man of consummate ability, eager ambition and worldly cynicism. When Charles James, his third and favourite son, was born, Henry Fox was secretary at war; he was later to win an unenviable reputation as paymaster-general of the forces. Although the post traditionally allowed its holder to pocket the proceeds from the skilful award of contracts, Henry Fox was commonly believed to have gone far beyond the generous limits tolerated by contemporary practice in exploiting public service for private gain. He was described as the defaulter of public millions, and in later life Charles Fox's political opponents made political capital out of the source of the wealth which his father had accumulated, and which he squandered so profusely. While Henry Fox was often denounced as an unscrupulous profiteer, his willingness to supervise the passage of the peace of Paris through the house of commons in 1763 earned him the even more dubious reputation of a political turncoat, a cynic capable of any deception and devoid of any loyalty except to furthering his own career. Much of the criticism was unfair and exaggerated. Fox saw himself as performing a necessary, if not particularly enjoyable, public duty. His attitude towards the practice of politics was functional not idealistic, and, as it fell out, his worldly rewards were disappointing. He had hoped for a viscounty; he was raised to the lords merely as Baron Holland. He could be forgiven for thinking that George III and Bute lacked generosity, and that his services, which had been performed at the cost of so much opprobrium, were lightly valued.

But with such a father it was hardly surprising that Charles Fox entered politics as much for personal advantage as public service, and with few illusions about the way in which the game was played.

Like many political cynics Henry Fox was a sentimentalist at heart. Where his own children were concerned he was indulgent to the point of excess, while his elopement with Lady Caroline Lennox in 1744 had itself demonstrated the self-will, passion, and disregard for convention which were so fundamental to his character. He was a devoted and kindly husband, and whatever taunts were heaped upon him by his opponents he was always able to take refuge within the warmth and understanding of his family. His wife was the daughter of the duke of Richmond, and a great-granddaughter of Charles II. Historians have sometimes traced a poignant irony in the fact that Charles James Fox, who eventually became the greatest critic of the influence of the crown and the avowed friend of the French revolution, was himself descended from the Stuarts and the Bourbons.

Loyalty to the crown had been marked among members of the Fox family during the troubles of the seventeenth century. Fox's grandfather, Sir Stephen Fox, had faithfully served Charles II, both when that prince was an impoverished exile and when he had happily come into his own again. As a youth Stephen Fox had entered the service of the Percys; he took part in the campaign which ended in defeat and flight at Worcester. Though Charles Fox's enemies claimed that his grandfather's management of Charles II's hounds and horses meant that he was descended from a stableboy, it was as a financial adviser that Sir Stephen had made his mark and his fortune. He served as paymaster-general and then as a lord commissioner of the treasury, and rich as he became it was nevertheless possible for John Evelyn to marvel at the fact that his wealth was honestly got, 'which is next to a miracle'. But Sir Stephen remembered the origins of his wealth, contributing generously to the founding of Chelsea Hospital.

But his sons by his first wife were all childless and as a vigorous and lusty widower of seventy-six Sir Stephen married again. His second wife, who outlived him by only three years, bore him four children. Sir Stephen died in 1716; he had remained active in business until the accession of Anne. Though he refused to play any active part against James II, and though the anniversary of the execution of Charles I (which he had witnessed as a young man) was always commemorated in his household, Sir Stephen came to terms with the political establishment after the revolution of 1688. He had laid the foundations of his family's fortune, and his tenure of the paymastership had established a precedent worthy of imitation. His elder son by his second wife, Stephen, eventually became earl of Ilchester; Henry Fox, who entered politics relatively late at the age of thirty after a dissolute youth and an early manhood distinguished more by a taste for pleasure than political ambition, began his public career as dutiful supporter of Robert Walpole. Like his master he believed that every man had his price, not least himself.

Henry Fox's second surviving son, Charles James, was born on 24 January 1749 in Conduit Street in London. At first his father was apprehensive, but though the child was weakly he consoled himself with the thought that he seemed likely to live. Henry Fox's anxiety was understandable. Infant mortality was a constant accompaniment to family life in the eighteenth century. Stephen, his first son, was delicate, and afflicted with St Vitus' dance, while Henry Charles, his second son, had survived for only two months. Once the risks of birth were surmounted smallpox, measles, whooping cough, pneumonia, and rickets were the scourges of the nursery. However severely children were disciplined, however callously they were exploited by parents who saw in them a valuable insurance against old age or a potential source of profit, their survival to adolescence was never taken for granted even in the wealthiest of households. Because parents were impatient for their children to leave the perils of childhood behind them they often treated them as if they were already adults, sometimes hastening them into contracting premature marriages which were thought desirable for the family. Only a later and more romantic age invested childhood with sentiment and marriage with glamour, suggesting that parents existed for the welfare and benefit of their children, rather than seeing children as a means of ensuring security in old age or infirmity and an insurance against poverty.

Henry Fox, however, was so benevolent a father as to become notorious for the profligacy with which he indulged his children. The stories which have so often been told about Charles Fox's childhood are evidence of the reputation which his father's ideas on the upbringing of children soon earned him. Many of the tales are second-hand and difficult to trace to any reliable source. Some may well be spurious. But however questionable their factual accuracy may be they testify to what most of his contemporaries chose to believe about the way in which Henry Fox brought up his sons. Even if the traditional anecdotes are no more than the most outrageous examples of Henry Fox's casual and affectionate indulgence they typify the general tenor of his performance of his duties as a parent.

Possibly Henry Fox's experience of the world explained his determination to ensure that his sons had a happy boyhood. He was aware of what might be waiting for Charles when he grew up. 'Let nothing be done to break his spirit,' he was fond of saying, 'the world will do that business fast enough.' It was natural therefore, for Charles to be allowed to smash his father's watch, 'because if you must I suppose you must,' or for a wall to be rebuilt in order to keep a promise which had been made to Charles that he would be able to enjoy the spectacle of its destruction, though in the latter case it was arguable that it was a good thing for the boy to be taught that promises, however lightly given, should be honoured. Much more dubious is the story of Charles urinating on a pig as it was being roasted in the kitchen: every instance of childish folly or parental slackness was avidly touched up and repeated. It was even claimed that Henry Fox had to redraft governmental despatches because Charles had wilfully thrown the first copies into the fire. Almost anything was deemed credible, and active imaginations provided everything that gossip demanded.

But there was no doubt of the delight which Henry Fox took in Charles's company. When Charles was only three years old his father confessed that it was much more pleasant to dine with him than to do business: 'I grow immoderately fond of him.' By the time Charles was five his father proudly described him as 'very well, very pert, very argumentative'. Even as a boy Charles exercised that charm to which contemporaries succumbed so often and which historians have found so difficult to recapture or to explain. He was 'all life, spirit, motion, and good humour.' When it suited him he submitted to the nauseous indignity of taking physic with bright-eyed cheerfulness. When his mother complained of his 'passionate' nature his father replied, 'He is a very sensible little boy and will learn to curb himself.'

There is ample evidence of the deep affection and regard which Charles Fox felt towards both his parents. Not even the turmoils of adolescence disturbed the ties of feeling which bound them together. When Fox was seventeen his cousin, Lady Sarah Lennox (with whom George III was head over heels in love as a young man) commented on the amiableness of his character; it was natural, she thought, for him to be loving and thoughtful: 'You cannot imagine the comfort he is to both his father and mother, and his constant attention to them is really beyond what I can describe.'

His education began at home, but when he found out his mother in a mistake in Roman history he was sent to school at Wandsworth. His master there was a Monsieur Pampelonne, and his training may possibly be responsible for the excellence of Charles's French accent, which impressed his friends so amazingly. At the age of eight he was writing to his brother Stephen, then at Eton:

I hope you are as well as I am. Mr and Mrs Farmer send their best respects, and hope to see you in a short time settled at Holland House. Harry sends his love and a kiss. I chose to come to school before the Fitzgeralds, and I am very glad of it for I don't loose my time as they do and I see my mama as often and oftener than they do, for I come home every Saturday and I shall be able to go to Eton before them. Pray send Fitzgerald's cricket bat as soon as you can.[1]

He retained his fondness for cricket to the end of his life, although he was never a skilful practitioner of the game, his impetuosity and bulk often getting him run out.

After a year at Wandsworth Charles went to Eton in June 1758. His father saw him off with mixed feelings. He hated to part with his favourite child, and he confided in his wife that whenever she thought London or Holland House better for Charles than Eton he would like it. 'There is no comparison', he continued, 'to be made between health and learning; besides that, I am sure enough for him of the latter; I wish to God I were so of the former.' Later Chatham, who had hated Eton himself and who believed that no boy who was there was not cowed for life, kept his own favourite son William, a more delicate child than Charles Fox, at home. But by that time Chatham was also convinced that the decline of English youth dated from the years Charles Fox spent at Eton. Political antipathies may here have distorted parental judgment, though there seems to have been little doubt in Chatham's mind that Charles Fox had initiated his companions into dissipations beyond their years. On two occasions he was taken from school to travel on the continent, where he was introduced to the wider world of politics, high fashion, and gambling. Both Chatham and Shelburne were of the opinion that Henry Fox educated his children with a total disregard for morality and a laxity which was tantamount to vulgar self-indulgence. Even as sympathetic an historian as Lord John Russell could not refrain from lamenting the nature and effects of Charles Fox's education and upbringing:

That this education enabled Mr Fox to read the Greek and Latin poets with facility, to make himself familiar with French and Italian literature, and to become very early a man of the world, cannot be disputed. But on the other hand it led to desultory habits of study, and what was much worse, to a fondness for the pleasures of unbridled youth, which in after life marred the effect of his brilliant talents, and prevented him acquiring the entire confidence of the moral and sober part of the nation.[2]

But this is possibly to endow the eighteenth century with Victorian opinions about the importance of education. Any lack of confidence which contemporaries showed towards Fox as a politician stemmed from his behaviour as an adult, not the stories which had gathered about his boyhood.

Henry Fox, in any case, would merely have wondered precisely what his son had to gain from the confidence of 'the moral and sober part of the nation'. His brilliance was undoubted. He was proficient in ancient and modern languages, and his enthusiasm for Homer, Theocritus, Virgil, Horace, Demosthenes, and Cicero, was to last a lifetime. He was popular with both his schoolmasters and his contemporaries. Nor was Charles called away from school only to attend the gambling table. He was taken to the house of commons to see and hear the debates and to acquire an early familiarity with the place in which it was assumed that he would cut a fine figure. Much of his education was a preparation for politics. The Greek and Latin classes were a training in rhetoric. Literature was the handmaid of oratory. His headmaster, Dr Barnard, was commonly regarded as one of the greatest elocutionists of his day, and Charles Fox himself referred to him as the English Quintilian. By eighteenth-century standards Barnard's views on discipline were liberal. He believed in encouraging originality among boys, even within the formal confines of Latin verse composition. He had been sorry to lose Fox on the first of his visits to Paris with his father. Like his pupil he enjoyed amateur dramatics, a branch of entertainment which might be regarded as a useful preliminary to the oratorical and emotional flourishes so necessary in parliamentary debate. Since the contrast between the education given to Charles Fox and William Pitt is often stressed it is worth noting that they both had a rigorous training in classical languages and literature, and that they both practised and enjoyed the popular vogue for private theatricals.

In May 1763 Lord Holland took Charles to Paris for four months. Another visit took place a year later. Lord Holland's conduct on these occasions is legendary and notorious; it is also perplexing. He is usually seen as encompassing not only his son's pleasure but his moral downfall. Not content with providing Charles with the means of enjoyment he seemed intent on corrupting him. The pleasures of gambling and of sex were allegedly arranged for the son by the doting father, who combined the professions of the bookmaker and pimp. Possibly historians have both exaggerated and misunderstood Holland's role. He wanted Charles to enjoy himself and he could hardly deny him the pleasures of games of chance. If the boy wanted to sow his wild oats the father was probably resigned to this as the inevitable accompaniment of growing up. Money was not to be hoarded but spent, and Holland's faults may have been those of carelessness or misjudgment, rather than of premeditated corruption. Charles was headstrong, feckless, wilful. He was an adolescent boy with powerful instincts. Throughout his life he had been taught to indulge his whims, not to control them. If Lord Holland thought that a few youthful indiscretions would teach Charles self-control and self-discipline he was wrong. But he found youthful follies amusing, and unlike many parents he did not forget the errors of his own youth. Perhaps he was reliving the excitements of his own debaucheries by observing those of his son with a shrewd and experienced sympathy. He was particularly entertained by Charles' extravagances in dress (which in itself would seem innocent enough). Others might be shocked at the sight of Charles decked out in red high-heels, Parisian velvet, and blue hair-powder, but Lord Holland knew that it would be a passing phase and that soon Charles would be a perfect schoolboy again. It would seem, however, that Charles' excesses on his return to Eton earned him at least one flogging.

But then Eton was dull after Paris. After imagining himself a man it was hard for Charles to remember that he was a boy. He had to force himself to settle down again to the routine of school life. Yet, frustrated as he was, he was capable of appreciating the value of carrying on with the more formal part of his education. He even pleaded the case for staying on at Eton with his father:

> Dr Barnard thanked me for his snuff box, and said it was very much against his interest to advise me to be absent in the summer rather than now, as that means the School lose so great an ornament at Election speeches. I cannot help saying that I find Eton more disagreeable than I had imagined: for which reason I think I am determined not to go to Paris at Christmas. My mother will not be sorry to hear this. ... I am so fully convinced of the use of being at Eton that I am afraid of running the risk of not returning. I am resolved to stay there until Christmas twelve month: by this you may see that the petit maitre de Paris is converted into an Oxford pedant. I am satisfied that you will not disapprove of this resolution, and I hope, therefore, you will not endeavour to dissuade me from it, as I am convinced you will willingly consent to spend six weeks less agreeably to make me a much better scholar than I should otherwise be, which is a glory you know I very much desire.[3]

From this it would seem that Charles deserved the tribute paid to him in 1764 by his father: that he had 'good sense, good nature, and as many good and amiable qualities as ever met in any one's composition'.

In October 1764 Charles went up to Hertford College, Oxford. His tutor was Dr Newcombe, who eventually became archbishop of Armagh, and who showed considerable tact in all his dealings with Fox. Charles enjoyed himself at Oxford, and he came to love the place warmly and affectionately. In February 1765 he told his friend George Macartney that he had not expected life at Oxford to be so pleasant. 'I really think,' he wrote, 'to a man who reads a great deal there cannot be a more agreeable place.' Since the picture of Charles Fox as the epitome of dissipated youth is so familiar it is worth remembering that he worked hard at Oxford. He gambled as well, it is true, but at times he worked nine or ten hours a day, and, as Sir George Otto Trevelyan pointed out many years ago, 'he read as hard as any young Englishman will ever read for reading's sake'. Possibly it was at Oxford that he first met Edmund Burke, who was not in the habit of seeking out rakes or young gentlemen of pleasure. Both of Charles's parents believed that he was working hard at Oxford and Dr Newcombe shared their opinion. When Fox took time off to accompany his parents to the continent his tutor thought he was wise to have a change of scene. 'Application like yours,' he assured his pupil, 'requires some intermission, and you are the only person with whom I have ever had connexion to whom I could say this. I expect that you will return with much keenness for Greek and for lines and angles ... You need not, therefore, interrupt your amusements by severe studies, for it is wholly unnecessary to take a step onwards without you, and therefore we shall stop until we have the pleasure of your company. All your acquaintances here, which I know, are well, but not much happier for your absence.'[4] In later life Fox was fond of producing Newcombe's letter to confound those who claimed that he had done nothing but idle his time away at Oxford. Since so much of his time was spent in reading the classics, as well as exploring Elizabethan and Jacobean drama, which was something of an adventure in those days, it is interesting to find that he devoted a good deal of effort to his mathematical studies, which he liked 'vastly'. Had his political career been conventionally successful more attention might have been paid to the evidence which showed that he was more than a young man about town. As it was the contrast between Fox and Pitt as the bad and good apprentices was quickly assimilated into most people's thinking, with the more sensational aspects of Fox's youth attracting a disproportionate share of attention in consequence. It was tempting to trace the frustrations of maturity back to the excesses of youth. But Fox was able to exert himself intellectually as well as giving vent to all the extravagances of pleasure. In the familiar adage Fox both worked hard and played hard, and no picture of his Oxford days would be just if it ignored one or other of these attributes.

But however much he liked Oxford his undergraduate days were soon over. In 1766 he went down, and accompanied his parents on a trip to France and Italy. It was from Florence that he wrote to Macartney in August 1767, summing up his feelings about his Oxford years, and telling his friend of his current enthusiasm for the Italian language. Curiously he claimed to have lost interest in politics, perhaps because most English news was unintelligible by the time it reached Italy. His reflections upon his experiences at Oxford showed how mixed his attitudes and reactions were:

> I employed almost my whole time at Oxford in the mathematical and classical knowledge, but more particularly in the latter, so that I understand Latin and Greek tolerably well. I am totally ignorant in every part of useful knowledge. I am more convinced every day how little advantage there is in being what at school and the university is called a good scholar: one receives a good deal of amusement from it, but that is all. At present I read nothing but Italian, which I am immoderately fond of, particularly of the poetry. You, who understand Italian so well yourself, will not at all wonder at this. As to French, I am far from being so thorough a master of it as I could wish, but I know so much of it that I could perfect myself in it at any time with very little trouble, especially if I pass three or four months in France. . . .[5]

He went on to explain his own natural idleness—'of which Lady Holland will tell you wonders. Indeed I am afraid it will in the end get the better of what little ambition I have, and that I never shall be anything but a lounging fellow.'

He anticipated that Macartney would make a brilliant debut in the house of commons; he was less certain of his own future. He was going through a period of self-questioning. This may have been the consequence of the continental tour. It had been physically exhausting and mentally tiring. Lyons, Marseilles, Naples, Turin, Genoa, Paris, Nice, Florence, and Rome had all followed each other in a wild whirl of excitement and pleasure. Besides the cruder pleasures the holiday was the occasion for cultural gourmandising of exceptional voracity. Paintings, sculptures, ruins, castles, palaces, and natural scenery were gaped at, catalogued, criticised and where appropriate acquired. There was even the thrill of meeting Voltaire at Ferney. Nor were the pleasures of the tour without variety, even if a price had to be paid for them. On 22 September 1767 he told Fitzpatrick, 'I have had one pox and one clap this summer. I believe I am the most unlucky rascal in the universe.'[6] But his appetite for sex was undiminished by his infection. On 23 January 1768 he wrote to Fitzpatrick from Nice, complaining of the disappointments of the town: 'We live at a mile's distance from the town of Nice which is perhaps the dullest town in the world, and what is a terrible thing there are no whores. I am now quite well; my poxes and claps have weakened me a good deal, but by means of the cold bath I recover apace. Je travaille toujours le matin, and in the evening read, lounge, play at chess, at cards, and talk.'[7] Even when referring to amateur theatricals a certain gloom crept into his letters; he expressed dissatisfaction with his last performance, 'I fell very short of my own expectations.' But despite his illnesses, and the exhaustion brought about by his sexual exertions, his spirit was not entirely broken. The run of pleasure was ceasing to satisfy him. The house of commons beckoned. In May 1768, while he was still under age, Charles Fox was returned in his absence for Midhurst in Sussex, and in November he took his seat.

It was natural for a young man of Fox's background to enter the house of commons at the earliest opportunity. Even for those who had little political ambition membership of the commons was an indispensable sign of prestige and social status. To be out of parliament was to be 'out of the world' and the majority of MPs prided themselves on being members of the most dignified and exclusive club in London. Men entered politics as much to establish their claim to social recognition as to play any part in government. For many backbenchers attendance at parliamentary debates was a wearisome formality. They cared little for the endless ebb and flow of debate. Only when a change of government seemed in the offing did they shoulder the burden of the parliamentary duties instead of enjoying the pleasures of their country seats. Though no government could survive once it had antagonised the country gentlemen it would be false to assume that the majority of eighteenth-century MPs eagerly followed the subtleties of classical oratory. Despite the plaudits of posterity Burke's speeches emptied the house instead of thrilling it. Something less intellectual and homely was preferred, especially by the country squires. However distinguished the great orators of the eighteenth century were they were exceptional men, not typical members of parliament. Often their most brilliant speeches were delivered to a house that was less than half full.

When Charles Fox took his seat the total membership of the house of commons numbered 558. These members represented the counties and those boroughs whose charters conceded the privilege of returning members of parliament, as well as two members for each of the English universities. Two 'knights of the shire' made up each of the counties' representation, whatever the difference in size or in population. The extremes were typified by Yorkshire with 15,000 electors and Rutland with just over 600. The franchise in the counties had not changed since the reign of Henry VI when the forty-shilling freeholders were invested with the privilege of choosing representatives in parliament. By Charles Fox's time this had become a fairly liberal qualification, though the system operated in an unpredictable manner.

In the boroughs the situation was confusing. A wide variety of franchises was in operation. Every attempt at overall categorisation runs the risk of misrepresentation, for every borough charter defined the franchise qualification for each borough in turn. Broadly speaking there were five types of borough franchise: those in which the vote was limited to members of the corporation; those in which the freemen had the vote; those in which everyone who paid local rates and taxes and who was not in receipt of alms voted; those in which the owners or occupiers of certain properties were enfranchised; and a small number of boroughs in which something much more like a democratic franchise was effective. This confused pattern of enfranchisement means that it is difficult to speak of the electorate in national terms in the eighteenth century. Local issues and regional loyalties counted for more than apparently national issues. Certainly eighteenth-century elections had no equivalent to the national swing so popular with the modern psephologist. Since voting was spread over as many as forty days, and since the poll took place on different days in different places, the pattern of voting was often very idiosyncratic in various areas and in particular constituencies. And especially in those boroughs where the number of electors was small the influence of dominant families or of single patrons was paramount. The burgage boroughs supplied most of the notoriously pocket or rotten boroughs, and yet there was little sense of resentment or injustice about the system.

Traditionally the right to vote was a privilege, invested in those classes of property owners who were thought to embody the lasting interests within the community. Parliamentary representation was as much the consequence of governmental and royal convenience as the outcome of any theory of politics. Most eighteenth-century theories of representation were explanations or justifications of a received pattern of behaviour; they were not abstract or speculative exercises in political philosophy. The theory was related to a familiar and trusted way of doing things; the pattern of representation was far more complex than the application of any single theory. Charles Fox was brought up in a world which thought of the representation of interests, not the rights of individuals. Men argued that the diversity of the traditional system was its greatest virtue. Every interest which contributed to the wellbeing of the community was represented in parliament. Politics were concerned, not with the transient differences of opinion which fluctuated with changing circumstances, but with the abiding interests which were the foundation of the nation's life. Since the levying of taxes was the governmental activity which most obviously impinged on the majority of the king's subjects, it was understandable that taxation should be so closely associated with representation and that those who paid taxes should feel particularly strongly about the way in which the interests of property were safeguarded. Property was also the simplest means of assessing that a man possessed at least a modicum of education and the ability to think about issues which lay beyond his immediate economic advantage. The house of commons was important, therefore, because all national interests were represented in it: the land, commerce, the professions, the armed forces, even (in eighteenth-century terms) the civil service and the church (the latter in the house of lords). In a pre-industrial age it was natural for men to assume that the predominance of the landed interest was the surest means of protecting the national interest and ensuring the nation's prosperity. It was possible to argue that, whatever the vagaries of the franchise, there was not a blade of grass which was unrepresented in the house of commons.

Associated with the representation of interests was the theory of virtual representation. This assumed that those who did not personally possess the vote, but who had similar interests with those who did, would identify themselves with the representative system because they could feel that their interests were taken into account, even if they did not themselves directly choose their representatives. This attitude confirms the subordinate status afforded to opinion in eighteenth-century constitutional practice. For most of Fox's lifetime the theory of virtual representation was used to defend the traditional pattern of representation from radical criticism. It assumed a union of hearts between those who had the vote, and those who did not, and for this reason it was particularly attractive to Burke. Later, at the time of the first reform act, the theory of virtual representation was invoked by the whig reformers to justify the enfranchisement of new forms of property and the admission of new classes within the ranks of the political nation.

Personality was of unique importance in eighteenth-century politics; personal relationships were more important than class relationships, and within the political community family ties were often more important than generalised social attitudes. Just as the constitutional theory assumed a relationship between those who had the vote and those who did not, so it was accepted that some forms of influence were legitimate and others illegitimate. Providing a landlord and his tenants were bound together by ties which transcended electoral convenience it was argued that they possessed a common interest in securing the welfare of the farming community. It was inevitable that a landlord should take a personal interest in how his tenants voted, but this did not necessarily imply intimidation. Their common interest often meant that they habitually and naturally preferred the same candidate, the man who by background and temperament seemed most likely to procure the prosperity of the landed classes. But should anyone seek to win votes by the offer of crude bribes or by the threat of personal violence, without having a concern for the prosperity of the county or borough, this type of behaviour, though widely practised, was stigmatised as illegitimate by contemporary theorists. It was seen as a concession to human weakness or political expediency, and though it might be tolerated it could hardly be defended.

The practice of influence in eighteenth-century elections was a more complex and more subtle affair than the familiar terminology of bribery and corruption would suggest. There was both violence and brutality; the voteless mob might terrify electors into casting their votes for the most popular candidate (though for some the fact that the populace could influence the outcome of an election was a defence of the traditional practice of open voting); individual electors might be assaulted, or cooped up in a drunken stupor until the poll was over; others might be waylaid or impersonated. But far more common than any of these was the uncontested return. Dominant and rival families found it to their mutual advantage to agree to share the representation, for contested elections, especially in some of the bigger counties and more populous boroughs, were often ruinously expensive. In many of the boroughs it made sense to do business with the corporation or the freemen or the men who owned the property which carried the franchise qualification. Sometimes a body of freemen could be elusive negotiators, skilful in the exploitation of every ruse to raise their price. They might bargain for a special gift to the town, some splendid act of munificence which would convince the people at large of the way in which their interests were being safeguarded. Men who had the vote often regarded it as a valuable economic asset which could be tapped at election time. The old practice of paying MPs had died out; now it was universally accepted that if men valued the prestige of being members of the house of commons highly enough they should be prepared to pay for it. Possibly the most open-minded in their approach to the problem of filling their seats were those boroughmongers who had acquired all the properties in some long-decayed borough. While keeping one seat for

members of the family with political ambitions they were sometimes prepared to return promising young men for the other vacancy. This brought
them the satisfaction of encouraging political ability and the prestige of
being conscious of their responsibilities towards the public. Their terms
were not always harsh. They were prepared to tolerate a wide measure of
political disagreement or a generous margin of freedom in political behaviour, providing essential points were met. Should any serious disagreement take place it was assumed that both parties would reconsider
the position in the light of their dissension. Thus, though many pocket
boroughs were used for the dutiful election of younger sons, there was
enough truth in the assertion that they were the nurseries of statesmen for
it to be a credible, though not necessarily a conclusive, argument.

But even by the standards of the time there were anomalies in the
eighteenth-century system of representation. The distribution of seats was
marked by the preponderance of the south, and especially the south-west,
as compared with the north. Many populous areas, including London,
and the towns of the north, were under-represented. Whatever might be
said about the wisdom of virtual representation it was difficult to see what
interest was represented by Dunwich, which had disappeared beneath
the sea, or Old Sarum, which had declined to a succession of grassy
mounds. For eighteenth-century reformers, therefore, the redistribution
of seats took precedence over any extension of the franchise. Even when
Grey and his colleagues reformed parliament in 1832 they were preoccupied with redistribution, rather than with enlarging the franchise. Historians have too often discussed the reform of parliament primarily in
terms of the extension of the right to vote and the coming of democracy.
This is to impose the priorities of a later age upon the past and to distort
the motivation of eighteenth-century reformers. Charles Fox himself, obsessed as he was by the need to curb the influence of the crown, was
chiefly interested in the purification of the house of commons by the
elimination of the worst of the rotten boroughs and like many other
reformers he liked to talk of restoring the constitution. Throughout his
life, both in his wayward youth and in his political maturity, he distrusted speculative opinions. He never lost sight of the physical im-
mediacy of the institutions he talked of improving. Representation was
inseparable from the tumult of the hustings, the excitement in following
each day's poll, the clamour and heat of parliamentary debate in the old
house of commons. He therefore sought to remove tangible abuses by
tangible means, without invoking a new ideology.

The house of commons, chosen in the manner described, was a different type of assembly from that which is familiar from twentieth-cen-

tury experience. It was not dominated by party, tyrannised by the whips, or even preoccupied with the strife of government and opposition. Though the words whig and tory remained in the vocabulary as expletives denoting praise or blame, by the time Fox was a youth they had ceased to have any precise or consistent political meaning. The long sway of Walpole and the acceptance of the Hanoverian settlement had emptied toryism of the old taint of royalism and Jacobitism. Old men, or sentimental high churchmen, might toast the king over the water, might even prefer claret to port, but in reality they deferred to King George and had no intention of doing anything to disturb either the reigning dynasty or the practice of politics. Whatever they called themselves, all active politicians—all with their eyes fixed on the lucrative rewards of office—were whigs. Within the house of commons there were three broad classes: the court or governmental interest, comprising all those minor officeholders who attached themselves to the government of the day so long as it had the confidence of the king; the country gentry, the permanent 'outs' of politics, who scorned office but who thought of themselves as the guardians of the national interest; and the 'professional' politicians, those who sought power and place, and who were intent either on discrediting the government, in the hope that in any reshuffle they would find a berth, or on so convincing the administration that their abilities were too outstanding or too dangerous to be left in opposition as to be brought within the government when next it embarked on the delicate procedure of broadening its parliamentary base.

It is wise, therefore, not merely to dispense with any notion of a two-party system in explaining mid-eighteenth-century politics, but also to reject any idea of an opposition in the modern sense, seeking to turn out the government of the day in order to get into office itself as a comprehensive and disciplined team. A systematic or formed opposition was distrusted as something faintly treasonable and certainly unpatriotic. To seek to impose a complete ministry upon the king was an affront to the balance of the constitution. The type of opposition approved in the eighteenth century was that typified by the country gentry, who would give any government the chance to prove itself in office, but who reserved the right to oppose the administration on particular issues. They were prepared to withdraw their support from any government whose credibility had been destroyed by events or which had lost the confidence of the king. The country gentlemen did not make governments; they did not conceive it as part of their duty to choose the king's ministers for him. But few governments could last for long without their benevolent neutrality and none could survive the withdrawal of their support or the exercise of consistent hostility on their part. In this sense the country gentlemen could be said to 'unmake' governments from time to time, and in their anxiety to preserve traditional liberties and to curtail any undue extension of governmental authority they were a patriotic opposition, untainted by self-seeking and uncorrupted by a lust for personal gain.

In Charles Fox's day no government had a majority in the modern sense. Though governments usually won eighteenth-century elections this did not mean that they could rely on an overall majority on every issue. It simply meant that the various groups making up the ministry and acting in concert with the court interest had a sufficient measure of support in the commons for most purposes, providing the attitude of the country gentlemen remained cooperative. On certain issues the country gentlemen might prove hostile; on others some of the MPs who normally supported the government might withdraw their favours. It was common, therefore, for governments to keep their eyes open for opportunities to widen their base of support in the house. Negotiation was the habitual accompaniment of government. Ministers were engaged in a ceaseless round of explanatory talks in the hope of making the government's relationship with the house of commons easier and more harmonious. Often the desired support could be won only by the granting of kindnesses—promotions in the church or army for relatives, the distribution of government contracts, elevations in the peerage, or knighthoods for faithful companions—but though patronage was the essential lubricant for the wheels of government, it was more effective in rewarding past services than in determining future conduct, and what often looks to modern susceptibilities like a desperate and selfish scramble for favours was no more than a desire to secure merited compensation for political fidelity. The family was more important than party, and while today a myriad host of minor party officials expect to be remembered when a party enters office, in the eighteenth-century politicians never forgot the duties they owed to their cousins and nephews.

Within the cabinet a diversity of views was tolerated: only on issues of finance and foreign policy was something akin to collective responsibility habitually expected. Ministers still regarded themselves as owing their primary loyalty to the king. The government was the king's government, and whatever the weaknesses of the elderly George III no Hanoverian monarch liked to think of himself as a cypher. A king could impose unity on a warring cabinet; by his influence he could reconcile those of his servants who had fallen out. Whenever a first lord of the treasury resigned it was assumed that the king would take the initiative in finding a successor. Most men believed that the revolution settlement had vested two inalienable rights in the monarch: the right to choose his ministers and the right to veto legislation. Although the royal veto had last been formally used by Queen Anne in withholding her assent from the Scots militia bill in 1708 no one would have dreamed that it was right for any set of ministers to ignore the wishes of the king on a matter of legislation. Similarly it was thought wrong for any single group of men to impose themselves collectively on the king, for this would lead to the rule of a faction, with the national interest prostituted for party advantage. It was assumed, despite experience and the bitter conflicts of politics, that there was a patriotic or national policy which would, in most situations be obvious to all men of goodwill. Unanimity was believed to be the natural and desirable state; the primary political assumption amounted to the negation of politics. But in an age when the central government's decisions affected the daily life of the majority of men only in times of war or distress such innocent attitudes could survive in a far from innocent world. For many men the real decisions were made in their locality; the attitudes of squire and parson, landlord and merchant, justice of the peace or lord mayor, counted for more than anything said or done by the great men in distant London. The eighteenth century had a robust distrust of great men, and the term great man was as likely to be applied to a highwayman as to a politician.

For any young man interested in a political career the cultivation of those in office, and the speedy acquisition of some administrative experience, were primary objectives. He could not hope to push himself forward merely by a display of oratorcal virtuosity, nor was he able to gain office merely by the support of the public or the affection of a party. The hostility of the king could delay any politician's admission to government, and royal antagonism could ensure that a distrusted individual could be kept at a safe distance among the more humble officeholders. The career of the elder Pitt demonstrated the liabilities of having incurred royal distaste and the limitations of popular support. Only the exigencies of war reconciled George II to the employment of the Great Commoner in a situation worthy of his talents. Though Pitt hated party as much as any man, was extremely deferential to the king, and affirmed the unoriginal creed of measures not men, the frustrations of his career were the consequence not only of his personal instability and arrogance but also of the constitutional assumptions which guided his political thinking, and which were typical of his age. During his own career Charles Fox was to challenge received ideas on the place of the king in government, the influence of the crown, the collective responsibility of the cabinet, the appointment and dismissal of ministers, the practice of party politics and the conduct of formed opposition, but even when he was quite near the end of his life he was nevertheless to experience how decisive the continued hostility of the king could be, when George III thwarted the younger Pitt's plans of bringing Fox into a truly national government as foreign secretary in 1804. George III's hostility towards Fox was both explicable and reprehensible but the king's success in excluding Fox from Pitt's second ministry is a reminder of the prevalence of old-fashioned notions about the place of the king in government even after Fox had questioned them for a quarter of a century. The originality of Fox's constitutional ideas can be appreciated only if they are firmly placed against a background of what his contemporaries unthinkingly believed and habitually practised.

When, therefore, the youthful Charles James Fox contemplated entering politics his vision was limited to the enclosed world of the professional politician. It was a world in which the governing classes shared common assumptions about the primacy of the landed interest and the virtues of the mixed constitution. When men talked of 'the people' they meant the respectable, propertied citizens who made up the political nation. The masses were synonymous with the mob, with all that implied of tumult, savagery and crime. The house of commons prided itself on its independence not only of the crown but of the people. The reporting and publication of parliamentary debates was for long regarded as fraught with constitutional dangers: the tyranny of opinion out of doors was held to be fully as dangerous as the influence of the crown. Some of Charles Fox's earliest speeches were devoted to praising the value of an independent house of commons, while descanting upon the iniquities of deferring to the wishes of the mob. He entered politics to enjoy the multifarious rumbustious conflicts of parliamentary debate, to feel that he was a man among men, and to savour the pleasures of knowing that he was a man of affairs who was able to influence events. He wanted to be loved, but it was better to be hated than to be ignored. Most of all he sought power, partly because he felt that it was naturally his, partly because he believed he had the judgment and intelligence to exercise it well. He was conscious, too, of how unpopular his father was, and he longed to achieve political distinction in order to gratify the ambition of his affectionate parent. It was hardly surprising that many men regarded him as an arrogant and presumptuous boy, impatient for the prestige and delights of office and contemptuous of the unglamorous routine which was a significant part of any political apprenticeship. Nor could they forget Henry Fox's ill-gotten wealth, his cynical opportunism, his disdain for those who were stupid enough to allow so-called principles to blind them to the political pickings which were theirs for the asking.

The 1760s had been a troubled decade. Since the accession of George III a succession of ministries had failed to win the confidence of the commons and the trust of the king. Yet men found it hard to explain why so many administrations had come and gone. It was tempting to believe that some sinister conspiracy accounted for the apparent breakdown. That the instability of ministries coincided with a new king's accession to the throne seemed to give a necessary clue. Politicians remembered the tales which had been prevalent about the king's upbringing at Leicester House, of how his mother had urged him, above all else, to be a king, while the handsome figure of Lord Bute flitted in and out of the corridors of scandal with a fascination which few gossip writers could resist. In the popular imagination Bute became at once the lover of the princess dowager of Wales and the sinister adviser to the youthful monarch. Though George III's constitutional ideas were merely those of the country gentry, held with tenacious obstinacy and expressed with self-righteous vehemence, men began to wonder whether the king's desire to purify politics and restore the patriotic virtues of disinterested service was a cloak, shielding an attempt to revive the personal prerogatives of the crown and to reduce the house of commons to abject servitude by the shameless distribution of patronage. Bute had been George III's tutor, and although there was nothing exceptional about the king bringing new men into the government, when Pitt and Newcastle resigned in quick succession and Bute was installed as first lord of the treasury it was argued that the king had intrigued against his ministers from the beginning in order to foist his favourite upon the nation. Bute's personal weakness and political incompetence were speedily revealed during his short tenure of power. Instead of being a strong first minister upon whom the king could rely he proved an abject failure. But even when he resigned in April 1763 men could not believe that his political career was over; there was talk of closet influence, of Bute continuing to guide the king, even though others now shouldered the public responsibility of advising the monarch.

The truth was less dramatic and less ominous. George III came to the throne obsessed with the need to perform those duties which providence had laid upon him. But he was also aware of his limitations, of his lack of self-confidence, his restricted intelligence, and his boyish indolence. Brought up as he had been within the stifling confines of Leicester House, ignorant of man and affairs, and deficient in political experience, he was dominated by his mother's rigid sense of propriety, while his emotional immaturity made him dependent upon the earl of Bute, 'his dearest friend', who became something of a father substitute, credited with insight and wisdom and complete reliability. In George's daydreams Bute

was destined to be at his side while together they cleansed politics of all
the corruption which his grandfather had tolerated and allowed to pro-
liferate. Far from seeking to subvert the constitution George III believed
that his mission was to restore it to all its pristine purity. He was convinced that his grandfather had been the senile dupe of shady adventurers;
that the Seven Years war was bloody and expensive; and that for too long
the government of Great Britain had been exploited to satisfy William
Pitt's insensate love of glory and the duke of Newcastle's passion for intrigue and electoral manipulation.

But the realities of political life soon shattered George's illusions.
Though Pitt resigned as secretary of state he did so, not because the king
had actively conspired to bring about his removal, but because he found
himself at odds with his cabinet colleagues over the wisdom of a pre-
ventive attack upon the Spanish treasure fleet. Indeed, far from seeing
George III at the centre of an unscrupulous intrigue, modern historians
have tended to criticise the king for failing to use his legitimate influence
within the government to reconcile the differences between his ministers.
Even when the duke of Newcastle resigned the king found that a reverence for the pious sentimentalities of constitutional theory did not enable
a government to control the house of commons. If the provisional peace
terms which were to end the war were to be approved then the arts of
management would have to be added to those of persuasion. The king
learned that patriotism was not enough, and instead of eliminating bribery
and corruption he was compelled to employ Henry Fox to pilot the
peace of Paris through the commons. Not only had the king discovered
(although too late) the wide divergence between his adulatory image of
Bute and the more mundane reality, he had been forced to call in bad
men to govern bad men, and to accept his constitutional responsibilities
not only as head of the executive but as the first of the electioneering
country gentlemen of England.

The absence of a reversionary interest, in that there was no prince of
Wales of mature years round whom disgruntled politicians could gather,
made it more difficult for men who regarded the rewards of office as
their birthright to come to terms with the new situation. They could
neither formulate a coherent doctrine of parliamentary opposition nor
carry into effect any cogent opposition based upon conventional notions of
parliamentary practice. In their confusion they overlooked the incompetence which had brought George Grenville's ministry to its close, and the
uncertain mixture of high principle and political ineptitude which had
finished Lord Rockingham's administration. It was acutely frustrating
that Pitt's return to office and his elevation to the lords as earl of Chatham

should be followed by his mental collapse, leaving the ministry in the fumbling hands of the duke of Grafton, but instead of seeking to grasp that the reasons for the instability of ministries lay as much with the foolishness or misjudgment of politicians and the inherent contradictions of contemporary constitutional conventions as with the efforts of George III to find a ministry which deserved his confidence, men preferred to seek a scapegoat in the king, and to talk of dark and mysterious plots against the constitution. The American controversy, which had been provoked by George Grenville's stamp act, and the Wilkes affair, which had began as a case of seditious libel laced with obscenity, but which eventually appeared as a struggle between the electors of Middlesex and the house of commons, both contributed to a further proliferation of rumour. The liberties of the subject, the rights of the Americans, and the preservation of the constitution, became blended in a series of massive misrepresentations and misunderstandings. It was easy to allege that the country's misfortunes sprang from the king's attempt to destroy the balance of the constitution. Colour was added to the debate by the free use of phrases such as ' prerogative power', 'the influence of the crown', 'closest influence', and 'the corruption of the commons'. Old fears of placemen in the house of commons were revived, and the notion gained ground that the king and his ministers were embarking on the wholesale corruption of the commons by the use of secret service money and the clandestine award of pensions, contracts, and divers promotions. George III and North were not only denounced as tyrants in America; at home they were charged with being enemies of constitutional government and the traditional liberties enjoyed by Englishmen.

It was nonsense, of course; but it was potent nonsense, and the mythology surrounding the early years of George III's reign was of lasting significance for Charles Fox's political career. Few could have guessed that the assertive young man who proved himself such a combative critic of John Wilkes and such an unrelenting defender of the privileges of the house of commons against the claims of the freeholders of Middlesex would spend so much of his later career denouncing the evils of the influence of the crown and advocating the practice of a formed parliamentary opposition. Fox entered politics as a member of the court interest, and though it would be an exaggeration to describe him as a protégé of Lord North he certainly looked to North for advancement. There is no need to look for any dramatic conversion to explain his later behaviour. When Fox entered parliament his ideas simply reflected his father's worldly wisdom, and like his father he had his eyes firmly fixed on office. The great themes which later inspired his oratory were irrelevant to the priorities dictated by the desire to follow an official and administrative career. The mature Fox was essentially a man formed in opposition. The bitter experience of years spent in fruitless opposition was a stimulus to the consideration of fundamental political beliefs. Fox was never an abstract thinker, but his disappointments saved him from cynicism. Much as he yearned for place and power his frustrations enabled him to take a broader view of affairs than had been possible in his brilliant but narrow-minded youth. When he was returned for Midhurst he was still a young man who habitually deferred to his father's political judgment. Filial loyalty was his principal inspiration. However fluent his invective, how-ever agile his mind he was politically inexperienced and naïve. He had hardly begun to think for himself. His speeches were the response of a gifted young man to the demands which the political situation made upon him; they did not express a considered or coherent viewpoint. Fox was content, for the first six years of his parliamentary career, to behave as any ambitious young man was expected to behave. He desired parental ap-proval and personal advancement; he needed to ingratiate himself with those who were in a position to distribute political largesse; and he en-joyed the plaudits of the house of commons. Only after his resignation in 1774 did Fox begin to formulate his own ideas. The exigencies of the parliamentary situation, and the expediency dictated by political tactics, were more important to him than anything smacking of idealism. Only when he was free from the restrictions and loyalties imposed by minor office, and only when he no longer felt bound by the responsibilities ex-pected of him if he sought advancement in the conventional style, did Fox's outlook become enriched with a wider vision and a generous com-passion. Rather than any deep-rooted transformation of his inner beliefs his years out of office saw him grope towards a better understanding of his own individuality while responding to a new set of demands which a new political situation made upon him. His verbal precocity disguised a fundamental immaturity. He seemed a man of the world, and older than in his years in his apprehension of the grubbier aspects of political be-haviour, but his early brilliance was divorced from both judgment and profound convictions, and he needed the rigours of disappointment be-fore he could achieve any significant measure of insight, self-reliance, and political wisdom.

Fox's early speeches have not survived. His maiden speech on 9 March 1769 was probably little more than an interjection, hastily made and quickly forgotten. Though there are many tributes to his brilliance on 14 April and 8 May 1769 the deficiencies of parliamentary reporting at that period mean that comment on Fox's speeches exceeds any sure evidence

2 'The Young Politician' *From a cartoon of 1771*

3 Charles James Fox (seated) and his opponent William Pitt, in the House of Commons *From a contemporary drawing*

for their real content. But opinion suggested that the young man's talents were extraordinary. Horace Walpole, the most avid political gossip of the age, thought that Charles Fox was abler than his brother, while not being inferior to him in insolence, while Lord Holland was told that few had spoken better than Charles on 14 April, his son's characteristics as a speaker being an off-hand manner, and a rapid and spirited delivery, allied to a knowledge of what he was talking about which surprised most people in so young a performer. Lord Holland prided himself on the fact that he could be forgiven for being proud of his son's success, and as Charles began so he continued. Walpole stated that he had answered Burke on 8 May 'with great quickness and parts, but with confidence equally premature', and Holland was delighted with the way in which Charles was impressing the House, not least because he thoroughly approved of Charles's style of speaking. On 11 May he wrote to Mr John Campbell about his son's speech:

> It was all off-hand, all argumentative, in reply to Mr Burke and Mr Wedderburn. . . . I hear it spoke of by everybody as a most extraordinary thing, and I am, you see, not a little pleased with it. My son Ste [Stephen] spoke too, and . . . very short and to the purpose. They neither of them aim at oratory, make apologies, or speak of themselves, but go directly to the purpose, so I do not doubt they will continue speakers; but I am told Charles can never make a better speech than he did on Monday. . . .[8]

On both of the occasions which won him such golden opinions Charles had been condoning the behaviour of the government and the house of commons in refusing to allow Wilkes to take his seat as the duly elected member for the county of Middlesex. Fox vehemently defended the expulsion of Wilkes and pertly and provocatively argued the case for the return of Colonel Luttrell as MP for Middlesex. Few attitudes were more congenial to the majority of backbench members at this time, and if he wanted favourable attention Fox had gone the right way about achieving it. He was able to say in scintillating fashion what many country gentlemen thought, and it was pleasant for them to feel that a young member was such a vigorous defender of the privileges of the house of commons.

The Wilkes case had already had a long history. Several important constitutional issues had been involved at various stages: the legality of general warrants, the freedom of the press, and, most of all when Charles Fox entered the controversy, the right of the house of commons to decide its own membership and scrutinise election returns.

John Wilkes was an unprepossessing candidate for any species of martyrdom. He was by temperament a man of pleasure; witty, amorous, and egocentric. But as well as indulging his taste for the refinements of aristocratic debauchery, he had been a savage critic of Bute, and the terms in which he had written of the king's speech from the throne on pro- roguing parliament on 19 April 1763 in his newspaper the *North Briton* had provoked the king and his ministers to take action. As a follower of the elder Pitt Wilkes despised the ministry for its foreign policy and for agreeing to the peace of Paris. Although in No 45 of the *North Briton* he had distinguished the person of the king from the words which the king's ministers had chosen to put into his mouth there was no doubt of the contempt he felt towards the sentiments expressed and for the policies which the speech represented. Wilkes claimed that the speech was an imposition on both the king and the nation: 'Every friend of this country must lament that a prince of so many great and admirable quali- ties, whom England truly reveres, can be brought to give the sanction of his sacred name to the most odious measures and the most unjustifiable declarations from a throne ever renowned for truth, honour, and an un- sullied virtue.'

The king and Grenville were stung by the imputation of lying, and, en- couraged by some ill-judged advice from the government's lawyers, they proceeded to issue a general warrant against the authors, publishers, and printers of No 45 of the *North Briton*. A confusing sequence of events followed. Wilkes was cleared on a legal technicality and eventually the use of general warrants was declared illegal, but what had originally been an attempt to discipline an unruly journalist became something of a vendetta. Wilkes was exposed as the author of a bawdy parody, an *Essay on Woman*, and he was accused of publishing an obscene libel. As a result of these revelations several of his political accomplices, Pitt among them, affirmed their horror at his excesses. After fighting a duel, and finding himself faced with mounting pressure from his creditors, Wilkes fled to France. Condemned in his absence he was outlawed, despite his plea that he was protected by parliamentary privilege as MP for Ayles- bury. Once he was abroad many people assumed that he would soon be- come a forgotten exile.

But deteriorating fortunes and rising debts in France drove him to re- turn to England. Technically he was still an outlaw, although he claimed that his original conviction was of questionable validity, but the best means by which he could protect himself against his creditors would be to become a member of parliament again. He therefore sought a seat in the house of commons. After failing in the City of London he was returned for the county of Middlesex, where the beginnings of urbanisation had made the forty-shilling freehold qualification a fairly liberal standard for admission to the franchise. Amid riot and all the violent excesses of eighteenth-century electioneering Wilkes was elected. But Wilkes had made the erroneous assumption that the government would allow by-gones to be bygones. In fact the ministers were in a quandary. They could neither forget nor forgive Wilkes' previous conduct. If Wilkes was an outlaw he could not be admitted as an MP. The commons had the right to scrutinise election returns and to survey its own membership. These ancient securities for the liberties of the house against the influence of the crown were invoked to keep Wilkes out of the commons. Four times Wilkes was chosen by the voters of Middlesex, on two occasions un-opposed. Every time he was returned the commons declared his election invalid; finally they pronounced that Colonel Luttrell, who had been far behind Wilkes in the poll, was the legally elected member for Middlesex.

This, in brief, was the background to Fox's speeches in April and May 1769. As a member of the privileged community of the house of commons he was determined to defend the privileges of the house to the last. If the Wilkes scandal implied a conflict between the rights of the freeholders of Middlesex and the privileges of the house of commons Fox did not hesi-tate to give priority to the claims of the house. On these, and on other occasions, he was content to accept the constitutional doctrine that the house of commons was the people's house, and that, for all political pur-poses, the decisions of the commons were the decisions of the people. It was a conventional attitude at the time, few troubling themselves about the legal fiction which the notion implied. There was certainly no trace of democratic thinking on Fox's part. The electors of Middlesex, which was merely one constituency among hundreds, could not presume to chal-lenge the wisdom of the house of commons, the embodiment of the political nation and the guardian of the national interest. If the commons became subordinate to any external interest its vaunted independence would be at an end and the rule of the mob would begin. There was nothing that Fox liked better than to hear the house roaring its applause as he laid into any suggestion that the privileges of the commons were not synonymous with the interests of the nation. In January 1770 he was lucky enough to outwit Wedderburn on a minor point of law as Wedderburn was pleading the Wilkite case; Fox invalidated one of Wedderburn's examples by drawing attention to a case which (he claimed) was ex-actly similar to Wilkes', and in which though there had been no precedent the court had gone on analogy. Possibly it was a cheap victory, a temporary advantage being seized by a born opportunist, but Fox was making his mark as a debater and, most of all, as a sound house of commons man.

In December 1770, for example, he used the opportunity of a debate on a motion calling for an inquiry into the administration of criminal justice to remind the house of its own superiority to the expression of opinions by those who were 'out of doors':

> For my own part, Sir, I am not disposed to take the voice of a miserable faction for the voice of my country. Were the people really dissatisfied I should be glad to know how I can ascertain the reality of that dissatisfaction. I must freely confess that I know of no other way but that of consulting this house. Here the people are represented, and here is their voice expressed. There is no other criterion but the majority of this assembly, by which we can judge their sentiments. This man, in order to answer one purpose, and that man, in order to answer another, will tell you that a general cry has gone abroad against certain men and certain measures: but will you be so credulous as to take him upon his word, when you can easily penetrate his interested views, and find him the original and prime mover of the clamour? ...[9]

Instead of trying to follow every whim of public opinion the members of the house ought to act 'according to the dictates of honour and conscience', being at peace with their own minds:

> It is thus that we shall sooner or later regain the confidence of our constituents, if we have lost it; and not by humouring, as foolish nurses humour great lubberly boys, the wayward whims of a misled multitude. The characteristic of this house should be a firm and manly steadiness, an unshaken perseverance in the pursuit of great and noble plans of general utility, and not a wavering, inconstant fluctuation of councils, regulated by the shifting of the popular breeze. If we are not to judge for ourselves, but to be ever at the command of the vulgar and their capricious shouts and hisses, I cannot see what advantage the nation will reap from a representative body, which they might not have reaped from a tumultuous assembly of themselves, collected at random on Salisbury plain or Runnymede. And it is very well known ... that such an irregular and riotous crowd are but ill-qualified to judge truly of their own interest, or to pursue it, even when they form a right judgment....[10]

This was the classical eighteenth-century argument for MPs to discharge their duties as representatives rather than delegates; it was, however, dressed up in a wilfully provocative and racy style. Fox had the ability to make respectable conventional views sound exciting and exhilarating, to convince men that the defence of the traditional way of doing things could be as thrilling as briskly challenging familiar assumptions about the primacy of the house of commons. Although Fox himself later paid more attention to extra-parliamentary opinion and organisation he never lost his reverence for the house of commons as the repository of political wisdom and the most effective safeguard against the extremes of democracy as well as the menace of a too powerful monarchy. Whatever may be thought of his adolescent sallies he was always dubious about appealing from the house of commons either to the electorate at large or to extra-parliamentary organisations. His understanding of the nature of representative government broadened with the years, but something of his passionate adulation for the house of commons remained a fundamental element in his political outlook to the end, despite all the vagaries of fortune.

By the time he delivered his speech on Glynn's motion about criminal justice, Fox had already attained minor office. On 23 February 1770 he was appointed a lord of the admiralty. He had earned his promotion, and his skilful contributions to debate had led North to note Fox's potentialities. North was busy forming his administration in succession to that of the unhappy duke of Grafton and he needed every debating talent he could recruit in the commons. Fox might be a difficult young man to handle from time to time; he was impetuous, self-willed, and unpredictable. But his parliamentary abilities were undeniable and he was thought a valuable acquisition to the ministry in that he strengthened its debating resources in the house of commons. As an astute and capable parliamentarian himself North had a shrewd appreciation of Fox's qualities; he did not anticipate that he was to enjoy little but embarrassment at the hands of Charles Fox, whether in office or opposition.

Fox's first brush with authority came about as a result of the government's desire to introduce legislation controlling the future marriages of members of the royal family. The king's brothers, the duke of Gloucester and the duke of Cumberland, had both married ladies who were unacceptable at court and George III was eager to prevent further injudicious marriages within his family. Though several ministers had misgivings about the proposed legislation it was decided that all descendants of King George II should require the permission of the reigning monarch in order to marry under the age of twenty-six. Fox saw the issue in a very personal light. He could not forget that his father's own marriage had been one of the most romantic elopements of a previous generation, and he recalled his father's intransigent opposition to Hardwicke's clandestine marriages act in 1753. He was oblivious to the fact that Hardwicke's act had been necessary to prevent the exploitation of immature young ladies (often of great wealth) by shady adventurers; he ignored the benefits which had undeniably followed the insistence upon the timely calling of the banns. Like his father he thought of himself as defending the right of true lovers to marry without the restraints imposed by hard-hearted and suspicious elders. So far as the royal marriages act was concerned Fox could not see why members of the royal family should be subjected to additional limitations upon their freedom, and in opposing the act he believed that he was renewing the struggle which his father had waged on behalf of romantic affection and the right of young people to have their unions blessed by the church and the state.

He was not content merely with opposing the new marriages bill. He moved the repeal of Hardwicke's act in the house of commons, a gesture which publicly linked the two pieces of legislation and which gave some measure of consistency to his own conduct; but his seriousness was called in question by his failure to read the act before moving its repeal and by his unwillingness to allow such a parliamentary chore to interfere with his own round of pleasure. The night before he had been gambling until dawn. He had lost heavily, and he was still suffering from the ill-effects of his night's exertions. But as always he was able to improvise skilfully. He was never at a loss for words and his effrontery carried him through. But his behaviour had irritated and offended Lord North and his colleagues in the government. They were justifiably angry at Fox's irresponsibility, at his willingness to allow what was little more than an ostentatious piece of filial affectation to carry him into courses of action embarrassing to the administration. His conduct threw doubts upon his loyalty. There was a petulant wilfulness about him which more experienced politicians found irksome. North had no desire, however, to humiliate Fox or to deny him legitimate freedom of speech and expression. What was depressing was Fox's lack of consideration for others. He apparently assumed that he had a right not only to governmental office but to behave in a manner which showed his indifference to the convictions of others. North admired his talents, but was increasingly ill at ease with his personality.

On 20 February 1772 Fox resigned as a lord of the admiralty. He found it difficult to explain or justify his conduct. He complained to his friends of North's coolness towards him, while arguing that this alone would not have brought about his resignation. He maintained that his determination to vote against the royal marriages bill was the real cause for his departure from office. He would have been ashamed, so he claimed, to have voted against the measure while retaining his post. Such was the version he gave to his friends. His pleas in mitigation lacked conviction. He was far from certain that he had made the right decision. He had acted in such a way as to provoke speculation about his political judgment. Many men were sceptical about any man who considered the marriages act of such importance as to risk his career, and Fox himself was conscious of how difficult it might be to get back into office once he had left it. He still thought of his political future primarily in terms of a ministerial career. His inexperience meant that he wondered about the wisdom of what he had done, although his egocentricity led him to defend himself vigorously and stubbornly. Whenever questions were asked about his departure from the admiralty he assured men that once they knew the whole story they would understand and condone what he had done. He longed for approbation, for the comfort of knowing that he had not, after all, made a fool of himself. Despite all the explanations he inflicted upon his friends he set their minds at rest on one issue: he affirmed that he was 'very safe from going into opposition, which is the only danger'. He did not mean to sever all ties with the ministry. He saw the situation as no more than a disagreement over one issue, rather than an irrevocable breach. Once the royal marriages bill was settled there was no reason why Fox should not be reconciled to the ministry. North hoped that a spell out of office would mature Fox by teaching him several elementary lessons about the rules governing political conduct. Perhaps in the future he would be a more amenable colleague.

But whatever calculations were going through Fox's mind, and whatever misgivings he had about his impetuosity, he did not moderate his opposition to the bill. His brilliance and resourcefulness dazzled his contemporaries. Even those who distrusted him as an unprincipled careerist were compelled to admire his fluency and wit. He argued that the bill should apply to descendants of George III, not of George II, making good use of the prevalent antipathy to anything savouring of retrospective legislation. He asked whether persons who were not British subjects came within the scope of the bill, and sneered at the notion that the dignity and security of the monarchy depended on the pitiful and disgraceful expedient of controlling the marriages contracted by members of the royal family. For centuries the crown had not needed such an arbitrary prop for its own survival. Fox's performance in the commons impressed MPs; they were amazed at the quickness of his mind, and the agility with which he contradicted the arguments of his opponents. Horace Walpole went so far as to say that it was universally agreed that Fox had outshone the memory of Charles Townshend as a parliamentarian, despite his 'inferiority in wit and variety of talents'. When he made another attempt in April 1772 to amend Hardwicke's act his combination of informality and lucidity took the fancy of the House. He also showed his capacity to do several things at once. During speeches by North and Burke Fox had been getting about the house, talking to friends and companions and apparently paying little attention to the debate. When he rose to reply he heaped ridicule on North, and shrewdly combatted the arguments of Burke, which had been presented in a speech distinguished by a wealth of information and a complex richness of language. Fox manufactured new reasons for his side in the controversy with a facility that bordered on the incredible. Words poured from him, and the contrast between Burke's deliberate and sophisticated style of speaking, and Fox's inspired spontaneity was for many a reflection of the difference of character between the two men, who within a few years were to begin a political association which lasted for almost twenty years. Horace Walpole defined the contrast: 'Burke was indefatigable, learned, and versed in every branch of eloquence; Fox was dissolute, dissipated, idle beyond measure. He was that very morning returned from Newmarket where he had lost some thousand pounds the preceding day; he ... had sat up all night drinking, and had not been in bed when he came to move his bill, which he had not even drawn upon. This was genius, was almost inspiration. . . .'[11]

But it was still genius at the service of private whims and parliamentary impulse. The unavailing struggle against the royal marriage act, which passed into law with relative ease, had been fun but politically it was wholly futile. However much men admired Fox's virtuosity they could not forget his questionable behaviour towards his colleagues, nor did they overlook the deficient political judgment which had led him to make so much of the issue. Even his resignation, instead of being interpreted, as it might reasonably have been, as a dilatory attempt to avoid embarrassing his ministerial colleagues more than was necessary, was seen as further evidence of Fox's intemperate impetuosity. Although his efforts to repeal or amend the clandestine marriages act had given ample proof of his gifts in debate they were politically worthless and seemed little more than an excessive display of family idiosyncrasy. His resignation was—at best— no more than a boyish prank, and this assessment of its significance was confirmed when in December 1772 Fox accepted a place as a member of the treasury board. He had had his fling; filial piety had been satisfied; now he could get back to the serious business of making his way up the administrative ladder. But he was now on probation. He had been forgiven once, but he was being sharply eyed lest he err again.

In one area of public controversy he had already taken a stand which was not to vary throughout his public life. From the start he supported the claims of the dissenters for the formal abrogation of the penal laws and the requests which were made by both Anglicans and dissenters for relief from the normal requirement of subscribing to all or some of the

Thirty-nine Articles. Under the toleration act of 1689 only those dissenting ministers who were willing to subscribe to those of the Thirty-nine Articles relating to the divinity of Christ were formally permitted to engage in their pastoral ministry. For most of the eighteenth century the provisions of the law were evaded or casually set aside, as the growth of unitarianism among English presbyterians showed, but whenever it was suggested that the enactments of the law should be brought into conformity with normal practice the proposed relaxation of the ecclesiastical provisions of the revolution settlement were staunchly resisted. It was argued that socinianism would flourish more vigorously without the securities afforded to orthodoxy by statute, and, more seriously, it was feared that any weakening of the traditional privileges of the church of England would destroy the habitual association of church and state which was deemed essential for political and social stability as well as for national morality. It was one thing generously to tolerate the practice of dissenting religions and even, within limits, the participation of dissenters in public life. It was another to deny the familiar links between the state and the church of England and the assertion that full citizenship implied membership of the Anglican church, with the acceptance of its liturgy, ecclesiastical government, and historic identification with the nation on its spiritual side. Even men whose Christian faith had been attenuated by rationalism or undermined by doubt saw the church of England as a valuable social institution. The idea that a man's religion was entirely a private affair was anathema; no religion could be divorced from its social context and no religion was held to be devoid of social and political significance. The church of England was regarded as a proven guardian of civil liberty, a defence against the errors of Rome and Geneva alike, and a bulwark against absolutism. Catholicism still bore the taint of Jacobitism, of a religion essentially foreign in temperament and ominously authoritarian in politics and dogma. Presbyterianism and independency, however genteel and inoffensive their contemporary adherents were, still smacked of republicanism, of dangerous levelling ideas, of a lack of respect for the establishment, and a disruptive and debasing egalitarianism. Much of the controversy was soured by ancient fears of Stuart apostasy and Cromwellian severity, but though the eighteenth century is so often described as above all else the century of reason, the idea of a secular state, and more particularly the idea of the separation of church and state, were foreign to the majority of those Englishmen who bothered to think about such matters. They had no wish to impose the law in all its ancient force; they were happy to neglect to enforce it; but to rescind the law was to remove a tested safeguard against unknown dangers. Toleration did not mean equality, nor did it yet imply indifference. However much it was softened in practice the law had still to remain as part of that establishment in church and state which had served England so well since the accession of William and Mary.

Charles Fox was impatient of conventional attitudes towards catholics and dissenters. Partly this was because for him religious controversies were particularly remote from his experience of life, and almost always virtually meaningless; partly his impatience was provoked by a sense of the obtuseness of his opponents. William Wilberforce, who was by no means unsympathetic to Fox and who thought him 'truly amiable' in private life, once lamented that Fox had not one religious friend 'or one who knows anything about it'. Possibly he was unintentionally doing an injustice to Elizabeth Armistead but, nevertheless, Fox's neglect of religious faith and practice was generally accepted by his contemporaries. Religion, he was fond of saying, was best understood when it was least talked of. Some men were distressed that such a kind and warm-hearted man should be untouched by religious orthodoxy or by a sense of sin; others tried to argue that Fox's generous and compassionate nature bore witness to the naturalness of his undogmatic brand of Christianity; but all were compelled to admit that in matters dealing with the imposition of religious tests Fox's convictions were unambiguous. He was opposed to all religious tests for public and political office, and whatever other changes of mind the years brought with them he never shrank from arguing for the relaxation of religious tests and the repeal of the penal laws. If there were times when he doubted the expediency of receiving petitions asking for relief from the necessity of subscribing to the Thirty-nine Articles, or when he thought that the reformers had mishandled their own case, he was always opposed to the exaction of declarations of religious belief as a preliminary to public service, especially in the instance of young people who were too young to comprehend the meaning of what they were to affirm.

He thought it regrettable that at Oxford, though the oaths of supremacy and allegiance could not be administered before the age of sixteen, an assent to the Thirty-nine Articles was required, no matter how youthful the individual concerned. He hoped that the universities might themselves take appropriate steps to eliminate this abuse. He also believed that the folly of imposing the Articles upon ministers of religion was exposed by the sight of men who had formally declared their assent afterwards preaching against the content of particular Articles or even against their overall meaning. Such men may be denounced as hypocrites or may make little impression upon their congregations or upon the public, but Fox deeply regretted that men who were otherwise sincere, upright and outspoken should be compelled to act in violation of their consciences and in conflict with their reputations.

On February 1773 Fox acted as teller on behalf of a motion calling for the establishment of a committee to consider the practice of demanding assent to the Thirty-nine Articles. Fox reminded the house of the seriousness of a practice which was all too often lightly regarded:

> This subscription ... is a solemn thing; it is a serious attestation of the truth of propositions, not a syllable of which ... a youth who subscribes can understand. Why, therefore, attest the truth of which he is ignorant? Is not this to teach our youth to prevaricate? And will not a habit of prevarication lead to the destruction of all that prompt, ingenuous frankness which ought to be the glory and pride of youth? ... Is it not a dangerous doctrine to teach, that because an oath is administered, a person may solemnly bear attestation to the truth of what may, for aught he can tell, be entirely false? I ... can relish no such doctrine; I think it has a highly injurious tendency; and I should therefore wish that the speaker should leave the chair, in order that we may discuss the advantages which can redound to the state, as well as to individuals, from our youth being trained solemnly to attest and subscribe to the truth of a string of propositions, all of which they are as entirely ignorant of as they are of the face of the country said to be in the moon....[12]

Fox was nevertheless reluctant to argue the case for complete religious liberty. His sympathies lay with those who were seeking a relaxation, if not a repeal, of the laws, but his early speeches are marked by a note of slight uncertainty, if not of ambivalence. There was little doubt about his dislike of the imposition of religious tests, but he had misgivings about the way in which his beliefs were to be given effective political expression. Though he was a friend to religious liberty Fox believed in maintaining an established church. He was not a forerunner of those nineteenth-century radicals who called for a free church in a free state. He did not object to the erastianism of the church of England or to the privileged position of the Anglican church as the church established by law. His primary objection was to the technique of using religious creeds, or conformity to certain defined religious practices, in order to determine political behaviour or to safeguard political institutions. As J. L. Hammond once wrote, 'he was resolutely opposed to any method of maintaining that establishment which pressed on any man's conscience'. He hated the thought of compelling men to say that they believed something which they neither believed nor understood, and he found the prospect of pretending to take some things seriously, while cynically exploiting them for worldly ends, offensive. If it was no hardship to insist that men pretended to assent to the Thirty-nine Articles, rather than attempting to ensure that their affirmation was sincere, then the formal subscription was no real security for those interests which it was intended to defend. Hypocrisy was as futile as it was repulsive. For Fox, even in the selfish days of his youth, the right of a man to his own opinions was fundamental and inalienable.

Ironically the decisive breach with North came on a matter connected with the old problem of the freedom of the press. Fox was unrepentant in arguing the sacrosanctity of parliamentary privilege. In the house of commons on 25 March 1771 he had given even more savage expression to his familiar beliefs about the house of commons and its relationship with public opinion and the press. The house was debating the committal of the lord mayor of London and Alderman Oliver to the Tower for their offence in discharging printers apprehended by order of the commons. Fox began by rebuking Dunning for suggesting that the house of commons was not the only judge of the sentiments of the nation: 'I say, Sir, what ought to be, because many laws are highly necessary for the public safety which excite the discontent of the people. If we were never to pass a law until it obtained the sanction of popular approbation we should never have a settled revenue to support either the establishment of our domestic policy or to defend ourselves against the invasion of a foreign enemy.' Every tax provoked an outcry from the public, no matter how necessary it was, and popular opinion often questioned the integrity of parliament.

Fox admitted that MPs could find themselves in conflict with their constituents, and with the people at large. He was willing to concede, for argument's sake, that nine-tenths of the people were at that moment in opposition to the government. But members had a higher obligation to perform than deference to the wishes of their constituents: 'We are bound to promote their true interests in preference to the dearest wishes of their hearts, and the constitution makes us the sole arbiters of those interests, notwithstanding the imaginary infallibility of the people.' In a torrent of invective Fox argued that MPs were elected to defend, not to destroy, the constitution. They were to keep the privileges of the people within their proper limits as well as to control any unwarrantable exercise of royal authority. He appealed to ideas of mixed monarchy, 'the pride and envy of the universe', in contrast to the dangers of democracy:

We have sworn to maintain this constitution in its present form; to maintain the privileges of parliament as a necessary part of that constitution, and neither to encroach upon the legal jurisdiction of the peers, nor the just prerogatives of the sovereign. Shall we then do what we are sensible is wrong, because the people desire it? Shall we sacrifice our reason, our honour, our conscience, for fear of incurring the popular resentment, and while we are appointed to watch the Hesperian fruit of liberty with a dragon's eye, be ourselves the only slaves of the whole community?

He did not accuse the people of deliberately seeking to destroy their own happiness, but he suspected their capacity to judge what was truly in their best interests. They were generally credulous, frequently misinformed, and all too often duped by appearances. The question was whether the people or the house of commons were the best judges of the public welfare:

> For my own part, sir, I shall not hesitate to pronounce positively in favour of this house. What acquaintance have the people at large with the arcana of political rectitude, with the connexions of kingdoms, the resources of national strength, the abilities of ministers, or even with their own dispositions? If we are to believe the very petitions which they have lately presented to the throne, they are unequal to those powers which the constitution has trusted to their hands. They have the power of electing their representatives, yet ... they constantly abuse that power, and appoint those as the guardians of their dearest rights whom they accuse of conspiring against the interests of their country. For these reasons ... I pay no regard whatever to the voice of the people....[13]

It was the duty of the people to choose members of parliament and it was the duty of the house of commons to act constitutionally and to maintain the independence of parliament.

> Whether that independency is attacked by the people or by the crown is a matter of little consequence; it is the attack, not the quarter it proceeds from which we are to punish; and if we are to be controlled in our necessary jurisdiction, can it signify much whether faction intimidate us with a rabble; or the king surround us with his guards? If we are driven from the direct line of justice by the threats of the mob, our existence is useless to the community. The minority within doors need only assault us by their myrmidons without to gain their ends

upon every occasion. . . . What must the consequence be? Universal
anarchy, sir. . . .[14]

It is tempting to disregard utterances such as these as the selfish and insincere trumpetings of a cynical and ambitious young man. But to do so
is to misrepresent Fox and to misunderstand his age. Few of his contemporaries could have expressed themselves so memorably; his gift for
pungent and aggressive invective as a rare and cleverly exploited talent;
but all the assumptions about the virtues of mixed government were the
common currency of constitutional debate. Fox had not yet formulated any
distinctive or personal view of the constitution. He was content to take
the prevalent forms of explanation on trust, giving them a new exhilaration
and potency by the fluent vehemence of his eloquence. But there is little
doubt that he sincerely believed the ideas about the constitution which he
propagated so enthusiastically. A desire to contrast his juvenile tory phase
with his later 'liberalism' should not obscure certain elements of continuity in his mental attitudes. He always subscribed to a theory of the constitution which approximated to that of mixed monarchy and a balanced
constitution. Restoration and purification, rather than innovation, were
the objects of his reforming zeal. The house of commons always took the
first place in his political affections, and even when he was prepared to
toast 'our sovereign the people' he was never a democrat. It was the house
of commons which was the guardian of English liberties, and the commons were a more trustworthy guide than the electorate. However unre-
flective Fox's early expositions of the benefits to the public of the privileges of the house of commons were, they were sincere and deeply-felt.
Later in his career he recurred to some of these early standpoints, but
only when the intensity of his commitment to the house of commons is
fully understood does the incident which led to his dismissal from the
treasury become comprehensible. Of course an ungovernable zest for
controversy, a restless ambition, and a desire to humiliate an enemy were
involved, but Fox's impatience with the misrepresentations and slanders
of the press was the product of a genuine commitment to the constitution
as he and many of his contemporaries understood it. Characteristically he
ignored the feelings of his superiors, and, most significantly of all, he succeeded in convincing the king of his total lack of honour, loyalty, and
scruple.

The appearance of an article criticising the speaker of the house of
commons in the *Public Advertiser* for 11 February 1774 incensed Fox and
other MPs, and the commons summoned William Woodfall the printer
to present himself at the bar of the house. The offensive article had been

written by the controversial radical parson John Horne (better known by his later name of Horne Tooke) and Woodfall claimed that because of the pressure of business he had not read the article, but had foolishly authorised its publication without realising the implications of what Horne had written. Woodfall had known that the article referred to the proceedings of the house of commons, but he had been unaware of its provocative and scurrilous nature. He was penitent and respectful, and expressed the hope that the fact that he had been a printer for twenty years without causing the house of commons any offence would be taken into account when his case was considered. Many members were impressed by Woodfall's demeanour; some who had been among the most eager to punish him severely were considerably softened by his sensible behaviour. But Charles Fox remained obdurate and adamant. He continued to call for the harshest penalties, moving that Woodfall should be committed to Newgate prison. North was acutely embarrassed by the affair. Until Woodfall's modesty had taken the sting out of the incident North had favoured imprisonment, but he recanted, thinking, with many members of the house, that it would be both impolitic and unjust to victimise Woodfall by subjecting him to an excessive punishment. But North reckoned without Fox's unrelenting vindictiveness. In a moment of hesitancy he had promised Fox that he would vote for Woodfall's imprisonment. To his horror he found that Fox wished to hold him to his promise. North solved the problem by voting with Fox in favour of Woodfall's committal while making it plain to the house that he did so under duress in obedience to a promise which had been extorted from him and from which Fox had refused to release him. North advised his friends to vote against Fox's motion. The commons were therefore treated to the unusual spectacle of the chief minister of the crown voting for a motion of which he disapproved, while urging his followers to go into the opposite lobby. North's personal honour remained unsullied, but he was intensely aware of the humiliation which Fox had inflicted upon him and of the absurdity of the situation which his good nature and Fox's selfish implacability had created. Fortunately the motion was defeated by 152 votes to 68 but the mortification lingered. Fox had behaved unreasonably. His failure to admit that Woodfall's penitent appearance at the bar of the house had changed the situation seemed to be new proof of his lack of judgment, while his insistence that North should accompany him into the 'Yea' lobby violated every principle of gentlemanly conduct. North had been irresolute and unimpressive, but Fox had been arrogant and abrasive and this added to his unpopularity while confirming men in thinking that he was incapable of respecting the restraints which a recognition for the normal courtesies of political life imposed on all politicians, no matter how ambitious.

But North was not the only eminent person who was indignant at Fox's behaviour. George III was outraged; all his worst suspicions, which had been inspired by Fox's first resignation and his opposition to the royal marriages bill as well as by the notorious excesses of Fox's private life, were confirmed. The king expected loyalty from all ministers of the crown, and he sought to stiffen North's resolution, as well as profferring consolation and comfort. On 15 February the king told North that he was greatly incensed by Fox's presumption in forcing North to vote with him the previous night, but that he approved of North's plea to his friends to vote the other way. George III's opinion of Fox could not have been lower: 'Indeed, that young man has so thoroughly cast off every principle of common honour and honesty that he must become as contemptible as he is odious.' He hoped that North would let Fox know of his feelings in the matter.

When retribution came to Fox it was brusque and pointed. After 15 February he had continued to vex the government by seeking further action against Woodfall and Horne, and on 23 February he further annoyed his colleagues by voting against the administration on a quite different matter (in which there was much more to be said for Fox's conduct): a dissenting petition for relief. For a week he had added one provocation to another. It was senseless and selfish; even where it was excusable it was unwise. But Fox found it gratifying and exciting. For purposeless insolence his conduct had no equal. There was a truculent, dare-devil aspect to his behaviour which his gambling companions found amusing and entertaining; when questions were asked as to whether North had yet turned him out Fox laughingly replied that he had not: 'But if he does, I will write to congratulate him, and tell him that if he had always acted with the same spirit, I should not have differed with him yesterday.' It was fun to plague his seniors, to see North squirming to avoid further trouble on the vexed question of the publication of parliamentary debates and to know that the king priggishly disapproved of the pranks of his junior lord of the treasury. But while Fox brazenly defied the frowns and warnings of his elders and betters the king solemnly noted the intolerableness of his behaviour. George III thought that Fox would have acted more becomingly if he had absented himself from the house after the Woodfall affair. As it was his conduct could not be attributed to conscience, which the king would have understood, having himself suffered deeply from the slanders of the press. Rather Fox's actions were explicable simply as the outcome of a congenital aversion to all restraints.

He could have satisfied any conscientious scruples of his own without heaping embarrassment upon poor North. In this, as in so many other ways, George III spoke for the majority of those silent backbenchers whose mute integrity made them the keepers of the conscience of the house. Fox's days were numbered, and few lamented the retribution which he had brought upon himself. On 24 February he received an unceremonious note from North: 'His majesty has thought proper to order a new commission of the treasury to be made out, in which I do not see your name.'

Fox's first reaction was to try to laugh the matter off. He was not surprised, and yet his mirth and flippancy had a hollow ring. George Selwyn seized the opportunity to make jokes about Fox as the new Charles the Martyr, the main contrast between him and his ancestor being that while King Charles' head could not be sown on again Fox's could and might be. But there could be no disguising the seriousness of Fox's plight. It was not only that he was out of place; he was out of favour with both government and opposition. The house of commons sympathised with North; Fox, it was generally agreed, had behaved in a contemptible fashion. His effrontery, his arrogance, his shameless disregard for the loyalties binding one minister to another, testified to the thoughtless rapacity of his ambition. He could hardly plead any depth of principle in extenuation of his conduct, for he could have pressed for firm action against Woodfall without wantonly humiliating North. To suggest that North dismissed Fox because he was apprehensive of the prospect of a colleague in the cabinet of whose abilities he was jealous was a sentimental fabrication manufactured in later years. North was not in the least jealous of Fox, nor was there any good reason for giving him accelerated promotion in ministerial rank. At this period it was North, not Fox, who was the darling of the house of commons. If Fox had behaved normally, accepting the need to temper his own desires by an understanding of the demands which the responsibilities of government made upon his colleagues there would have been no trouble. Nor is it adequate to see Fox as the victim of the king's vengeful hostility and distrust. George III's anger was a reflection of the horror which he felt concerning the insult which had been gratuitously offered to his first minister. The king was sensitive about the reputation of the administration, and anxious to enforce a respect for the conventions of public life. He was not following a personal vendetta or seeking to make Fox a scapegoat for his own frustrations or for those of the government. George III's response to Fox's outrageous conduct was honest, sane and almost universally approved.

Apologists for Fox later argued that his dismissal in 1774 was a blessing for the country, liberating him as it did from adherence to North's ministry on the eve of the American crisis. His folly over the Woodfall incident could be seen as a blessed fall from grace, in that it allowed 'the enlightened conclusions of his own judgment' free rein. His opposition to the American policies of the king and of North could be interpreted as giving retrospective justification to his earlier breach with North. But this is to glamorise Fox's dismissal, investing it with more significance than it possessed at the time, while giving the wholly misleading impression that there was an ineluctable connexion between his departure from the ministry and his later opposition to the American war. But when Fox left office he had not challenged North or any of his colleagues on any aspect of colonial policy. His nephew, the third Lord Holland, was wiser in suggesting that it was fortunate for Fox that no decisive clash had taken place over the government's American policy at the time of his dismissal. Holland saw that it was possible that Fox would have defended the American policy of any government in which he served. His truculence, indifference to popular feeling, and regard for the privileges of parliament, might have made him an intransigent and vehement apologist for coercion, had he not been able, in the freedom of the back benches, to take time to consider what the new situation demanded of him. It would also be false to see him as moving speedily and promptly into the Rockinghamite camp. He did not substitute adherence to opposition for his previous membership of the administration. The political considerations governing his behaviour were too complex for that. His evolution as an opposition spokesman, the development of his own ideas about the American dispute and the practice of formed opposition, and his relationship with the other politicians who opposed the American war, were the product of time and chance, not the inevitable outcome of an independent and selfless idealism.

In retrospect it was easy for Fox and his friends to clothe his dismissal in February 1774 with an irrevocable significance it did not possess. His breach with North assumed decisive proportions because of events which succeeded it, not because there was any inherent finality in the episode. Nor should Fox's early excursions into vigorous opposition be deemed evidence of any profound political conversion. If he made himself sufficient of a nuisance to his former colleagues he could hope that, with promises of future good conduct, he might once again be forgiven and admitted to minor office. But if he were not forgiven the future looked black. He was a lonely and distrusted political figure, however popular he might be with close friends and gambling companions. He was identified with no connexion, and he represented no transcendent political principle. His reputation was that of a gifted but unreliable braggart, a scintillating debater who had no sense of loyalty and who had no one's confidence. He seemed too fond of place and too eager for profit, too insolent to his seniors and too contemptuous of his contemporaries. In addition to political disaster he was experiencing personal anguish, first because of his gambling debts, and then during a series of family bereavements.

His reputation as a man of pleasure was an unenviable one. Gossip and scandal abounded, but all too often there was a basis in fact for the rumours which were so maliciously circulated. Fox followed the races and indulged in games of chance with abnormal zest. He had learned nothing from the experiences of his youth. Instead of being inoculated against excessive gambling by the premature indulgences of his adolescence he became a helpless addict, who allowed nothing, neither the warnings of his friends nor the threats of his creditors, to deter him from gratifying his restless appetite for extravagance and excitement. He was notorious for the complete involvement with which he followed any horse race. Whenever he watched a race with any fancy in one of the runners he was highly tensed in a state of nervous excitement. He was always eager for a race to begin, and impatiently anxious for it to be settled. He was often confident of winning, but he could not tear himself away from the race for a moment. He well knew the bitter-sweet anguish of watching an apparently certain winner go down to defeat amid the cries of disappointment emanating from its backers. He liked to station himself at the final, decisive stretch of the course. At the beginning of a race he might appear calm, but as the horses galloped towards him Fox's breathing increased, and as they rushed past him he imitated the actions of jockey, imaginatively whipping the horses on to new efforts and wheezing and blowing as if he was in the race himself. He became totally indifferent to his surroundings and oblivious of his friends. Afterwards he might joke about his winnings or even more frequently about his losses, tearfully bewailing his bad luck while laughing at his poor judgment. He might denounce his competitors as winning only by a low cheat, or he might praise the skill with which the race had been won, his chivalrous instinct triumphing over his disappointment. It was this propensity to give himself freely, openly, and unrestrainedly which charmed Fox's friends, leading them to be forgiving in circumstances which would have led other friendships to founder in recrimination and disgust. But though Fox's uninhibited emotions helped him to win friends they were disastrous for his pocket.

Like many compulsive gamblers Fox was consistently unlucky, and his bad luck became famous. One contemporary rhyme put it nicely:

At Almack's of pigeons I am told there are flocks;
But it's thought the completest is one Mr Fox.
If he touches a card, if he rattles a box,
Away fly the guineas of this Mr Fox.
He has met, I'm afraid, with so many bad knocks,
The cash is not plenty with this Mr Fox;
In gaming 'tis said he's the stoutest of cocks,
No man can play deeper than this Mr Fox,
And he always must lose, for the strongest of locks
Cannot keep any money for this Mr Fox.
No doubt such behaviour exceedingly shocks
The friends and relations of this Mr Fox.

All night gambling was an exhausting as well as an expensive pastime. It was a marvel that Fox was so often seen in the house of commons after spending the previous night at Almack's, Brooks', or White's. It was said that he sometimes lost £10,000 in a night. On one occasion he and his brother Stephen lost £32,000 on three successive nights. As his losses mounted so Charles Fox's excitement increased. If he was going through a bad spell he seemed almost to play as much to lose as to win. The losses were made good by borrowing sums at high rates from Jewish moneylenders, to whom Fox was soon deeply in debt. He gleefully called his antechamber his Jerusalem Chamber, and when Henry Vassal Fox, the future third Lord Holland, was born to his elder brother Stephen and his wife, Charles cheerfully called the boy a second Messiah, but born for the destruction not the salvation of the Jews. But he had small grounds for mirth. So long as his brother Stephen was without an heir it was possible for Charles to borrow money with the chance that he might succeed to his father's title affording some prospect to his creditors that they might eventually be paid. Stephen Fox enjoyed poor health, and it was commonly believed that he would not long outlive his father. But with the birth of Stephen's son Charles was in a compromising situation. His creditors, angry at the changed outlook, became impatient for payment, and when Charles sought to raise loans he found the terms stiffer and the brokers less generous. High interest rates were thought some compensation for the unlikely possibility of being repaid. Fox had become a financial liability without either present or future wealth. By the winter of 1773-4 his debts totalled £140,000. He was in desperate straits, and he did not know what to do to avert imminent catastrophe. In desperation he turned to his father. Lord Holland dutifully came to the rescue, settling the problem by discharging Charles' debts from his own estate. This was virtually the last service he performed for his son; the seeds which he had so casually sown in Charles' boyhood had ripened to a distressingly fruitful harvest. But Holland bore it bravely. 'Never', he commented, 'let Charles know how excessively he afflicts me.'

Fox's gambling has sometimes been seen as the reflection of an essential instability of character which afflicted his public as well as his private career. Certainly he took risks throughout his political life, risks which were all too often proved wrong by the sequence of events and which exposed him to the charge of reckless impetuosity. It was true that Fox's political judgment was defective, but to suggest that he was no more than a gambler, indulging in risks which were without any political excuse and which were totally inexplicable, is a gross and misleading over-simplification. It would be truer to say that at decisive moments he made significant miscalculations, which, however plausible they seemed at the time, proved disastrous and irretrievable. In this context, as in others, the contrast between Fox, the idle apprentice, and Pitt, the industrious apprentice, has been overplayed. In office Fox could be hard-working, sober-minded and impressively assured. His gambling may, in some ways, have been a means of compensating for his political frustrations, rather than their cause. The excitements of the casino may have gratified those surging energies whose natural sphere of fulfilment was the exercise of supreme political power. Ironically, Fox's temperament might have become more disciplined, his energies more purposefully directed, his longing for political mastery more controlled, had he been given the chance to mature his talents within the demanding context of major governmental responsibilities. Reprehensible though his gambling was it does not of itself explain his political disappointments. He was a victim of the values of the society in which he habitually moved. It was easy for him to assume that the indulgence of every whim and the gratification of every passion was his natural birthright as a well-born Englishman. His incapacity to learn from his errors, and his tendency to make the same feckless mistakes again and again, even at the cost of wounding those whom he most loved, may be evidence of a weakness of character but they should not be given an excessive place in the explanation of the futilities which dogged Fox's political career.

The crisis over his debts had distressed Fox's family. His parents were loving and affectionate to the end but they were now less confident of Charles' ability to deal with the problems with which life could confront him. His political prospects and his private life seemed clouded with uncertainty and improvidence. He was still unmarried, despite grotesque rumours that, in an attempt to salvage his fortunes by marrying an heir-ess who was said to prefer fair men, he had powdered his eyebrows. His relationships with women had been casual, undemanding, and all too often discreditable. He lacked both public respect and private virtue, and he could no longer be regarded with charitable tolerance as an unusually promising boy, whose foibles could be forgiven as the understandable and inevitable accompaniments of growing up.

On 1 July 1774 Fox experienced the first of an unhappy series of be-reavements with the death of his father, Lord Holland. Within a month his mother followed her husband to the grave, and in November Stephen Fox died, having enjoyed the hereditary dignity of Baron Holland for a mere four months. His small son, Henry Vassal Fox, whose companion-ship was later to be one of the joys of Charles Fox's life, succeeded to the title. Such a succession of deaths within a family which had always been bound closely together by the closest emotional ties affected Charles Fox deeply. In almost every way his life had reached a crisis. But his private circumstances improved slightly. After his father's death he was assured of an annual income of £900, as well as inheriting £20,000 and estates at Thanet and Sheppey, and his beloved Kingsgate. When Stephen Fox died he left Charles the clerkship of the pells, worth £2,300 a year; but Charles, whose misgivings about sinecures were beginning to have political sig-nificance, chose to sell the reversion to the government, his price being an annual income of £1,700 for thirty-one years. If he could restrain his itch to gamble there was a chance that he would be able to live within his means, but this proved a vain hope. He had lost three people who were very dear to him, and his private griefs added personal anguish to the other disappointments he had had to bear. It was hard for him to detect any break in the clouds, or to take hope from any omen. He was con-scious of the worries and anxieties which he had inflicted upon his parents in their last year of life. He could not forget that he had had to call upon his father to save him from his follies, and the memory of the sufferings endured by his mother during her final illness was often with him. He could no longer take either life or success for granted.

Politically he was in the doldrums. He had to work his passage with the Rockinghamites and that ill-assorted collection of disgruntled politi-cians who, like Fox, found themselves being drawn into more consistent opposition to the government's American policy. But it would be wrong to suggest that Fox was warmly welcomed into the ranks of the opposition. His previous record made men sceptical about his new attitudes and ap-prehensive about becoming too closely allied with him. He did not 'cross the floor of the house' in the conventional sense. Such a step was an impossibility in the absence of a party system and a formulated pattern of government and opposition. On Fox's side, too, there were good reasons for hesitancy and mistrust. He had no desire to follow Chatham, his father's old rival, whose individualistic interventions in politics spread such consternation among both his friends and foes. Nor could Fox look to Shelburne, whom his father had always disliked, and who was commonly regarded as being too fond of the company of eccentric intellectuals. Shelburne was intelligent, but he was unreliable and devious. The originality of his ideas, and the high quality of his mind, contributed to the suspicion that he was too subtle and too clever: a man of uncommon abilities who lacked the common touch and the gift of winning the confidence of back-bench opinion. Nor was Fox immediately attracted to Rockingham, that faint and elusive symbol of high whiggery, who relied so trustingly upon Edmund Burke for his political ideas. Only the ineluctable pressure of events forced men who were dissimilar in temperament and diverse in outlook to act together, and only the deterioration of the situation in America enabled Charles Fox to emerge as the most brilliant and the most individualistic of the government's parliamentary opponents. He had still to reach political maturity, and he had yet to articulate those ideas which came to be so closely identified with his name. Only a changing political climate afforded him the opportunity to redeem the follies of youth, but in his response to events Fox proved himself an opportunist of genius.

2 The Champion of America

It was an historical accident that Charles Fox became the spokesman for the American colonists in their struggle against the British parliament. Like most English politicians he had been indifferent to the fate of the American colonies until the dispute over the right of the British government to levy taxes in America erupted in violence. Fox was drawn into the controversy by the exigencies of parliamentary politics. He had made no substantial study of the relationship between the colonies and Great Britain, and he at first sought to expose inconsistencies in the government's case, rather than committing himself to any distinctive interpretation of the constitutional issues involved in the denial of the British parliament's claim that it was vested with a legislative supremacy empowering it to raise taxation in any part of the empire, as its responsibilities of regulating trade in the interests of the whole demanded from time to time. Fox approached the controversy from the standpoint of a lonely and independent-minded member of the commons who was seeking to discover the political stance which made most sense for himself, placed as he was in a situation of acute embarrassment and uncertainty. He viewed the American conflict in political terms, without any unique grasp of abstract considerations or of theoretical principle, and with an indifference to any vague talk of moral issues. He lacked any profound insight into the more complex aspects of the problem, and his inspiration was essentially pragmatic not ideological.

Fox could be forgiven for his hesitancy. The American controversy was more complicated than men at first realised, and while there was from the start a clarity (if not always a consistency) on the American side of the dispute, the assumptions governing the conduct of British politicians, the objectives of policy guiding North and his colleagues, and the criticisms voiced by parliamentary critics of the administration, were frequently contradictory, obscure and perplexing, taking on new forms with each shift in the balance of power in America.

Far from the British government following a policy of wilful provocation, and lightly entering into a conflict with the Americans, the king's ministers were slowly dragged into a war which none of them desired. Nor had they systematically attempted to impose a fully thought-out policy upon the colonists. Although the restoration of British authority by force of arms might seem the logical outcome of the principles which most Englishmen took for granted in the dispute, many men, including members of North's administration, were reluctant to believe that war would eventually become a reality. Even the advocates of a tough line thought that it was the surest means of preventing armed conflict. Perhaps it was impossible for war to be averted, once the initial challenge to the British parliament had been made, but it was still thought that in some unforeseen and unexpected way both sides might draw back from the irrevocable act of rebellion or repression. Most Englishmen were ignorant of America, and forgetful of the historical reasons for English colonisation. It was difficult to conceive of the immense differences of outlook which enabled Americans to make allegations of harsh and grasping tyranny and Englishmen to argue that above all else the unity of the empire and the legislative supremacy of the British parliament had to be preserved. Englishmen felt that the Americans had benefited from British victories in the Seven Years war, and that it was legitimate that the colonists should bear some part of the cost. Americans deeply resented the suggestion that they were the passive beneficiaries of English military genius, and regarded the imposition of taxes without the consent of colonial assemblies as reminiscent of those attempts to raise extra-parliamentary taxation which had finally brought the Stuarts into conflict with the house of commons. While Englishmen talked of the advantages to the colonies of the imperial connexion Americans pointed out the incompetence and incomprehension which the British had often shown in their dealings with the colonists. Government apologists in London talked of the need to regulate trade; the Americans writhed under what they considered to be obsolete economic restrictions which held back American industrial development in obedience to the outdated assumption that the chief function of the colonies was the production of raw materials and primary products deemed essential for British manufacturers and naval supremacy. The 'old colonial system' was never a fully integrated method of economic planning, and mercantilist ideas were as much an explanation of how pressing needs were to be met as a coherent exposition of an economic doctrine, but the restrictions imposed upon the colonies were sufficiently cramping for the Americans to feel angry and frustrated and for the alleged virtues of commercial control from London to be decried as the unrealistic imaginings of those who knew little of the territories whose prosperity they claimed to be protecting, and who cared less for the susceptibilities of men whom they despised as raw colonials. The problem of the Indians, and the British government's apprehension about expansion west of the Alleghany mountains, exacerbated the situation still further.

But important though these points of view were, there was no reason why they should inevitably erupt in a squabble which raised issues of constitutional theory and practice for which all parties to the dispute were ill-prepared. The legitimate demands of colonial economic development, and the powerful attraction of virgin territories which were ripe for exploitation, would have called in question most of the assumptions governing the policy of successive British governments; but differences of opinion about commerce and colonisation would not, by themselves, have provoked a constitutional controversy which revealed the great gulf separating the more articulate and assertive colonists from the king and his ministers. George Grenville and Charles Townshend, the one an energetic pedant, the other a brilliant political adventurer, succeeded in planting the American controversy on a basis which made the denial of received constitutional ideas inseparable from the discussion of those matters of taxation and the control of trade which were the focal points for dissension and conflict. George Grenville's stamp act, defensible as it was from the British point of view as a means of ensuring a reasonable American contribution towards imperial defence, was to the Americans a dangerous innovation, which deprived the colonists of their money while denying them opportunity to control or consent to the taxation to which they were being subjected. The spectre of 'no taxation without representation' allowed the dispute to be vitiated by the misleading notion that the colonists were as clearly the victims of the abuse of the prerogatives of the crown as the mutinous subjects of King Charles I. Since in England the 1760s had been dominated by fears of closet influence and a royal conspiracy against the constitution, for reasons which had nothing to do with America and little to do with the facts of the case, the false parallel between ship-money in the reigns of the first two Stuarts and the stamp tax in the reign of the third Hanoverian was hastily exploited by journalists and politicians in order to explain what they could not understand. Instead of being a difference of opinion over the efficacy or justification of particular forms of taxation the American quarrel took on the proportions and the temper of a struggle between tyranny and arbitrary rule, on the one hand, and traditional liberties and representative government on the other. This was a double misfortune, for it meant that both sides invoked high-sounding constitutional principles whenever they had to cover up a weakness in their case, and what was explicable as an instance of misunderstanding and confusion was denounced as the premeditated violation of habitual constitutional practice.

Once the issue of no taxation without representation had been injected into the dispute the evil could not be undone. Only superlative political skill on the part of the British government and charitable patience on the American side could have saved the day, and these qualities were dramatically lacking just when they were most desperately needed. Once the nature of representation was discussed it was impossible to bring together two disputants who had lost all sense of agreement on fundamental beliefs. Dutiful attempts to mollify American indignation by invoking ideas of virtual representation revealed the contradictions in traditional thinking without reconciling American opinion. It was impossible to visualise American participation in the British house of commons and yet it was equally impossible to see how the principle of the sovereignty of parliament could be affirmed without it once the Americans rejected the argument that the British parliament was supreme, in all countries owing allegiance to the crown, by virtue of historical development. To the British no taxation without representation meant no taxation, since the Americans were hostile to those notions of representation which were acceptable to the British. To the Americans the first objective was to compel the British government to rescind those taxes which had been so arbitrarily imposed; once this had been achieved the definition of representation and the effort to give it practicable expression could be tackled in a less contentious atmosphere. But so long as one of the offensive taxes was officially levied no fruitful negotiation was possible with a British government which seemed intent on demanding obedience to the wilful assertion of arbitrary authority. Conciliatory gestures were often nullified by a determination to justify previous affirmations of principle, while arguments which had alleged the necessity for certain taxes on grounds of utility were exposed as fallacious whenever the tax in question was abandoned in the hope of achieving a measure of conciliation. This was the background against which the tragedy of the American war was played out.

Nothing is a greater travesty of historical truth than the suggestion (perhaps accusation would be a more appropriate word) that Britain lost the American colonies because George III sought to revive the personal prerogatives of the crown by levying taxation in America. If the king had been interested in strengthening the position of the crown he might have stumbled upon a workable solution to what was an intractable constitutional dilemma. But George III was devoted to the defence and maintenance of the legislative authority of the British parliament. This he

believed to be fundamental to the constitution which the house of Hanover had been called in to secure. Any suggestion that parliament should
yield some of its legislative supremacy in the interests of peace was, for
the king, a meaningless as well as a reprehensible gesture. If the Americans
questioned the validity of the constitution which the king was formally
pledged to preserve this did not mean that it was right to allow constitutional proprieties to be perverted by expedient opportunism. For
George III the prestige and powers of the British parliament were so
fundamental to the future well-being of the country, and were so intimately associated with the promises which he had solemnly made at his
coronation, that to talk of yielding on any point of principle was tantamount to treachery, if not treason. The king could conceive of the necessity of accepting defeat; but in his view military reverses did not turn a
sound constitutional argument into a bad one.

He was, therefore, the most determined and most uncompromising
apologist for the right of parliament to legislate for any part of his domin-
ions; on that point there could be no compromises and no concessions. Nor
was it easy for George III to envisage the possibility of defeat; his confidence in the justice of his cause was so unshakable that whatever reverses
had to be endured the prospect of final and irreparable defeat was unthinkable. George III was profoundly aware of the responsibilities of
kingship; he believed it to be of the essence of the trust vested in him that
he should preserve the unity of the empire, handing it on intact to his
successor. He could not grasp any notion that he might be king of
Massachusetts rather than king of the United Kingdom and all her
colonies beyond the seas. Yet without the utilisation of the crown as a
formal link (and this was an intangible shadow to eighteenth-century
minds) it was difficult to see what were the alternatives to the penitent
return of the Americans to their allegiance, or the granting of independence to the recalcitrant colonies.

The confusions in the attitudes of most British politicians towards the
American colonies had been mirrored in the policies of successive governments. George Grenville had been preoccupied with raising money in
America for the cost of maintaining military garrisons, and though many
Americans were sceptical about the need for a British military presence
after the defeat of France and the acquisition of Canada by the British
crown, Grenville's objective, however criticised, was at least comprehensible. The tumult caused by the stamp act surprised many British observers,
who suspected that the colonists were making a fuss over something of
minor importance, and although the troubles in the colonies persuaded
men that it would be expedient to repeal the stamp act, the declaratory

act, affirming the legal claim of the British parliament to legislate for the colonies, was passed. A practical concession was accompanied by a more explicit and tougher pronouncement on the theoretical aspects of the question. The declaratory act was clear and uncompromising, stating 'that the said colonies and plantations in America have been, are, and of right ought to be, subordinate unto, and dependant upon the imperial crown and parliament of Great Britain; and that the king's majesty, by and with the advice and consent of the lords spiritual and temporal, and commons of Great Britain, in parliament assembled, had, hath, and of right ought to have, full power and authority to make laws and statutes of sufficient force and validity to bind the colonies and people of America, subjects of the crown of Great Britain, in all cases whatever'. Furthermore, the act condemned all the resolutions which had passed in the colonial assemblies questioning or denying the authority of the British Parliament as 'utterly null and void'.[1]

But, although the Rockinghamites flattered themselves that they had solved the problem by refusing to exercise a right which they specifically endorsed, more agile minds were looking out for a means of raising taxes in America without provoking the outcry which had greeted Grenville's stamp act. Charles Townshend was just the sort of quicksilver opportunist to seize on the distinction which was commonly made between taxation for the purposes of revenue and taxation for the control of trade, in the hope of exploiting it to the advantage of the British government. He cheerfully hit on the expedient of imposing duties on such items as paper, tea, glass and printers' colours, ostensibly for the direction of commerce, while having the satisfaction of gaining a considerable revenue in the process. Such tactics might appeal to those who enjoyed sophistical subtleties in the heady atmosphere of St Stephen's, but the subtlety seemed dishonest to the point of crudity so far as the Americans were concerned; as well as creating a determination to resist Townshend's duties the ruse discredited what had previously been a widely respected distinction between the two main functions of colonial taxation.

While the Rockinghamites favoured a 'sleeping sovereignty' as the answer to the American problem, Chatham, who had always regarded the declaratory act as theoretically unacceptable and politically inept, was willing to concede that the sovereignty of the British parliament was, in certain significant respects, limited. He argued that the British parliament had not the right to levy taxes in the colonies or to maintain armed forces in the American dependencies without the consent of the colonists. He was prepared to put the distinction between taxation for the purposes of revenue and taxation for the purposes of trade on a firmer theoretical foundation. Possibly he was less open to the accusation of expediency than the Rockinghamites were. Even Burke, despite the famous phrases about a great empire and little minds going ill together, and magnanimity in politics often being the greatest wisdom, was doing little more than arguing the case for expediency on a high level. The Rockinghamites were far less impressive as constitutional theorists than they liked to pretend, and though they were, in a genuine sense, friends of America their conduct was not always consistent. Neither Burke nor Chatham had a completely satisfactory answer to the problems of constitutional theory which the American dispute had exposed, and, when American resistance to the British government took a more violent turn, not even those who sympathised with the Americans were prepared to condone acts of defiance and reprisal which showed little respect for legitimately constituted authority or for the person and property of the king's representatives in the colonies.

North felt that he had done his best to be conciliatory. The Grafton ministry had already given up all the obnoxious duties which Townshend had introduced, with the single, glaring example of that on tea. Not only had it been agreed that some tangible manifestation of the government's right to levy duties should remain in evidence, but there was also the conviction that the tea duty could be convincingly defended as a sign of the government's solicitude for the welfare of the empire as a whole, and a proof of the willingness of the government to perform its obligations to the East India company. The continued intransigence of the Americans was especially galling, and it was impossible for North and his colleagues to understand it. To make further concessions seemed unwise and untimely, and with some misgiving and reluctance the British government felt compelled to reassert its authority in disaffected areas, particularly in the colony of Massachusetts and the port of Boston. The notorious Boston Tea Party in December 1773, when colonists disguised as Indians boarded the ships of the East India company and threw their hated cargoes into the sea, was so outrageous a provocation that George III and his ministers believed that they had little alternative but to respond. They were heartened by optimistic forecasts of the likely success of a tougher policy in America, and by the general disgust expressed in England for the Boston Tea Party. Chatham condemned the behaviour of the Americans as 'criminal' and a violation of 'the most indispensable ties of civil society'. Lord John Cavendish, a prominent Rockinghamite, thought it impossible to defend what the Bostonians had done. But despite the chorus of disapproval there were still definite limits on the lengths to which the Rockinghamites were prepared to go in punishing the Americans. The friends of America regretted what had happened, but they believed that erroneous policies on the part of the British government were chiefly to blame for the current unhappy situation. The Americans had erred, but they merited charity not retribution. Rockingham summed up the position when writing to Burke on 30 January 1774: 'The conduct of the Americans cannot be justified, but the folly and impolicy of the provocation deserve the fullest arraignments, and notwithstanding all that has passed, I can never give my assent to proceeding to actual force against the colonies.'[2]

Despite the hesitancy or hostility shown by many of the opposition leaders to the policy of coercion in America, the opportunity for a debater as vigorous, as resourceful, and as uninhibited as Charles James Fox to make his mark in the controversy was richly inviting. The friends of America were not in good order to do battle on behalf of their wayward protégés. Chatham was isolated, wracked by spells of mental instability and physical decrepitude, and incapable of giving any consistent lead. His distrust of the Rockinghamites, which dated back to the declaratory act, coloured his attitude towards Rockingham and his friends. The Rockinghamite contingent was equally incapable of pursuing a coherent and thoroughly prepared strategy in the house of commons. Rockingham himself was ill-fitted to provide decisive leadership, and though Edmund Burke liked to use the Rockinghamite group as the focus of his ideas on party the reality invariably fell short of the ambitious visions nurtured by his powerful imagination. Charles Fox could act as an independent critic of the government, courting the favour of the Rockinghamites without irrevocably committing himself to their cause. The jauntiness of his conduct in opposition would remind North of the ally he had lost. Initially Fox's technique in opposition looked back to the years when Walpole had successfully impressed himself upon the government by the ingenuity and lack of scruple which he had shown in opposition. It was possible that North would come to regret the dismissal of the incorrigible junior lord of the treasury; no one could foresee how long the American controversy would last. The length of the conflict, the growing intransigence on both sides, the influence of habitual opposition focused on one major issue of policy—all of these governed the evolution of Fox as an exponent and practitioner of the craft of systematic opposition. His political beliefs underwent no revolutionary convulsion. Above all else a house of commons man, it was as a house of commons man that his initial flirtation with opposition to the policy of coercion in America took place.

North's proposals for the punishment of the Americans were embodied in the Boston port bill and another bill for the regulation of the government of the Massachusetts colony. The port of Boston was to be closed, pending the payment of compensation to the East India company and the crown; the constitution of Massachusetts was to be amended by substituting the nomination of the upper legislative house by the crown for election by the house of representatives; troops were to be stationed in barracks in the town of Boston; and, at the Governor's discretion, controversial trials were to be remanded to England, in order to ensure that those indulging in smuggling and acts of defiance would be brought to justice. North argued that he was restoring law and order, and that events would show that the majority of Americans would dissociate themselves from events in Boston. Other American ports would, in any case, benefit from the diversion of traffic previously dealt with at Boston.

The Boston port bill passed the commons with little trouble, but Charles Fox expressed his misgivings forcefully and lucidly. Shrewdly he questioned the advisability of entrusting the crown with the power to close a port in the way proposed. In criticising the bill he cleverly concentrated upon the constitutional aspects of the proposed legislation:

> The bill ... was calculated for three purposes: the first for securing trade, the second for punishing the Bostonians, and the third for satisfaction to the East India company. He said the first clause did not give a true and exact distinction by what means, and at what period, the crown was to exercise the power vested in it; he thought that application for relief should come to parliament only, and that the power of affording such relief should not be lodged in the crown. The quarrel was with parliament, and parliament was the proper power to end it; not, said he ironically, that there is any need to distrust his majesty's ministers, that they will not restore the port when it shall be proper; but I want to hear the reason why this clause should be so left in the judgment of the crown, and the next clause should be so particularly granted, with such a guard upon his majesty to prevent him from restoring the port until the East India company should be fully satisfied.[3]

The first occasion when Fox went into the same lobby as the Rockinghamites was on 19 April 1774 in support of a motion calling for the repeal of the American tea duty. The motion was defeated by 182 votes to 49, but during the debate Fox argued that the Americans would once again become useful and loyal subjects, providing they were treated with appropriate generosity and moderation. But, even while warning the government of the risks of pushing the colonists further along the road to outright revolt, Fox was capable of invoking the doctrine of virtual representation, an indication of the limitations of his own outlook at this period:

> When the stamp act was repealed murmurs ceased and quiet succeeded. Taxes have produced a contrary behaviour; quiet has been succeeded by riots and disturbances. Here is an absolute dereliction of the authority of this country. It has been said, that America is not represented in this house, but the Americans are full as virtually taxed as virtually represented. A tax can only be laid for three purposes; the first for a commercial regulation, the second for a revenue, and the third for asserting your right. As to the two first, it has been clearly denied that it is for either; as to the latter, it is only done with a view to irritate and declare war against the Americans, which, if you persist in, I am clearly of the opinion you will effect, or force them, into open rebellion.[4]

Fox was merely reiterating the Rockinghamite solution: no abrogation of the legislative supremacy of the British coupled with a willingness to refrain from exercising the right should it offend the susceptibilities of the colonists or embitter the relationship between the mother country and America. The tea duty was expendable because it had become the symbol of subjection, and because it was bringing the British crown, the British parliament, and even the British connexion itself into bad odour and ill repute. But merely to jettison the tea duty would not heal the breach; the revision of the Massachusetts constitution had roused the deepest suspicions in America, where it was likened to James II's attack on borough charters, and the extension of the quarrel to cover matters of constitutional procedure raised issues which were more heavily charged with emotion and with memories of historic struggles for constitutional liberties, so that on both sides self-righteousness stiffened the determination to resist.

Fox's own attitudes were still in a formative stage. Even during the debates on the Massachusetts government bill he shifted his ground when referring to the legislative supremacy of parliament. He responded to each new piece of news from America and he was sensitive to the ebb and flow of passion within the house of commons. Matters of constitutional theory were secondary to the daily transformations of politics. On 22 April 1774 he stated that, while he did not believe Britain had any right to tax the Americans, he was convinced that the Americans were wrong in resisting the legislative authority of the British parliament. But when the Massachusetts government bill was debated again on 2 May he argued that the question was whether America was to be governed by force or by management, and he likened the bill to legislative coercion, as contrasted with law, for it was tantamount to taking

away the colony's charter. It was far from clear whether or not this involved some diminution of the right to legislate. Fox was probably aware
that he was in some danger of going further than his Rockinghamite
allies—further than the majority of MPs—in yielding some point of
principle over the contentious claim of legislative supremacy vested in
the British parliament. He therefore returned to the efficacy of laying
aside the right to tax as the best means of convincing Americans that they
were deeply attached by ties of sentiment and affection to Great Britain.
He discovered that his most reliable source of support and encouragement in the commons came from the Rockinghamites; he therefore fell
back on their distinction between the validity of a legislative right and
the political wisdom of exercising such a right.

He was happier in explaining how affairs had deteriorated to their
sorry state than in dealing with the constitutional enigma which now
lay at the heart of the dispute. He was also active in warning the commons of the likely consequences of government policy. In March 1775
he reminded the house of the way in which the Americans had been
compelled to abandon the original distinction between internal and external taxation by the realisation that external taxation could be made
'to answer all the purposes, and to produce all the mischiefs, of internal
taxation'. The Americans had denied parliament's right of taxing for
supply; when parliament had sought to deprive them of their charters
and to regulate their forms of government they had denounced its power
of internal legislation. Yet, despite the provocation to which they had
been subjected, and the violence which had broken out, the Americans
had never formally rejected the power of parliament to bind their trade.
For Britain to reduce the colonies to submission by restricting the commerce of the New England colonies would do nothing but exasperate the
colonies into open and direct rebellion. North's policy was giving the
Americans no alternative to starvation but rebellion, worst of all 'an
opportunity for drawing the sword and throwing away the scabbard'.
Fox was justly apprehensive about the type of war which would follow
armed risings in the colonies. Because of the vastness of distance it would
be a difficult war to control. Deep convictions had awakened passions
on both sides which would render such a war immune from the normal
restraints of conflict between civilised states. It would be a hard war to
bring to an end by means of conventional diplomacy and negotiation.
Considerations such as these made Fox regard the follies of the government with mounting apprehension.

The Americans were being goaded into extremism by the stupidity of
the government. When the commons debated a motion of Burke's to

receive a remonstrance from the colony of New York on 5 May 1775 Fox warned members of the dangers of forcing the colonists to take extreme measures, but he also revived the familiar distinction between the recognition of a right and the exercise of that right:

> The right of parliament to tax America was not simply denied in the remonstrance but only as coupled with the exercise of it. The exercise was the thing complained of, not the right itself. When the declaratory act was passed, asserting the right in the fullest extent, there were no tumults in America, no opposition to government in any part of that country: but when the right came to be exercised in the manner we have seen, the whole country was alarmed, and there was a unanimous determination to oppose it. The right simply is not regarded; it is the exercise of it that is the object of opposition. It is this exercise that has irritated, and made almost desperate several of the colonies; but the noble lord chooses to be consistent; he is determined to make them all mad alike.[5]

Events were moving beyond the scope of constitutional debates, theoretical refinements, and even judicious warnings. In April 1775 the first shots were fired at Concord and Lexington; the government had to deal with armed rebellion, not merely with isolated acts of disobedience. It was becoming increasingly difficult to hold out even the possibility of fruitful negotiations. Distrust and resentment and mutual suspicion flourished with every scuffle between the colonists and British troops, and, with every life that was lost, the temptation to insist on a final outcome which would be justification both of the taking of life and the willingness to sacrifice one's own life grew stronger and more compelling for both sides. Englishmen who had talked lightly of restoring law and order and a respect for the king's name in America were faced with the task of waging a special type of war, with its own problems of strategy and tactics, of supply and logistics. There was always a sense of unease in men's minds. Fighting the Americans was not the same as fighting the French, and the British were hampered by a disturbing reluctance to accept that it had, after all, come to war. It was this failure to come to terms with the unpleasantnesses of reality, as much as any innate arrogance, which led Englishmen eagerly to grasp at suggestions that American resistance would speedily wither away, that the rebels were merely a handful of rascally and cowardly eccentrics, and that hostilities would soon end with the colonists asking to be forgiven, family harmony being duly restored. Ignorance of the terrain, and disdain for the informal tactics of insurgent warfare, bred their own species of false optimism.

But until military defeat brought its own brand of disillusionment the outbreak of hostilities precipitated a reaction which rallied support for the king and for North. Many men who had had doubts about the justice or wisdom of British policy towards the Americans felt it to be their patriotic duty to rally round the flag: disputes about the nature of a settlement with the colonists could wait until rebellion and disorder had been crushed.

It was more difficult for Fox and his associates to carry on anything resembling a 'patriotic' opposition once the quarrel with the Americans had ended in war. Debates about the causes of the war, and even proposals for conciliation, had been rendered irrelevant by events. To criticise the conduct of war, even to plead for continued attempts to understand the American point of view, were tainted with treasonable half-heartedness. Things became rather easier when France joined the conflict as an ally of the Americans: conciliation with the Americans could be linked with demands for the more resolute waging of the war against the French. Fox was grateful for sympathy wherever he could find it. He yearned for public support. An example of the approach which he made to those of friends who had not declared themselves may be taken from a letter which he wrote to Lord Ossory on 5 November 1775:

> ... I am glad to inform you that, on Friday next, Burke will move to bring in a bill to secure the colonies against parliamentary taxation, and to repeal the obnoxious laws. I say I am very glad that Burke is to move such a bill, because it will be the fairest test in the world to try who is really for war and who for peace. It is conceived in the most moderate terms imaginable, and states no more than that the Americans have considered themselves as aggrieved by taxation, not that they are actually so; and upon the ground of their having been *in their conception* injured, is founded the repeal of the tea act, etc., and a general pardon and indemnity. I am sure, my dear Ossory, if you do think seriously enough of this matter to let your opinion regulate your conduct, it is impossible but you must consider this as the true opportunity of declaring yourself. And, indeed, if party does not blind me very much more than I am aware of, this is an occasion when a man not overscrupulous ought to think for himself. It does not need surely the tenth part of your good sense to see how cruel and intolerable a thing it is to sacrifice thousands of lives almost without prospect of advantage.[6]

It was unthinkable for the opposition to contemplate any complete change of ministry at this stage. All they could hope for was a moderation of government policy, and, should any members of the government be particularly discredited, for some partial reshuffle which would bring some liberally disposed men into the administration. But there were peculiar handicaps in opposing the war against the Americans. The opposition could not restrict themselves to criticising the inefficiency with which the war was being fought; they were inevitably drawn into a discussion of the aims of the war, of the conditions in which a peace could be negotiated, and of the means by which the colonists could be reconciled with Britain. In each of these instances the criticisms which the opposition made of the government's policy could be denounced as giving comfort to the king's enemies and inspiration to rebels in the field. It was, therefore, less probable that North would accept opposition criticisms or amend his approach towards any possible negotiations with the Americans in the light of what Fox and his friends had said in the house of commons. A further complication was the tendency for hopes to be raised or dashed by every victory or reverse. It was always possible for the government to argue that victory was just round the corner, that only one more effort was needed to convince the Americans that whatever the outcome of negotiations there was no purpose in continuing to resist lawful authority by force of arms. Fox knew, too, how imperative it was to avoid greeting defeats inflicted on the British army with too obvious enthusiasm: as it was his impetuosity often got the better of him, and his critics frequently claimed that he gloated over the sufferings and humiliations endured by his countrymen. It was convenient for the government that the opponents of the war could be discredited by the charge that they were too sympathetic to the Americans to be good British patriots.

Although contemporary political ideas could not condone anything savouring of a formed opposition, and although party was for most men synonymous with faction, the opposition to the American war had a deceptive appearance of unity, which allowed the misleading impression to be gained that all those who denounced the policies of the government belonged to the same party. For as long as the war continued this illusion was fostered by the accidents of circumstance, though once the war was over the divisions between the various whig groups became all too apparent. But in truth the tensions which caused so much strain during and after Rockingham's second ministry were there all the time, obscured by a common hostility to the policy of coercion in America but undiminished by the enforced alliances of politics.

Chatham always remained disdainfully independent; contemptuous of men whom he hated as the destroyers of his life's work, but indefatigably opposed to any tactics implying that he was a party man, he went his own way, wilfully and magnificently, to the end. Shelburne, who saw himself as Chatham's political heir, had ideas of his own about the handling of the American problem: he had hoped to evade the problem of revenue by arranging for the Americans to pay quit-rents to the crown in areas of new colonisation, and unlike many Englishmen he acknowledged the inevitability of American expansion west of the Alleghanies. Nor did he accept the suggestion that American political independence would sever all ties with Britain. He envisaged commercial and economic reciprocity and the possibility of a common foreign policy. The originality of his proposals did not commend them to the attention of the commons. The opposition were divided on the nature of British sovereignty in America and once the Americans had declared themselves independent of Britain in July 1776 the friends of America could not agree on whether recognition of American independence should be conceded at all, or on the wisdom of recognising the independence of the United States merely as part of an overall peace settlement or as a preliminary to peace negotiations. Once France had declared war the opposition were able to cover up their differences of opinion by vehemently urging the government to give priority to the war against France, allowing the war against the colonists to fall into desuetude. Such a standpoint was more explicable as an answer to the exigencies of parliamentary politics than as a serious military concept. The war with France was inextricably bound up with that in America and, attractive though the idea of concentrating on the foreign enemy rather than on the unruly colonists was, it did not represent military realities.

Despite their differences and despite Rockingham's pallid leadership, the opposition was given both dignity and a sense of purpose by Edmund Burke's propensity to weave his theories about the party from the none too robust threads of the Rockinghamite group. Burke had defended the necessity for party in his *Thoughts on the Cause of the Present Discontents*, published in 1770. For him party was the means of restoring integrity to political life. Far from reducing politics to a scramble for place and profit party would allow convictions and ideas to mould political controversy, putting disagreements to positive use and allowing a fertile continuity to enrich political conflict. Burke's definition of party has become an integral part of liberal political theory, but in his own day his ideas were bold and controversial and all too rarely understood:

Party is a body of men united, for promoting by their joint endeavours the national interest, upon some particular principle in which they are all agreed. For my part, I find it impossible to conceive, that any one believes in his own politics, or thinks them to be of any weight, who refuses to adopt the means of having them reduced into practice. It is the business of the speculative philosopher to mark the proper ends of government. It is the business of the politician, who is the philosopher in action, to find out proper means towards those ends, and to employ them with effect. Therefore every honourable connexion will avow it is their first purpose, to pursue every just method to put the men who hold their opinions into such a condition as may enable them to carry their common plans into execution, with all the power and authority of the state.

The Rockinghamites, however honourable they believed themselves to be as a connexion, were not always agreed upon particular principles, and the opposition as a whole bore even less resemblance to Burke's vision. But for Charles Fox, still a lonely figure, and not by any means a fully fledged Rockinghamite, Burke's ideas provided the general context in which his own notions of party and opposition, more closely related as they were to the immediate demands of politics, could mature. With the bracing expansiveness of Burke's thought to goad him on, Fox came to identify himself, not with a closely wrought political ideology, but with a set of attitudes and assumptions which determined the shape of his future outlook.

Fox and Burke were associated with the struggle against the American war and with pleas for a negotiated settlement. Later they were to work together on plans for economic reform and for the reform of the government of India. But though their association was of crucial significance in Fox's emergence as a major political figure, and though many of the ideas to which Fox gave expression in such fields as the appointment of ministers and the collective responsibility of the cabinet were a tribute to how much he had learned from Burke, it is important not to exaggerate the intimacy of their personal friendship. Forged in the heat of political controversy it later broke under the strain of political dissension. Fox was a political associate who echoed many of the insights of Burke's thought. He took what was relevant to his needs, and, often vulgarising the ideas in the process, he made what he had acquired into his own. But it was not a formal relationship of master and pupil, any more than it was a harmonious personal union. Fox's language was always more earthy than Burke's, and though he often invoked the loftiest of Burke's ideas he never attained anything like the same intellectual profundity, the same philosophical insight, or the same immense and perplexing consistency. Burke subordinated politics to transcendent ideas, seeing political behaviour as a reflection of moral principles and as a mode of satisfying the moral law. Fox liked to discuss issues of general principle, but he was always ruled by the needs of the moment, the opportunities which each political situation gave for seizing an advantage or defeating an opponent. For Fox political ideas, however deeply held and however ennobling, were part of the eternal conflict of politics; they were expressions of invincible common sense rather than of immortal truth. Fox saw politics as a struggle for power and a clash of interests. He was no theorist, seeking to reduce the political order to any systematised abstract philosophy. He was a practising politician, for whom the exchange of ideas was an important but incidental part of the unceasing tumult of politics.

He had chosen to defend the Americans and to explain the errors of government policy in America. He did so, not only because of his devotion to liberty, but because he was deeply apprehensive of the political consequences of antagonising the Americans. He saw English interests as the major victims of the American conflict. He had persuaded himself that the crisis was the outcome of an attack on the independence of the house of commons by the abuse of the prerogatives and influence of the crown, but he was also worried by the disturbance in the balance of power which the loss of the American colonies would bring about. Like George III he had no wish to see the British empire destroyed. The difference between Fox and his king was that Fox believed that only by refraining from exercising a legitimate legislative supremacy could Britain hope to retain the affection and loyalty of the Americans, and that on such affections the true unity of the empire depended. Whether it is permissible to argue that Fox had a fully articulated theory of empire, similar to some of those which emerged in the reign of Victoria, is doubtful. Fox was neither an imperialist nor an anti-imperialist in the nineteenth-century sense. He did not move from dogma to politics; he judged each political situation on its merits. Though he was prepared to recognise the independence of the United States, and though he favoured granting legislative autonomy to the Irish parliament in Dublin, he had no desire to abandon British responsibilities in India, however much he wanted to improve the control exercised by the British government over the East India company.

Possibly his first attacks on North and the government's policy in America were motivated as much by a desire to shine in opposition as by any real concern for the welfare of the American colonies as such. For a man in Fox's situation such behaviour was understandable, given his political isolation and the peculiar problems of opposition in the eighteenth century. But as the situation in America worsened, and as the more gloomy predictions of the government's critics were fulfilled, a note of profounder conviction and more passionate commitment entered into Fox's speeches. As the government's incompetence was more cruelly exposed he threw himself ever more vigorously into the attack, and whenever the outlook was black for the Americans his sense of loyalty was roused, leading him to assert that whoever else might desert the Americans when things were going badly for them he would remain faithful (even in moments of despondency he was capable of strange spasms of defiant optimism). Writing to Ossory in June 1776 he gave vent to his confused feelings on hearing of American reverses in Canada:

I am still convinced the Americans will finally succeed, whether by victories or defeats; and if they do not, I am sure ... that it will check all future enterprise to such a degree as to give the completest triumph to toryism that it ever had.... Whatever happens, for God's sake let us all resolve to stick by them as handsomely (or more so) in their adversity as we have done in their glory, and still maintain the whig cause, however discredited by defeats, to be the only true principle for this country. The serieux of this letter may probably make you think me more dispirited than I am by this news. I am really not much so myself; but I see such strange dispositions in others to despond on every trifling disadvantage, that I fear the effect it may have upon them....[7]

Fox was firmly of the opinion that it was physically and therefore militarily impossible for Britain to subdue the American colonies. The war was not to be won by a few set-piece battles; once order was restored in one area insurrection would break out in another. Unless the confidence of the Americans in the good intentions of the British government and in the benefits of the British connexion was restored the attempt to compel the colonists to submit once more to the British crown was bound to fail. He made his position clear on 18 November 1777 when taking part in the debate on the king's speech:

Mr Fox asserted that the idea of conquering America was absurd; and that such an event was, in the nature of things, absolutely impossible. He proved his assertion from the situation of the country, the disposition of the people, and the distance from Great Britain. He said, that though the resources of this empire might be such as to enable us to carry on the war for several campaigns more, there was a fundamental error in the proceedings, which would forever prevent our generals from acting with success; that no man of common sense would have placed the two armies in such a position as from their distance made it utterly impossible that one should receive any assistance from the other. That the war carried on by General Burgoyne was a war of posts: that the taking of one did not subdue the country, but that it would be necessary to conquer it inch by inch: that his army was not equal to the task, for the numerous skirmishes with the enemy, and the natural difficulties of the country, would so retard his motions, that the campaign must be ended before the object of it was fulfilled; and that if he was happy enough to join Sir William Howe it must be with nothing more than the shattered remains of an army mouldered away.[8]

Fox was fully justified in his criticisms of the strategy which was to splutter out in humiliation at Saratoga. Indeed, as Fox spoke he was unaware that Burgoyne had already surrendered; events had confirmed Fox's prescience. The Saratoga compaign was a perfect example of those military inspirations which look impressive on a map, in some headquarters far from the front, but which are rendered futile by the conditions in which the troops have to march and fight. The attractions of dividing the troublesome northern seaboard colonies from the other American settlements were obvious, but the distances which Burgoyne's force had to cover were immense, while the cooperation of Clinton and Howe, on which the success of the venture depended, was not forthcoming, partly because of deficient communications between London and America, partly because the details of the campaign were never fully coordinated and conveyed to the generals on the spot. Instead of concentrating all their resources on one objective the British generals dispersed them on a number of sideshows. Hypothetical political advantages lured the military leaders into misjudgments. The most ominous consequence of the Saratoga capitulation, news of which reached London in late November, was the almost certain entry of France into the war.

Fox was worried by the lack of realism governing the direction of the war in the colonies; he was also deeply shocked by the readiness of the government to authorise the employment of Indian auxiliaries. There was nothing new in this, just as there was nothing new about the use of German mercenaries. During the wars against the French, Indians had acted as scouts and guides, and both sides were appreciative of the advantages of gaining help from the Indians. The problem was that it was difficult to control Indian tribesmen; they were often unreliable, and in the heat of battle it was virtually impossible to discipline them. Fox found it repulsive that Indians should be used against the colonists, expressing his horror at 'arming the Indians and letting them loose, not only against the troops of America, but also against the defenceless women and children, whose bodies even death could not rescue from the insults and barbarity of the savages'. He was aware of the propaganda value to the Americans of the British employment of Indians, regretting that 'a prince so famed for his humanity, benevolence, and sanctity of manners, as his present majesty was' could allow Indian troops to serve in his army.

Saratoga was a desperate blow for the morale of North's government. In an effort to avert calamity North sought to conciliate the Americans. Though preparations continued to be made for the prosecution of the war the British government offered to recognise the American Congress, to abandon any right to tax the colonies, and even to discuss the possibility of American representatives sitting at Westminster. But it was still argued that the British parliament should control trade, and this, coupled with the insistence that loyal colonists should be restored to their properties, was enough to ensure the failure of the negotiations. The hope that the Americans were longing to return to their allegiance was exposed as a shallow mockery. With the intervention of the French fleet, and a more bitter atmosphere in America, the future was indeed sombre.

But Fox was driven to welcome every attempt at conciliation. Although the division of opinion within the opposition now tended to be over the advisability of recognising the independence of the United States, which was vehemently opposed by Chatham and Shelburne, no one could condemn efforts to reach a negotiated settlement with the Americans, however much men doubted the likelihood of such a negotiation being successful. On 17 February 1778 Fox told the house of commons that North's proposals for conciliation would be supported by those with whom he had the honour to act. The terms set before the house did not differ to any significant extent from those which Burke had put forward three years earlier. Fox was particularly happy that the government had at last seen the wisdom of relinquishing the right of taxation, and that the traditional liberties which the Americans had enjoyed under their charters would be restored. He reminded the house that the Americans were as jealous of the rights of their assemblies as they were apprehensive about taxation; their chief objection to the latter was that it adversely affected the former. But he was concerned about the failure to make these concessions in time. He told a stunned house that he was in possession of information stating that France had concluded a treaty with the independent United States of America. Did the government know anything about this treaty? Had they any inkling, while making their proposals for conciliation, of the treaty which made those proposals as useless to the cause of peace as they were now seen to be humiliating to the dignity of Great Britain? Fox was in the fortunate position of having been given private information by Thomas Walpole about the outcome of Franco-American negotiations which were taking place in Paris. North could only tell the House that he had no definite information, but that it had to be admitted that a treaty between France and America was a possibility which could not be ruled out. Fox had shown, not only that the government were doing the right thing too late, but that their incompetence was equalled only by their ignorance.

Fox was in determined mood; during the previous two years he had often taken some of his associates to task for failing to show sufficient toughness in opposition. Rockingham had been rebuked for his faint-heartedness. Fox had combated the idea of a secession from parliament as long ago as October 1776, warning Rockingham that a secession would be interpreted as no more than the opposition running away, possibly as the abandonment of an untenable course. Whether in good fortune or bad he believed 'firmness' to be necessary. Fox assured Rockingham that he intended to adhere 'still more if possible ... to those principles of government which we have always recommended with respect to America, and to maintain that if America should be at our feet (which God forbid!) we ought to give them as good terms (at least) as those offered in Burke's propositions'.[9] But in February 1777, despite his exhortations, Fox found himself virtually alone in opposing the second reading of the bill suspending habeas corpus in America. Rockingham, Cavendish, and Burke had all absented themselves from parliament, though Fox did have the comfort of Sir George Savile's support. The close of the year left him convinced that the country would be 'totally demolished' by the government's 'folly, obstinacy, and insensibility'. But he also felt that the opposition were slowly making inroads into public opinion, as well as opinion within the house of commons, and he flattered himself that, in the long run, opinions would influence votes.

His contempt for the government was boundless. The king's ministers seemed intent on keeping their places, though they had little idea of how to grapple with the problems facing the country. They were as ignorant of how to make peace as they were incapable of waging war. Yet their hold on the house of commons was as firm as ever. In February 1778 Fox lamented to his friend, Richard Fitzpatrick, who was then in

America, that although the opposition was gaining more votes than in previous divisions, he was disappointed, considering the state of the country, that the administration continued to secure substantial majorities. In the house Fox sought to exploit the mood of the hour by overlooking the question of the justice of the war and concentrating his criticism upon the folly with which it was being fought and 'the absolute madness of continuing it'. He was especially outraged and disgusted by the tendency of the ministers to throw all the blame for the failure of the Saratoga campaign upon Burgoyne, 'a baseness', so he told Fitzpatrick, 'beyond what even you or I could have expected from them'. He was looking forward to leading the opposition attack on the government's military incompetence, but, much as he enjoyed debate in the house of commons, he hated the preparatory business of looking at accounts, drawing up motions, and checking information. Although he was optimistic about the degree of support the critics of the government would receive he recognised the unlikelihood of their being a change of ministry:

> *I am convinced we shall so far succeed as to get great divisions* in the house of commons, and to convince all the world that the ministers deserve all possible contempt; *but when we have done that, I think we shall have done all we can do, and the ministers, though despised everywhere, and by everybody, will still continue ministers. I am thoroughly persuaded of this,* but the general opinion is otherwise.[10]

Fox discounted reports that Chatham was about to form a ministry: he regarded these as the unrealistic daydreams of people who were looking for a deliverer who would turn the tide of defeat and lead the country to victory over the French, while miraculously restoring the situation in America.

At this period Fox was torn by conflicting hopes and various anxieties. He knew that his reputation as a speaker, particularly as a master of the debating techniques so necessary for success in the house of commons, was rising, and yet he wondered whether he would ever be given the chance to prove himself in office. He recognised the attractions of power: a growing sense of his maturing talents made his frustrations all the more galling. But he was also conscious of his continued isolation in politics. He had acted in concert with the Rockinghamites, but he had not been fully assimilated to that party. He was still a freelance; any one with more definite party ties would have found it more difficult to be so bold and so wantonly defiant in exploiting every governmental weakness. The knowledge that he was very much his own master made Fox a more appealing figure than a more conventional party man would have been to those backbenchers who obstinately regarded the Rockinghamites as a suspicious faction.

Yet Fox had been subjected to considerable pressures to identify himself more closely and more obediently with Rockingham and his followers. On 8 October 1777 Burke wrote a long letter to Fox expounding the need for men to act in concert in public life, surveying the opposition groups with a critical as well as a sympathetic eye. Burke pleaded with Fox to behave with greater consistency, despite his own awareness of the limitations of Rockingham and the Cavendishes and of the obstacles towards having any 'settled, preconceived plan'. He was conscious that the divisions within the opposition, and the disagreements between the various leaders, had contributed to the depressing situation in which they found themselves. The opposition's plight was obvious: 'What we are is now pretty evidently experienced, and it is certain, that partly by our own common faults, but much more by the difficulties of our Situation, and some circumstances of unavoidable misfortune, we are in little better than a sort of Cul-de-Sac.'[11]

Burke understood Fox's burning sense of disappointment. With considerable compassion he warned Fox of the dangers of being over-zealous or too passionate. He knew from his own experience of the high price which had to be paid for outbursts of enthusiasm. Patience was indispensable to a politician, and discussion of this point led Burke to raise the question of party:

If you should grow too earnest, you will be still more inexcusable than I was. Your having entered into affairs so much younger ought to make them too familiar to you, to be a cause of much agitation, and you have much more day before you for your work. Do not be in haste. Lay your foundations deep in public opinion. Though (as you are sensible) I have never given you the least hint of advice about joining yourself in a declared connexion with our party, nor do I now—yet as I love that party very well, and am clear that you are better able to serve than any man I know, I wish that things should be so kept, as to leave you mutually open to one another in all changes and exigencies. And I wish this the rather, because in order to be very great, as I am anxious that you should be, (always presuming that you are disposed to make a good use of power) you will certainly want some better support than merely that of the crown. For I much doubt whether, with all your parts, you are the man formed for acquiring real interior favour in this court or in any. I therefore wish you a firm ground in the country; and I do not know so firm and sound a bottom to build upon as our party....[12]

Fox had already told Lord John Townshend that he had decided to co-operate with Rockingham, but his attitude was far from settled, and in some ways it was uncertain and ambivalent. He knew that a common opposition to the American war made it natural and inevitable that he should work with the Rockinghamites, but he was hesitant about moving forward from common action combating particular aspects of government policy to complete membership of the Rockingham group. Unlike the Rockinghamites Fox was, at this stage, sceptical of both the desirability and practicality of procuring a complete change of ministry. He wanted to remain open to any approaches from the government side. He saw any change of heart on the ministers' part as being reflected in the dropping of those ministers who were personally identified with the policy of coercion in America. At this stage he did not anticipate collective resignation by North and his colleagues; such a step was rare in eighteenth-century politics, and Fox preferred the idea of the administration opening its ranks to admit some of those who had distinguished themselves as critics of the American war. By keeping at some distance from the Rockinghamites Fox flattered himself that he would thereby become more acceptable as a potential member of the ministry. By pinning his hopes on a cabinet reshuffle, and by concentrating his attacks on particular ministers, of whom Lord George Germain was the prime example, he believed himself to be conforming to the known realities of contemporary politics; but this meant that his relationship with the Rockinghamites was a curious one. He consoled himself with the thought that Burke's advice had been far from clear, and that while encouraging him to act with 'the honestest public men' Burke had also charged him to retain sufficient freedom of manoeuvre for all future emergencies. He was also torn by the awareness that any invitation to join a reformed and repentant government would be dependent on his speaking for a body of opinion more broadly based than the Rockinghamite contingent, and representative of opinion outside parliament. But even here there were dangers. If he took too many pains to cultivate extra-parliamentary support he would make himself less acceptable to George III and his ministers.

There were times when he tried hard to rationalise his political frustrations, and to reconcile the often divergent impulses dictated by his mind and his feelings. He sought advice from his friends only to ignore much of the advice which he was given. He was preoccupied with the

call of honour, yet sensitive to the demands of interest. Admiring some
of his political allies, he despised others, and despite the vigour of his
onslaughts on North and his colleagues, there were some members of
the cabinet—North himself being the most obvious example—for whom
he retained a lingering regard. To an old friend like Fitzpatrick he unburdened himself in an uninhibited and rather bewildering way:

I am certainly ambitious by nature, but I really have, or think I have
totally subdued the passion. I have still as much vanity as ever, which
is a happier passion by far: because great reputation I think I may
acquire and *keep*, great situation I *never* can acquire, nor if acquired,
keep without making sacrifices that I never will make. If I am wrong,
and more sanguine people right, *tant mieux*, and I shall be as happy
as they can be, but if I am right, I am sure I shall be the happier,
for having made up my mind to my situation. I need not say how
happy I am at the thoughts of your coming; I should be so at all times,
but I really want you at present to a great degree. I have other friends
whom I love, and who I believe love me, but I foresee possible cases
where I am determined to act against all the advice that they are
likely to give me. I know they will not shake me, for nothing ever shall;
but yet it would be a great satisfaction to have you here, who I know
would be of my opinion. You guess, I may say, the sort of cases I mean.
I shall be told by prudent friends that I am under no sort of engage-
ments to any set of men. *I certainly am not*, but there are many cases,
where there is no engagement, and yet it is dishonourable not to act as
if there was one. But even suppose it were quite honourable, is it possible to be happy in acting with people of whom one has the worst
opinions, and being on a cold-footing (which must be the case) with all
those whom one loves best, and with whom one passes one's life? I
have talked to you a great deal about myself, but I know it will interest
you, and I have really little else to tell you....[13]

He warned Fitzpatrick not to expect any change in politics when he
arrived home; if he did so, he would almost certainly be disappointed.
Curiously Fox felt that only Lord Camden and Burke shared his pessimism about the future, but he was more than ever convinced that they were
right to be despondent. He anticipated a period of intense unpopularity:
'we are, *and ever shall be*, as much proscribed as ever the Jacobites were
formerly.'[14]

Thus, though Fox was more open to any approach from the government
than his colleagues in opposition, he was gloomy about the outcome of
any negotiation. He sensed that the government's motives, like his own,

would be mixed, and that the need to minimise the impact of defeat was more of an impetus than any desire to broaden the ministry for its own sake. Military reverses were more persuasive than any of Fox's speeches in the commons, but although defeat was the most convincing argument in favour of ministerial readjustment, it was hardly calculated to increase the popularity of men who were already distrusted as friends of the Americans and lukewarm patriots. A deterioration in the military situation was a necessary preliminary for the entry of Fox and his companions into office, but it would create a hideous complex of diplomatic and other problems for the new administration to face. Furthermore, the war ensured that the motives of government and opposition in entering any discussions for admitting new men into the ministry were contradictory: the administration sought to win renewed public confidence by strengthening its ranks in order to prosecute the war with greater vigour and efficiency, while the opposition wanted to end the war, at least so far as hostilities against the American colonists were concerned, some scaling down of the conflict being in their view an indispensable pre-condition for the victorious conclusion of the struggle against France. The problem of American independence not only embarrassed the government, it divided the opposition, and although the negotiation of March 1778 was a characteristic example of the methods which eighteenth-century governments habitually resorted to in moments of crisis it was carried out against a background of exceptional difficulty and with little prospect of success.

The government contacted Fox and Shelburne with a view to a possible agreement being worked out with the ministers of the crown. William Eden was the agent employed on these confidential meetings. Shelburne was seen as the representative of the Chatham interest, and since the government was seeking to stimulate a greater sense of national confidence on the eve of the extension of the war through French intervention, any sign that Chatham was prepared either to join the ministry or to allow his followers to do so was eagerly looked for. Shelburne reminded Eden that, in his opinion, Rockingham ought to be approached about any broadening of the administration, and that, above all else, it was essential for Chatham to become the effective head of the government. He pointed out that Chatham would be dissatisfied with any proposals 'which did not comprehend and annihilate every party in the kingdom'. Chatham favoured the inclusion of both Grafton and Rockingham, while Shelburne particularly condemned Lord George Germain, among the current ministers. Lord Sandwich was also criticised; clearly here were two scapegoats who could be sacrificed with impunity. But Shelburne was dubious about whether any government could withstand the military reverses which he felt would probably follow France's entry into the war, and during the discussions with Eden he became more outspoken in advocating an entirely new cabinet under Chatham, with most of the important offices changing hands. Though Shelburne sought to mollify Eden's anxiety by arguing that the complete change of personnel would apply only to posts of cabinet rank, Eden could not but complain of the harshness of Shelburne's proposals. He condemned the attempt which he believed Chatham was making of dictating terms which would lead to the removal of servants of the crown, who had faithfully striven to defend and secure the interests of king and parliament. Shelburne claimed that Chatham was in good health and high spirits, but finally the stringency of Chatham's terms terminated the negotiation. Shelburne abruptly told Eden that the time was not ripe for Chatham and himself to take office, and he repeated familiar assurances that he was much happier in a retired situation.

Although in theory Chatham's dislike of party and his desire to form a truly national government had much in common with the king's desire to end the unhappy distinctions of party, his determination to be the dominant figure in any new government and his insistence on a clean sweep in the upper reaches of the administration revealed that he was interested, not in stabilising the ministry by bringing in new talent, but in substituting a ministry which would, for all practical purposes, be controlled by himself. Though Chatham disowned Rockinghamite apologies for 'party' ministries, the consequences of his own demands approximated, in the eyes of the king, to much the same thing.

Fox behaved throughout the negotiations in an open and straightforward way. On receiving a note from Eden, inquiring if he could spare 'five minutes from the politics of the day,' he immediately went to Eden's house, where the two of them dined alone. Eden pledged Fox to secrecy, and then went on to talk generally about the advisability of strengthening the government. He refrained from making specific proposals, preferring to speculate on any ministerial changes rather than proposing any. He discovered that Fox was in favour of removing Lord George Germain, the secretary of state responsible for the American colonies, and that he believed a post such as treasurer of the navy was more appropriate for himself than a major appointment. Fox approved of bringing in the Shelburne group, which he thought by no means improbable, but, though he was at pains to state that he was 'unconnected and at liberty,' he disavowed any possibility of accepting office 'singly and alone.' With the exception of Germain he was prepared to serve with the present ministers, but he believed that his own situation depended on at least one other opposition figure being amenable to coming into the government. In some ways he expected little to come of the conversations, but he begged Eden to keep him well informed of what arrangements might be agreed with other interested parties.

Eden had sufficient confidence in Fox to be satisfied that he would not put these private discussions to any political use, but he felt that there was no immediate prospect of making Fox less hostile to the policies of the government in the house. Fox had kept his head in a situation of political confusion. He had indicated his willingness to accept office, without seeking to impose excessive conditions. He had realised the foolishness of entering North's ministry without bringing some allies with him; since he saw the main hope of changing government policy as stemming from the exercise of influence within the government he never forgot the dangers of isolation. But he knew something of the rigidity of the Rockinghamites, with their insistence upon a complete change of ministry, and it was therefore reasonable for him to suggest that the Shelburne group should be approached. He was not to know that Chatham's terms would be scarcely less unrealistic than Rockingham's. Of course there was the perennial difference of opinion with the Chathamites over the recognition of American independence, but since Shelburne wished to concentrate on waging war against France, while evacuating Pennsylvania and standing on the defensive in America, Fox could be forgiven for thinking that the practicalities of fighting the French, and the collective sharing of the responsibilities of office, would ensure that what was in theory a substantial difference would be resolved by the march of events. Furthermore, Fox had been modest (perhaps unduly so) in asking for nothing more distinguished than the treasurership of the navy; he had shown a shrewd appreciation of not pressing for too much too soon. He had his past to live down, and he knew that his enemies would be on the alert for any evidence of excessive ambition on his part. The king would not accept his return lightly; it would have to be free from any suspicion of arrogance, self-seeking or ostentation. Once he had proved himself in office promotion would come in due course. The first priority was to get into office, providing the right conditions were obtained. By making a distinction between coming in with other members of the opposition, and on the other hand conniving at any proposals demanding a complete change of ministry, Fox showed a more perceptive comprehension of the realities of politics than either Chatham or Rockingham, while his conduct was much more frank than that of Shelburne, who was suspected of using Chatham as a means of obscuring changes of attitude on his own behalf. Fox rightly differentiated between broadening the basis of the government and bringing a wholly new ministry into power. George III was quick to sense what Chatham's terms implied, and he assured North that he was resolved to run any risk, rather than submitting to the opposition, 'which every plan deviating from strengthening the present administration is more or less tending to.' The king complained of the insincerity of politicians; he could not regard public life simply as a game, and, acting as he invariably did from conviction, he was shocked at 'the base arts these men have used'. If they were prepared to come to North's assistance he would accept them, but he saw no reason to go out of his way to beg for their services.

So the negotiations came to nothing, and both government and opposition staggered on, seeking to make the best of a situation fraught with anxiety and uncertainty on all sides. Chatham's collapse in the house of lords on 7 April 1778, while begging the nation not to concede American independence but to fight the war against the French with unrelenting courage, shocked his hearers and filled them with apprehension. On 11 May he died, and although Shelburne sought to win recognition as the political heir of Chatham he was not in politics on his own account, not as the mistrusted spokesman for an absentee genius. The Rockinghamites thought of themselves more than ever as the repositories of national wisdom. Fox could only brood over lost opportunities. Chatham's death emphasized the folly of his intransigence during the March negotiations, and this Fox found hard to bear.

He still sought to save the country from falling prey to wishful thinking, both about the war and American independence. It was impossible to compel the Americans to resume any dependent status. France had recognised the United States, and had entered into commercial and diplomatic relations with the Americans, Every attempt—whether by concession or coercion—to restore British sovereignty in America would bring Britain into conflict with France and possibly other powers, such as Spain. It was far wiser to recognise the independence of the Americans. Commercially the country might do better in cultivating good relations with the United States, than by seeking to restore a shattered and illusory suzerainty. It was foolish to delude oneself by claiming that the majority of Americans did not support independence. The experience of the war should have cured Englishmen of that particular delusion. Futhermore, it was dangerous to talk of solving the American problem by depriving parliament of the right to levy taxes in the colonies; this could easily lead to a diminution of the importance of the legislature, and consequent inflation of the executive, and, in Fox's opinion, the influence of the crown had been increasing for some years. Thus, the American controversy was given another twist, entwining it ever more closely with the legend of the rise of the influence of the crown and the alleged assault on the independency of parliament and the stability of the balanced constitution and the mixed form of government.

Whatever the theoretical problems involved in persuading the king, his ministers, the lords and the commons, of the necessity of recognising the independence of the United States, the most sensible course seemed to be to divert the major part of the country's military and naval resources to fighting the war against the French. Fox argued that the advantages of tacitly submitting to the fact of America's independence were considerable. He returned to this theme again and again, both in private correspondence and in his public speeches. He confided his hopes to Fitzpatrick on 11 November 1778:

> ... If the acknowledgement of independence would not procure peace, it is certainly useless. I own my present idea (considering all things as well at home as abroad) is rather with Lord Shelburne for being silent on that subject, but acting as if it were acknowledged, withdrawing our troops from North America, and making the most vigorous attacks upon France, or possibly Spain too. Whatever may be the conditions of alliance between the States and France, I cannot help thinking that they would act very lukewarmly against us, when they found themselves wholly uninterested in the war and engaged merely by a point of honour. That this would be much surer of producing the effect proposed, if the independence were acknowledged, I see very clearly; but we must consider a little the state of things at home, and think what is practicable as well as what is best. This is at present my opinion, but it is very liable to be altered by a thousand circumstances, of which it is impossible for me to judge, and therefore I need not say that it is an opinion I could by no means wish to have known.[15]

Fox was always conscious of the need to be realistic. Much as he had to believe in the essential justice of the American cause he had always been as preoccupied with the practical consequences of British policy in America as with issues of constitution-propriety. He was as committed to securing British interests as he was anxious to protect American rights. He recognised that a conflict of interests might necessitate a recourse to war, but he was willing to exploit different American and French interests in the hope of thrusting the new allies apart. He knew how difficult it was to carry British opinion with him on any matter of abstract right which lent credence to the American cause, and he was constantly aware of the impossibility of putting any pressure on the government unless he could convince the king's ministers that he was carrying opinion with him.

Because the war was a different type of war to that previously waged against the French, opinion at home was intimately linked with the conduct of operations abroad. The justice of the war against the Americans was questioned; the aims of the conflict against the colonists were criticised by some, and rejected by others. This confusion of attitudes adversely affected the other war, which all Englishmen wanted to win; the war against Bourbon France, the traditional enemy and colonial rival. But it was one thing to talk of giving preference to the French war, quite another to advocate the recognition of American independence. Even George III favoured withdrawing the greater part of British troops from America in order to employ them against France and Spain, aware as the king was of the impossibility of carrying on the land war against the American rebels and a sea war against France and probably Spain as well. But it was beyond the capacity of North and Germain to carry such a policy into effect. In America every local success led to a dispersal of forces and the indulgence of every comforting illusion. Without any firm grasp of strategy, and exposed to every upsurge of optimism as well as to every despondency of defeat, the government failed to impose any overall pattern on the direction of the war. Furthermore it was tempting to believe that something could be saved from the wreck, and that calls for the recognition of the United States ignored the possibility of retaining at least some of the former colonies for the British crown.

A typical instance of Fox's public stance in the autumn and winter of 1778-9 was his speech in the commons on 26 November on the address to the king's speech. He took care to emphasize, not only that the country was fighting two wars simultaneously, but also that the two wars differed in character. Even when fighting the colonists when they were alone the mother country had been unable to compel them to return to their allegiance. There was less chance of success now that France had given succour to the Americans. The logic of Britain's geographical position was that she should attack France; it was impossible even to stand on the defensive in America with any hope of success; therefore British troops should be withdrawn from the former colonies entirely. The war against America was a war against their own countrymen, Fox told the commons; that against France was a war against 'your inveterate enemy and rival'. Every blow against the Americans was a blow struck against themselves; every blow against France was of advantage to Britain. America might be conquered in France; France could not be conquered in America.

But Fox also defined the contrast between the war against America and the war against France as one between a war of passion and a war of interest:

The war of the Americans is a war of passion; it is of such a nature as to be supported by the most powerful virtues, love of liberty and of country, and at the same time by those passions in the human heart which give courage, strength, and perseverance to man; the spirit of revenge for the injuries you have done them, of retaliation for the hardships inflicted on them, and of opposition to the injust powers you would have exercised over them; everything combines to animate them to this war, and such a war is without end; for whatever obstinacy enthusiasm ever inspired man with, you will now have to contend with in America; no matter what gives birth to that enthusiasm, whether the name of religion or of liberty, the effects are the same; it inspires a spirit that is unconquerable and solicitous to undergo difficulties and dangers; and as long as there is a man in America, so long will you have him against you in the field.

The war of France is of another sort; the war of France is a war of interest; it was interest that first induced her to engage in it, and it is by that same interest that she will measure its continuance; turn your face at once against her, attack her wherever she is exposed, crush her commerce wherever you can, make her feel heavy and immediate distress throughout the nation, and the people will soon cry out to their government. Whilst the advantages she promises herself are remote and uncertain, inflict present evils and distresses upon her subjects; the people will become discontented and clamorous, she will find the having entered into this business a bad bargain, and you will force her to desert an ally that brings so much trouble and distress, and the advantages of whose alliance may never take effect....[16]

Here forceful rhetoric was skilfully employed to give force and vitality to what was in any case an attractive argument. Fox took care to make up in his denunciations of the French for any suspected leniency towards the Americans. He deliberately avoided going over familiar arguments about the legislative supremacy of the British parliament, choosing instead to lament the folly of the American war on the grounds of impracticality. With an eighteenth-century preference for limited wars for definable objectives Fox bewailed the uncontrollable nature of the war in America, the distressing way in which it defied conventional restraints. Though men might deplore enthusiasm they could not deny its resilience and strength. But the war against France was one in which the advantages of the national self-interest were combined with those of control: there was no danger of becoming involved in a struggle in which all the benefits of conviction and patriotism lay with the other side. In a war of interest the balance of superiority could be assessed, the significance or decisiveness of victories or defeats could be calculated, and the war could therefore be limited or terminated by the normal practices of negotiation. In a war of passion even military victories were rendered hollow by the psychological aspects of the conflict. Fox shrewdly sought to convince his fellow MPs that the American war was against the best interests of the nation, and that it was fraught with disruptive and imponderable consequences, as well as tainted with the awesome and unusual prospect of defeat.

Despite the continued controversy about the war, and the furious exchanges that took place within the house of commons, the possibility of some negotiation by which the government could be strengthened lingered on. Strangely attractive, and yet singularly elusive, it could not be discounted. Chatham's death had removed the most inspiring and impressive of patriots, and the balance of forces within the opposition had been altered in consequence. In the spring of 1778 Fox had thought of the Shelburne group as possible associates within a rearranged ministry. By the end of the year he realised that he would have to improve his standing with the Rockinghamites, and, what was more important, that he would have to persuade Rockingham to come round to his own position on the advisability of renewed negotiations with the administration and the conditions on which members of the opposition would be willing to accede to the government.

On 24 January 1779 Fox discussed the question of the possible entry of the whigs into office in a long and frank letter to Rockingham. He regretted that in the past they had differed so fundamentally, each holding to his original opinions, yet it was not easy to reconcile their divergent beliefs:

What you considered as a step of the most dangerous tendency to the whig party, I looked upon as a most favourable opportunity for restoring it to that power and influence which I wish to have as earnestly as you can do. The very circumstances which you thought likely to render the proposed arrangement weak, I considered as means of strength and stability; because it has always been, and I believe always will be, my opinion that power (whether over a people or a king) obtained by gentle means, by the goodwill of the person to be governed, and, above all, by degrees, rather than by a sudden exertion of strength, is in its nature more durable and firm than any advantage that can be obtained by contrary means. I do not say all this in hopes of convincing you, but only in my own justification for entertaining sentiments so opposite to those of the person in the world I most respect.

Fox was remarkably sensitive to the dangers of trying to impose a complete change of ministry upon the king. With his astute sense of the realities of politics he was concious of the need for the king's confidence to be fully and openly extended to any new administration. If the king's wishes were respected the new government would have a greater chance of gaining support from all quarters of the house of commons. Fox was thinking of a truly national government, not of a purely party ministry. He was aware of the need to replace the most obnoxious members of North's government, but he was convinced that it would be both necessary and possible for some members of the current administration to remain in office and for members of the opposition groups to work amicably with them. Fox was defending the traditional means of changing the personnel of a government against the more advanced ideas put forward by Rockingham. It is a valuable reminder of the gradualness with which Fox's own constitutional assumptions developed, and of the way in which they were transformed by changing political circumstances rather than by abstract speculations divorced from a precise political context.

Regretfully Fox confessed to Rockingham that he thought their difference of opinion was 'quite complete':

> You think you can best serve the country by continuing in a fruitless opposition; I think it is impossible to serve it at all but by coming into power, and go even so far as to think it irreconcilable with the duty of a public man to refuse it, if offered to him in a manner consistent with his private honour, and so as to enable him to form fair hopes of doing essential service. I know there are some people, and perhaps you may be one, who will say that these opinions are the consequences of my particular situation, or, at best, that I am warped towards them by that situation. All I can say is, that I have done all I could do to examine my heart on that question, and do not feel myself doubtful upon it.[17]

Fox was wounded by accusations that he was seeking to get back into office without regard for those with whom he had been allied in opposition to the policy of coercion in America. He was independent of any political group, but he was honestly trying to fulfil the obligations which he had incurred towards other members of the opposition. He assured Rockingham that he was not over-eager to accept office, and that he was anxious for the Rockinghamites to be part of any new arrangement; their presence was necessary for the formation of the best possible government, and, what was perhaps even more crucial, if present opportunities were missed, it was extremely unlikely that any similar opportunity would recur. Though Fox had defended the patriotic nature of the opposition to the American war, and though he had argued that the opposition performed a valuable political service, he did not, like some of the Rockinghamites, take a doctrinaire position on negotiations with the government. He did not see opposition as a means of securing the total replacement of the ministry. The function of opposition could not be divided from the pursuit of power, but there were significant differences between Rockingham and himself on just this point. Opposition was not an end in itself. Fox strove hard to convey the depth of his feelings and the nature of his objections to Rockingham:

> But I do beg of you, my dear Lord, to consider how very impracticable it is either for me or for many other parts of the opposition to go on together upon the ideas upon which you maintain your refusal. For it is, is it not, a fair and open declaration that you will never have anything to do with any ministry that is *not entirely* of your own forming? and do you not in some instances rest your refusal upon grounds to which we are so far from pledged, that we are in some instances pledged directly to the contrary side? I do not mention this as a matter of reproach, but only to show you how very impossible it is for anybody who is not *one of you* to enter into your ideas and objects of opposition.

Fox knew that the assumption on the part of the Rockinghamites that they spoke for the whole opposition was bitterly resented, especially by Shelburne, who, though he was scrupulous in giving the Rockinghamites their due whenever he was approached on the delicate matter of possible negotiations, nevertheless did not feel that he had given up his own freedom of action or that he had ever authorised Rockingham to speak on his behalf. While the Rockinghamites would play a decisive role in the formation of any new ministry, Fox believed that there was a very real danger that by arrogating the supreme position among the opposition groups to themselves the Rockinghamites would make any negotiation futile, disappointing and unnecessarily bitter, not least to the other members of the opposition. Instead of a reshaped ministry embarking upon a policy of withdrawal from America and the more vigorous prosecution of the war against France, the government would be left to carry on those policies which had already proved disastrous, while the opposition, even more divided among themselves as a result of allegations of deception which thwarted hopes of office would engender, would be incapable of effectively challenging the government or of bringing about a revision of government policy.

Fox wanted to wring out of Rockingham specific answers to two questions: would he persist in rejecting the offers previously made if the government repeated them? and, if Rockingham refused to engage in negotiations of the type which had already failed, would he be prepared to give approval to a ministry which might be formed by some members of the opposition agreeing to serve in company with some of the king's present ministers? Fox named North, Sandwich, and Germain as those with whom political cooperation would be impossible; there were definite limits to the tolerance which could be extended to the authors of the country's misfortunes. But it was important that he knew whether Rockingham would allow some of his followers to align themselves with a new administration even if he would not join it himself. Fox accepted that the individuals concerned would each have stipulations of their own which would have to be met during negotiations, but the future would look brighter if he knew that Rockingham would not insist that all his followers held aloof on principle. He affirmed the confidential nature of their correspondence, promising not to make any rash or improper use of any information which had been given to him. He appealed to Rockingham's sense of honour and patriotism, reminding him, 'If ever there was a crisis where a country demanded all the efforts of its best men, it is the present, and surely some blame must lie at the doors of those who, from mistrust or suspicion, deprive it of the best assistance it can have.'[18]

The Rockinghamites were flustered and embarrassed by Fox's willingness to embark on another round of discussions, if there was any chance of forming a more broadly-based government. They felt that he had misunderstood their conduct during the negotiations of the previous year, and Rockingham urged the duke of Richmond to put Fox right on these points. Richmond denied that there had been an absolute refusal to treat except on the basis of a total change of ministry. He argued that it was the particular terms of the coalition to which the Rockinghamites had objected, not to the principle of a coalition as such. The king's desire to protect his ministers, and even to bestow additional honours upon those members of the government such as North, Sandwich and Germain, who were especially obnoxious to the Rockinghamites, had rendered the whole negotiation null and void, but, Richmond maintained, the Rockinghamites could hardly be expected to allow themselves to be parties to the showering of marks of favour and approbation on those whose conduct merited disgrace. Nor had the Rockinghamites insisted on any particular items of policy as the condition of office; though there was general agreement that preference should be given to the war against France, the recognition of American independence had been left open, while no specific foreign alliances had been proposed. Indian affairs were not even discussed.

Yet there was an undeniable element of special pleading about Richmond's apology for Rockingham and his friends. The fact that the duke had been asked to reply to Fox's inquiries was itself significant. Richmond was, like Fox, something of an independent. In some ways more radical than most of the Rockinghamites he was not in their innermost councils. He was proudly self-reliant and often unpredictable, and in his attempt to justify Rockingham to Fox he was inconsistent. After claiming that the Rockinghamites had not gone beyond normal conventions in the conditions which they had laid down for their accession to the ministry he reminded Fox of the virtues of making conditions before entering office:

> I may be told that, meaning to make us ministers, measures were to be in our hands, and would be a more proper subject for discussion when the new arrangement should have actually taken place. If the change of men were to be a *total change,* and the new ministry—instead of consenting to rewards to those whose conduct they had been condemning for years past—bore the complexion of a new system, there might be some weight in the argument of the propriety of leaving it till they were fixed in office, to determine on the precise mode by which they would support their consistency of character; and yet, even in such circumstances, I should think it more fair and honourable to the king to let him know, before he took us into his service, at least the general plan of measures we meant to pursue, especially as some of them must strike directly at what he may have been told is his interest, and certainly at his civil list—I mean, at its present extent. But in a ministry to be composed of men who have hitherto professedly differed in principles, as well as in the modes of conducting them, it is surely necessary, unless men look at nothing but employment, to begin by having a right understanding of the conduct to be pursued.[19]

All this, so far as Fox was concerned, epitomised the mixture of wishful thinking and self-righteousness which made Rockingham and his associates so infuriating. Despite their qualities and the desirability of the principles for which they stood, they helped to keep North's government in office because they ignored the only means of changing the composition of the ministry and the bias of government policy. Fox hated being lectured on the virtues of political consistency. He saw the moral integrity of Rockingham as one reason why North, Sandwich and Germain survived all the catastrophes which were the inevitable outcome of their policies and the proofs of their incompetence. Fox did not doubt that in a perfect world it would be pleasant to lay down the conditions upon which one would enter the government and the principles of public policy before accepting office; but in the imperfect world, the world in which actual decisions had to be taken, such an attitude seemed to him to smack of priggish complacency. It was impossible for any negotiation to succeed on such terms. Yet something had to be rescued immediately from the wreck and if it was necessary to accept certain members of North's administration as colleagues this price was worth paying in return for an effective voice in the formulation of policy and the implementation of decisions. Fox recognised, in a way which the Rockinghamites did not, the essential weakness of the opposition's position. He knew of the suspicion, both in the house of commons and in the country at large, with which the friends of America were habitually regarded. He knew that the country gentlemen would resent any conspiracy to impose a faction on the king, and he was sufficiently acquainted with the psychology of the commons to appreciate the critical value of royal confidence in stabilising support for any administration. If North's critics were to enter the government they had to be above suspicions that they were exploiting national difficulties for personal advancement. They would have to shun the temptation to glory in their own probity or to exult in their own far-sightedness. Instead of humiliating their opponents they would have to be chivalrous and generous. Fox was too good a house of commons man to take too seriously the violent accusations bandied to and fro in debate. He was too much of a patriot to place his self-esteem before the public welfare. If the rescue of the nation from its predicament demanded that he sink his pride in going into office without a total purge of ministers, and without cast-iron pledges on policy, he was prepared to take the risk, and bear any criticisms with a clear conscience.

He was not unaware of the dangers, nor did he need Richmond to warn him that everything depended on the balance of personnel and attitudes within the cabinet. But he did not believe that it was either desirable or possible to settle all this beforehand. He was confident of his own powers of persuasion, once he could plead his case with his colleagues, sharing the burdens of responsibility instead of appealing to generalised political sentiments. He resented Richmond's suggestion that he was going too far to meet North by agreeing to the removal of only 'the lowest tide-waiters' from the government. Fox sympathised with Richmond's principles, but he was impatient with Rockingham's tendency to disregard the practicalities of politics. Fox recognised the unreality of asking George III to send for Rockingham to form a ministry. When Richmond talked of such a step he justified all Fox's anxieties. Richmond seemed to think that the Rockinghamites were the only politicians unsullied by a lust for place, but Fox had a more magnanimous comprehension of the motives and pressures to which men succumbed when high-minded idealism mingled with the hope of office and became exposed to the mundane requirements of compromise and expediency. He had himself to come to terms with the knowledge that he could look for little understanding of his own attitude among the Rockinghamites, and with the growing conviction that because of Rockingham's obstinacy the chances of reshaping the ministry by negotiation, with the consequent reformation of government policy from within, were negligible. It was doubly irritating when Richmond condescendingly assured Fox that he did not impute his conduct to 'any improper desire for the emoluments of office' while condemning his 'want of patience' and 'natural eagerness of temper' in the present 'difficult situation'.

The period 1779-80 marks a decisive epoch in Fox's career. With the frustration of his hopes for office he was compelled to take stock of the political situation and of his prospects. He had experienced all the restrictions imposed upon a man of boundless ambition and dazzling talent by the received pattern of political conduct. He had remained faithful to the primacy of the house of commons as the major political arena and he had sought to exploit the proven techniques of negotiation: all without success. He was regarded with apprehension and distrust by the Rockinghamites, despite their association on opposition to the American war, and he returned their mistrust by a withering disdain for their self-righteous unrealism. Yet without an understanding with the Rockinghamites, where could he turn for support? He could not rely upon Shelburne, whose own conduct had played its part in wrecking former plans for a coalition. Ironically, Fox, whose youth had been distinguished by his denunciations of extra-parliamentary politics, was to find in new forms of association and new fields of activity compensation for the frustrations of conventional politics, as well as the opportunity to win a reputation as 'a man of the people'. In the circumstances in which he was placed it was understandable that he should turn away, almost in desperation, from tactics which had proved so fruitless and seek to exploit new methods of winning that wider measure of support, without which the way to office was permanently barred. Fox was the beneficiary of events. He responded to developments which he had done nothing to stimulate and which were beyond his control. But, though he exploited the opportunities offered with his usual skill, he found that even on subjects where they had at first seemed united there were significant differences between himself and the Rockingham group.

The country faced an appalling combination of calamities in the summer of 1779. There was a danger of invasion, with the navy overstrained by the tasks of controlling American waters and maintaining command of the English channel. When Spain came into the war the menace of the Franco-Spanish fleets was considerable and ominous. Memories of the disappointment off Ushant in July 1778, and the consequent quarrel between Admiral Keppel and Sir Hugh Palliser, sapped public confidence in the navy. It was easy to unload all frustrations onto Lord Sandwich, who was better fitted than any other politician to be first lord of the admiralty, but whom contemporaries savagely blamed for every disappointment at sea, many of which were the results of the neglect of the navy by previous administrations, before Sandwich had taken over in 1775. The navy was torn apart by political hatreds, and though the crisis of the summer was survived there was a persistent climate of suspicion and mistrust. Doubts about the navy's ability to protect the country from invasion seemed to confirm the government's incompetence. Furthermore, knowledge that the government was itself stricken with rivalry and strife heightened convictions that catastrophe was imminent. In Ireland the invasion scare had stimulated the growth of the volunteer movement, and this in turn fired the Irish with the desire to wring legislative independence and commercial concessions out of the British government. The Irish felt that they suffered from similar abuses to those which had provoked the American revolt; they sympathised with the Americans and they hoped to win for themselves at least a measure of free trade. The outbreak of the war caused distress in Ireland by disrupting normal trade with the American colonies, and constitutional and economic considerations united to encourage Irish agitation. The government was divided and uncertain what to do. It was aware of its own inability to secure Ireland from invasion, and apprehensive as to the uses to which the volunteers might be put. Behind the constitutional and economic grievances in Ireland loomed the spectre of the religious problem. North languished in indecision, and then sought to buy time by conciliation and concession. Undignified as his Irish policy was it averted a full-scale catastrophe, but it also contributed towards a growing feeling that such a combination of ills reflected a fundamental corruption in the institutions of government. The dark conspiracy to extend the influence of the crown and destroy the independence of the house of commons seemed the obvious explanation. The destruction of the constitution was the primary cause of the American débâcle, the humiliations of war, and the Irish problem. The cost of the war, which necessitated higher taxation, added a further spur to action. Men conveniently forgot that a desire to keep the land tax down had been one of the reasons why the attempt to tax the Americans had been initially popular in England. Now the theory was that the country's woes were caused by excessive public spending, especially in the dubious award of pensions, contracts and places by the crown in order to heighten the control of the executive over the house of commons.

The Yorkshire freeholders, with the Reverend Christopher Wyvill as their leader, took the initiative in calling meetings to protest at wasteful expenditure. At a meeting at York on 30 December 1779 a petition was approved by the freeholders with only one adverse vote. It denounced the waste of public money, alleging that in this way the crown had built up 'a great and unconstitutional influence, which, if not checked, may soon prove fatal to the liberties of this country', and asked the commons to correct gross abuses in the expenditure of public funds, to reduce excessive emoluments, and to abolish all sinecures and undeserved pensions. What was more significant, a second resolution was passed late in the meeting, appointing a committee 'to carry on the necessary correspondence for effectually promoting the object of the petition and to support that laudable reform and such other measures as may conduce to restore the freedom of parliament'. Wyvill was astute enough to declare both peers and MPs ineligible for this committee of management: the Yorkshire association was to remain the instrument by which the wishes of the people were to be communicated to the house of lords and the house of commons; it was not to be exploited by the politicians merely as an accessory to their parliamentary activities.

The Yorkshire association pressed on collecting signatures for their petition. Their example was followed in sixteen other counties. In Middlesex, under the inspiration of Dr John Jebb, the freeholders committed themselves to approving of a national association to restore the freedom and independence of parliament, to curb public expenditure, and to prune all extravagance and exorbitance. Like the Yorkshiremen they set up a committee to carry on necessary correspondence for the furtherance of the petition and to propose a plan 'to support that laudable reform, and such other measures as may conduce to restore the freedom of parliament'. Meetings were held in Huntingdonshire, Hertfordshire, and Bedfordshire, while the Yorkshire committee supported—in addition to economic reform—shorter parliaments and a purification of parliamentary representation. Wyvill reassured his supporters that he disapproved of anything savouring of revolution, but he was soon in London discussing future action with the leaders of the petitioning movement in other counties.

At a great meeting of Westminster freeholders on 2 February 1780 Charles Fox threw himself behind the movement by delivering a vehement speech urging the formation of a Westminster committee on

the lines of that set up in Yorkshire, and the adoption of a petition calling
for economic and parliamentary reform. Overnight he became the hero of
the radicals. He had now abandoned any hope of an understanding with
the government. It seemed that he had plunged into the most extreme
popular politics. He was adopted as a parliamentary candidate in Westminster on the basis of his performance. But, however, violent his
language, his actions must be set against the disappointments of the
previous year. In some ways he was driven to do what he did by a growing
conviction of his own isolation. With the patching-up of North's government in the previous November there was little prospect of advancement
through negotiation, and less chance of the government falling to pieces
under the pressure of its own incompetence and self-doubt. Fox's emergence as a radical was as much the result of thwarted political expectations
as of any profound belief in the reformers' cause. His appeal to the people
of Westminster was a calculated act of desperation, and in so far as it
provided him with a new audience it was a success. But what he hoped
to tap was a new source of power, confident in his power to exploit mass
emotions and his ability to subordinate extra-parliamentary politics to
parliamentary ends. He could not afford to ignore the chance of injecting
a new element of unpredictability into a political situation which, from
his point of view, was showing depressing signs of settling down. He was
eager to shatter the government's will to survive; for this purpose the
petitioning movement was worth exploiting. It held out the prospect of
a more fluid political situation in which his ingenuity would have full and
unfettered scope. Nor could he allow the Rockinghamites to monopolise
attention as the alternatives to North and his colleagues.

   The interest of the petitioners in curbing the influence of the crown was
a happy coincidence. Fox and the Rockinghamites had been deploring the
increase of wasteful expenditure, and associating it with the debasement
of the house of commons, throughout the previous parliamentary session.
The facts do not support their allegations of a sustained and malignant
increase of the proportion of placemen in the commons or their charge
that George III was distributing pensions and favours on an unprecedented scale. Far from the first twenty years of George III's reign
seeing a huge increase in the number of placemen it would seem that
their numbers declined after reaching a peak of about 260 in 1761. 'Secret
influence' was a convenient allegation to make against the king and his
ministers; it could neither be proved nor disproved, but it provided a
satisfactory explanation of those ills which called for some extraordinary
circumstances to make them intelligible. Since the extent of secret
influence could be deduced from almost any unhappy chain of events

afflicting the government it enabled the critics of the king and North to feel that their worst suspicions were justified. Fox was, therefore, puzzled by the opposition's lack of success. Though he thought Rockingham unrealistic in his disdain for the inevitable compromises of politics Fox had been disappointed by his failure to make greater inroads into the government's parliamentary majority. It was not that he expected known supporters of the administration to desert the ministers; he was too closely acquainted with the actualities of political life to look for the impossible. But he was perturbed by the indifference of many of the country gentlemen and independent members of the house of commons. He sensed the impact which his speeches often made, the waves of emotion his invective unleashed, and he looked for the gradual conversion of movements of opinion into the casting of votes. Here he was disillusioned: the only explanation for the failure of these men, whom he sensed responding to his words, to follow him in divisions must be that they were bound to the government by ties of secret interest.

But the insistence on the secret influence of the crown as the explanation of the country's ills had the additional advantage of appealing to the country gentlemen, who were always sensitive towards any suggestions that public money was being wasted. They resented any increase in taxation, and they always argued that the costs of fighting a war weighed unfairly on the landed interest. They were equally suspicious of anything which threatened the independence of the house of commons, and they loathed any sign of the increase of the executive's influence upon the legislature. It was not surprising, therefore, that Fox should utilise those arguments which appealed most strongly to the prejudices and convictions of that section of the House without which no government could long survive or any opposition triumph. A shift towards the denunciation of the influence of the crown as the major source of national humiliation also avoided getting bogged down in the endless repetitions of familiar arguments about American taxation and the legislative supremacy of the British house of commons, which were much less congenial so far as the country gentlemen were concerned.

Fox's speech in Westminster Hall, to a meeting of the freeholders of Westminster, on 2 February 1780, went far beyond what he had previously urged in his public speeches and was more far-reaching in its implications than anything which the more cautious Rockinghamites were prepared to advocate in their own flirtation with the petitioning movement. Previously Fox had staunchly asserted the primacy and independency of parliament; now he invoked ideas which subordinated the house of commons to the people:

What is the government of this country? Does it not consist of king, lords, and people? Is the house of commons more or less than the delegate or representation of the people, who intrust, for a limited time, their power, their rights, and their interests, in their hands? The moment that delegated body becomes perfidious, the interests of their constituents are abandoned, and they, instead of being the representatives of the people, become the slaves or passive instruments of the crown. Is this then the case?

The problem was who was to judge when the house of commons had so far deteriorated as to forfeit any claim to represent the people, and although Fox cleverly exploited this idea he skirted round any implication of some permanent extra-parliamentary body sitting in judgment upon the commons. He chose vigorously to defend petitioning the house; far from petitions leading to anarchy and confusion they were a security against excessive government expenditure and crippling taxation. Everything that was saved from 'the sink of corruption' was a contribution to the public service; economy was the best means of securing efficient government.

Fox reminded his hearers that they were to be the authors of their own deliverance. He cited the examples of America and Ireland to demonstrate how good men should act when provoked beyond endurance by bad men. He hoped that the people of Westminster had as great a veneration for the liberties transmitted to them by their forefathers and which it was their duty to bequeath to their posterity. Life without freedom was to be spurned, and since the people were the vitals of the body politic it was to be hoped that corruption had not yet extended its debilitating influence to them.

This was why the association movement was so important, for it was the most powerful means of resisting corruption:

Without association you must fall a sacrifice to that corruption which has given the crown an influence unknown to any former period of our history. Permit this influence to increase, and the country is enslaved, freedom destroyed, and the English constitution completely overthrown. You may be told, association, in the present instance, has the appearance of controlling parliament, who have always deemed it an infringement of their privileges for subjects to interfere in the regulation of taxes. Happy had it been for this country, fortunate and honourable had it been for us all, had parliament listened in time to the interfering voice of America, and suffered itself to be controlled by the temperate admonitions of a brave and free people.[20]

But though Fox's audience was carried away by the emotional force of his diatribe they ignored the implied limits which Fox was setting to the control of parliament by extra-parliamentary opinion. He linked the petitioning movement to the American dispute, infusing the struggle with the dramatic histrionics of a fight for the preservation of the constitution. Yet, by referring to the validity of agitation for the better scrutiny of public expenditure in the context of a more regular survey of the grant of taxation, he sought to avoid extending the principle of extra-parliamentary control to general legislation. Fox was playing a dangerous game. Despite his fervour he was no convert to democratic theories of representation, and much as he supported the petitioning movement's demand for the more stringent control of expenditure he was too experienced and too wily a politician to chain himself unconditionally to the wheels of a popular juggernaut. He carefully laced his provocative appeals to the populace with references to the restoration of the constitution and to the notion of traditional liberties as an inheritance from the past. He accepted the need to asset popular control of parliament only within the confines of an exceptional political situation. The constitution was in danger: therefore it was necessary for the people to take the initiative, temporarily revoking those powers which they normally delegated to the house of commons in order to save the commons from the effects of corruption and to liberate MPs from the servitude enforced and maintained by the influence of the crown. The justification for the petitioners' actions lay in the extraordinary threat to fundamental constitutional liberties which the current situation posed. Parliament was empowered to perform certain trusts on behalf of the people; since it was incapable of adequately performing these trusts the people were justified in revoking their mandate. The problem was that for many of Fox's radical associates this principle was of universal application; they claimed that extra-parliamentary assemblies should act as perpetual watchdogs of the constitution, goading MPs to fulfil the promises made to their constituents and ensuring that the house of commons was, in a more literal sense than that implicit in Fox's thought, the people's house of parliament.

Rockingham and Burke were principally interested in the petitioning movement as an agency for economic reform—the attack on the resources of patronage available to the crown—and they shrank back from any scheme for the reform of parliament. They were uneasy for the proposal for shorter parliaments (though there was nothing new about such proposals in principle) and they were worried by any interference with the traditional pattern of representation. Though they wanted to exploit popular agitation in order to embarrass and humiliate North they were shocked by the extremism of radicals such as Jebb, and deeply distressed by demagogic performances such as that in which Fox had so shamelessly indulged on 2 February. They wanted to purify the commons, exclude contractors from the house, and rescind the worst type of pensions in the gift of the crown; and in all this they were of one mind with Wyvill and the petitioners. But they deplored any subordination—however carefully phrased—of the commons to the electorate, and they rejected any notion that extra-parliamentary associations ought to dictate their terms to members of parliament, or act as any sort of permanent control over the house of commons.

Fox was just as interested in exploiting the mood of the moment, but, though he was far from insensitive to the anxieties felt by the Rockinghamites, he was sufficiently appreciative of the uniqueness of the situation to realise that if a large enough volume of popular agitation was to be released to put serious pressures upon the government it was necessary to outbid the radical leaders in order to retain some measure of control over the movement. It was wiser to take the risk of plumping for parliamentary reform than to hang back: by exaggerating the constitutional crisis it would be possible to bluff the radical thinkers into thinking that one was prepared to go all the way, but, since it could be argued that once a satisfactory measure of parliamentary reform had been implemented the constitution had been restored, the more extreme demands for some permanent control over parliament could be quietly passed over as redundant. It was important, too, that the agitation should be made to resemble the agitation in Ireland, even possibly the resistance of the Americans, so that it would appear as part of a universal and interrelated rejection of a government whose policies were decried as a consistent repudiation of traditional liberties, both at home and overseas. Only by breaking the government's will to continue in office could Fox envisage any possibility of winning place and power himself. He had tried negotiation, and he had failed; now believing that the intransigent self-deception of the Rockinghamites ruled out any coalition, he was convinced that only the complete break-up of North's government would allow a new ministry to come in on anything like the terms favoured by the Rockinghamites. The petitioning movement held some prospect of so frightening the administration that North's will would break. In many ways all this conflicted with Fox's private preferences and previous utterances, but a desperate man, whose every effort had been frustrated, could not afford to ignore any development which promised so to transform the political situation that power would once again be within his grasp. If he failed he might be discredited; if he succeeded he would have the ticklish job of unburdening himself of those temporary allies who would prove a long-term embarrassment. But both for the country's and his own sake he could not risk being overtaken by events. Unlike Rockingham he did not mind sullying himself in the more muddy waters of politics, and unlike Burke he could not allow fidelity to any ideology to blind him to the chance of securing decisive political advantages.

Outside the house Fox used language which stimulated heat and passion; within the commons he was anxious to convince members of the reasonableness of the petitioners' demands and of the validity of the act of petitioning itself. He rebuffed North's attempt to cast doubt on the good faith of the petitioners: it was nonsense to suggest that the people were in arms or were threatening civil war or were trying to overawe the house. They were simply seeking to exercise their legal rights, and peaceably to use their constitutional privileges. In Fox's opinion the danger was not civil war but the breakdown of the people's faith in the house of commons. If the petition from the county of York were to be insolently thrown out the people would lose all confidence in their representatives and all reverence for parliament.

> The consequences of such a situation I need not point out: let not the contemplation of necessary effects from certain causes be considered as a denunciation of vengeance ... It is the duty of members of parliament to conform to the sentiments, and in some degree even to the prejudices of the people. In their legislative capacity, the wishes and wants of the people ought, in this land of liberty, to be their grand rule of conduct. I say in their legislative capacity: for I make a distinction between that and their judicial capacity; in which last they must give judgment according to the letter of the law, and in this, too, they consult the interests of liberty ...

Fox argued that the ministry would be wise to hearken to the petitions of the people, whatever misgivings they had of deferring to the judgment of members of the opposition. The advantages of proper economy in public expenditure, and the value of a proper scrutiny of the public purse, were self-evident. There was even something in it for the government:

> On the whole economy will strengthen the hands of government, relieve the people from hardships, be a source of fame and triumph to the ministry over their adversaries; for who will dare to say, or who will not be abhorred for saying anything to the prejudice of so honest and upright an administration, as those men who shall redress in so satisfactory a manner, the grievances of an oppressed people?[21]

Throughout the first three months of 1780 it seemed that the opposition might be successful in pushing through a significant measure of economic reform, and in so discrediting North's administration that the government would be forced to resign. The most dramatic opposition success was the passing of Dunning's famous resolution on 6 April, 'that the influence of the crown has increased, is increasing and ought to be diminished'. But however striking its phraseology the motion marked the final stages of a period of opposition optimism, other than being the prelude to further and more specific triumphs. North and his colleagues exploited every trick in the parliamentary pack; they fell back on the house of lords to block motions which had proved too popular to stop in the commons, and by concentrating on some clauses in bills proposing economical reforms, while allowing others to go through, they succeeded in frustrating the opposition. The technique of amendment was skilfully utilised, and though the opposition seemed to stand on the threshold of success, final victory was denied to them.

One example of the means by which North defied the opposition and eventually denied everything to them, except for a handful of hollow triumphs, may be seen in the fate of Burke's disestablishment bill. On the face of things this was one of the most formidable assaults mounted by the opposition. Burke's proposals were comprehensive, embracing as they did the abolition of many sinecures and offices and the termination of the board of trade, the pruning of the royal household, and the reduction of expenditure on public appointments by £200,000 and the reduction of the privy purse by twenty-five per cent. The government fell back on delaying tactics with considerable success and although Burke abolished the board of trade and came within seven votes of eliminating the third secretaryship of state, he ruefully saw 'the pith and marrow' of his bill destroyed, largely because of the reluctance of the country gentlemen to interfere with the king's use of his civil list. Burke lost heart; he had no wish to 'put his weak and disordered frame ... to the torture, in order to fight his bill ... inch by inch, clause by clause, line by line.' Yet there was no other way of ensuring success when opposed by a parliamentarian of North's proven skill.

Fox was disappointed by the lack of fight shown by some of his colleagues. He had taken great risks in committing himself to the campaign for economical reform and to the association movement. On the Westminster committee he was doing sterling work, sustaining the morale of the reformers while keeping their demands within the bounds of sense and practicability and ensuring that they remained amenable to parliamentary influences. Although many of his colleagues on the Westminster

committee were more doctrinaire and more advanced than Fox in their
ideas of parliamentary reform, and though the Westminster association
had a more dogmatic flavour than its Yorkshire counterpart, Fox felt that
at least the link between the parliamentarians and the radicals had, as yet,
remained unbroken, and for that he could take much of the credit. He
had often to work hard to retain the confidence of the more extreme
agitators, even running risks within the house of commons to satisfy
the expectations of his motley crowd of associates.

He had spoken in favour of Burke's bill, but he had done so in
language which Burke had not condoned. Fox was bold enough to ask
whether the king had any hereditary right to the throne, and the response
of the commons was so querulous that he was driven to explain himself:

> Parliament, indeed, had made him the successor to the throne, but
> hereditary right he had none. He was, as an honourable friend near
> him (Mr Burke) had declared, the mere creature of the people's institu-
> tions, and held nothing but what he held in trust for the people, for
> their use and benefit.... The king, it was true was the sovereign of
> the people, but the king was to hold the crown only as long as the people
> should choose. This, he trusted, he might advance without offence.
> He felt himself warm, and he knew it. But, he trusted, he was neither
> unparliamentary nor disorderly. He again asserted that the king was no
> longer king than while he should be found to wear the crown for the
> good of his people, for that all power lodged in the crown, or elsewhere,
> could only centre in that one great fundamental point.

He was, of course, preparing the way for a justification of Burke's reduction of the civil list, but strange and imprecise ramblings in the more
questionable fields of constitutional theory were hardly likely to soothe the
fears of those members who had already detected in Burke's proposals
ominous proofs of aggression by the commons upon the legitimate rights
of the crown. In fact, MPs were as much bewildered as enlightened by
Fox's verbosity, particularly when he discussed methods of proving the
scope and nature of the influence of the crown:

> How was the influence of the crown to be proved? He had almost made
> a blunder, for he was going to say that the influence of the crown
> showed itself only in the dark, or it appeared so rarely in the light, that
> it was not one of those things so capable of proving any otherwise than
> by the notoriety of the fact.[22]

The truth was that the strain of the campaign, both within parliament and out of doors, was beginning to tell, not merely on Fox, but upon the other members of the opposition. North remained on the strategic defensive, using all the arts of procrastination and of procedure to delay the consideration of bills which were decisive for the success of the opposition's plans; but the whigs had to maintain the pressure if they were to have any hope of success. This was a difficult task within the confines of the contemporary political system. Popular agitation and the association movement had seemed valuable allies in wearing out the government, but like most allies they had added tensions and strains to those already weighing so heavily on the parliamentary opposition. That even Fox's resilience was showing signs of fatigue was an indication of the immense stresses which were exhausting the resources of both mind and body. The longer the campaign lasted the more difficult it would be to disguise the differences of conviction and the diversity of aims which were already contributing to the discomfiture of the opposition. Rockingham and Burke would have preferred to concentrate simply and solely upon economical reform, with the overriding objective of curbing the influence of the crown. Shelburne shared a desire for the reform of administration, but he was more interested in securing more efficient government than in curbing the influence of the crown. He also advocated triennial parliaments, and, as a faithful Chathamite, he called for a substantial increase of county representation in the house of commons in order to purify the house and safeguard its independence. These proposals were sufficient in themselves to mark Shelburne off from the Rockinghamites, but he was also almost as convinced as Fox of the need to stimulate popular agitation in order to maintain government apprehensions at their peak, and he was consequently impatient with the half-hearted attitude of Rockingham and the Cavendishes towards the petitioning movement.

No one could accuse Fox of being half-hearted. When presenting the Westminster petition for economical reform on 13 March 1780 he vigorously defended the respectability and responsibility of the petitioners, and the peaceful and constitutional character of their demands. But he warned the house of the necessity of paying a proper attention to the petitions of the people. Over 5,000 electors had signed the Westminster petition; they were temperate and law-abiding citizens but they were firm in seeking redress of their grievances. Though Lord North had defeated Burke's bill he could not stand long against the people; he might delay reform, but he could not prevent it. Possibly because he sensed that he had already ruffled the susceptibilities of members, Fox disavowed any intention of 'menacing' parliament; when he said that they dare not but comply with the prayer of the petitioners, he wished to be understood as saying that they dared not because it would be unjust to refuse the demands of the petitioners.

While the Rockinghamites trembled at the prospect of parliamentary reform Fox blithely pushed forward, speaking in support of Sawbridge's bill for shortening the duration of parliaments on 8 May 1780. He confessed that for years he had been opposed to the proposal, but, though he still felt that, in its time, the septennial act had been a laudable measure, the situation had now changed out of all recognition. The people of England, in whom the sole right to determine the lifetime of parliament lay, desired the commons to shorten the duration of parliaments, and while for himself this was a sufficient justification he was convinced that the bill would have the additional advantage of lessening the influence of the crown. He rejected the argument that over-frequent elections would impose an unacceptable level of expenditure upon independent men, who sought to exercise a legitimate political influence. As it was, it was possible for the crown to use its power of dissolution to call an election at times inconvenient to members of the house.

Fox was committed to a plan of parliamentary reform, involving not only shorter parliaments but the addition of 100 county members to the commons; but his colleagues in Westminster had gone far beyond this, a sub-committee of the Westminster association recommending the adoption of single member seats, universal male suffrage, the payment of MPs, the abolition of the property qualification, and the ballot, as well as annual elections and the exclusion of placemen from the house of commons. Opinion within the Westminster committee was divided on a scheme as far-reaching, and as improbable of fulfilment, as this; but even the decision to circulate propaganda on these lines was a sufficient embarrassment to Fox. He himself never adopted the radical position of Cartwright or Jebb. He sensed the dangers in the situation, for in some ways the airing of more extreme demands was a further confirmation of the failure of the association movement to gain any decisive victory in parliament. With the thwarting of the opposition's attempts to carry a measure of economical reform the theoretical attractions of a radical reform of parliament increased; the people's house had refused the just demands of the people, and this confirmed the allegations of those who argued that a reformed parliament was a necessary preliminary to the purification of administration and the improvement of government. Fox had failed to defeat the ministry by invoking popular agitation. He had driven North against the ropes, but he had been unable to knock him out. Rockingham and his group lost stomach for the fight; in June they ceased to attend parliament, much to Shelburne's disgust.

Fox had earned himself an unenviable reputation as an extreme reformer. This went beyond what the facts of the case justified, but it was
understandable nevertheless. For Fox the situation was galling; he had
received all the odium which his association with the petitioning movement had provoked in some quarters, but the glittering prize for which
he had risked his good name was as far off as ever. Both the parliamentary
campaign and the popular agitation had failed. The only consolation for
the opposition was the hope that their fortunes would take a turn for
the better should the government suffer new reverses in America. But
even there North's luck held. Cornwallis' invasion of Georgia and the
Carolinas went well at first, heartening the ministers and lulling them into
the comforting belief that whatever happened to the northern colonies
there was a real chance of retaining the southern colonies. For a brief,
heady period Lord George Germain's obstinate confidence in the ubiquity
and fidelity of countless American loyalists seemed to be borne out by
events. It was easy to overlook the difficulties confronting Cornwallis; he
had to cover immense distances with inadequate forces; he was short of
necessary stores and equipment; he could not hope for reinforcements.
Although he might defeat the Americans in the field he could not control
the country through which he was passing. But North and Germain ignored the handicaps which Cornwallis was struggling with so manfully;
for them the campaign in the Carolinas promised to compensate for all
former military disappointments.

In June the outbreak of the Gordon riots jolted many men out of a vague
sympathy with popular agitation and into a shrill and angry horror of
all mass disturbances. Although the riots had their root in demonstrations
organised by Lord George Gordon's protestant association against a very
moderate measure of catholic relief permitting the recruitment of catholics
for the army, they speedily became a senseless outbreak threatening the
existence of fundamental law and order within the capital. The mob
cloaked its depredations under the historic cry of 'No popery!'. Catholic
chapels were looted and desecrated and the lust for destruction and booty
spread the sacking to private houses. For eleven days the government
trembled. Only characteristically firm action by the king, and intelligent
intervention by John Wilkes, whose anxiety to secure property confirmed
his transformation into a pillar of the establishment, saved the day. Ironically, however feebly the ministers had responded to the crisis, the riots
rallied opinion round the government. The excesses of the mob were a
brutal warning against the exploitation of mass emotions. Protest became
identified with lawlessness. It seemed that even the most cautious modification of the status quo would be fraught with dangers of the most appall-

ing kind. With the charred and burning wreckage of houses and chapels before their eyes, men became more doubtful about generalised invocations of the people's right to control and scrutinise parliament. The tendency for popular agitation to degenerate into riot had been amply demonstrated by events. Even those who claimed to speak for the people had to admit that the people's leaders could not always control their followers. After 1780 the fear of the mob was burned deep in the public consciousness. Men were determined to avoid any repetition of those ghastly days and more fearful nights when London was torn by pillage, ravaged by fire, and at the mercy of a ferocious mob.

So a year which had begun with the opposition in good spirits passed into high summer with North and his colleagues more firmly entrenched in office than ever. During the summer it was the whigs who bewailed their lot, asked what had gone wrong, and sought to pass their share of the blame onto others. When North requested the king to dissolve parliament in September 1780 he was confident of a satisfactory result. Fox and the Rockinghamites denounced the breach of the septennial convention, but their ardour for constitutional propriety was inspired by a knowledge that everything pointed to a victory for the government. No one expected the ministry to be turned out at a general election. The elections, as it happened, went less well for the government than John Robinson, the king's election manager, had anticipated, but for all that only disaster in America could turn North out and bring the opposition in.

For Fox the election of 1780 was especially significant: he was elected for the city of Westminster. Previously he had represented the pocket boroughs of Midhurst and Malmesbury; now he sat for one of the open constituencies. He could claim with much greater justification to speak for the people, and he retained the affection and support of his Westminster constituents until his death. His new constituency was his reward for zealous support of the petitioning movement and his work in the Westminster association was the prelude to his becoming one of Westminster's MPs.

It was a lively and noisy campaign. Fox confessed to his friend Lord Ossory that he expected a 'very sharp' contest. Despite his newly discovered fondness for the people he was anxious to have the support of titled and propertied gentlemen. He wanted Ossory to propose him on the hustings, 'especially as there is so great a scarcity of gentlemen here'. There were two other candidates: Admiral Rodney and Lord Lincoln. From shortly after the start Rodney built up a commanding lead as the front runner; the real struggle was between Fox and Lincoln. Fox canvassed incessantly, and spoke vehemently and often. He reminded the voters that Lincoln's father, the duke of Newcastle, enjoyed the perquisites of office; in reply, he had to defend himself the charge of being the beneficiary of his own father's shameless profiteering. Day by day Fox pulled ahead. Despite Lincoln's demands for a recount, and his threat to call for a scrutiny of the return, Fox was elected by a comfortable, though not an overwhelming, majority. He polled 4,878 votes to Lincoln's 4,157. Rodney came head of the poll with 5,298 votes.

For much of the election Fox was in fine fettle. He was cheerfully optimistic, and the enthusiasm of his supporters maintained his buoyant spirits. There was no time to lose nor was any submission to laziness or despair condoned. Everything depended on the outcome of the elections. Despite the confidence shown by the king's ministers Fox anticipated a series of close results. He was so swept along by the fury of electioneering that he looked for opposition gains, whatever the overall verdict might be. All his pent-up feelings, which the disappointments of the association agitation had damped down, erupted anew. In the middle of his campaign in Westminster he wrote to Burke telling him that things were going along 'swimmingly'. He was overjoyed by Sheridan's election at Stafford, though apprehensive about Burgoyne's fate at Preston. He need not have worried. Burgoyne was successful, though there was a petition against his return. His anxieties about Alderman Sawbridge were better grounded. Sawbridge lost his seat because of the hostility of the sugar interest, although Fox attributed his defeat to the catholic issue, still a delicate matter with the memory of the Gordon riots in everyone's mind. In his own campaign Fox had frequently been pressed on the subject of catholic relief and he confided his misgivings and intentions to Burke:

A voter asked me publicly today upon the hustings whether I would do my endeavours for the repeal of the popish bill declaring that his vote should be guided by my answer. I told him I would not, upon which, though he had already taken the oath, he went away and would not vote at all. They have at last persuaded me to declare publicly in an advertisement this much, viz: 'that I never have supported nor ever will support any measure prejudicial to the protestant religion, or tending to *establish* popery in this kingdom'. I think that by referring for my future conduct to my past nobody can accuse me of having done anything mean, or gone at all from the ground which I would not give up for all the elections in the world. I was afraid and I told my friends so, that by saying 'I never had supported etc.' it would be thought as is the truth that I maintain and defend that very bill they complain of and

so do me more harm than good in the election; but they thought otherwise and I gave way.[23]

He dwelt on the subject at length because if anyone thought that he
had allowed electoral advantage to persuade him to give up 'in the smallest
degree the great cause of toleration' he would be 'the most miserable man
in the world'. Not even the acclamations which were ringing in his ears,
and for which he freely confessed his partiality, would compensate him for
his deep sense of shame, yet he was sufficiently uncertain of what he had
done to beg Burke to judge him severely, and to say whether he thought he
had done wrong. Fox's supporters had urged him to leave out the
words 'have supported' but whatever its likely effects on the result of the
election he had refused to do so. But he was acutely conscious of the
calculated ambivalence of his disclaimer. Though he had resisted pressures to go further to mollify popular feelings, without in any sense giving
up his own basic convictions, he occasionally wished that he had been even
more unyielding on an issue about which he felt so deeply. The episode
was a reminder of the complex difficulty of combining fidelity to unpopular causes with a realistic appraisal of the needs of practical politics.

The overall result of the 1780 elections justified Fox's belief that the
outcome would be 'very near'. Though several members of the government had urged North to go to the country in the hope of making the
most of a swing of opinion back to the ministry the failure of the administration to improve their performance in the more open constituencies
proved a severe disappointment. North's initial hesitancy seemed to be
justified, though the deterioration which soon took place in the situation
in America would have made a later dissolution either unthinkable or disastrous. It is probable that in about ten of the popular boroughs a candidate
critical of the government replaced a member who had been faithful in
supporting the ministry. In the counties the government decline was more
marked. Before the dissolution twenty-six county members were estim-
ated to be sympathetic to the ministry; after the election only fifteen county
members were placed in this category. Fox was right in arguing that there
were signs of a genuine shift of public opinion away from the government.
It was probable that the country gentlemen were increasingly weary of
the war, and more convinced than ever that they bore an unfair proportion of the taxation necessary to pay for the conduct of military operations in America. It was not that the opposition could claim that they could
force North's resignation any more easily in the new house of commons
than in the old; but the government was being eyed more critically, and
the policy of coercion in America was being regarded more sceptically by

those members whose confidence or goodwill was essential to the survival of any administration.

But while the government was regretfully assessing the significance of the general election, and seeking to come to terms with the new house of commons, the opposition were uncertain about the tactics which they should adopt in attacking the government. Rockingham and his friends favoured another attempt to pass a measure of economical reform, but Fox was unconvinced that what had failed to break up the government a year earlier—even when supported by the fervour of the petitioning movement—would have any decisive impact in the new situation. He was sure now that the course of the American war was the only factor which would enable the opposition to do more than strike poses in the house. With the entry of Holland into the war at the beginning of 1781 the prospect looked more gloomy. In the Baltic the armed neutrality of the north took up a stance which embarrassed the British government, disrupted Britain's naval strategy, and interfered with British commerce. It was becoming increasingly apparent that Cornwallis' victories were barren of any lasting benefits. His victory at Camden had not been decisive, and in March 1781, although he had won another victory at Guilford Courthouse in North Carolina, he was becoming more apprehensive about the outcome of his campaign.

Fox supported a motion to restore peace with America in the commons on 30 May 1781, but although he made a long and animated speech in which he exposed the contradictory justifications for the war given by the king's ministers and took the opportunity of inveighing against the influence of the crown, he found that the house was not disposed to attend such a debate in any large numbers. Only 178 MPs voted in the division, and the government had a comfortable majority of 34. There seemed an overwhelming sense of futility in the air, whatever efforts were made to discomfit the government. Only when more members began to doubt the wisdom of the campaign in the Carolinas would it be worth the opposition's while to press the American issue once again. But Fox was able to urge the unavoidability of conceding American independence; he argued convincingly that in their refusal to contemplate recognising the United States the ministry were merely running away from unpalatable but inescapable facts.

While the political future remained dismal, and while men waited for news from America to confirm their worst fears or to stiffen their weakening resolve, Fox revived a subject which was always a favourite with him and which he always approached with a keen sense of filial obligation. He made another attempt to amend the marriages act, and although he failed

to change the law his speech was among his most charming and characteristic. He indulged all his innate romanticism in painting a verbal picture
of the joys of youthful marriage and the benefits it brought both to the
individuals concerned and to society at large. Fox's sentimentality ran riot;
his fondness for exaggeration tempted him into portraying an indulgent
version of young love and the evils of preventing early marriage:

> In that generous season ... a young man, a farmer or an artisan, becomes
> enamoured of a female, possessing, like himself, all the honest and
> warm affections of the heart. They have youth, they have virtue, they
> have love, but they have not fortune. Prudence, with her cold train of
> associates, points out a variety of obstacles to their union; but passion
> surmounts them all, and the couple are wedded. What are the con-
> sequences? Happy to themselves, and favourable to their country. Their
> love is the sweetener of domestic life. Their prospect of a rising family
> becomes the incentive to industry. Their natural cares and their toils are
> softened by the natural ecstasy of affording protection and nourishment
> to their children.... Thus, while they secure to themselves the most
> able and tranquil felicity, they become, by their marriage, amiable,
> active, and virtuous members of society.

Fox contrasted this blissful situation with the lot of a similar couple, who,
being under the age of twenty-one, were prevented from marrying by
their parents.

> But they have it not in their power to prevent their intercourse....
> What are the consequences? Enjoyment satiates the man and ruins the
> woman; she becomes pregnant; he, prosecuted by the parish for the
> maintenance of the child, is initiated into a course of unsettled pursuits
> and of licentious gratifications. Having no incitement to industry he
> loses the disposition, and he either flies the place of his residence, or he
> remains the corrupter and disgrace of his neighbourhood. The unhappy
> female, after suffering all the contemptuous reproach of relations, and all
> the exulting censure of female acquaintances, is turned out of doors, and
> doomed to struggle with all the ills and difficulties of a strange and
> severe world. The miserable wanderer comes to London, and here, after
> waiting, perhaps, in vain to secure some hospitable service, in which
> she might be able to retrieve or conceal her misfortune, she is forced,
> much oftener by necessity than inclination, to join that unfortunate de-
> scription of women, who seek a precarious subsistence in the gratifica-
> tion of loose desire. Good God! what are the miseries that she is not to
> undergo—what are the evils that do not result to society! But, above all,

what must be the consolation of that legislature who, from pride and cowardice, are mean enough to inflict such misfortunes on their country![24]

All this was typical of Fox's rhetoric: the warmth of feeling and the generous impulses often clouding a deficiency in argument. Interestingly, Fox's technique was frequently to exploit a particular case, not merely to illustrate an argument, but sometimes to do duty for a logical exposition of it. He liked to swoop on the human aspect of any situation, and he was usually happier in dealing with the way in which a particular principle affected the lives of people than in discussing the speculative justifications of or objections to a point of policy. He elevated illustration to the level of exposition, and although the method sometimes revealed limitations in his thought or an impatient narrowness in his outlook, it equipped him to excel in the circumstances of parliamentary debate. When the arguments were forgotten Fox's copious illustrations were remembered, and when they recalled his vivid details men called to mind his generosity, his compassion and his uninhibited depth of feeling.

But more serious matters soon intruded, thrusting themselves upon his attention. North's Indian summer was drawing to its close. The strategic failure and political frustrations of Cornwallis' campaign in the Carolinas were becoming more apparent. Far from creating conditions in which a favourable compromise settlement could be negotiated with perhaps some of the colonies being retained for the British crown, it was petering out with ominous indications of ultimate disaster. On 12 June 1781 Fox moved for a committee to consider the state of the American war. He boldly cited Cornwallis himself as his authority for arguing that a reconquest of America was impracticable. He reminded the house that the government had talked of a victory which would recall the rebels to the British standard; the victory had been confirmed, 'but what then were the predicted fruits of what he was tempted to call this pretended victory? Nothing but disappointment, nothing but misfortune.... The truth was the victory of Guilford ... drew after it all the consequences of something very nearly allied to a decisive defeat.'

Fox savagely exposed the futility of British strategy. It was impossible to remain on the defensive in America with any prospect of success, but it was equally impossible to act offensively. The task of preserving law and order in those areas through which the British army had passed imposed excessive burdens on resources both of administration and of manpower. It was absurd to contend with France in America, and although it was often said that during the Seven Years war Britain had conquered France in Germany, even that conflict had ended chiefly because of mutual exhaustion. Fox reminded members of the dangers of the influence of the crown, and of the importance of 'the supreme rights of the legislature to direct, propound, and finally determine, on what or ought not to be asserted or conceded in respect of the rights or claims of this country over America'. In order to vindicate parliament's authority Fox had to return to the original issue of the legislative supremacy of the British parliament. All he could do was to fall back on the familiar Rockinghamite approach, perhaps because he was now more dependent on Rockingham's approval for any chance of gaining office:

> I am ready to appeal to every impartial person in this house, whether there is not an immense difference between a speculative assertion of a right, and the enforcing that right with the point of the bayonet? I would appeal to those who hear me, whether there is any similarity between regulations of commerce and actual taxes?

Fox defended himself against the charge of equivocation over the recognition of American independence. There was no doubt in his mind that the colonies were irrevocably lost, but he recognised that several considerations went against a 'naked' recognition of American independence. Such a declaration, if hastily issued at the wrong moment, might have had the effect of stimulating 'still higher pretensions in the minds of the people of America'. It was, therefore, wise, before holding out an offer of independence, to become better informed about the connexion between France and America, so that the recognition by Britain of the United States would not tempt the French to exploit the situation to their own advantage. Fox deplored talk of the American war as a holy war; such an attitude would prolong and intensify hostilities. He believed it to be in Britain's interests for the war to be brought to an end, and for American independence to be recognised, but he did not overlook the diplomatic difficulties of bringing this about. In reply to critics who denounced his speech because it would lead to American independence he predicted that 'in the course of six months from this day' the government itself would be compelled to make an offer similar to that which he had laid before the house.[25]

During the autumn of 1781 Fox's attitude towards the North administration hardened. Gone were the days when he had envisaged the possibility of entering North's ministry. Whereas previously he had thought Rockingham too uncompromising in holding out for a complete change of ministers, he now believed that nothing less would accomplish anything of lasting benefit to the nation. An increasingly bitter tone crept into both his public speeches and his private correspondence. Though his wrath was directed principally against the king and his ministers he could not forget that public opinion had either approved of the policy of taxing the Americans or had condoned the tactics of coercion for too long. It was galling to feel that the destinies of the country were in the hands of incompetent fools. Writing to Fitzpatrick on 9 September Fox's anger boiled over:

> I agree with you thinking that the people of this country in general deserve no pity, and certainly the king still less. But is it not a little hard upon us, who expected to play some part upon the stage of the world, and who had certainly at least the shares of individuals in the greatness of our country, to be obliged to bound our hopes, nay our wishes, to being able some way or other to heal the wounds made by others, and to put this country, which was the first in Europe, upon a footing to be one amongst the other nations of the world? I dare say you think even this more than we can do; but to those who ever had any ambition, good God! what is this? Indeed, indeed, it is intolerable to think that it should be in the power of one blockhead to do so much mischief. The more I think of the whole of the business, the more I feel averse to coming in upon any terms, unless on those of parliamentary condemnation of what is past....[26]

Yet, for all Fox's oratory, interest both within the house and in the country at large had fallen away from the excited intensity of the previous year. Fox's motion was defeated by the comfortable margin of 172 votes to 99. After their efforts of the previous eighteen months the opposition were weary and uncertain which way to go. Most men were sceptical of any short-cut to success; only the news from America could transform the situation. It seemed wiser to wait and see. Apprehension about the final outcome of the war was still tinged with the hope of retaining some consoling foothold in America. A tired disillusionment with the war against the colonists did not overcome a repugnance towards submitting to defeat at the hands of France.

On 19 October 1781 Cornwallis' army surrendered to the French and Americans at Yorktown; on 25 November the news reached London. 'Oh, God! It's all over!' cried North, recognising the collapse of all his hopes and the impossibility of salvaging any military compensations from the débâcle. The catastrophe which had overwhelmed the British army in Virginia confirmed the delusions on which Cornwallis' campaign in the Carolinas had been built. Whatever reverses might be inflicted on the French, there was no prospect of restoring British sovereignty in America. But men did not altogether despair. The king set his face firmly against any talk of surrender. There were hurried conversations as to how best the government could be strengthened. Though the number of MPs supporting Fox during the debate on the address to the king's speech on 27 November rose to 129 there were still 218 who were faithful to North in the division.

Possibly in the immediate aftermath of Yorktown men could not bring themselves to go to the lengths which Fox was urging so vigorously. The very sprightliness with which Fox exploited the ministry's humiliation was more than some members could bear. Though Fox could claim that all his warnings had been amply justified by events and that he had anticipated every misfortune which now crowded in upon the dejected and discredited administration, it was difficult for backbench MPs to be enthusiastic in recognising Fox's insight and their own folly. There was, after all, a tone of exultant triumph in much of Fox's speech:

> It was his opinion that the day was now approaching, that it was at hand, when the public would no longer submit, nor the ministry escape. Their conduct was unprecedented in any age of our history; it beggared the records of nations: for in all the annals of kingdoms ruined by weakness or treachery, there was not an instance so glaring as the present, of a country ruined by a set of men, without the confidence, the love, or the opinion of the people, and who yet remained secure amidst the storms of public disaster. The honourable gentleman who had seconded the motion had called for unanimity. He demanded to know if they meant to insult that side of the house when they asked for unanimity, and designed to continue the American war? They had opposed it from its commencement; they had opposed it in all its progress; they had warned, supplicated, and threatened; they had predicted every event, and in no one instance had they failed in predicting the fatal consequences that had ensued from their obstinacy or from their treason. If in a moment like the present, a moment of impending ruin, men who loved their country could have any comfort, he confessed he must feel it as a comfort and consolation, that when the history of this dreadful period should come to be written by a candid and impartial hand, he must proclaim to posterity, that the friends with whom he had the honour to act were not to be charged with the calamities of the system.[27]

Fox argued that the ministers, 'overruled by that high and secret authority which they durst not disobey and from which they derive their situations', had deluded both parliament and people. Rather than admit the deceptions which they were practising they had plunged the country into war with France, Spain and Holland. There was 'one grand domestic evil' from which all the country's misfortunes and miseries, whether foreign or domestic, had sprung: 'the influence of the crown'.

> To the influence of the crown we must attribute the loss of the army in Virginia; to the influence of the crown we must attribute the loss of the thirteen provinces of America; for it was the influence of the crown in the two houses of parliament that enabled his Majesty's ministers to persevere against the voice of reason, the voice of truth, the voice of the people. This was the grand parent spring from which all our misfortunes flowed. . . .[28]

Here Fox was expounding the fully fledged Rockinghamite thesis. It was not a viewpoint which he had always held, but in the circumstances it was understandable that he should identify himself so explicitly with the group which had been the most insistent on a complete change of ministers as the necessary precondition for coming into office. The attack on the influence of the crown gave greater coherence to the opposition attack. It linked domestic troubles with colonial tragedy and by promising a change of system it clothed the opposition case with dignity and a nobler stature than could have been attained by arguments drawn from pure expediency. The opposition had been thwarted for so long that its various members could not afford to temporise with their opponents in government now that it seemed they were to be totally discredited. Yet the demand for a total change of ministers was so unconventional and so distasteful to the majority of members, that only the theory that a fundamental attack had already been made on the essentials of the constitution could make it palatable.

There were attempts to save the government. Dundas argued that the sacrifice of Sandwich or Germain or both was necessary if the ministry was to enter into negotiations with the Rockinghamites with any hope of success. But though Germain was dropped the hopes for a fruitful understanding leading to the broadening of the ministry proved futile. Inexorably the tide moved against the government. Fox kept up his assault on Sandwich, affirming the primacy of parliament in securing the dismissal of unpopular ministers as well as exposing weaknesses in naval policy and administration. Then the opposition widened its scope to include the overall purposes and conduct of the American war. On 22 February only one vote saved the government from defeat; five days later, a resolution moved by Conway calling for an end to the war was carried without a division after the opposition had defeated a government motion to adjourn by nineteen votes. Amidst a scurry of rumour and intrigue the government fought desperately to restore its position in the house. But though North saw a flicker of recovery in subsequent divisions he knew that Rockingham remained obdurate in demanding a clean sweep of ministers and the freedom to recognise American independence and to introduce a measure of economical reform. The country gentlemen finally decided to withdraw their confidence from the government, and this news meant that North could at last procure his release from office. George III gave way reluctantly, reminding North that it was he who was deserting his post, and the king showed ill grace in the manner with which he parted with his minister. On 20 March 1782 North told the house of commons that the ministry had ceased to exist and that the ministers were merely remaining to do their official duties until others were appointed to fill their places. When a surprised house adjourned North turned cheerfully to those members standing waiting for their carriages in the falling sleet and snow and said brightly, as he climbed into his own vehicle, 'Good night, gentlemen, you see what it is to be in the secret'.

With the departure of North Fox was at last on the threshold of power. Despite his independence of the Rockinghamites he knew that he could expect office in the new administration. Though the king chose to use Shelburne as his go-between there was no doubt that Rockingham would head the new government and that his terms would have to be met by the king, however much he detested them. For Fox the future looked bright. He had retained his political independence, yet with the triumph of the Rockinghamites his ministerial career could be resumed. Though he would be happiest as secretary of state there was no reason to anticipate any insuperable barrier to his attaining one of the major offices. The long years of opposition had now reached the moment of fulfilment—or so it seemed.

It is nevertheless important to restrain any tendency to glamorise Fox's conduct during the American war. He constantly opposed the government, but his opposition was prompted as much by the exigencies of parliamentary politics as by any regard for principle. His insight into the American controversy was limited, and his understanding of the constitutional aspects of the conflict was defective. If Fox's attitude towards the American problem changed it did so because of the pressure of circumstances, not because of any devotion to a transcendent ideal. Fox had certain basic attitudes which did not change; he believed that the simple fact of conflict between the colonists and Great Britain undermined any advantages gained by affirming constitutional principles even when there was much to be said for the latter on theoretical grounds. He wanted to conciliate the colonists, regardless of ideological consistency, for he was bitterly aware of the potential benefits for France in any struggle between the Americans and the British government. But he tended to ignore or play down the genuine constitutional issues which had to be faced, and towards the end of the war he exaggerated the ease with which recognition of the independence of the United States could be implemented, and the speed with which such a recognition would affect the relations between the Americans and their French allies.

Far from being a noble exponent of a highly principled and altruistic policy Fox was all too often the brilliant debater, exploiting weaknesses in the government's case with fertile inventiveness and skilfully using whatever arguments were at hand for his purpose. Even in his conduct of opposition Fox was far less of a party man, and far less preoccupied with defending the practice of a formed opposition, than he was to be in the years after the death of Rockingham and the disaster of the Fox-North coalition. He attacked North, Sandwich and Germain with savage and resourceful invective, but he accepted the need for demanding a total change of ministers only after the disappointment of his hopes for a coalition ministry in 1778. For four years at least he regarded the insistence of Rockingham on a total dismissal of those ministers who were responsible for government policy in America as unrealistic and a positive hindrance to the reshaping of the ministry and the reversal of British policy towards the colonists. The ferocity with which he assailed the ministry was inspired by an old-fashioned expectation that outstanding skill in opposition would lure the government to seek an accommodation by bringing its most vociferous critic into the administration. If Fox was preoccupied with any constitutional issue during these years it was the alleged influence of the crown (from which all evils, including the conflict in America, sprang), not the issue of American taxation or the legislative supremacy of the British parliament. He was as much interested in the political utility of emphasising an issue such as the influence of the crown as in any abstract considerations. Though historians have failed to discover any evidence justifying the allegations which Fox and Burke made during their years of opposition that George III and North were subverting the independence of the commons on an unprecedented scale, the influence of the crown was a potent rallying cry, partly because it could not, in the nature of things, be proved. The failure of North's policy in America and the humiliations suffered by the country during the war against France were deemed sufficient evidence of a fundamental malaise, sinister and malignant, afflicting the practice of politics. It was as a critic of the influence of the crown, even more than as a friend of the Americans, that Fox finally succeeded in winning a measure of support and confidence from the country gentry. Just as the country gentlemen had once supported the policy of taxing the Americans because it promised to lead to a reduction in the land tax, so they now regarded the increase of the influence of the crown as the explanation for a war which had increased the burden of taxation. But, as Fox knew, without the humiliating experience of defeat, most MPs would have supported the king and North to the end.

Fox's career during the years of opposition to the American war must be seen in terms of maturing political skills, rather than the vindication of idealism. Fox's anguish at the policy of coercion in America was as much the outcome of a shrewd anticipation of the depressing consequences of government policy for British interests as the result of a sense of moral outrage. It was as a political practitioner that he earned the admiration of his contemporaries, and to many it appeared that his ingenuity, quickness of thought, and keen appreciation of the realities of politics, would be well suited to the responsibilities of office. The skills which Fox had shown in opposition were valued only because they held out the promise of high achievement in government, and it was with eager impatience to prove himself in office that Fox accepted the invitation to serve as secretary of state for foreign affairs in Rockingham's second administration.

Fox's political abilities earned the respect of contemporaries, even when they feared and distrusted him, but his reputation as a dissolute gambler was something which he lived down only slowly. The contrast between the hard-working, public-spirited Pitt and the extravagant, self-indulgent Fox attracted historians, who liked to see the contrast in private life mirrored in the public fortunes of the two rivals. When men came to estimate Fox's place in history a veil was cast over much of his early life, and what he lacked in public achievement he was deemed to make up for in high principle, far-sightedness, and enlightened reformism. Others preferred to see in the happiness of his domestic circle some compensation for the frustrations of Fox's political career; the warmth and generosity of the man were used to condone the more dubious stratagems of the politician. His notorious impetuosity was interpreted as the political expression of his well-known susceptibility of heart, and broad and lofty principles were discerned behind the countless twists and confusions of political conflict.

It was once claimed that Fox's career was dominated by three passions: women, play and politics, and that he formed no honourable connexion with any woman, gambled away his vast wealth, and spent most of his public life in futile opposition. Whether Fox's relationship with Elizabeth Armistead merits the taint of dishonour is questionable, but his reputation as a profligate and a womaniser rested on much hearsay as well as some evidence. The tales which Horace Walpole repeated and embroidered with such avid zeal belong, in any event, to the earlier part of Fox's career. Only as a young man did he contemplate mending his fortunes by making a suitable marriage, powdering his swarthy jowls to win the favour of an heiress who liked fair and ruddy men; his failure to carry off the lady meant that he never attempted to repeat the performance. As a youth his relations with women were sensual, affairs of pleasure, not of the heart. He accepted sexual gratification as part of life, and he took it where he found it, and as a young man this tendency to indulge in casual relationships offended the more thoughtful of his contemporaries.

But the tributes to his overpowering charm and the attraction of his personality are legion. Burke once remarked that Fox was a man made to be loved and even as scathing a commentator as Brougham paid a considerable tribute to Fox's character, maintaining that the impulses of a great and benevolent soul were uppermost in his personality: 'A life of gambling, and intrigue, and faction, left the nature of Charles Fox as little tainted with selfishness or falsehood, and his heart as little hardened, as if he had lived and died in a farmhouse; or rather as if he had not outlived his childish years.' Wordsworth noted in Fox 'a constant predominance of sensibility of heart', and he believed that this saved him from falling victim to the politician's besetting sin of regarding men only in groups, ignoring their individuality. Even Wilberforce, who lamented that Fox had not one religious friend or one who knew anything about religion, affirmed that he was truly amiable in private life. Even when allowance is made for old men looking back to the exciting world of their maturity and the great figures who were no more, Fox's personality must have been especially powerful and outstandingly lovable for him to inspire so much affection so many years after his death.

But there was another side to the picture. Where friends talked of the manly and honest warmth of Fox's heart, others were less enthusiastic. Even when George Selwyn praised Fox's debating skill during the closing months of North's ministry he could not refrain from adding, 'If he had any judgment or ... character he would ... be the first man in the country'. Dr Richard Price, who was more advanced in his political thinking than Fox, and who cannot be accused of being unsympathetic to many of the causes which Fox advocated, was antipathetic: 'Can you imagine that a spendthrift in his own concerns will make an economist in managing the concerns of others? That a wild gamester will take due care of the state of a kingdom? Treachery, venality, and corruption must be the effects of dissipation, voluptuousness, and impiety. These sap the foundations of virtue. They render men necessitous and supple, and ready at any time to sacrifice their consciences, or to fly to a court in order to repair a shattered fortune and procure supplies for prodigality.' One of the chief reasons for George III's dislike of Fox was the belief that Fox's influence had lured the prince of Wales to the gambling tables and the company of women such as 'Perdita' Robinson, the actress with whom the prince had a flamboyant affair. Nor did the king forget the selfish irresponsibility which Fox had displayed when he had been a junior member of North's administration. Charm is a quality which often evades the historian; what to one witness is lovable spontaneity looks more like sloppy sentimentality or self-indulgence to another.

Whatever the differences of opinion over Fox's character there was almost complete agreement over his distinction as an orator. His heavy figure, with its gross body and short, stout legs, and his dark-jowled face, dominated by bushy eyebrows, were as unmistakable as were the fire and vehemence with which he spoke. Fox was a master of impromptu speech. There was nothing of the midnight oil about his eloquence. He was usually repetitive, sometimes excessively so, and the excitement which he engendered was occasionally vulgar and cheap. His exuberance merited the innocent remark of the young girl who asked her father, when watching a debate in the commons, 'what is that fat gentleman in a state about?' Yet men listened with rapt attention to what he said. Pitt talked of Fox as wielding the wand of a magician, and said that only those who had experienced Fox in the commons could appreciate the magnetism of his oratory. Sir James Mackintosh thought that when Fox began to speak he was often awkward, but that once he had warmed to his task he was transformed. He forgot himself and everything round him. He 'darted fire' into his audience: 'torrents of impetuous and irresistible eloquence swept along their feelings and convictions'. Lord Erskine maintained that Fox 'no more premeditated the particular language he should employ ... than he contemplated the hour he was to die'. It was the vigour of his ideas, the breadth of his information, the retentiveness of his memory and the exuberance of his invention which cast such a spell over his audience. Erskine thought that Fox's habit of returning again and again to his themes in an unmethodical way added its own fascination to any subject, since the issues being discussed were often illuminated in an unexpected and original fashion. This quality of infusing debate with inspiration was a happy gift which Fox never lost, although Grattan believed that after the coalition with North there was a change in Fox's style: 'The mouth still spoke great things, but the swell of soul was no more.'

Fox's emotional power gave his oratory its unique distinctiveness. Erskine believed that intellect alone, devoid of strong feelings, was like a magazine of gunpowder without the flame necessary to ignite it. 'It is the *heart* which is the spring and fountain of eloquence. A cold-blooded, learned man might, for anything I know, compose in his closet an eloquent book: but in public discourse, arising out of sudden occasions, could by no possibility be eloquent.' Fox was the reverse of Erskine's cold and learned scholar. He combined mental agility with 'the most gentle and yet the most ardent spirit—a rare and happy combination'. Mackintosh commented on the contrast between the vehement orator and the private man: 'In private life he was gentle, modest, placable, kind, of simple manners, and so averse from dogmatism, as to be not only unostentatious, but even something inactive in conversation.' Fox disliked political conversation, and never willingly took part in it. Few could be as witty as Fox when he was in the mood, but he preferred literature to politics in the peace of his home. Yet there were times when his impetuosity in the house of commons had unpleasant consequences. His duel with William Adam was the most colourful instance of his words bringing a nemesis which was far from his thoughts and remote from his intentions. Sometimes he failed to appreciate the searing nature of the wound which his wit and debating skill inflicted on less talented men.

He hated carrying public disagreements into private intercourse. He was distressed when men expected him to show hostility towards North, for however much he deplored North's politics he could not loathe him as a man. Fox regarded the postures of politics as an inescapable part of public life, but he saw no reason to allow the antagonisms of controversy to sour personal relationships. Much as he loved politics they were never his only passion. Nor did women and gambling comprise his complete range of interests. He never lost a boyish enthusiasm for cricket, and he enjoyed games of tennis, though he had no aptitude for ball games. For some orators the classics were storehouses of useful quotations; for Fox they were an abiding source of refreshment and delight. He never allowed familiarity to stale his enjoyment of the Greek and Latin authors, and poetry was an inspiration to him throughout his life. He was interested in French, Spanish, and Italian literature, although Italian seems to have been his chief joy among modern tongues, and Ariosto his primary enthusiasm. Whenever the strain of politics or the seemingly endless disappointments of public life became unbearable, Fox found solace in reading Homer, Virgil, Theocritus, Dante, Shakespeare and Chaucer. As the years went by his literary interests became more profound, more searching, more absorbing; the gambler became a connoisseur of verse and prose, discussing the significance of the nightingale in poets as different as Chaucer and Theocritus and stoutly maintaining his contention that the nightingale had often been regarded as a cheerful, not a melancholy, bird. He retained the ability to lose himself in an author and there was a universality about his literary tastes which was remarkable.

One of the chief influences in taming Fox's early wildness was his mistress, Elizabeth Armistead, whose association with Fox seems to have begun about 1783, and which lasted until his death, although in 1778 there is a reference to Mrs Armistead in Fox's correspondence. She was not Fox's first mistress, nor was he her first companion. For a while in 1782 Fox shared the favours of 'Perdita' Robinson with the prince of Wales, which led George Selwyn to remark, 'Who should the man of the people live with, but with the woman of the people.' But there was no rival to Mrs Armistead in Fox's affections. Throughout their long partnership Fox retained his ardent admiration for her. She provided him with understanding, security, fidelity and selfless love, and in return she received his boundless devotion. When writing to her he often turned away from politics in anger or disgust or boredom, his passionate feelings erupting in intense outbursts of emotion. When writing to Mrs Armistead about the result of the Westminster election in May 1784 he ended by saying, 'Adieu, my dearest Liz. It may sound ridiculous, but it is true that I feel every day how much more I love you than I know. You are *all* to me. You can always make me happy in circumstances apparently unpleasant and miserable in the most prosperous. Indeed, my dearest Angel, the whole happiness of my life depends upon you. Pray do not abuse your power. Adieu.'[29] Three years later he still felt as passionately; in June 1787 he assured Mrs Armistead, 'I never can be happy now I have known you but with you. I have known many men and many women and for many of them I have great friendship and esteem, but I never did know nor ever shall man or woman who deserves to be loved like Liz and I am so convinced of this that having you for my wife appears to me a full compensation for every disappointment.'[30] Even when the depressing experiences of the war years made him wish that he could retire from politics completely Mrs Armistead's companionship and faithfulness were great comforts to him: 'My Liz says she wishes she could shoot too, and so do I with all my heart, and when I have made a good shot I often think how I should like to turn round and see my dear Liz's lovely face smiling and encouraging me, and even when I do ill, I should like to hear her find fault with me, and see her look contemptuously as she does when I am awkward at carving.'[31]

Considerable mystery surrounds Mrs Armistead's origins and early career. She was born in 1751 and in 1773 she was already well-known as a lady of easy virtue associated with 'a notorious establishment' in Marlborough Street. She was the duke of Dorset's mistress for three years, and for short periods she was on intimate relations with Lord Derby and Lord Cholmondeley. In the summer of 1782 the prince of Wales was infatuated by her, calling upon her every morning, and after the prince Charles Fox became her lover. By this time both Fox and his new mistress had outgrown a taste for the more extravagant and lavish forms of self-indulgence; both were seeking affectionate companionship, not erotic excitement.

For Fox the relationship quickly assumed all the qualities of a permanent partnership. Ironically it was Mrs Armistead who held back and postponed formal marriage. She was sufficiently experienced, and sufficiently unselfish to have a kindly scepticism towards masculine protestations of eternal devotion, nor did she wish to impose herself on Fox, or exploit his good nature. There may have been other obstacles to a marriage, though these are purely speculative. The identity of Mr Armistead has never been established, and there are considerable doubts about his existence. Some historians have suggested that he was a polite fiction, the assumption of a married status being a ruse adopted by the more respectable type of prostitute to give herself a certain dignity in the eyes of the world, and to assure her clients that they were not exploiting the innocence of an inexperienced girl. Elizabeth Fox signed the marriage register as Elizabeth B. Cane when she and Charles Fox were married, very quietly, on 28 September 1795, but it is still possible that some form of marriage— perhaps of doubtful legality—had bound her to one of her early associates at a previous stage of her career, and that some misgivings following from this made her uneasy at the thought of submitting to a wedding ceremony with Fox. Mrs Armistead was a sensitive woman, aware of the ambivalence with which she was regarded in polite society. She had no wish to embarrass Fox, and while an informal relationship was permissible she knew that some would look askance at a public figure such as Charles Fox marrying a woman with her history to live down. But she eventually gave way to Fox's entreaties to allow the church to bless and the law to recognise their union. Even so the marriage was a jealously guarded secret for many years. Charles and Elizabeth Fox were married at the parish church at Wyton in Huntingdonshire, the rector, the Reverend J. Pery, being a friend of Fox. Only in 1802, on the eve of their visit to France after the peace of Amiens, did Mr and Mrs Fox tell the world that they had been legally man and wife for seven years. Their motives for announcing the marriage were simple: Fox wanted to ensure that his wife would be accepted in any company during their time abroad. The motives for secrecy are more difficult to ascertain. Perhaps it was Fox's way of assuring his wife that his desire to legitimise their union sprang from a respect for her, not a deference to social convention or a sensitivity to society gossip. By keeping their marriage secret Fox and his wife could feel superior to the scandalmongers, and faithful to their previous attitude of regarding their relationship as a matter of concern to no one but themselves.

Few marriages have been as happy, so blessed with affection and loyalty. From the beginning Fox referred to Mrs Armistead as his wife; he never doubted the permanence of their relationship. He cherished Elizabeth as the guardian of his home and the provider of domestic peace. Doubtless he regretted that there were no children; certainly there were no legitimate offspring, though for many years tales were occasionally heard that Mrs Armistead had borne Fox two daughters, both of whom were later said to have lived to a ripe old age. Possibly this is no more than another instance of high society gossip, adding another element of mystery to Fox's private life. No trace of these daughters has survived, and there is even less evidence about them than the deaf-and-dumb boy whom Fox begot on an earlier mistress, and of whom he was said to be inordinately fond. But the most serious complication of any illicit union is the issue of children (as Fox himself reminded the prince of Wales when warning him against marrying Mrs Fitzherbert) and it would be easy for fertile imaginations and ready tongues to manufacture stories of forgotten, ignored, or disinherited children.

Mrs Fox was by temperament a woman of simple and unassuming religious faith. Whatever the sins of her youth or the waywardness of her life she was a devoted Christian; her diaries are marked by brief bursts of prayer. When Fox was dying she prevailed upon him to allow the local vicar to visit him. Trust and fidelity, charity and compassion, were her most deep-seated characteristics. Many years after Fox's death she always recalled the joys of living with her 'angel', never failing to remember his birthday, the anniversary of their wedding, and the day on which he died. She outlived Fox by thirty-six years, dying in 1842 in her ninety-second year; she was buried in Chertsey parish church.

Such was the woman who played so constant and so prominent a part in Fox's life from the early 1780s onwards. She brought about the transition from feckless instability to domestic calm and fulfilment. Fox's devotion to his wife, and the happiness of their life together, is one of the finest things in Fox's career. The tragedy for Fox was that, while his private life became more assured and benign, there was no similar fulfilment in his public life during the years when his love for Elizabeth Armistead was maturing into a lifelong commitment.

He never lost a fondness for gambling, though he dropped the habit when in office, and he became much more cautious after his failure to set up as a professional gambler. During the 1780s he became more interested in horse-racing, fancying himself as a potentially successful owner of racehorses. He knew good days and bad days, and sadly for Fox the bad days outnumbered the good. He had several famous wins, one of the most sensational being when his horse Seagull won 6,000 guineas at Ascot. But he knew anger and disappointment too. In October 1791 he told Mrs Armistead of the frustrations he had experienced at Newmarket:

> I thank you kindly for your nice ... letters without which I really should feel very much out of humour at all my bad luck at this place, and still more at the ... things that happen here. Instead of leaving it by degrees I am determined to get rid of my horses as soon as possible and even if I cannot do that I will send down the money for them and come as seldom as possible. It is very difficult to explain to you by letter but such a thing has been done by the prince's people here as in my opinion amounts to an absolute cheat....[32]

Fox's relations with the prince of Wales and the other dignitaries within the whig party such as Portland, Shelburne, Burke, Sheridan, Grey and Fitzwilliam were complex and often subject to intense fluctuations. He always suspected that Shelburne had an excessive partiality for royal favour and he was always suspicious of Shelburne's loyalty to his colleagues. Portland earned Fox's respect as an honest, straightforward and dependable public servant, and it was the confidence which Portland won from all parts of the house of commons which made him so attractive to Fox as a head of government. Portland was slow-witted, and far from scintillating in debate in the house of lords or in discussions in the cabinet, but he never forfeited the regard of his contemporaries and in his undramatic way he was competent in those aspects of politics which Fox found so boring: negotiation, the cultivation of electoral and constituency interests, and the patient creation of a viable party organisation.

Though Fox appreciated the profundity of Burke's genius and the richness of his mind, the two men were never close personal friends. They were thrown together by the exigencies of politics and by a common concern for the constitution; both were outraged by the folly of a British policy in the American colonies and both responded to the need to meet the grievances of the Irish and the Indians. Burke sympathised with catholic requests for the remission of outmoded penal laws; Fox went further and extended his generous advocacy to the cause of the protestant dissenters. But despite all this Burke was never a member of Fox's personal circle. He was bored by card play and horse racing, and however much he admired the aristocracy, venerating them for the stability and continuity which they supplied in society, he was repelled by raffish self-indulgence in high places. Perhaps he could retain his reverence for noble families only by ignoring the petty behaviour of those who bore high-sounding names. The seventies were the years in which Burke and Fox were closest in political outlook and friendship, but after the death of Rockingham Burke became ever more isolated. The breach with Fox—distressing as it was for both men—was the culmination of a period of growing coolness, not an abrupt termination of an intimate friendship. Yet Fox always retained a regard for Burke, even when he thought that like most Irishmen he had a piece of potato in his head. When Burke lay dying Fox tried to see him; but Burke refused to see him, believing that if he did so his sincerity about their disagreement over the French revolution might be impugned. When Fox heard of Burke's death he wept bitterly. He was never reconciled to the loss of friends, and to be denied access as Burke lay on his deathbed hurt him deeply.

Sheridan was a colleague towards whom Fox's attitude was ambivalent. Initially they had much in common. They both knew the excitements of high living and the embarrassments of financial catastrophe. But Fox came to distrust Sheridan's familiarity with the prince of Wales and to despise, sometimes quite unfairly, his political judgment. He eventually believed that Sheridan's vanity was his gravest weakness and towards the end of their long association there was little love between them. For Grey, on the other hand, Fox always retained a warm and deep affection. He held Grey in high esteem, although there were occasions when he tried his patience, as over the formation of the Friends of the People. But throughout the depressing 1790s Fox's enthusiasm for Grey remained a powerful, and consoling, force. Fitzwilliam was in some ways Fox's favourite associate, and it was Fitzwilliam from whom he found it hardest to part over the French revolution and the war. What is interesting is that Fox's deepest friendships with political colleagues belonged to the earlier stages of his career; from the time he began to live with Elizabeth Armistead a greater distinction can be traced between his political associations and his personal affections. As he became a less familiar figure in the casinos and clubs, so the unpretentious joys of St Anne's Hill made him less dependent on the friendship of those with whom he was acting in politics.

3 *The Breach with Shelburne*

A casual observer might have been forgiven for assuming that Rockingham and his friends would remain in power for the foreseeable future
when they took office in the spring of 1782. The ministry comprised
virtually all those whose talents and industry had been devoted to denouncing North and the American policy with which he had been
associated, and what was perhaps more significant Rockingham had
imposed his own terms on the king. There was to be no royal veto on
the recognition of American independence or upon the economical
reforms which the Rockinghamites intended to introduce in order to
honour their pledge to Wyvill and the reformers. But there were nevertheless serious problems which would have taxed the skill of the most
able of statesmen. The ministry was not a party ministry. Despite the
unanimity with which the new ministers criticised their predecessors they
were less agreed on the actual means by which peace was to be achieved
than at first appeared. Nor was it easy to see how the United States could
be recognised without reference to the views of their French allies, and
without causing complex repercussions in Ireland where the volunteer
movement was still agitating for the granting of full legislative independence to the Dublin parliament. These difficult issues were made all the
more troublesome by personal hostility between Fox and Shelburne, and
inherited confusions about the precise responsibilities of each of the two
secretaries of state.

Despite the new division of the work associated with the two secretaryships into home and foreign departments, with Shelburne being responsible for domestic and colonial affairs and Fox being primarily concerned
with foreign affairs, there was uncertainty as to the precise allocation
of responsibility for the former British colonies. Shelburne argued that
until the British government formally recognised the independence of the
United States his department could not be excluded from discussions of
the American problem. Fox believed that, whatever the technicalities, the

4 King George III *Bust by Joseph Nollekens*

5 Lord North *From the portrait by N. Dance*

6 William Pitt *From the portrait by John Hoppner*

7 Edmund Burke *From a portrait after Joshua Reynolds, 1771*

8 Richard Brinsley Sheridan *From a pastel portrait by J. Russell, 1788*

9 The Prince of Wales *From the portrait by Joshua Reynolds*

10 Charles Grey *From the portrait by Thomas Lawrence*

11 W. W. Grenville *From the portrait by John Hoppner*

American colonies had effectively secured their independence and that the primary responsibility for dealing with them lay with the foreign office. But these were not the only divisions within the cabinet; there were differences of opinion over the scope of the proposed economical reforms and the best means of bringing them into effect. The Rockinghamites could not forget that George III had preferred Shelburne as a mediator during the negotiations leading to the formation of the ministry and they still suspected that the king wished to see Shelburne as his first minister and that Shelburne was deliberately cultivating the king in an attempt to ingratiate himself still further with his monarch. It was tempting to believe that Shelburne was playing a double game, and that he was giving the king advice and information which conflicted with his attitudes within the cabinet. Because of their obsession with the influence of the crown the Rockinghamites were quick to explain legitimate divergences of opinion as the expression of sinister intrigues to restore the so-called personal rule of George III. Rockingham's death came at a time when only the most ingenious diplomacy on the part of the first minister would have saved the administration, and it is doubtful whether Rockingham, if he had lived, would have risen to the occasion. Whatever criticisms may be made of Charles Fox's decision to resign after Rockingham's death (and there are good reasons for regarding it as the crucial error of his political career) there is no doubt that he was justified in claiming that the conflict within the cabinet was already critical before Rockingham died. Partly out of respect for Rockingham Fox had restrained his inclination to bring things to a head; after Rockingham's death he abandoned such restraint, with imponderable consequences for his own future.

Fox was suspicious of both Shelburne and the lord chancellor, Thurlow, from the start. On 12 April 1782 he confided his anxieties to Fitzpatrick. In cabinet discussions there had been more evidence of those sympathies with the royal prerogative which he had always mistrusted in Shelburne. Thurlow had vehemently criticised Burke's bill, and Shelburne had given him some support; the consequence was a very heated discussion, in which Fox told his colleagues that he was determined to bring the matter to a crisis. Worried though he was Fox was still optimistic. He believed that Shelburne and Thurlow would be forced to yield, but experienced members of the government such as Camden were apprehensive of the significance of the differences within the cabinet. Conway was sounding out the possibility of putting reforms in administration into effect by using the king's prerogative and thus evading the necessity to pass a bill through the commons. Fox did not regard this tactic as inherently objectionable, but he thought it unwise to risk delay since this would be imputed as lukewarmness by those who already harboured doubts about the government's good faith or ability to carry reforming legislation through parliament. The only real consolation was the king's apparent good humour: Fox thought that George III's spirits were rising every day, and there was some evidence to suggest that having reconciled himself to the change of ministry George III was coming to approve of his new ministers. But on 15 April Fox had more unhappy news for Fitzpatrick:

> We have had another very teasing and wrangling cabinet, but I rather think everything is or will be settled tonight. I am to carry a message today to the house of commons, which looks and points to Burke's bill. The king is, in the first instance, to abolish of his own accord the offices, but that abolition is in every instance to have sanction of an act of parliament for the appropriation of the money, the preventing their revival etc. Lord chancellor, as you may imagine, dislikes it. Lord Shelburne seems more *bothered* about it than anything else, does not understand it, but, in conjunction with Lord Ashburton, rather throws difficulties in its way. General Conway, quite with us in the general view, but unfortunately *doubts* in almost every particular instance. Lord Camden, evidently with us in his mind, yet is so terribly afraid of dissensions that he does not do us all the good he might. The duke of Grafton rather hostile, though professing *right principles* in the strongest terms, but full of little projects of his own, and troublesome in the extreme; the remaining five [Rockingham, Richmond, Lord John Cavendish, Keppel, Fox] just as you would expect and wish. This is a tolerably accurate sketch of our councils, but I have no doubt things will jumble themselves into something more to our mind, to come to a crisis the other way. Indeed, if they do not, it will be very uneasy to me, and to everybody. We met yesterday at eleven, and did not get to the drawing-room till four, when it was over. All this time the king seems in perfect good humour, and does not seem to make any of those difficulties which others make for him.[1]

In the light of the lurid assertions which Fox was to make only a few weeks later his emphasis on the cheerful demeanour of George III is of particular interest; there seems little evidence of that sinister influence of the crown which Fox was later to indict in justification of his resignation from the administration after the death of Rockingham. Perhaps Fox believed that the king was being unscrupulously exploited by Shelburne, but if this was the case then he ought to have made it more apparent just what he was complaining about. It was possible to argue that the influence of the crown was worrying because it could be utilised by a subtle and ruthless minister, but since he did not exempt the king from the accusations which he made Fox can hardly have been surprised at George III's pained and angry response to his allegations.

Within a fortnight of his letter to Fitzpatrick describing the wrangles within the cabinet over economical reform Fox's pessimism reasserted itself. Increasingly he identified Shelburne as the most dangerous threat to governmental policy, even to the very existence of the ministry. He could not wholly explain his depression; but he felt that every day confirmed his suspicions and mistrust of Shelburne. In addition to their differences of opinion over domestic reform Fox hated Shelburne for his jealous defence of his own department against any encroachment while using every ruse in the game in order to encroach upon Fox's departmental responsibilities. Fox thought that Shelburne behaved as if he were already head of the government, while it seemed all too obvious that he believed that he would soon become the king's first minister in name as well as in fact. Fox told Fitzpatrick that he was convinced that Shelburne was 'perfectly confident' that the king intended to make him first lord of the treasury. Already Fox's thoughts were turning to the prospect of leaving office. He was strangely defeatist in this respect, for although Shelburne had the support of a substantial number of cabinet ministers he was far short of commanding a majority. Fox was confusing the range of support which Shelburne was receiving on particular issues with the chance of his acquiring a workable majority as head of the government. Fox's anxieties and resentments about Shelburne's intervention in the peace negotiations in Paris were understandable, but he was losing all sense of proportion over Shelburne's influence within the cabinet and more especially his influence on the king. Perhaps Fox had always underestimated the tensions and disagreements within any cabinet, foolishly expecting a degree of unanimity which no eighteenth-century cabinet could hope to attain. In his perplexity he clutched at familiar explanations, invoking memories of former controversies and making charges which he could not substantiate with any real conviction. Mistakenly he came to see the government's function in a curiously narrow and restricted light, telling Fitzpatrick, 'Provided we can stay in long enough to have given a good stout blow to the influence of the crown, I do not think it much signifies how soon we go out after, and leave him [Shelburne] and the chancellor to make such a government as they can, and this I think we shall be able to do.'[2]

Fox was also concerned with the arrangements necessary to carry into effect the government's declared intention of recognising the independence of the American colonies, and of making peace with France and the

United States. On 23 April the cabinet agreed to send Mr Oswald back to Paris with the authority to settle with Benjamin Franklin the most convenient time for setting on foot negotiations for a general peace, with two main considerations, the recognition of American independence and the restoration of Britain to the position in which she had been placed by the peace settlement of 1763. It was agreed that Fox should submit to the king for approval the name of the diplomatist to make similar approaches to Vergennes, the French minister. The government must have known that they were being optimistic in suggesting the treaties of Paris as the starting point for future negotiations. The balance of power now favoured the French and they were bound to press for territorial rewards for their military successes. The tasks facing the British representatives in Paris were complex and difficult. The willingness of the United Kingdom to recognise the independence of the American colonies was an essential prerequisite to any negotiations, but such a willingness could also become a factor in the pattern of negotiation itself. It was possible to hope that Britain would win the confidence, perhaps even the gratitude of the United States, and certainly Shelburne favoured a generous settlement with the Americans in order to wean them from an undue dependence upon France and to secure Anglo-American cooperation in the future. But in the circumstances it was unrealistic to imagine that any simple and speedy solution to the American problem could be arrived at without the vigorous participation of the French.

Instead of choosing a diplomat of experience and skill Fox settled on Thomas Grenville, the younger son of George Grenville of stamp act fame. Grenville's instructions were to propose the negotiation of peace terms on the basis of the independence of the thirteen American colonies and of the peace of Paris. If these preliminary overtures were well received he was then to call on Vergennes to make counter-proposals of his own. But the situation in Paris was all the more confusing because Britain seemed to be speaking with two voices. Neither of her representatives seemed to be fully informed of what the other was doing. The French and the Americans found it easy to play off Oswald against Grenville, but they were also genuinely uncertain of what the British government's real intentions were. The king warned Fox on 22 May that until he saw Shelburne and heard from him all that Oswald had told him of Franklin's attitude he could not hope that the Americans were prepared to conclude a peace without the concurrence of France. George went on, 'Peace is the object of my heart if it can be obtained without forfeiting either the Honour or the essential rights of my kingdom; I do not think myself at liberty to hazard any opinion. I must see my way clear before me.'³ The king was not alone in finding it impossible to discern what was likely to happen.

Yet on the following day the cabinet agreed to instruct Grenville to propose the negotiation of American independence, 'in the first instance, instead of making it a condition of a general Treaty'.⁴ This was a victory for Fox, but he could not take too much comfort from the fact that Shelburne had acquiesced in the decision. Grenville was sending him details of the shrewd delaying tactics which Vergennes was exploiting to the full, and which Fox believed to be partly stimulated by Shelburne's duplicity and the behaviour of his envoy in Paris. Grenville found both the French and Spanish negotiators very trying; he thought Vergennes' manner ominous, resenting 'those little expressions which it is easier to feel the force of than to put into a despatch'. The French minister believed that Britain would have to make peace on virtually any conditions, and that the divisions within the new administration made it impossible for the British government to hold out for better terms. If the ministry failed to end the war confidence in it in the house of commons would crumble. Grenville told Fox of the difficulties of finding out exactly what proposals the French were willing to consider. If the French propositions followed Grenville's expectations he sadly confessed that they were likely to be so disgraceful that it would be impossible for Britain to accept them. Would it not, he inquired, 'be more manly and more dignified to state at once the extent of what reasonable and supportable concessions can be made'? Grenville thought concessions were inevitable, and it was embarrassing for him to be asked whether it was true that there was great dissension within the British government between Shelburne and the duke of Richmond.

Rodney's defeat of De Grasse at the battle of the Saints (12 April 1782) heartened the ministry, though while congratulating the king upon the event Fox told George III that the ministers were still doubtful about the outcome of the peace negotiations. The ministers were basing their plans upon the supposition that the peace talks would fail and they were chiefly preoccupied with detaching France from her allies and with conciliating the other European powers. If Vergennes rejected the British proposals Fox thought it likely that such conduct would produce 'the most salutary effects with regard both to Europe and to America and possibly to the exertions of Great Britain herself'.⁵

But Grenville remained gloomy. Vergennes claimed that he was unable to enter into prolonged or binding negotiations until he had had full consultation with his Spanish and Dutch allies, and Grenville became more than ever convinced that the demands of France and Spain would be ruinous and dishonourable to Great Britain. Even Rodney's victory failed to make the French more amenable in negotiation. The news of the British victory had only made the French more peevish, without making them more inclined to making peace. The general opinion in Paris was that peace was as far away as ever. Grenville was trying to make a good impression upon Franklin, but the chances of a separate treaty with the Americans were remote. Franklin was profuse in affirming his favourable opinion of Fox but even when passing on this item of news Grenville warned Fox not to be sanguine in expecting that America would be detached from France during the negotiations: 'Franklin seems too jealous of the faith of his first treaty to hear of anything that looks like abandoning it.'[16]

The beginning of June saw things take a turn for the worse, from Grenville's point of view. One of his few consolations during his frustrating time in Paris had been his belief that he had earned the confidence of Franklin, and that there was a surer prospect for a future reconciliation between Britain and the United States. Grenville had never been optimistic about the chances for an immediate improvement in Anglo-American relations, but he believed that there were grounds for thinking that Franklin would communicate to him his own ideas as to the best means of achieving an understanding between Britain and America. Unhappily for Grenville, Franklin was also having discussions with Oswald. This meant that when Grenville offered recognition for American independence in the first instance, instead of making it dependent on a general treaty, he found Franklin's response disappointing and strangely contradictory. Franklin was pleased that independence had been dissociated from the general peace settlement, but he refused to be drawn on precisely those issues on which he had promised to let Grenville have his ideas in full. Franklin's hesitancy was the outcome of his having been told by Oswald that he was the commissioner appointed to deal with the American representatives. Grenville thus found himself excluded from negotiations with Franklin, and it was all the more galling to know that Lafayette had gaily referred to Oswald as Lord Shelburne's ambassador. Suspicions that Shelburne and Oswald had been less than frank with their colleagues were confirmed by what passed between Oswald and Franklin on the subject of Canada. Franklin had entrusted Oswald with a paper suggesting that England should 'spontaneously' cede Canada to the United States. The document was to be shown only to Shelburne, since the proposal to yield Canada to the Americans was unlikely to commend itself to the French. Shelburne showed the paper to no one but the king, and whatever one's views about Franklin's suggestion it was apparent that Shelburne had deceived his cabinet colleagues. While keeping his associates in the dark he was seeking to curry favour with George III on the one hand and Franklin on the other. From the American viewpoint the acquisition of Canada was attractive. Congress hoped to make considerable sums by selling unappropriated lands, and this fund could be used to compensate those who had suffered from the forays of the British army, as well as offering some compensation to the American loyalists, whose treatment was one of the principal sources of contention between the British and American governments.

Grenville thought the cession of Canada unthinkable. It was folly, having lost thirteen colonies, to throw away a fourteenth, and the proposal raised all sorts of complications with respect to the Newfoundland fisheries. But most ugly of all was the clear evidence of the way Shelburne and his emissary in Paris had undermined the confidence of the American ambassador in the official representative of the British foreign secretary. Grenville felt unable to carry on; he had been humiliated and slighted. It was imperative for Britain to be represented by one diplomatist in Paris. As long as two envoys were present confusion and deception would ensue, with Fox himself being effectively excluded from the most essential aspects of negotiations. Grenville's choice for the supreme British representative in Paris was Earl Fitzwilliam.

Fox was angry at hearing of the frustrations and slights which had been heaped upon his representative in Paris. He was incapable of seeing that the most sinister interpretation of Shelburne's conduct was not necessarily the most convincing or even the only explanation. Possibly Shelburne was trying to be too subtle in his dealings with Franklin, but it did not follow that he was betraying his colleagues. The divisions within the cabinet were themselves arguments in favour of discretion in negotiations which were intended to drive a wedge between the Americans and their French allies. The truth was that the sophistications of Shelburne's policy were lost on his colleagues. He wanted to preserve commercial links with America, possibly even to work out a common foreign policy, but although the cabinet had agreed on 8 April to open the question of reciprocal trade agreements with the Americans they had little grasp of the complexity of the issues which they were raising. It was inevitable that the cession of Canada was repugnant to the British government, and if Franklin's proposals had been communicated to the cabinet they would have been hotly rejected. But this would have prejudiced further discussions with the American ambassador in Paris, and by receiving Franklin's paper while insisting that it remained in the category of a confidential and semi-personal interchange, Shelburne was hoping to keep the lines of communication open for further negotiations on issues which were particularly dear to himself. Perhaps he was seeking to save his colleagues from embarrassment rather than to deceive them. By faithfully adhering to the request which Franklin had made of him (with the understandable exception of the king) Shelburne could claim that he had behaved with all due propriety. But the distrust with which he was regarded in the cabinet was too powerful, and his direct dealings with the king (although fully in line with conventional practice) were seen as proof of sinister motives. Within the cabinet no one was more convinced that he had been deceived and betrayed than Fox.

Fox showed Grenville's letter to Rockingham, Richmond and Cavendish, all of whom were shocked and indignant. Fox respected the confidential nature of Grenville's letter but two questions demanded action. The first was the suggestion that Canada should be ceded to the United States; the second was the role of Oswald, since Shelburne seemed intent on investing him with full powers. Fox wished to challenge Shelburne with his conduct directly; but it was thought advisable for the ministers not to stir until they had heard further from Grenville. Fox was acutely sensitive to the dangers of the intrigue becoming public knowledge. It was impossible to mention Canada by name during any public controversy but it was permissible to claim that it had been discovered that Shelburne had withheld matters of significance for the outcome of the peace negotiations from his colleagues and that the authority of one of the king's accredited plenipotentiaries had been undermined. In the meantime Fox begged Grenville to be on the alert for further evidence of Shelburne's duplicity:

> When the object is attained, that is, when the duplicity is proved, to what consequences we ought to drive, whether to an absolute rupture, or merely to the recall of Oswald and the simplification of this negotiation, is a point that may be afterwards considered. I own I incline to the more decisive measure, and so, I think, do those with whom I must act in concert. I am very happy indeed that you did not come yourself; the mischiefs that would have happened from it to our affairs are incredible, and I must beg of you, nay entreat and conjure you, not to think of taking any precipitate step of this nature. As to the idea of replacing you with Lord Fitzwilliam, not only would it be very objectionable on account of the mistaken notion it would convey of things being much riper than they are; but it would, as I conceive, be no remedy to the evil.[7]

Fox begged Grenville, as a personal kindness, to remain a little longer at

Paris. If Grenville were to leave all sorts of suspicions would be raised. It was of 'infinite consequence' for Fox and his friends to be able to say that they had done all in their power to make peace, both in America and Europe. Fox fully recognised the immensity of what he was asking Grenville to do:

> I know your situation cannot be pleasant, but as you first undertook it in great measure from friendship to me, so let me hope that the same motive will induce you to continue in it, at least for some time. What will be the end of this, God knows; but I am sure you will agree with me that we cannot suffer a system to go on, which is not only dishonourable to us, but evidently ruinous to the affairs of the country....[8]

Both Fox and Grenville were bitterly conscious of the political dangers of the French becoming too familiar with the differences of opinion and clashes of temperament within the British government. Yet they were so incensed by Shelburne's behaviour and so infuriated by what seemed to be an attempt by Shelburne to usurp at least some of the functions reserved for the head of an administration, that they found it impossible not to view the matter in the gravest light. But Grenville was also mindful of his responsibilities towards Franklin. To accuse Shelburne of having diverted from Grenville to himself a communication which Franklin had promised to send to Grenville would be to publicise Franklin's promise to Grenville, thus violating the confidence which Franklin had originally reposed in Grenville. As Grenville reminded Fox, 'The delicacy of Franklin's situation with respect to the French court was, as he said, the ground of the caution which he observed; and which nevertheless he was inclined to risk in my trust; he would certainly have both to repent and complain, if anything on my part should lead to betray even the confidential disposition he had entertained.'

The Canada paper was rather different. Grenville knew of it only from Oswald, though he suspected that Oswald's only reason for telling him of its existence was a fear that Grenville would, in any case, hear of it from Franklin. Grenville had made no promises of secrecy in the matter of the Canada memorandum, but the risk in making public any reference to it was simply that Franklin's name would be brought into the discussion in a way which he would find embarrassing and which would be a poor reward to Franklin for the attempt he had made to initiate discussions with the British government independently of his commitments to the French.

But there were no similar scruples when dealing with Shelburne's promise to Oswald that he would be empowered to act as the sole British emissary to the American minister in Paris. Grenville had been shocked to discover that Shelburne had not broached this subject with his colleagues. He had assumed that Shelburne had discussed his intention with other ministers, citing his responsibility for the American side of the negotiations. Grenville thought that it was possible that Fox had not found it easy to object to such a reading of the division of duties between the two secretaries of state. Grenville had made the suggestion that Fitzwilliam should take his place, 'not to prevent a *clandestine* negotiation, but to unite a *separated* one, always imagining that you knew of, but did not resist, the intended commission to Mr Oswald'.[9]

For Fox the situation was now intolerable. Not only had negotiations in Paris been singularly barren of any results but the ministry was torn with suspicions, intrigue and rivalry. Yet it was important for the ministry to remain in office if the economical reforms upon which so much emphasis had been placed were to be carried into effect. In Ireland the situation was critical. The crisis of 1779-80 had stimulated the creation of the Irish volunteers and now Grattan and his friends were pressing hard for the restoration of full legislative supremacy to the Dublin parliament. There was also talk of purifying Irish politics by the same sort of administrative reforms on which the Rockinghamites had staked their reputations in England, and of improving the efficiency of the lord lieutenant's administration by introducing something like a cabinet council. Fox was sympathetic to these suggestions, but Fitzpatrick was careful to warn him of the risks inherent in the Irish imbroglio and to emphasize the need for caution in communicating the information being passed on to him to his colleagues in London. Fitzpatrick asked Fox to send his letters by messenger, since there was a considerable likelihood that his letters had been opened by post office officials. Fitzpatrick's chief anxiety was to caution Fox against trusting Grattan too unthinkingly:

> For though everybody seems to argue that he is honest, I am sure he is an enthusiast and impracticable as the most impracticable of our friends in the Westminster Committee; his situation is enough to turn the head of any man fond of popular applause, but the brilliancy of it can only subsist by carrying points in opposition to Government, and though he chose to make a comparison yesterday between Ireland and America, giving the preference to his own country, I confess I think the wise, temperate, systematic conduct of the other, if adopted by Ireland, would bring all these difficulties to a very short and happy conclusion, to the satisfaction and advantage of both parties.[10]

Fitzpatrick could not refrain from noting that Shelburne's speech in the lords, declaring that the claims of Ireland must be acceded to, had given great satisfaction in Dublin.

It was helpful to Fox to have the benefit of Fitzpatrick's shrewd advice, especially since he was in direct correspondence with Grattan. The Irish leader stressed the fact that he and his countrymen were asking for no more than what was indispensable for their freedom. He told Fox that Irishmen particularly objected to having to submit to a foreign legislature, a foreign judicature, a legislative privy council, and the presence of a British army. He pointed out the impossibility of Irishmen having any respect for the English constitution in such circumstances, and he urged the abandonment of the British claim to legislative supremacy. Not surprisingly, Grattan reminded Fox of the parallel with America:

> Can England cede with dignity? I submit she can; for if she has consented to enable his majesty to repeal all the laws respecting America, among which the declaratory act is one, she can with more majesty repeal the declaratory act against Ireland, who has declared her resolution to stand and fall with the British nation, and has stated her own rights by appealing not to your fears but to your magnanimity.[11]

Fox was cautious in replying to Grattan. He excused himself from answering the precise questions which Grattan had raised by referring to the fact that they were not within his department. He contented himself by saying that it was his 'ardent wish' that matters might be settled to the satisfaction of both countries, hoping that an agreed settlement would preclude all future occasions of dispute between the two nations 'upon whose mutual union the prosperity of both so unquestionably depends'. He continued:

> That as close a connexion may subsist between us, as the nature of the case will admit, must be my wish as an Englishman. That this connexion may be such as may consist with the liberty and happiness of Ireland, I must wish as a whig, and as one who professes to hold the natural right of mankind far more sacred than any local prejudices whatever. I am sure I share those feelings in common with your lord lieutenant and his secretary, and if ever you should think it worth while to inquire into my political sentiments upon any point, you may always be pretty sure of them when you know those of these two persons.[12]

But Fox was uneasy about the best means of dealing with Irish grievances. He lacked nothing by way of sympathy and a keen desire to solve the problems confronting the government quickly and amicably, but he sensed his own ignorance, his inexperience of Irish conditions, and the dangers of blundering in such a complex situation, whatever his intentions and despite his good will. He lamented that he and Fitzpatrick had misunderstood each other. Fitzpatrick was impatient for Rockingham to declare himself; Fox and his colleagues were waiting for further proposals from Portland, the lord lieutenant. Fox criticised Portland's hesitancy, wondering whether a simple repeal of the act passed in the sixth year of George I's reign reaffirming the control of the British parliament over Irish legislation would be adequate to meet the needs of the situation. Yet his own inclination—for once—was to risk criticism because of delay, rather than taking up positions which might prove temporary or embarrassing. He even toyed with the notion of a parliamentary commission. Much as he wanted a lasting solution, as distinct from a makeshift expedient, he was anxious not to give away 'everything' without a treaty or agreement binding on both countries. To do so would merely obtain peace and quiet for a few months. He wanted to be generous to the Irish but he was conscious of the consequences of appeasement and he was determined to avoid them. He assured Fitzpatrick of his firmness and resolution:

> My opinion is clear for giving them all that they ask, but for giving it to them so as to secure us from further demands, and at the same time to have some clear understanding with respect to what we are to expect from Ireland, in return for the protection and assistance which she receives from those fleets which cost us such enormous sums, and her nothing. If they mean really well to their country, they must wish some *final adjustment* which may preclude further disputes; if they mean nothing but consequence to themselves, they will insist upon these points being given up, simply without any reciprocal engagement, and as soon as this is done, begin to attack whatever little is left in order to continue the ferment of the country. In one word, what I want to guard against is Jonathan Wild's plan of seizing one part in order to dispute afterwards about the remainder....[13]

Broad as his sympathies were, and eager as he was to remove the Irish question from political controversy, Fox had no illusions about the slowness with which the confused tangle of racial, religious, and political antagonisms in Ireland could be smoothed out into some semblance of order and justice. Fox had no wish to see successive British governments immersed in the stifling hatreds of Irish politics or to forget that if there had been conflicts of interest between the two countries in the past there were also common interests which were vital to the future prosperity of both nations. He thought about the matter deeply in the intervals of following the course of the negotiations in Paris, eventually concluding that the immediate concession of freedom of internal legislation to the Irish, coupled with a modification of Poynings' law and a temporary mutiny bill, would enable amicable negotiations to be started, which he was confident would terminate in an arrangement which would preserve the connexion between Britain and Ireland.

Fox made his standpoint clear in his speech in the house of commons on 17 May 1782. It had always been his opinion that it was wrong for Britain to legislate for the internal regulation of Irish affairs. Though he had not been opposed to the declaratory act relating to America he had always made a distinction between internal and external legislation. Though the ultimate sovereignty rested with the British parliament this power ought to be exercised with discretion:

> The great superintending power of the state ought not to be called into action, but in the aid of the local legislature, and for the good of the empire at large; but when ministers ... carried the principle of external to internal legislation, and attempted to bind the internal government of its colonies by acts, in the passing of which the colonies had no voice, that power, which, on proper occasions, would have been cheerfully obeyed, created animosity and hatred, and had produced the dismemberment of an empire, which, if properly exerted, it would have served to unite and bind in the firmest manner.

Fox was careful to place his discussion of Irish affairs against a background invoking all the memories associated with the American dispute. By doing so he could play on apprehensions of the future as well as on echoes from the past. He was also able to pin the blame for the deterioration in Anglo-Irish relations on those who had antagonised the Irish by abusing a power which would have provoked no hostility had it been correctly applied. Unfortunately, the power of external legislation had been employed against Ireland as an instrument of oppression. An 'impolitic monopoly' in trade had been established, enriching one country at the expense of the other, and the insensitivity of the British government and parliament had compelled the Irish to resort to extreme measures. But Fox emphasized that only by dealing justly with Ireland would the British prevail upon the Irish willingly to render obedience to the British crown. He warned against the dire consequences of a policy of coercion, reminding the house that unwilling subjects were little better than enemies:

> It would be better not to have subjects at all, than to have such as would be continually on the watch, to seize opportunities of making them-

selves free. If this country should attempt to coerce Ireland, and succeed in that attempt, the consequence would be that, at the breaking
out of every war with any foreign power, the first step must be to send
troops over to secure Ireland, instead of calling upon her to give a
willing support to the common cause.

It would be better to see Ireland totally separated from the English crown
than for the Irish to be kept in obedience only by force. He did not believe
that total separation was desirable or likely, providing just policies were
followed by the British in their dealings with Ireland. He thought it
was wrong to suggest that by making legislative concessions to the Irish
the government were allowing themselves to be humiliated. Britain was
merely giving up what it was just that she should give up. Policy and
justice, principle and expediency, united to approve the wisdom of giving
the Irish parliament greater control over Irish affairs. The only real
danger was not that of humiliation for England: it was that the prevalent
and mistaken idea would be that England yielded out of fear what she
would not have given out of a sense of justice. Fox was not gloomy about
the future: he had no doubts that Ireland would be satisfied with the
manner in which England was about to comply with her demands. In
affection and in interest the English and the Irish would remain one
people, but it ought also to be remembered that important as the crown
was in uniting the two nations, it was not the king who was the chief
bond of union: 'it was a communion of affection, of regard, of brotherly
love, of consanguinity, and of constitution'.[14]

Fox had deftly appealed to Irish sentiment without ignoring the
anxieties harboured by many of the country gentlemen about Irish affairs.
He sought to convince the commons that the government's policy towards
Ireland stemmed from the fundamental principles which were guiding its
efforts to reach a peaceful and just solution to the American conflict. The
proposed concessions were part of a comprehensive and liberal application
of the constitutional ideas which he and his colleagues had advocated for
so long in opposition. But he had also been eager to demonstrate that
self-interest as well as idealism justified the government's approach to the
Irish problem. Throughout, Fox had never lost his appreciation of political
realities: though he cultivated Grattan he refrained from becoming too
closely associated with him and he was careful not to defer too easily to
Grattan's opinions. However responsive Fox was to the demands of the
Irish he never lost his freedom of manoeuvre by allowing them to dictate
terms to him or by permitting them to take his support for granted. He

balanced the demands of politics and the calls of morality with scrupulous and judicious discernment.

The ministry were of one mind on the necessity of implementing the economical reforms which had played so great a part in the popular agitations of 1779-80. Various ministers had different preferences as to the best ways of initiating administrative reforms, but there was little disagreement in principle. But the Rockinghamites remained deeply divided over proposals to reform parliament. Fox, Richmond, Sheridan, and Shelburne were sympathetic to the purification of the house of commons by the suppression of the most decayed boroughs and the redistribution of seats to under-represented cities and to the most populous counties. Rockingham, Portland, and Burke were hostile to any measure of parliamentary reform, believing that it would create a dangerous precedent and that far from securing the better representation of interests it might seriously disturb the natural balance which had been built up over the years. There was, of course, no suggestion that there should be any massive extension of the franchise; the whigs were preoccupied with eliminating corruption and illegitimate influence and with restoring the much vaunted independence of the house of commons; they were by temperament averse to anything savouring of the rule of numbers. There was no prospect of the ministry pushing through a reform of parliament, but private members were free to bring reform resolutions before the house.

On 7 May William Pitt, the younger son of the great earl of Chatham and the new member for Sir James Lowther's pocket borough of Appleby, introduced a motion calling for an inquiry into the state of representation. Fox gave the resolution his warmest support. He generously complimented Pitt on his attachment to parliamentary principles though he feared that only crisis or catastrophe would rouse the people to a sense of the dangers threatening representative government. Interestingly enough Fox sought to turn the familiar argument that all interests and all people in Britain were virtually represented in the house of commons to reformist uses. He admitted that in the present house the people were, in a loose sense, virtually represented, whatever the vagaries of the franchise and the eccentricities of the distribution of seats; but he reminded the house of the exaggerations and misrepresentations which had so often disfigured the theory of virtual representation in the past. Some had argued that the people of America were as effectively represented in the commons as the people of Birmingham. Virtual representation was, in truth, only 'a mere succedaneum' for 'an equal representation'. Those who urged that the constitution was perfect should visualise the effect upon the electorate if those who did not possess estates comparable in real terms to what comprised a forty shilling freehold in the reign of Henry VI were to be excluded from the franchise. He also emphasized the dangers to the constitutional independence of the house of commons from an excess of members from rotten and pocket boroughs. In reply to those who said that to increase the number of county members would be to increase aristocratic influence he admitted that in once sense it would, although he himself interpreted aristocratic in a way which embraced a fuller representation of the monied interest, not the aggregation of the influence of peers. He believed that those who had a stake in the country ought to be more effectively represented, for their natural anxiety to preserve their interests would add stability as well as liberality to the pattern of representation. He favoured the actual, as well as the theoretical or virtual, representation of every interest in the community in the house of commons, and he cited the examples of the county of Middlesex and of his own constituency, Westminster, to demonstrate some of the glaring anomalies of the traditional system. Not that Fox wished to supplant the historic pattern of representation by some wholly abstract conception: far from it. He was anxious for the principles of the constitution to be effectively applied and for the corruptions which had crept into the representative system to be pruned away. In brief, his attitude was that, accepting the representation of interests as the primary purpose of the electoral system, it was all the more urgent for the commons to ensure that all interests were fully and fairly represented, and that this meant the regular reform of the constituencies by legislation. Though Fox became more interested in proposals to extend the franchise at a later stage of his career his approach to parliamentary reform was thoroughly traditionalist, and however vigorously he inveighed against the influence of the crown or however persuasively he defended the rights of the people, he was never a democrat. His reformism was rooted in a strong, even a romantic, sense of tradition.

But motions calling for the reform of parliament, however powerfully they appealed to Fox's instincts, were hardly of primary political importance. Fox's anxieties were provoked by fears that the existence of the ministry was in jeopardy; the suspicions which Shelburne's conduct over the negotiations in Paris had fermented were heightened by recurrent disputes within the cabinet about the precise meaning of the unconditional nature of the promised recognition of American independence. The overall peace settlement could not be said directly to relate to a prior recognition of American independence, but it could not realistically be completely dissociated from it, and while it was possible to argue that the recognition of the United States had been agreed without prejudice to the negotiation of a peace treaty it could be claimed that the future boundaries of the United States and any possibility of a commercial agreement with the Americans were interrelated to wider issues affecting the peace settlement. One of the chief arguments for the unconditional recognition of the United States had been the expectation that such a step would allow the Americans to act more independently of the French, but, though the Americans were impatient with the lethargic conduct of negotiations by Vergennes, they could not act too freely, and their powers of initiative were limited. Much of the argument within the British cabinet was strangely unrealistic; a good deal of the heat engendered by the American issue was as much the result of deep-rooted, though not always fully admitted, personal antagonisms, and clashes of personality and difficulties of temperament were more to blame for the strains upon the ministry's coherence than the finer implications of a decision to recognise American independence.

Shelburne believed that though the decision to recognise the United States had been taken in principle it could not be formally accomplished until the peace negotiations were complete; the acceptance of the need to concede American independence did not absolve the government from keeping a watchful eye on how problems such as the balance of trade and westward expansion were to be settled. As long as the Americans were allied to the French the British government's conduct of negotiations with the Americans could not be divorced from a due consideration of their likely impact on Franco-American relations. By deftly managing the precise concessions which followed from a recognition of American independence Britain could hope to do better in the general peace settlement than had at one time seemed probable. The Americans could not become allies overnight, but if it was made clear that despite the war there were considerable mutual advantages in a measure of Anglo-American cooperation at the conference table then both countries would benefit from the peace treaties.

Fox thought that much of this was over-subtle and dangerously ambivalent. Any suggestion that there was any hesitancy about recognising the United States would make the Americans more irreconcilable and more dependent than ever upon the French. Fox suspected that Vergennes' perplexing dilatoriness might be explicable in so far as he hoped that a deadlock between the British and Americans would make the Americans all the more hostile to Britain, American intransigence and the disappointment of British expectations of a quick and amicable settlement with the former colonies making it easier for France to impose a harsh peace upon Great Britain. In Fox's view, any ambiguity about the unconditional commitment to American independence (which was an accomplished fact, whatever British feelings were on the matter) would have disastrous effects, not only upon Anglo-American relations, but also on the prospect for softening the terms which France and Spain were preparing to offer Britain. More annoying still was Shelburne's agreement on 23 May with the cabinet's decision to instruct Grenville to propose 'the independency of America in the first instance, instead of making it a condition of a general treaty'. All Shelburne's sophistries could not alter the fact that he had submitted to the opinion of his colleagues. Despite Shelburne's apprehensiveness about the peace terms Fox argued that as foreign secretary they were primarily his responsibility, whatever might be said about the legitimacy of Shelburne's interest in the former thirteen colonies. Fox linked Shelburne's conduct with his closeness to the king and, in turn, with the reluctance of George III to recognise the independence of the United States. He wondered whether Shelburne was subordinating public policy to his desire to mollify George III's feelings. Perhaps Shelburne was seeking to become the most powerful figure in the government by exploiting the king's favour; perhaps he was seeking to become head of the ministry. Such were the fears (many of them unjust) which were in Fox's mind, and which explained his behaviour during the summer of 1782. It was in an atmosphere heavy with suspicions such as these that the cabinet learned that the marquis of Rockingham was ill.

Rockingham had never been robust and his frail health had worsened during office. On 23 June it became known that he was ill; immediately rumours threw members of the government into a state of anxiety and confusion. Expectations fluctuated with every reported change in Rockingham's condition. On 29 June Fox wrote to Portland, claiming that Rockingham was a good deal better, but this cheerful news proved false. On Monday, 1 July, Rockingham died, and all the tensions and antagonisms which had been straining his government almost to breaking point now erupted with new vigour and intensity.

Even before Rockingham died Fox had been seriously contemplating resignation. On Sunday, 30 June he had found himself in a minority in the cabinet on the interpretation of the minute referring to the 'unconditional' recognition of American independence. He did not resign, but he talked in a manner which implied that it was almost certain that he would do so. Yet it was understandable that he should hesitate. With Rockingham's life hanging in the balance Fox did not want to lay himself open to the accusation of wilfully disturbing the delicate harmony of forces within the cabinet. If Rockingham recovered Fox's conduct would appear dubious. His critics would accuse him of resigning in a fit of offended vanity and of showing no sense of loyalty to his stricken chief. Nor would it be easy to explain the differences of opinion within the cabinet. To provoke public controversy on the meaning of a minute referring to the recognition of American independence would be denounced as adding new difficulties to those facing British diplomatists in Paris. Fox regarded the difference with Shelburne as one of principle, but the majority of his colleagues, including some who were sympathetic to Fox, thought of the divergence as one of emphasis, and in the debates on his resignation Fox had later formally to refute this charge. Furthermore, for Fox to resign by himself would be futile. The assertion that some important principle had been at stake would appear ludicrous if none of Fox's colleagues followed him into opposition. For his resignation to have any political significance he would have to be accompanied by a number of other ministers. Only after George III asked Shelburne to succeed Rockingham as first lord of the treasury was it possible for several other members of the government to feel, like Fox, that they had no alternative but to resign.

But the issue of principle became even more confused. Fox shifted the emphasis to the constitutional issues involved in the choice of a successor to Rockingham, talking darkly of Shelburne as something of an advocate and practitioner of the principles of government associated with North; instead of concentrating on the conduct of negotiations in Paris and the most judicious approach to the final recognition of American independence, Fox preferred to expatiate on conflicting 'systems' of government. Without the change at the head of the government necessitated by Rockingham's untimely death Fox would have been unable to discuss his resignation in this context. Had Rockingham lived Fox would have been compelled to carry on as foreign secretary, despite his loathing for Shelburne. Resignation would have been tantamount to political suicide. Fox's motives for choosing to emphasise the constitutional aspects of the crisis were mixed. Perhaps he felt this was the most convincing means of persuading the house of commons that he had not resigned for personal reasons, and that he and his friends were the true heirs to Rockingham and were defending all the political principles associated with Rockingham. But he might also have been genuinely reluctant to initiate a public discussion of the real meaning of the recognition of American independence, knowing as he did that this might jeopardise the outcome of the negotiations. He knew enough about the embarrassments which Grenville had already experienced to be anxious to avoid multiplying them. Possibly his decision was fortified by the suspicion that self-interest and patriotic duty were both satisfied by his self-restraint and the nature of the controversy which he provoked.

But it was difficult to argue that there was anything questionable either in the king's use of his constitutional powers in asking Shelburne to become his chief minister or in Shelburne's response to the king's invitation. The day after Rockingham's death Shelburne told his colleagues that the king had asked him to become first lord of the treasury. In the circumstances Shelburne felt that he could not refuse, although in many ways he would have preferred the post to have gone to a friend of Rockingham. Fox and his friends boldly suggested the duke of Portland as the best successor to Rockingham, and because of their obvious aversion to his own appointment Shelburne requested that no precipitate decision should be taken, promising to draw the king's attention to the misgivings of certain members of the cabinet. Both Fox and Lord John Cavendish, the chancellor of the exchequer, were determined to resign should the king insist on Shelburne heading the ministry, but other ministers were uncertain of what they would do. Richmond vigorously argued for the wisdom of staying in office, despite his own doubts about whether he himself could stay on if a majority of the Rockinghamites were unable to do so. Conway was personally in favour of Portland rather than Shelburne, but he was convinced that it was his duty to carry on as commander-in-chief. All the ministers felt the contradictory pulls of loyalty to their friends and of their responsibilities as servants of the crown who owed their first obligation to the king. They were also aware of the respect which Shelburne had shown to the opinions of his opponents within the cabinet; whatever their own views as to the person best fitted to succeed Rockingham they had a sincere regard for Shelburne's integrity and a willingness to allow the king to take the initiative in finding a new chief minister. Many of the cabinet thought it presumptuous to impose the head of an administration on the king; others found it convenient to avoid assuming any responsibility in the matter, thankfully congratulating themselves that the decision was not theirs to make.

Fox told the king that in his opinion the support of Rockingham's old friends for the government could only be secured by the appointment of a first minister in whom the Rockinghamites could place absolute confidence. George III replied that when North had resigned he had hoped and intended to make Shelburne first lord of the treasury. Shelburne had then declined the invitation in favour of Rockingham. It now seemed natural that after Rockingham's death the leadership of the government should fall to Shelburne. In reply Fox could do no more than say that Shelburne did not meet the conditions which he had previously stated.

The ebb and flow of negotiation and intrigue within the government was unabated. Richmond became more convinced of the folly of resigning and decided to remain as master-general of the ordnance, whatever some of his colleagues might do. He even induced Fox to promise to stay on, providing that Cavendish agreed to fill the secretaryship of state which Shelburne would vacate on his promotion. But Cavendish was obdurate in refusing to contemplate becoming home secretary and Fox consequently resigned from the foreign office. He argued that Shelburne's appointment was a violation of the principles upon which the Rockinghamites had entered office. When giving up the seals of office on Thursday 4 July he told the king of his feelings, adding that Shelburne's appointment would create the sort of distrust and disaffection among the king's servants which had been one of the misfortunes of his reign. George III was taken aback by Fox's comments; he was also displeased by his resignation. Far from eagerly dispensing with Fox the king asked him to reconsider his decision. George could not grasp what all the fuss was about. He was firm in his own conviction that Shelburne was the best fitted of his ministers for promotion to the highest office, and he saw no good reason for the other ministers to refuse to perform their obvious constitutional duty by continuing to serve under the new first minister. They had been prepared to serve with him; they ought now to serve under him. While Fox suspected a plot on the king's part to impose Shelburne on the cabinet, George III discerned a conspiracy of disappointed men seeking to hound his chosen minister to destruction by denying to their sovereign his legitimate right of choosing his own servants. Certainly the king had ample grounds for believing that Shelburne was a better choice as head of the government than Portland. It was inevitable therefore that he should be disposed to take a poor view of those who, however much they prated about principle, ran away from their constitutional obligations for no better reasons than personal spite and thwarted ambition.

However much he sought to put a brave face upon events, Fox was uneasy in his own mind about the wisdom of his actions. He had no doubts about the impracticability of serving under Shelburne but he was acutely sensitive to the change of arbitrarily throwing the government into confusion. With the negotiations in Paris in a delicate state the country could ill afford a governmental crisis. Fox was also disturbed by the hesitant attitude of his colleagues. Even those who resigned with him—and of these only Cavendish held cabinet rank—did so out of affection for Rockingham's memory and personal loyalty to Fox rather than any firm conviction that their resignations were politically justifiable.

Burke was convinced of the 'utter impossibility' of Fox's acting for any length of time 'as a clerk in Lord Shelburne's administration', but nevertheless he had drawn Fox's attention to two alternative courses of action which were open to him. He could insist on Portland (or himself) as first lord of the treasury; or he could tell the king that much as he distrusted Shelburne he had no wish to throw public affairs into confusion and that he would remain in office until the sense of parliament was taken on the matter. Burke's advice, attractive though it appeared in theory, was hardly realistic: he must have known that if Fox agreed to serve under Shelburne even for a limited period, it would be difficult for him to leave the ministry without additional good reasons at a later date. Though his suggestion that the outcome of the crisis should be dependent upon the opinions of parliament was theoretically attractive, since it would satisfy both conventional practice and Rockinghamite sentiment, it was by no means an answer to the immediate questions which were pressing so relentlessly upon Fox for a decision. He knew that if a breach was to be made with Shelburne it would be best done at once. But he was also depressingly aware of the unlikelihood of his motives being properly understood, while he was conscious of the folly of putting himself forward as the head of a ministry, whatever Burke might think.

It was understandable, therefore, that when Fox sought to explain his conduct in the house of commons he should seek to place his resignation within a wider context than the events immediately following the death of Rockingham. He compared his situation with that of Lord North. He had criticised North for remaining in office when he had lost all confidence in the policies which were being pursued by the administration of which he was chief; Fox could hardly do anything other than resign when he found himself in a similar situation. He was not head of the ministry, but throughout his career in opposition he had warned against the dangers of divided counsels within the cabinet. He had therefore resigned 'to prevent disunion, to prevent the distraction which he conceived to be so ruinous'. But he went further than this, claiming that he had acted consistently with those principles which had guided the Rockinghamites when forming their ministry. He identified the Rockinghamites with the practice of collective responsibility within the cabinet, and he argued that this principle had been violated by several members of Shelburne's government. Shelburne's appointment heralded, not merely a change of ministry, but a change of 'system', a return to the bad old system of departmental government as carried on by North. Fox made much of the notion that the constitution was in danger; though his language was suitably veiled its implications were clear. He affirmed that he felt a special responsibility to the house of commons in answering his critics and in justifying his actions: it was 'indispensably necessary that he should

come forward and ring the alarm bell and tell this country that the principle on which they had with due deliberation formed this administration
was abandoned, and that the old system was to be revived, most probably
with the old men, or indeed with any men that could be found'.[15]

This was both untrue and malicious. The confusions over protocol at
Paris had sprung from the overlapping responsibilities of the secretaries
of state, not from any sinister attempt to revive the influence of the crown,
and the differences of opinion over the recognition of American independence and the extent to which it should precede the conclusion of a comprehensive peace settlement had no connexion with any conspiracy to
smash the Rockinghamites and destroy an allegedly harmonious cabinet
system. The tensions within the ministry had existed from the start. It
was misleading to suggest that the type of collective responsibility which
Fox was advocating had been in operation during Rockingham's few
months at the head of the government. Shelburne and Fox disagreed about
a number of constitutional issues: Shelburne deeply respected the king
as the effective head of the executive and he had no wish to deprive him of
his legitimate place in government; as a Chathamite he did not believe in
party politics and he had never disguised his regret at the prospect of the
total separation of the American colonies from Britain. He thought it
right that the king should be free to choose his own ministers and that
the house of commons should judge the wisdom of the king's choice on results rather than by prejudice. Again, though Shelburne valued a wide
measure of agreement within the cabinet he accepted the inevitability of
divergent viewpoints and he distrusted ideas of exaggerated collective responsibility as potentially dangerous to the balance of the constitution. The
imposition of a head of the ministry upon the king by the cabinet was repugnant to him.

What was really significant here was that the weight of prevalent opinion among practising politicians and the whole of previous constitutional
practice were on Shelburne's side of the dispute. Far from Shelburne acting
as the agent of a royal plot to disrupt the continuity of constitutional development he was the apologist for accepted constitutional conventions.
It was Fox who was the innovator, and though he desired to seem to stand
within the Rockinghamite tradition he went beyond it. He was particularly mischievous in suggesting that Shelburne was contemplating bringing
back the 'old guard' into his government. The idea that Shelburne was
merely an agent through whose activities North would return to power
was wilfully perverse. In some ways Shelburne's hostility to North was
more fundamental than Fox's (as events were soon to show), and although Shelburne thought of himself as acting independently of all groups

he was more interested in strengthening his administration's appeal by bringing in new men, such as the young William Pitt, rather than by turning to former opponents for support. Fox's gibe about 'any men that could be found' had more pertinence with reference to Shelburne's recruitment of new and inexperienced talent than to any familiar faces. When Fox proceeded to join forces with North in order to push Shelburne out of office men recalled that he was doing precisely what he had accused Shelburne of contemplating. It was unnecessary for men to cast their minds back to the most ferocious of Fox's attacks on North during their long contest during the darkest days of the American war: Fox's duplicity stood revealed when he acted as he had so unscrupulously charged Shelburne with intending to act.

The cruellest aspect, from Fox's viewpoint, was that he had gone out upon pique, and that the dissensions within the ministry were primarily concerned with the distribution of places which it was argued should follow the replacement of Rockingham by Shelburne. Fox prided himself upon the fact that he had consciously turned his back upon office arguing that the placehunters were those who rallied to Shelburne's support, while Burke, Cavendish, and himself had chosen all the uncertainties of resignation rather than compromising their principles. He freely admitted that he had not left the foreign office without a pang: he was 'neither incapable of vanity nor of ambition'. But there were considerations superior to both his vanity and his ambition, 'the considerations of duty and conscience'. His willingness to resign before Rockingham's death seemed to prove that he was untainted by any squabble over the distribution of offices in the new government. His delay in resigning was explained as springing from his deference to the need to comfort Rockingham in his last days of life; he had no wish 'to embitter the last moments of a venerable friend by taking a step which he knew would give him the greatest uneasiness'.

It was important, too, for him to refute the charge that he had exaggerated mere 'shades' of meaning to the level of high principle. The issue was of the same magnitude as the choice between peace and war. He stood by the principle of granting full, unconditional, and unlimited independence to America; if this was the opinion of the cabinet after his resignation then he could claim that his departure had had some real influence upon events. But the handling of the negotiations relating to American independence was not the only issue which had separated him from Shelburne. Fox hinted that Shelburne was too inclined to screen from justice the 'delinquents' who had been responsible for the calamities which had so afflicted the nation. Shelburne claimed to be in favour of economic and administrative reform, but he had been lukewarm and condescending about Burke's bill. Fox accused Shelburne of being lavish in making promises but magnanimous only in the ease with which he broke them.

Nor could he disguise the relevance of Shelburne's appointment as first lord of the treasury to his own resignation. Fox reminded the commons of the patronage habitually attached to the office and the overriding power vested in it. He continued:

> Now it was but just and fair, that those who went into office, upon certain public principles, should be satisfied that none were introduced into the cabinet, who were hostile to those principles; and they either should have a right to retire, or to have a voice in the appointments of all persons who should be nominated to fill those vacancies that might happen: when that power was taken from them, their power was at an end; and if the king had a right to nominate his ministers, his counsellors had a right to retire, whenever they thought fit.

Fox was being less than frank, despite the determination with which he sought to persuade the house that he was taking members into his confidence. It was one thing to argue that members of the cabinet should be consulted about the acceptability of those who were soon to be of their number; it was another to claim that the cabinet should effectively replace the king in choosing the head of a ministry. Perhaps by confusing the issue Fox was attempting to win a wider acceptance for his ideas than would otherwise be the case. Nor was his argument materially advanced by resorting to an analysis of the personal fitness of the duke of Portland to be Rockingham's successor:

> One would naturally imagine, in an administration formed on the principles of the men distinguished by the name of Rockingham, that upon the decease of that great man ... the man would be sought and appointed to succeed him, who most resembled him in character, in influence, in popularity ... and the eyes of all men were naturally turned to the duke of Portland. Instead of that noble person, however, the earl of Shelburne was selected, of whom, if he meant to describe the character, he could not truly say he bore any resemblance to his predecessor; perhaps the exact reverse might come nearer to the picture.[16]

But Fox soon realised the weakness of attacking Shelburne on grounds of personality. It was easy for men to wonder why, thinking as he did of Shelburne, Fox had come into office with him at all. Fox could only reply by admitting that he had had strong reservations about Shelburne and the lord chancellor, Thurlow, and that the only thing which had persuaded him to associate with them in office, was 'the satisfactory pledge which he had for the integrity of the administration ... the noble marquis being at the head of it'. In order to make his resignation appear more convincing Fox was driven into exaggerating both his admiration for, and his closeness to, Rockingham. Furthermore he had to argue that Shelburne represented a denial of all those principles with which the Rockinghamites had publicly identified themselves. It was not surprising (although it was scarcely just) for him to pander to the prevalent impression that Shelburne was, above everything else, an arch dissembler, and a consummate hypocrite:

> The country had now an administration which could not be that popular administration to which his honourable friend had alluded; it was now the administration of a man who could not think of reformation with temper, however loudly he might speak of it; a man who would declare that the influence of the crown ought to be diminished, but who would, at the same time, say that the king had a right to use his negative in passing laws, and would threaten with the exercise of that negative all those who should attempt to move any bills that went to retrenchment. Such was the man now at the head of the treasury; the principles of the late ministry were now in the cabinet; and the next thing he should look for, would be to see the late ministers again in office. But perhaps he would be said to be too apprehensive and that his suspicions were vague; probably they were so; it would, however, be acknowledged to him, that thinking conscientiously that he saw such a danger, it was fit for him to come forward and to warn his country in time....[17]

Fox was so bitter about Shelburne's promotion that he sneered at Conway's suggestion that Shelburne had persuaded the king that American independence had to be granted. Despite all the appeals to principle, to consistency, to loyalty, and to scrupulosity, it was all too apparent that the biggest factor in compelling Fox to resign had been his consuming hatred of Shelburne. His anger and frustration were understandable; his decision to resign had been wrought through tears and a minor nervous collapse. But in laying so much emphasis on the sinister character of Shelburne and his alleged fondness for the principles and personnel of 'the late ministry' Fox was misjudging the popular mood and laying up criticisms which were to be cast at himself in the not too distant future. It was also a calculated mischief deliberately to confuse Shelburne's well-known respect for the legitimate place of the crown in government with any condonation on his part of the increase of royal influence in the house of commons. In this Fox was behaving in a manner wholly unworthy of those principles of public integrity for which he claimed to stand, and for which he asserted he was continuing to fight.

It is difficult not to believe that Fox's political judgment at this crucial juncture was deficient. Richmond and those who were sympathetic to Fox and just as seriously committed to the cause of reform were genuinely perturbed by his resignation and its possible consequences for the future of the administration. They believed that Fox's major error was in acting as if he would have found himself in a permanent minority within Shelburne's cabinet. They were sincerely incapable of seeing the complex squabble over the recognition of American independence and the conduct of the peace negotiations in Paris as more than a difference of opinion over tactics rather than a fundamental difference of principle. They were anxious, too, not to antagonise the king or to prejudice the peace negotiations. They could not view Shelburne as the embodiment of a sinister conspiracy to restore the influence of the crown, and much as they appreciated the resentment which Fox had shown over the confusions governing the instructions given to Grenville and Oswald in Paris they did not see these as anything more than the unhappy administrative errors consequent upon the uncertain responsibilities of the secretaries of state. Once the peace had been settled Fox would be free to conduct foreign policy without the risk of interference from the home secretary. If Lord John Cavendish had been willing to succeed Shelburne as home secretary the balance of power within the cabinet would have favoured the Rockinghamites, in that both the secretaryships would have been held by men who belonged to that wing of the government. It was understandable that Richmond and Conway thought that Fox had acted hastily, and that his personal aversion to Shelburne had counted for more in bringing him to his decision to resign than more far-sighted considerations of honour and duty. Nor could they overlook the patience which Shelburne had displayed during the formation of his ministry: he had throughout shown a sensible and statesmanlike consideration for the feelings of his colleagues. They did not feel that Fox had shown a similar charity or good temper.

Fox had challenged the king's right to choose his own ministry, and in particular the royal prerogative of selecting the head of a ministry, but he was sufficiently sensitive to the conservative outlook of the majority of MPs on such issues to be less than forthright in spelling out the full significance of his viewpoint in the commons. His efforts to revive fears of the influence of the crown and to bid for the sympathy and support of those who had approved of Rockingham compelled him to exaggerate his own links with the Rockinghamite party. But he failed to convince the majority of backbenchers, while succeeding in heightening all of George III's blackest suspicions. The king simply despised Fox's behaviour as unworthy of any minister of the crown. Fox's apparent indifference to the stability of the ministry reminded George III of the wayward youth who had goaded North into anger by his perverse and wilful individualism in the early 1770s. Now a no less wilful temperament and an intense ambition urged Fox to jeopardise the future of the government and to dispute the validity of accepted standards of constitutional behaviour rather than tolerating the most polite check on the ambitious yearnings of a man who had still fully to discipline himself to the restraints of office.

But Fox was right in emphasising the different approaches which he and Shelburne made towards the essential constitutional problem of the place of the king in government. Shelburne had never been a Rockinghamite. He was in many ways more far-sighted and more original. His interest in economical reform went far beyond the dutiful repetition of clichés about the influence of the crown, just as his understanding of the American issue went deeper than a fondness for the declaratory act, providing it was never invoked. His mind was the most subtle of any practising politician of the time, the most open to new ideas and the freest from outworn prejudices. While Fox sought to enter into Rockingham's political inheritance Shelburne pictured himself as the heir to Chatham. It was in this mood that Shelburne, speaking in the house of lords on 10 July 1782, defended himself against the innuendoes which had been so pervasive in Fox's speech in the commons the previous day.

Shelburne admitted that he had had differences of principle from some of his former colleagues, but 'when they pleaded consistency, it was but fair that he should stand upon his consistency as firmly as they did upon theirs'.

> It would have been very singular indeed, if he should have given up to them all those constitutional ideas, which for seventeen years he had imbibed from his mentor in politics, the late earl of Chatham; that noble earl had always declared, that this country ought not to be governed by any party or faction; that if it was to be so governed, the constitution must necessarily expire; with these principles he had always acted, they were not merely taken up for ambitious purposes; their lordships might recollect a particular expression that he had used some time ago, when speaking of party, he declared that he never would consent that the 'king of England should be king of the Mahrattas' among whom it was a custom for a certain number of great lords to elect a

peshaw, who was the creature of an aristocracy, and who was vested with the plenitude of power, while the king was, in fact, nothing more than a royal pageant or puppet.

These being his principles, it was natural for him to stand up for the prerogative of the crown and insist upon the king's right to appoint his own servants. If the power which others wished to assume, of vesting in the cabinet the right of appointing to all places, and filling up all vacancies, should once be established, the king must then resemble the king of the Mahrattas, who had nothing of the sovereignty but the name: in that case the monarchical part of the constitution would be absorbed by the aristocracy, and the famed constitution of England would be no more.[18]

The conflict was not, as historians once imagined, between the constitutional ideas of George III and those of Fox, but between the prevalent outlook of the time, symbolised in the lifelong hostility of Chatham towards anything savouring of 'party' politics, and ideas which Fox expressed, not so much as a coherent and thoroughly thought out challenge to the dominant theories of the day, but as a necessary verbal accompaniment to and articulate apology for actions which he was compelled to take because of the exigencies of the current political situation. Fox's resignation in 1782 typifies the primacy of practical politics in his career. Far from representing a sustained attempt to carry a new philosophy of politics into effect his constitutional ideas were the response of an agile, fertile, but not highly original mind, to the need to make some sort of sense out of a situation in which his political instincts had already told him how he must act. His demand for a greater recognition of collective responsibility within the cabinet was an attempt to give a more than partisan or tactical significance to his determination not to accept Shelburne as the head of the ministry. Thus it is misleading to suggest that because Fox advocated a greater measure of collective responsibility, and because in the nineteenth century a greater degree of collective responsibility became the accepted norm of government, Fox was thereby ahead of his time, and blessed with an appreciation of the needs of government in the century which followed his own, or equipped with a consistent doctrine of parliamentary democracy and party politics. It is true that Fox argued that constitutional developments should take one direction rather than another, and that many of his ideas were incorporated into later constitutional practice. But Fox was preoccupied with the contemporary political scene, and his ideas were a reflection of the frustrations which he endured as a practising politician, not the expression of any concern for abstract theories of government.

Had Fox's resignation been the consequence of a profoundly thought-out interpretation of the constitutional issues raised by the crisis which followed Rockingham's death he would have been less uneasy in his own mind after giving up the seals. He was convinced of the impossibility of serving under Shelburne, but he was apprehensive of the reactions of those whom he knew and respected and uncertain of the future. His very anxiety to justify himself, whether in private to his friends or in public to a confused and bewildered house of commons, was a sign of his own inner doubts. Emotionally he had made his decision and he was loath to retract it. But intellectually and politically he was guiltily sensitive to the criticisms which he knew were being made of his actions and motives. On 4 July he confided his anxieties to his friend Fitzpatrick:

> Last night I thought everything finally and rightly settled. This morning I am again afraid. The duke of R[ichmond] has been with me, and says he thinks Lord S[helburne] willing (as I thought he would be) to give up the point of America. He is now gone to persuade Lord John to be secretary of state in which, if he succeeds, I shall have a hard task to refuse, but am still of opinion *that even in that case I shall do it*. One of the many mischiefs of all these negotiations is, that when it breaks, it will prevent such of our friends as differ in opinion with us upon the prudence of the measure from acting heartily with us hereafter. I wish I could see you. I shall be about all morning. I did not think it had been in the power of politics to make me so miserable as this cursed anxiety and suspense does.[19]

Fox was allowing his friends to attempt conciliation yet in the depths of his being he had decided to go out, whatever happened. He was doing less than justice to those, such as Richmond, who were honestly trying to find some means of keeping the ministry together while meeting the just demands of the interested parties. In the light of Fox's letter to Fitzpatrick it is difficult to take too seriously the sincerity of his public avowals that the differences of opinion over America were an insuperable division over fundamental principles. He was exploiting the good nature of Richmond in allowing him to believe that Fox was willing to stay on if Cavendish became secretary of state, and in permitting this notion to dominate the abortive negotiations Fox was trusting in Cavendish's own distaste for office to provide him with a convenient and respectable alibi. Yet he was still smitten with remorse, not so much over his decision to resign, as over the consequences which it would have for those of his friends who could not see any justification for his conduct. He was determined to leave office, but he could not bring himself boldly to damn the consequences.

He did not hope to bring the government down, at least not immediately, but he was bitterly resentful of those, such as William Pitt, who rallied to Shelburne's support. He discerned in Pitt's acceptance of the chancellorship of the exchequer proof of a selfish and voracious ambition: he ignored the common attitudes binding together Pitt and Shelburne. The political situation was confused. The cabinet had remained substantially faithful to Shelburne, but in the commons the new administration's basis of support was weak. Much would depend on any possible reconciliation between the various groups in the house; much, too, would depend on the way in which Shelburne handled events, particularly the peace negotiations, which held out the prospect of resentment, differences of opinion, and ample opportunities for attacking the government, whatever the terms of the final settlement might be.

But for Fox the future looked bleak and depressing. His resignation left him dangerously isolated, cut off from former friends, closely identified with the inner segment of the Rockinghamite group, and apprehensive that his motives would remain dubious and his explanations unconvincing to most men. It seemed that irresponsibility had triumphed again, that he had put personal feelings before public service, and that he had cracked under the strains and stresses which were inseparable from ministerial appointment. His claims to represent constitutional rectitude impressed few: his ideas of collective responsibility and the right of the cabinet to choose the head of a ministry seemed disturbingly novel and too clearly designed to further his own advancement. His allegations that Shelburne would bring back the former ministers into his administration were exposed as vapid and deceitful nonsense by the eagerness with which Shelburne brought new talent into his government. Far from being the martyred representative of future enlightenment, worsted in a struggle with the forces of obscurantism, Fox was all too obviously a worldly-wise politician who had blundered in taking an immense political gamble and who had lost. He had made his calculations, but they were faulty, and the obstinacy with which he allowed his emotions to drive him into even more vehement hostility to Shelburne lost him the support of those who had initially sympathised with him. He had cruelly tested the faithfulness of his friends; he was soon to try their patience still further, outraging not only his sworn enemies but many of the independents whose support he desperately needed if he was to broaden his appeal and regain office with a prospect of a lengthy and fruitful tenure.

4 *The Coalition with North*

'England', claimed Disraeli in one of his most famous aphorisms, 'does not love coalitions.' The most spectacular example of this maxim would seem to be Charles Fox's coalition with Lord North, the most notorious and most disastrous combination of unlikely partners in the history of English politics. Conceived as the means of enabling Fox to entrench himself securely in office it brought well-merited judgment in its train, contributing to that melancholy exclusion from power which was to last until a few months before his death. Yet simply because the Fox-North coalition has figured so prominently in the mythology of party politics it must be placed firmly in its context. Dramatic and provocative though Fox's union with North was, coalition was a constant and inescapable accompaniment of eighteenth-century parliamentary life. All ministries—even the Rockingham administration of 1782, as the presence of Shelburne and Fox within its ranks testifies—were coalition ministries, associations of a number of groups, sometimes loosely, sometimes closely allied, owing their primary loyalty not to any party affiliation but to the king himself. Ministers were first and foremost servants of the crown, and most men found the idea of any single faction imposing its will upon the king repugnant. Coalition, with its ceaseless round of negotiations, was the inevitable outcome of the diffuse pattern of loyalties reflected in the eighteenth-century house of commons. The Fox-North coalition was not, therefore, shocking to contemporary tastes because it violated contemporary practice; paradoxically it conformed to it. It was held to be especially obnoxious because of the particular circumstances from which it sprang, the personalities who stood at its head, the methods it employed to force its way into power, and the means which it adopted in an effort to retain power and place and the fruits of office.

Shelburne sought to appeal to the patriotic instincts of the house of commons. Glorying in his weakness he sought to make a virtue out of necessity by governing without any concessions to the petty ambitions of

12 'Shelb—ne, badgered & Foxed' *Cartoon of 28 February 1783*

13 'A transfer of East India Stock' *Cartoon of 25 November 1783*

rival groups. He was by temperament an audacious intellectual, and soon he made it clear that he was in earnest about the reform of governmental machinery. He favoured a generous peace with America in the hope of achieving a speedy reconciliation and a forward-looking understanding with the former colonists. However devious he was about the precise timing of formal recognition of the United States he shocked the prejudices of contemporaries by the lengths to which he was prepared to go in order to create a real and voluntary partnership with the Americans. Though he disclaimed the squalid details of political intrigue he was eager to broaden his ministry's appeal by admitting able men, regardless of their prior loyalties, sometimes in defiance of them. He was eager to reduce taxation and to rescind obsolete customs duties; he wished to stimulate rather than to control trade.

But neither Fox nor Shelburne could escape the crude mathematics of power. In the house of commons Shelburne commanded no more than 140 supporters, and not all of these were committed to him personally. Fox had about 90 followers, many (but not all) of the old Rockinghamites having accepted him as the actual though not the titular leader of their party. About 120 members still looked to North, partly in sentimental affection, partly as an enduring symbol of decent conservatism and common sense. As the time approached for the draft peace treaty to be approved by the commons it was imperative for Shelburne to broaden the base of his parliamentary support. The peace was bound to be unpopular: it would allow men who agreed on little else to join forces in attacking a settlement which however necessary was certain to be denounced as the consummation of the country's degradation and defeat.

The obvious means of placing the government on a more secure footing in the house of commons was a reconciliation between Fox and Shelburne. Attempts were made to bring the two factions together but these foundered because of Fox's determination not to serve under Shelburne. He had so far muted his hatred of Shelburne as to be willing to serve in the same ministry, but he was determined not to submit to what he considered the indignity of accepting Shelburne as head of the administration. When Pitt, acting as Shelburne's emissary, heard of Fox's insistence that Shelburne should resign as first lord of the treasury his response was firm and unflinching: 'I did not come here to betray Lord Shelburne.' Fox could not claim that his attitude to Shelburne was untainted by either personal aversion or private ambition and the failure of efforts to patch up the quarrel with Shelburne meant only one thing: the inevitability of seeking some understanding with North. It is ironic that Fox should find a reconciliation with North more acceptable than service under Shelburne.

The sense of having suffered from personal treachery was strong in all Fox's reactions to Shelburne's approaches for a reunion of the whig groups. Whatever their former disagreements over policy and despite the savagery of Fox's attacks upon him during the American war there was no personal hostility between Fox and North. North was the most easy-going of men; providing some measure of agreement on the distribution of offices and on the main lines of policy was possible there were no emotional or personal obstacles to a union of the Foxite and Northite groups.

A number of intermediaries were involved in bringing the new alignment into existence. North's son, George, Lord John Townshend, William Adam, and William Eden were chiefly responsible. The chief difficulty during the negotiations was not the attitude of the leaders of the two parties, but doubts as to the extent to which the rank and file would follow their leaders in their new alliance. Townshend was especially anxious about the reactions which were likely among North's followers, who were more hostile to the junction of the two groups than the whigs. Eden was particularly assiduous in smoothing the fears and anxieties of the Northites, but among the Rockinghamites Burke held aloof from the negotiations. There had been apprehensions lest his well-known passionate temperament would inspire him either to oppose the coalition with North root and branch, or, even if he accepted it, to betray the secret consultations by some tactless outburst of impatience. In the event Burke succumbed to the necessity of coming to terms with North, but he played little part in the preliminary discussions and, fortunately for his colleagues, he remained silent. Another of Fox's associates who rather surprised his friends by coming out in support of the coalition was Sheridan. Although he was fond of claiming, after the coalition had fallen from power, that he was always against the junction with North, Sheridan was, in Townshend's words, 'one of the most eager and clamorous for it' at the time, chiefly because of his loathing for Pitt and his own impatience for office.

With the collapse of negotiations intended to bring Fox and his friends back into the ministry Shelburne was compelled, very much against his better judgment, to contemplate seeking out support from North and his following. Like other ministers who had trusted too confidently in their reputation and their policies to win them the support of the house of commons Shelburne was driven to come to grips with the intractable realities of eighteenth-century politics. But he had left it too late: the Fox-North coalition was already in existence. Some ministers, of whom Pitt was one, were not too worried about the consequences for the government of a possible understanding between Fox and North; perhaps the ministry would gain support from disgruntled adherents of both men. But in the prevailing uncertainty, with one rumour following another and various individuals revealing confidences to tactfully chosen acquaintances, especially in opposing camps, it was impossible accurately to predict likely events.

On 14 February, after the ground had been thoroughly prepared by various intermediaries, Fox and North had their first meeting. Fox appealed for that goodwill and confidence without which no ministry could long survive. It was agreed that there was no need to reduce the influence of the crown still further by another instalment of economical reform. Parliamentary reform was to be an open question, with every member of the government free to act as he saw fit. There was no prospect, therefore, of any ministerial initiative on either of the two issues most widely publicised by the reform lobby. Fox was going far to meet the requirements of the more conservative of North's followers. Perhaps he sensed that reform was more likely to lose than to win votes in the house of commons, and that Shelburne's interest in further schemes of reform would probably antagonise back-bench opinion, not rally it. Despite the emphasis which Fox had placed on the continued existence of a revival of the influence of the crown during his various attempts to explain his resignation he was abandoning the principle that economical reform was the most effective means of curbing the patronage of the crown. Possibly he was aware of the exaggerated place which the influence of crown and economical reform occupied in conventional Rockinghamite thinking. He explained the danger of a revived form of personal government on the king's part almost entirely in terms of Shelburne's personality and his relationship with George III; change the ministers and all would be well. Furthermore, Fox was aware of the value of patronage in securing support for any new ministry, and once he and North were again in office there were many faithful followers who would be looking for some tangible reward for their fidelity.

Fox cloaked his abandonment of any immediate reform programme by virtue of the undertaking on cabinet government which he coaxed from North. He emphasized to North the overriding necessity that under no circumstances should the king be allowed to be his own first minister. North confessed that if Fox was referring to 'government by departments' he agreed with him; he now thought it a very bad system. 'There should be one man, or a cabinet, to govern the whole and direct every measure. Government by departments was not brought in by me. I found it so, and had not vigour or resolution to put an end to it. The king ought to be treated with all sort of respect and attention, but the appearance of power is all that a king of this country can have. Though the government in my time was a government by departments, the whole was done by the ministers, except in a few instances.'

But, though Fox had imposed his view of cabinet government upon North, his new ally had carefully defended his own reputation; he had tacitly denied that he had aided the king to implement any system of personal rule; whatever his misgivings about departmental government he had quickly drawn Fox's attention to the fact that it was already in operation when he had taken office, and whatever criticisms might be made of his administration North had put the record straight by reminding Fox that the ministers had been responsible for the decisions which had been taken; they had not been mere agents of the king. On the other hand Fox could argue that North's acceptance of a greater degree of oversight within the cabinet and over the policies of the government in general ensured that there would be no risk of reviving the former system. This was the surest pledge for the security of the principles of government affirmed by Rockingham. North could defend his conduct as providing the only possibility for a stable government, able to command the confidence of the majority of the house of commons. Fox could claim that, once personalities were not allowed to prejudice a calm consideration of the political situation, what he had done would ensure the peaceful development of cabinet government along the lines which he had indicated during the wrangles within the ministry over Shelburne's appointment.

The allies, still rather nervous of the public's reaction once their junction became public, and still understandably embarrassed by the unusual spectacle of Fox and North acting in collusion, made their decisive attack upon the ministry during the debates on the preliminary articles of peace in February 1783. Shelburne's position was unenviable. He had made the best peace possible in the circumstances, but he was open to the charge that he had been unnecessarily generous in the concessions he had made to the United States, and too weak in yielding to the demands of Britain's continental enemies. He did not attempt fully to expound his hopes of a far-reaching commercial understanding with America; even if he had done so it is unlikely that his sophisticated schemes would have won him many friends. Men were grudgingly willing to admit the unavoidable necessity of recognising American independence, but they could not see why Shelburne should be so anxious to flatter the self-esteem and stimulate the prosperity of the rebellious colonists. Those who had advocated the unconditional recognition of the United States, independently of any overall peace settlement, believed that that gesture was sufficiently magnanimous. A peace was unavoidable and a better peace than that which Shelburne had negotiated was highly improbable, but the sense of national humiliation was strong, and the obvious scapegoat was Shelburne. He had added to his reputation for subtle casuistry, and some members of his government were complaining of his arrogance and deviousness. It was not surprising, therefore, that Shelburne found himself in a minority of 16 in the commons on 17 February; on 21 February the government was defeated by 207 votes to 190. The government had polled respectably: the victory of the Fox-North coalition was far from overwhelming. Possibly some of the independents and doubters had rallied to the government, but Shelburne felt let down by the substantial body of absentees and he lacked the will to fight it out. He was bitterly conscious of the continued divisions within his ministry and on 24 February he resigned. All looked set for the triumphant re-entry of Fox and North into office.

But already some ominous rumblings had been heard. During the debate on the proposed articles of peace on 17 February Fox had found it necessary to go out of his way to refute accusations of foul play and dishonesty in allying himself with North. He was sufficiently embarrassed to refrain from openly confessing that he and North were formally associated. With a greater sense of political expediency than a respect for truth he attempted to convince his audience that he and North had merely found themselves in happy agreement on the issue of the peace settlement:

> That I shall have the honour of concurring with the noble lord in the blue ribbon on the present question is very certain; and if men of honour can meet on points of general national concern, I see no reason for calling such a meeting an unnatural junction. It is neither wise nor noble to keep up animosities forever. It is neither just nor candid to keep up animosity when the cause of it is no more. It is not in my nature to bear malice, or to live in ill will. My friendships are perpetual, my enmities are not so. 'Amicitae sempiternae, inimicitae placabiles.' I disdain to keep alive in my bosom the enmities which I may bear to men, when the cause of those enmities is no more. When a man ceases to be what he was, when the opinions which made him obnoxious are changed, he then is no more my enemy, but my friend.[1]

Fox reminded the house that the American war was the cause of enmity between North and himself, but the American question was no longer of political significance, and it would be folly to treat North as if it were. Fox went so far as to argue that North had learned much from the 'fatal experience' of the American war. So long as the system which had led to the American controversy was maintained no two men could be more bitterly divided than North and himself, but now that it was a thing of the past it was 'wise and candid' to put an end to 'the ill will, the animosity, the rancour, and the feuds which it occasioned'. Fox added a warm tribute to North's personal character:

> I am free to acknowledge that when I was the friend of the noble lord in the blue ribbon I found him open and sincere; when the enemy, honourable and manly. I never had reason to say of the noble lord in the blue ribbon, that he practised any of those little subterfuges, tricks and stratagems, which I found in others; any of those behindhand and paltry manoeuvres which destroy confidence between human beings, and degrade the character of the statesman and the man. . . .[2]

Obviously North's virtues were a convenient pretext for implying the contrast between North and Shelburne, and pointing the moral of how wise it was for Fox, their old enmity buried in the ruins of North's own American policy, to seek out North as his political ally and to act with him on a basis of mutual trust and respect.

There were still misgivings, however. Men disliked and feared Shelburne but they found the sight of Fox acting in collusion with North disturbing. Despite all his good qualities North was no man of iron will; even those who were fond of him thought him seriously lacking in determination. Fitzpatrick complained of North's weakness and indecision, when gleefully telling his brother of the reverses suffered by Shelburne in the commons and the inevitability of a change of ministry. Possibly North was having doubts about what was already being described as 'the unnatural alliance'; he must have been perturbed by tales of the king's shocked disapproval—which, strangely enough, he does not seem to have anticipated. Fitzpatrick put his finger on the crucial issue affecting Fox's career and reputation at this crucial period, telling his brother, Lord Ossory:

> Unless a *real good government* is the consequence of this juncture, nothing can justify it to the public. . . . The good to be expected from all this is, that no one will venture to undertake the government after Lord Shelburne's example. Lord Gower makes almost as ridiculous a figure as the minister, having thought fit to oppose the last question after having shabbily supported the first. The duke of Marlborough equally so, by having deserted Lord Shelburne after the first defeat. . . . I wish you had been present to have talked over these matters, for there never was a case more full of difficulties and dangers to the real friends of whiggism and good principles.[3]

It had proved relatively easy to get rid of Shelburne, but it was not quite so easy for Fox and North to push themselves into his place. George III thrashed about frantically in an effort to avoid submitting to the hated coalition. He despised Shelburne for deserting his post without putting up a tougher fight, but he fiercely resented suggestions that he had not supported his minister sufficiently vigorously. He saw Fox as another vain and vindictive politician, eager for power but contemptuous of the loyalties and responsibilities which rightly accompanied office. As for North, he had nothing for him but contempt, resenting that he should be so oblivious of every debt of private honour and public duty as to be willing to foist himself upon his king in the unconvincing role of a crony of Charles Fox and the Rockinghamites. George III begged Pitt to accept the first lordship of the treasury, but Pitt refused. The king hawked the office round from one unlikely contender to another; he even hoped that North might be prevailed upon to accept the chief responsibility himself, without bringing his newly acquired allies in with him. For six weeks the king fought gamely against the inevitable: Fox and North as secretaries of state in a ministry headed by the duke of Portland.

But even when the king was prevailed upon to ask Portland to form a ministry 'upon a broad bottom' it was not easy for the administration to be formed. Although Fox, North, and their followers had agreed on broad principles as guides to their conduct and on the overall division of appointments, the detailed allocation of all governmental offices provoked considerable rivalry, suspicion, and tension among those who were sensitive to any slight or suggestion that their just claims were being passed over. Even when Fox and North had sorted out some of the dissensions within their own ranks their refusal to allow Thurlow to stay on as lord chancellor provoked the king to say that if they were not prepared to work with the lord chancellor a truly 'broad bottomed' ministry was an impossibility. George III further complicated matters at one stage by insisting upon Lord Stormont as secretary of state. So the long rigmarole continued, with the king trying elsewhere, and Fox and his friends buoying themselves up with the thought that he was foredoomed to fail, and that he would have to accept them upon their own terms. The king had shown his usual astuteness, however; the lord chancellor was conventionally regarded as 'the keeper of the royal conscience' and it was accepted that the king should take a particular interest in the appointment. If Fox was unwilling to acquiesce in the king's choice for lord chancellor it could be cited as further evidence of the way in which he and North had violated to bring about the downfall of Shelburne without giving his ministry the opportunity to prove itself in office; now, they were disregarding the wishes of the king even with respect to those appointments in which it was customary for him to have a direct and personal say.

Finally the king had to submit to the inescapable pressure of events. Fox and North kissed hands as secretaries of state, with Portland as first lord of the treasury, and Loughborough presiding uneasily over the commission vested with the task of performing the duties of the lord chancellorship, since Fox had remained obstinate in his determination not to endure Thurlow's presence in the cabinet and the king had been similarly obdurate in refusing to have anyone but Thurlow as his lord chancellor. The king made no effort to disguise his loathing for the new ministry. When Fox kissed hands the king was observed to 'turn back his ears and eyes just like the horse at Astley's when the tailor he had determined to throw was getting on him'. George III refused to do anything other than the bare necessities of constitutional practice and the rudimentary routine of government. He declined to demonstrate his confidence in his new ministers by the distribution of peerages, honours and dignified promotions.

The hostility of the king was a grave handicap to any administration seeking to win public confidence and to establish itself firmly in office. But until George III had an alternative minister or set of ministers he could hardly throw the government out. Before he could rid himself of Fox and North he needed an issue on which either he or the lords or the commons could credibly challenge the government's reputation and its handling of events. Difficult though the entry into office had been for Fox and his allies, once they were appointed it was no simple task to get rid of them, unless they offended public sentiment, outraged the independent back-benchers in the commons, or antagonised some major interest group. The king could not actively intrigue against his ministers from the start. He needed the right sort of issue which would allow him to exploit anti-government feeling with a sufficiently convincing show of respect for constitutional convention and an appropriate degree of self-righteousness. The longer the government lasted the more likely men would be to forget or forgive the circumstances surrounding its formation. Opinion was becoming weary of endless governmental crises. Since the fall of North the political world had been dominated by ministerial instability and endless speculation about the future. If the Fox-North coalition achieved a practicable measure of stability and a modest and unassuming level of competence its prospects were reasonably good. Only if the ministers behaved in ways recalling the intrigue which had brought them into office would they experience renewed difficulty in the house of commons; only if their actions confirmed the lingering suspicions of their integrity and their motives would they find themselves faced with renewed hostility.

Fox's primary task was to push on with the formal conclusion of the peace treaties with America, France, Spain and Holland. The final outcome was essentially the peace settlement arranged by Shelburne and for which he had suffered so unjustly. In his dealings with the Americans Fox had at first sought to subject American trade to the restrictions imposed on shipping to British and West Indian ports; but he was compelled to take refuge in the ruse of stating that complicated details could be postponed until after the formal conclusion of the peace treaty. The Americans discovered that Fox was much less generous, and much more conventional, than Shelburne in his attitude towards the regulation of Anglo-American trade. Whereas Shelburne had seen the opportunities for the expansion of commerce Fox was preoccupied with its control. Nor did the Americans overlook Fox's savage criticisms of the terms proposed by Shelburne and the part he had played in defeating Shelburne's government in the debates on the articles of peace. They could hardly be expected to view North's return to office with equanimity even if he was now in Fox's company.

Fox did his best to wring more favourable terms out of the French, Spanish and Dutch, but however much he wrangled (as over the concessions to British logwood cutters in the Bahamas) he could only amend the precise terms on points of minor importance. When Pitt criticised the government's handling of the peace negotiations in the house of commons he emphasized the irony in the situation: ministers who had come to power by securing the defeat of the Shelburne government over the preliminary articles of peace were now seeking parliamentary approval for a peace settlement which was to all intents and purposes identical with that which they had so vehemently denounced. Nor could the government flatter themselves with the speed or the expertise which they had shown in their conduct of affairs: they had taken six months to finalise the peace treaties, and, taking into account the additional delay caused by the ministerial crisis following Shelburne's resignation, almost nine months had elapsed without any material benefit to the country. Opponents of the government could see all this as further proof of the essential hypocrisy which was at the heart of the Fox-North coalition. The failure of the ministry significantly to improve the peace treaties made the fall of Shelburne look all the more questionable: the conspiratorial nature of the political realignment which had brought Fox and North back into power seemed all the more evident. It was impossible to view the peace as anything other than a national humiliation. Tobago,

St Lucia, Senegal, and Goree were ceded to France, together with some of the former French factories in India. Spain recovered Minorca and Florida. Although Canada and Gibraltar were retained many men felt that the gains of the Seven Years war had been needlessly squandered. Few consoled themselves with the thought that the peace might have been worse. Fox could scarcely take refuge in such sophistries. He could hardly boast of how much he had saved from the wreck when he had criticised Shelburne for not doing better. The loss of the American colonies was the most dramatic proof of the depths to which the country had sunk. Shelburne was almost alone in possessing sufficient imagination to sense the dazzling new opportunities which an intelligent and boldly cooperative policy with the United States held out for Britain. But Shelburne's political career was virtually over, and his American policies were incomprehensible to his contemporaries. Only those who had grasped the basic motive of replacing old-fashioned restrictionist policies by those of free trade and commercial reciprocity could appreciate the import of Shelburne's ideas. Fox always remained crudely mercantilist in his economic outlook; he was impatient with the new commercial theories being adumbrated by Adam Smith and he was always suspicious of free trade, as his opposition to Pitt's attempt to liberalise Anglo-Irish commerce and to Pitt's free trade treaty with France later confirmed.

But whatever misgivings men had about the peace treaties they knew that there was no alternative but to accept them. It was better to end the long miserable controversy over the American colonies, and the war which it had provoked, and to try to come to terms with the realities of the political situation. The government was in no danger over the peace settlement; the house of commons sullenly submitted to cruel necessity. But for a brief period in the summer of 1783 it looked as if an attempt to deal with the delicate question of the prince of Wales' debts might embarrass the government sufficiently for the king to wonder if the moment had come to rid himself of a set of ministers whose presence in office was a permanent insult to his sense of constitutional propriety and a standing affront to his self-respect.

George III was bitterly disappointed in the character and behaviour of the prince of Wales. Where the king had looked for sobriety, self-discipline, and a devotion to duty he found that his eldest son was feckless, selfish, fond of wine, women and song, and addicted to gambling, whether at the card table, the faro board, or the racecourse. The prince's aesthetic sense, and intermittent outbursts of shallow charm and self-pitying emotion, did little to endear him to his parents. Worst of all was his political association with Fox and the whigs. Nor did he limit his favours to the more respectable of the whigs, as his fondness for Sheridan showed. Instead of being a comfort to his father, a supporter in times of peril and a consolation in times of distress, he was a hideous embarrassment, whose self-indulgence and ostentatious defiance added to the king's public and private anxieties. George III was scrupulous, even stingy, in his management of his financial affairs; he had a deep sense of public responsibility for the way in which he spent his money. No such scruples bothered the prince of Wales, who thoughtlessly squandered money on every form of extravagance. The prince's debts had become more than a private embarrassment or a social scandal; they were a political nuisance, a convenient pretext for those sturdy backbench members of parliament who were on the alert for any sign of extravagance which justified their accusations that the government was allowing money to be squandered at the whim of a royal debauchee.

It was understandable that Fox and his friends should want to do something for the prince. Affection and expediency alike prompted them to want to ease both the prince's financial anxieties and their own embarrassment, as the well-known advocates of public economy, at their royal patron's profuse expenditure. But Fox had hinted to the prince that he would be able to settle his financial arrangements in generous terms, and once the prince came of age it seemed sensible to tackle the problem even at the risk of becoming embroiled in the confusions of the prince's private affairs. The initial proposal was to give the prince a settlement of £100,000 a year, to be voted by parliament.

But when Portland suggested to the king that parliament should vote £50,000 a year, with the other £50,000 coming from the civil list, George III angrily denounced the whole scheme. Though the ministry was under the impression that the king had been willing to accept the original sum of £100,000 as being appropriate for the prince, George III claimed that he had never approved of granting such a large sum out of public funds. He thought it wrong to impose such a burden upon the public. He urged that £50,000 a year was sufficient for the prince's needs, and said that he was willing to give this sum from the civil list. Despite all the protestations which the ministers had made about economy they were sacrificing the interests of the public, so the king reminded them, 'to the wishes of an ill-advised young man'. He would never forget or forgive the ministers for their deplorable conduct towards him. In the face of the king's anger the ministers began to wonder if he had decided to challenge them on the issue of the prince's debts with the intention of forcing them out of office.

Fox was certainly very anxious about the ministry's viability. On 17

June he told Northington of the ominous turn which events had taken:

> Lest in the hurry of this day nobody should have had time to write to you, I just steal a minute to tell you there is great reason to think that an administration will not outlive tomorrow, or, at least, that it will be at an end in a very few days.... The whole is quite sudden and was never dreamt of by me, at least till yesterday. You will, of course, not mention this till it is confirmed. The immediate cause of the quarrel is the prince of Wales' establishment, which we thought perfectly agreed upon a week ago....[4]

It was said that the king intended to dismiss the ministry, calling upon Lord Temple to form a new one. But though the king's hostility was all too apparent, there were several restraints on both sides which prevented the crisis from coming to a head. The king realised that though public sentiment supported him in his desire to curb the extravagance of the prince the issue of his son's debts was hardly one which would justify, in the eyes of the independents, a change of government. Nor was it clear that the quarrel over the prince's establishment would initiate any significant or decisive shift of political opinion or loyalty. It was the sort of an issue on which men felt strongly, but it was not sufficiently important for MPs to be willing to bring down the administration.

On the government side Loughborough was particularly eager to meet the king's misgivings. He assured Fox that submission was the only course, but 'it would be much better, and much handsomer, if it were possible to dispose his royal highness to give way respectfully, and with a dutiful remonstrance profess himself ready to show his obedience'. However close they were to the prince of Wales, and however much they valued his patronage as an insurance against the uncertainties of politics, few members of the government were prepared to leave office on the issue of the prince's establishment. So a compromise was worked out: the prince received a private establishment of £50,000 a year out of the civil list, £30,000 down, and the duchy of Cornwall. Honour, if not avarice, had been satisfied.

Fox had himself pleaded with the prince to be reasonable and not to push his demands to the point where they would provoke a political furore in circumstances which would favour the king and embarrass, perhaps even discredit, his friends. In any confrontation with his father it was advisable for the prince to have 'the world' on his side. On 17 July Fox told Northington the inside story of the crisis from the government's point of view:

> As to the opinion of our having gained strength by it, the only rational

foundation for such an opinion is, that this event has proved that there subsists no such understanding between the king and Lord Temple as to enable them to form an administration, because if there did, it is impossible but that they must have seized an occasion in many respects so fortunate for them. They would have had on their side the various cries of *paternal authority, economy, moderate establishment, mischief-making between father and son,* and many other plausible topics. As therefore they did not avail themselves of all these advantages, it seems reasonable to suppose that there is as yet nothing settled and understood amongst them, and in this sense, and inasmuch as this is so felt and understood in the world, I think we may flatter ourselves that we are somewhat stronger than we were....[5]

Fox was underestimating the potential dangers stemming from the king's confidence in Temple, but he was anxious about the weaknesses in the government's situation, going on to list them for Northington's benefit:

The king has certainly carried one point against us, and the notoriety that he has done so may lead people to suppose that he might be successful in others, if he were to attempt them. Everybody will not see the distinction between this and political points so strong as the ministers have done. Perhaps I do not myself, but yet no man was more convinced of the necessity of yielding than I. The truth is, that excepting the duke of Portland and Lord Keppel, there was not one minister *who would have fought with any heart in this cause.* I could see clearly from the beginning, long before the difficulties appeared, that Lord North and Lord John [Cavendish], though they did not say so, thought the large establishment extravagant, and you will, I am sure, agree with me that to fight a cause, where the latter especially was not hearty, would have been a most desperate measure. Indeed, all the advantages we have hitherto derived, and are every day deriving, from the deserved and universal good opinion which is entertained of Lord J. Cavendish, would not only have been flung away, but his name would have been used against us; for it is quite certain ... that his sentiments would have been known enough to have this effect. Under all these circumstances there appeared to me no alternative in common sense but to yield with the best grace possible, if the prince of Wales could be brought to be of that mind....[6]

Yet Fox felt constrained to confess that if the prince had remained obdurate he would have considered himself 'bound to follow his royal highness's line upon the subject', although he knew that by so doing he would have destroyed the ministry 'in the worst possible way', while subjecting himself to the interpretation of extreme wrongheadedness. It was very fortunate therefore that the prince had yielded, and Fox was deeply grateful to him for doing so. He had been in a most embarrassing situation. He had vaguely promised the prince that he would see that his establishment was settled in a handsome and generous fashion, yet, in the particular circumstances surrounding the affair, he was disposed to press for compromise. Consequently, had the prince insisted on the original proposals Fox would have followed the dictates of private honour in supporting the prince; perhaps this was in itself an indication of his belief that if no compromise could be amicably worked out nothing could save the ministry in a direct clash with the king. Inconclusive as it was the crisis over the prince's establishment is a reminder of the importance of royal confidence in endowing eighteenth-century ministries with stability. Fox's determination not to lose the trust of the prince of Wales is a testimony to the continuing significance of the reversionary interest. Though Fox had so recently advocated conventions regarding the appointment of ministers and the conduct of cabinet business which foreshadowed later developments appropriate to an era of party, he was still appreciative of the crucial role of the king in government. He never allowed his advocacy of new and innovating constitutional ideas to blind him to the persistence of familiar political practices. Occasionally the discrepancy between his theories and his actions added a lurid suspicion of paradox, or even hypocrisy, to his conduct. The accusation is unjust: Fox could never afford the questionable luxury of permitting abstract theories, however attractive, to inspire or control the practice of politics.

Sensitive as he had been to the dangers implicit in the clash with the king over the prince's establishment, Fox nevertheless found his hopes and his confidence rising throughout the summer. Once the crisis had been averted he thought that the government was gaining both in strength and credit. Providing the coalition stuck together he felt there was little danger from a divided opposition. He rightly refused to regard Temple, Thurlow, Shelburne and Pitt as having a common interest sufficiently powerful to make them act together against the government. Once the ministry lasted long enough for people to forget how it was formed, and for the belief to be prevalent that the king had reconciled himself to his new ministers, the opposition could become even more futile. Deprived as it would be of the prospect of the king taking the initiative to get rid of the coalition the opposition would begin to suffer from desertions to the ministerial side. But even when he was cheerfully contemplating the political future with pardonable confidence Fox was aware that the East

India bill would require the most careful handling, involving as it did a variety of powerful interests and a number of political groupings.

Long after the event the survivors of the coalition sought to evade responsibility for the India bill which, it was generally agreed, was chiefly to blame for the expulsion of Fox and North from office. Although he had been an eager supporter of the Indian legislation at the time Sheridan was fond of charging Burke with the primary burden of guilt. Similarly it was possible to exonerate Fox from his complicity in the collapse of the ministry either by claiming that he was drawn into supporting Burke's proposals only against his better judgment or that he was inspired by such a noble vision of a reformed Indian administration that he became selflessly indifferent to calculations of squalid self-interest. The truth is less simple and less dramatic. Fox believed that the degree of control exercised by the British crown over the East India company needed to be refined and strengthened. But he never shared Burke's obsessive emotionalism over India and much as he valued the opportunity to improve the government of British India he was by no means averse to combining administrative reform with the shrewd manipulation of patronage. If he could make the administration more secure while reforming the East India company so much the better. Far from being insensitive to the need to calculate the likely effect of the India bill on current political loyalties he simply miscalculated the response of many of the independent members to the government's proposals. Fox was neither an inspired visionary nor a shady conspirator. He thought it possible to combine necessary governmental reforms with party advantage. The error which Fox and his friends made was not one of principle, for there was widespread agreement that something would have to be done to supervise the East India company's management of Indian affairs. They simply assumed that the house of commons and the public would be more acquiescent in the creation of new sources of patronage than turned out to be the case. Fox completely misjudged the reaction of all interested parties; this in itself was a sign of his isolation from backbench opinion, and an example of his recurrent tendency to allow wishful thinking to warp his political judgment.

But Fox was sufficiently cognisant of political realities to justify the government's proposals on the grounds of necessity, not of choice. He knew only too well how suspicious his contemporaries were of anything savouring of the arbitrary assertion of abstract principle. He assured the house of commons on 18 November 1783 that the Indian business had forced itself upon him, and far from appealing to the altruism of MPs he claimed that the government was attempting to protect the interests of

both the East India company and the British nation. It was impossible for
the government to postpone any legislative intervention in Indian affairs:

> The deplorable situation of the East India company was well known
> and universally admitted; their extreme distress, and the embarrassed
> state of their affairs not only called for the aid of government, but re-
> quired its immediate assistance, as the only possible means of averting
> and preventing the final and complete destruction of the company's
> interests, and with them, of materially injuring, if not entirely ruining,
> the interests of the nation, as far as they were connected with our
> territorial acquisitions in India. . . . It was some consolation and some
> satisfaction for him to know, that he was merely discharging an act of
> indispensable duty as a minister, that there was no choice or option
> before him, that he was not about to obtrude any idle, visionary, or
> speculative projects of his own upon their notice, but was in the act of
> offering to the consideration of parliament the best propositions for the
> preservation of the India company, and the restoration of the welfare
> of their concerns, that his most deliberate attention could suggest; and
> that he did it for no other reason upon earth than because the necessity
> that called for it was so urgent, that it pressed itself forwards irresist-
> ibly, and as a matter that would not admit of further delay.[7]

This was the sort of language which most members understood, but they
were sufficiently experienced in the ways of the world to be apprehensive
about the detailed proposals which were foreshadowed by such a prologue.
Fox was careful to remind the house of the contradictory character of the
East India company; it was both a commercial venture and a political
institution, and sometimes the interests of those who were seeking a good
return for their investments and those who were primarily concerned with
the conduct of government in India conflicted. At other times the dual
nature of the company was an incitement to corruption, Fox lamenting
that the unhappy Indians 'might undergo a second fleecing for the benefit
of the proprietors; so that they were to be robbed first to enrich their
governor, and afterwards they were to be plundered to furnish means to
prevent a discovery of his speculations'. Even those who were most appalled
by the situation found it almost impossible to know how best to eliminate
corruption, embezzlement, and the exploitation of the natives. The
directors could not offend the court of proprietors to whom they owed their
situation, while the proprietors would never be easily persuaded to sacrifice
servants by whose efforts their profits were created. The finances of the
East India company were in as parlous a state as the administration of
the company's Indian territories, and only intervention by the govern-

ment could bring order and decency into the conduct of Indian affairs.

But Fox sought to refute allegations that the government was trespassing upon the legitimate rights of the East India company by discounting any suggestion that the British government was seeking to assume direct responsibility for the company's overseas territories. Even if the ministry ever took the territorial possessions into its own hands it would be under the necessity of keeping up a company to carry on a trade 'by which alone the revenues of India could be converted to the benefit of Great Britain'. Fox's idea was to form 'a mixed system of government', adapted to the particular needs of the Indian situation. Statesmen were hardly qualified to conduct the complicated branches of a remote trade, yet some greater measure of political oversight had to be devised.

His plan was to set up a board of seven commissioners, vested with the power to appoint and dismiss officers in India, and under whose control the government of India was to be placed. Eight assistants would be responsible for the management of the company's commercial concerns, but they would be subject to the control of the first seven. The commissioners would remain in England 'under the very eye of parliament', but they would have considerable discretion in assessing the actions of the company's representatives in India. At the same time the fact that they had to justify their own behaviour to parliament would ensure effective scrutiny by both lords and commons.

Whatever misgivings might be entertained about the wisdom of Fox's proposals there was so far nothing which could conceivably provoke a widespread sense of outrage, either on the part of the East India company or of the government's political opponents. Even when Fox affirmed that in the first instance parliament should nominate the board of seven commissioners exception could hardly be taken to his suggestion. A known critic of the influence of the crown and a defender of parliamentary control could not be expected to act otherwise. But when he went on to talk about 'the inconvenience of parliamentary appointments' and to admit that the board should be established for an initial period of four years without parliament having the power to change any of its personnel, men immediately suspected a ruse to protect seven government appointees from the turbulent uncertainties of politics. Furthermore, it was all too obvious that the commissioners would be able to use the patronage of the East India company for political purposes. With such a vast source of patronage available Fox and his colleagues could well establish their predominance in the house of commons for the foreseeable future, if not for good. Nor did Fox's ominous warnings of the dangers of the company exploiting its resources to thwart government reforms do more than confirm his critics in their suspicion that his proposals were the outcome of an itching desire to get his hands on a rich fund of patronage which would guarantee the government's independence of either parliamentary scrutiny or royal disfavour.

Instead of interpreting the bill as the most serious attempt for some years to restore responsibility to the government of British India Fox's enemies argued that the legislation was primarily an invasion of the charter and property rights of the East India company. Perhaps Burke's sincerity in urging the more humane conduct of Indian administration could be conceded, though possibly only as further confirmation of his outrageously unrealistic attitude to politics, a sign of that incipient hysteria which led so many contemporaries to doubt his sanity; but Fox's motives were denounced with self-righteous frenzy as the hypocritical abuse of politics in the cause of greed and ambition. All Fox's preoccupations with curbing the influence of the crown seemed specious when he embarked on such a concerted plan to subvert the independence of the commons in order to prolong his own tenure of office. He was accused of replacing the legitimate influence of the crown with the illegitimate influence of faction financed by robbery; he was also accused of seeking to exploit the influence of the crown on his own behalf. Contradictory though these accusations were they were made with repetitive fury, and the chorus of condemnation grew louder with each day that passed. What was worse for Fox was the fact that he had united so many interests against himself, providing his opponents with a cause which appealed both to the highest notions of political probity and the lowest and most vindictive manifestations of political spite.

North had warned Fox of the dangers. With his shrewd and kindly insight into the behaviour of backbenchers North reminded Fox on the morning of the first reading of the India bill of the likely mode of attack: 'Influence of the crown, and influence of party against crown and people, are two of the many topics which will be urged against your plan. The latter of the two objections will not be sounded so high and loudly in the house of commons, but it may be one of the most fatal objections to your measure. It certainly ought to be obviated as much as possible.'[8] But perceptive though he was North could not indicate exactly how the misfortunes he saw were to be averted. Within the cabinet the Northites were less enthusiastic than the Foxites about the provisions of the bill. Perhaps North's reference to 'your plan' was a discreet reminder of their differences, though the Northites were going to get a generous share of the pickings once the bill went through. North's own advice was tainted by the misgivings he felt about the measure, however kindly meant. The bill sprang from Burke's researches into the management of Indian affairs, but it was not the product of careful and comprehensive deliberation within the government. The bill smacked too strongly of an over-confident attempt to grapple too easily with an intractable problem. Defensible in principle it proved disastrous in practice. Nor was this simply the price to pay for Fox's impetuosity; it was symptom of the endemic weakness of eighteenth-century governments. Lacking skilled professional advice, ignorant of essential facts, and compelled by deficiencies of information to trust their fortunes to bold guesswork, they were often cut off from those sources of opinion and of knowledge which were indispensable for the framing of practicable and efficacious legislation. Often what was admirable in theory was marred beyond recognition in the confused intricacies of its application. Fox responded to the broad affirmation of essential principle; similarly he had a keen eye for immediate political advantage within the confines of the parliamentary system. But he was less certain in gauging the reactions of classes and interests outside the house of commons and impatient with the technicalities of government and legislation. He was indifferent to the needs of the rudimentary party organisation of his day, contenting himself with leadership in parliamentary debate while leaving the intricacies of negotiation and co-ordination to Portland and Adam. It was not surprising, therefore, that dazzling initiatives often petered out in confusion and despair. The tragedy for Fox was not that he was a martyr in the cause of more enlightened Indian administration, but that he could have achieved much without risking defeat and humiliation had he taken a little more care to soothe ruffled susceptibilities and to consult interested parties. There was nothing inevitable about his discomfiture over the India bill. With more thought and a little luck he might have defied his enemies and remained serene in the enjoyment and exercise of supreme political power.

Fox quickly realised his mistake. He needed no one to tell him of the powerful influence wielded by the formidable combination of the king and the East India company. He sensed the impact of his enemies' slogan: 'Our charter and privileges are invaded, look to your own!' He knew how indifferent men were to the management of either commerce or government in India, and how sensitive they were to any infringement, real or imagined, of the rights of property. Yet he never fully appreciated the tremendous swing against the government amongst genuinely independent and uncommitted voters which the controversy over the India bill provoked and which the 1784 election registered. He recognised that his motives were mixed, but if perhaps they were no better they were certainly no worse than other men's, and to be pilloried as a scoundrel because he had taken certain realistic precautions against the tides of fortune was hard for him to bear. He sincerely believed that what he was proposing was right, that it would lead to greater prosperity both for the East India company and the natives, and this raw sense of being wilfully misrepresented explains the note of self-justification which became so audible in Fox's speeches and correspondence during the crisis which the India bill precipitated and which brought the Younger Pitt to power.

That his opponents would use every available innuendo to blacken his name was an unhappy certainty. Fox confided to Mrs Armistead that his enemies were trying to whip up a great public outcry against the government, and he sadly confessed that they would succeed in making the ministers very unpopular in the city. But there was no alternative but to stick it out:

> ... I know I am right, and must bear the consequences, though I dislike unpopularity as much as any man. Indeed, it is no hypocrisy in me to say, that the consciousness of having always acted upon principle in public matters, and my determination always to be so, is the great comfort of my life. I know I never did act more upon principle than at this moment, when they are abusing me so. If I had considered nothing but keeping my power, it was the safest way to leave things as they are, or to propose some trifling alteration, and I am not at all ignorant of the political danger which I run by this bold measure; but whether I succeed or no, I shall always be glad that I attempted, because I know I have done no more than I was bound to do, in risking my power and that of my friends when the happiness of so many millions is at stake. I write very gravely, because the amazing abuse which is heaped upon me makes me feel so. I have the weakness of disliking abuse but that weakness shall never prevent me from doing what I think right. Do not fancy from this that I am out of spirits, or even that I am much alarmed for the success of our scheme. On the contrary, I am very sanguine; but the reflection of how much depends at the moment on me, is enough to make any man who has any feeling serious. ...[9]

Despite his assurances to Mrs Armistead Fox's spirits fluctuated throughout November and December as the commons debated the India bill and as the scale of the controversy which it had provoked became more evident. He consistently reiterated his claim that only pressing necessity had led the government to intervene in the business of the East India company at all, and he sought to refute charges that the board of commissioners was a ruse by which his colleagues and himself were feathering their nests.

He reminded the house that the commissioners were to be under the immediate eye of parliament: 'where, then, was the danger so loudly trumpeted forth to the world, and so industriously made the subject of popular clamour?'

Confronted as he was by savage criticism and increasingly conscious as he became of the possibility that the bill might be defeated in the lords, if not in the commons, with the government falling in consequence, Fox rose to great heights in defending the government's proposals and in rejecting the charge that he had been motivated throughout by the basest political considerations. On 1 December he eloquently justified the India bill as the expression of a concern for civilised and responsible government as well as an intelligent piece of reforming legislation. It was during this debate that Burke paid generous tribute to the purity of Fox's motives and to the integrity of his character. Burke had, of course, a unique personal interest in the India bill and the policies which it represented, but he was moved to conclude his own speech by eulogising Fox because the unworthy attacks which had been made upon him went far beyond the generous freedoms of customary debate. Rarely has one politician spoken so feelingly and so warmly of another:

I must say then, that it will be a distinction honourable to the age, that the rescue of the greatest number of the human race that ever were so grievously oppressed, from the greatest tyranny that was ever exercised, has fallen to the lot of abilities and dispositions equal to the task; that it has fallen to one who has the enlargement to comprehend, the spirit to undertake, and the eloquence to support, so great a measure of hazardous benevolence. His spirit is not owing to his ignorance of the state of men and things; he well knows what snares are spread about his path, from personal animosity, from court intrigues, and possibly from popular delusion. But he has put to hazard his ease, his security, his interest, his power, even his darling popularity, for the benefit of a people whom he has never seen. This is the road that all heroes have trod before him. He is traduced and abused for his supposed motives. He will remember that obloquy is a necessary ingredient in the composition of all true glory; he will remember that it was not only in the Roman customs, but it is in the nature and constitution of things, that calumny and abuse are essential parts of triumph. These thoughts will support a mind, which only exists for honour, under the burthen of temporary reproach. He is doing indeed a great good; such as rarely falls to the lot, and almost as rarely coincides with the desires, of any man. Let him use his time. Let him give the whole length of the reins to his benevolence. He is now on a great eminence, where the eyes of mankind are turned to him. He may live long, he may do much. But here is the summit. He can never exceed what he does this day.[10]

Burke confessed that Fox had faults, but there was nothing in them 'to extinguish the fire of great virtue'; there was 'no mixture of deceit, of hypocrisy, of pride, of ferocity, of complexional despotism, or want of feeling for the distresses of mankind'. Burke's passionate advocacy of Fox's cause was more than an expression of friendship; it sprang from his own conviction that the India bill represented a transcendent political issue. Fox was praised not only as a close political colleague but as an agent of benevolence, the instrument by which great wrongs could be avenged and noble ideals vindicated. It would be misleading to interpret Burke's tribute as evidence of real intimacy between the two men. With all its splendid rhetoric Burke's eulogy was the expression of a public sentiment rather than an avowal of private friendship. It was meant to convey beyond all possible doubt the conviction of the most idealistic practitioner in English politics that Fox was serving the ultimate good of mankind. Yet however deeply posterity has been moved by Burke's magnificent language many of his audience shrugged off his peroration as additional evidence of the lengths to which the government was prepared to go to disguise its true intentions from the people.

In his own speech on 1 December Fox sought to place the government's policy and the provisions of the India bill within the context of those ideas which the bill was said to be denying. He was anxious to defend his reputation as a friend of political and civil liberty, while showing that the liberty which he valued was no shallow abstraction but a living reality, apprehended through the life of politics and a received pattern of public probity and behaviour:

> Freedom, according to my conception of it, consists in the safe and sound possession of a man's property, governed by laws defined and certain; with many personal privileges, natural, civil, and religious, which he cannot surrender without ruin to himself; and of which to be deprived by any other power is despotism. This bill, instead of subverting, is destined to give stability to these principles; instead of narrowing the basis of freedom it tends to enlarge it; instead of suppressing its object is to infuse and circulate the spirit of liberty.[11]

The most odious form of tyranny was that which allowed a handful of men to hold despotic sway over millions of their fellow creatures without being answerable for their actions. It was wrong that the Indian peasant should sweat, not for his own benefit, but for the luxury of those who ruled him as tyrants, filling their own pockets with their ill-gotten gains. The end of all government was the happiness of the governed. It was against this background that the dispute over charter rights was properly understood. A charter was a trust for some given benefit; if those entrusted with charter privileges abused the trust reposed in them, or if the expected benefit to the public was not obtained, whether the cause was ignorance or mismanagement or corruption, it was only right that the trust should be delivered to others who would honourably perform the duties expected of them. In the case of the East India company whose laxity and languor had too often produced consequences opposed to the general good, it was all the more necessary for parliament to take action to ensure that the purposes for which charter privileges were granted were in fact accomplished. Far from undermining charter rights the government was anxious that they should be properly observed, and that the reciprocal character of charter privileges should be fully appreciated. Fox was determined to show that the enjoyment of charter privileges was irrevocably linked with the performance of public services; the public good, of which parliament was the guardian and the judge, was more important than the narrow technicalities of charter rights, and parliament must always protect and safeguard it. 'Those who condemn the present bill as a violation of the chartered rights of the East India company,' Fox solemnly warned the house, 'condemn, on the same ground ... the revolution, as a violation of the chartered rights of King James II.' The analogy was inexact but the moral was plain.

In addition to defending the India bill as an example of justifiable legislation, morally, politically and technically, Fox was compelled to reply to the allegations which his opponents had made about his conduct as a party leader. Since the bill was denounced as a party measure for the achievement of party advantage, Fox sought to justify party as a valid element in political behaviour, an agency of continuity, harmony and stability. He was not ashamed of party; he even went so far as to claim that he had always acknowledged himself to be a party man. He had always acted with a party in whose principles he had had confidence, and if he had the same opinion of any ministry as that which his parliamentary critics claimed to have of the present administration he would undoubtedly feel it his duty to overthrow it by systematic opposition. He was bold enough to claim, somewhat fancifully, that he had already been able to accomplish this more than once.

His opponents exploited the phrase 'systematic opposition' in an effort to discredit Fox and his friends. Fox retorted by drawing a contrast between 'peevish, capricious objections' to everything which the government proposed and the correct conduct of opposition when properly understood. He cheerfully affirmed his own liking for systematic opposition: a systematic opposition to a dangerous government was a noble employment of the highest faculties:

> Opposition is natural in such a political system as ours; it has subsisted in all such governments; and perhaps it is necessary. But to those who oppose it, it is extremely essential that their manner of conducting it should not incur a suspicion of their motives. If they appear to oppose from disappointment, from mortification, from pique, from whim, the people will be against them. If they oppose from public principle, from love of their country rather than hatred to administration, from evident conviction of the badness of measures, and a full persuasion that in their resistance to men they are aiming at the public welfare, the people will be with them. We opposed upon these principles, and the people were with us; if we are opposed upon other principles, they will not be against us.[12]

The fear that the people might after all be deserting him was never far from Fox's mind. Throughout the India bill debates he was anxious for some unmistakable sign of public confidence, and perhaps because too little was known of reactions to the India bill outside parliament, Fox swung from careless optimism to wild apprehension and back again. He found it impossible to conceive of any genuinely free movement of opinion going against the government; with his usual incapacity for self-criticism he explained every reverse as a triumph for conspiracy. His opponents had sought to infuse prejudice into the controversy over the India bill; he consoled himself with the thought that such labours had been fruitless.

He was aware that many of the charges which were made against the government as a whole were in effect denunciations of his own character. He grieved that his critics accused him of being motivated by avarice or ambition or party spirit. His integrity was traduced and his character impugned. Experienced as he was in the tumult of politics he found this hard to bear at a time when he sincerely felt that he had risked his career and reputation in a noble cause. He forgot that many men could not forgive him for allying himself with North. Only if the coalition's deeds transcended its origins would Fox and his friends earn forgiveness. But the India bill, despite its many virtues, aroused old suspicions and fanned familiar passions into flame. The tactlessness of the proposal about the board of commissioners, and worse still the disclosure that all of the first batch of nominees were good coalitionists, confirmed every perplexed doubter in his belief that a dangerous confidence trick was being perpetrated for the pecuniary and political benefit of Fox and his companions. However much it is possible to sympathise with Fox's anguish at seeing the most far-sighted of his Indian proposals obscured under a fog of abuse about patronage, it is nevertheless inescapable that by his mishandling of the situation he had invited this sort of misunderstanding. The ministers had omitted to ensure that their proposals were acceptable to the East India company; only by doing so could they have averted open hostility from that most powerful of political interests. Nor were they entirely free from a willingness to combine public service with party advantage if not with private gain. In this they were not unusual, but the extreme delicacy of the political situation called for a subtlety of political technique which neither Fox nor his colleagues possessed. At a time when they should have taken every precaution to avoid offending public susceptibilities they behaved with a bland disdain for the misgivings felt by many MPs and country gentlemen. By doing so they jeopardised the lofty purposes for which they claimed to stand.

Fox eloquently defended himself from the cruel misrepresentations to which he was subjected. He found it easy to justify both his ambition and his party spirit:

> Ambition I confess I have, but not ambition upon a narrow bottom, or built upon paltry principles. If, from the devotion of my life to political objects, if from the direction of my industry to the attainment of some knowledge of the constitution, and the true interests of the British empire, the ambition of taking no mean part in those acts that elevate nations and make a people happy, be criminal, that ambition I acknowledge. And as to party spirit—that I feel it, that I have been even under its impulse, and that I ever shall, is what I proclaim to the world. That I am one of a party, a party never known to sacrifice the interests, or barter the liberties of the nation for mercenary purposes, emolument or honours: a party linked together upon principles which comprehend whatever is dear and most precious to free men, and essential to a free constitution, is my pride and my boast.[13]

But however satisfying language such as this was, it was more effective in keeping up the spirits of his supporters than in disarming his critics or in convincing the public that the board of commissioners was more than a ruse to divert East India company patronage to the service of the coalitionists. Though the government retained a comfortable majority of about a hundred in the house of commons it was also becoming increasingly apparent that the real threat to the bill would come from the lords.

The outcome there would depend on more tangible political factors than the declamation of lofty principles. The king's known hostility to the ministry and to the India bill was stimulating talk of intrigues, cabinet reshuffles, changes of ministry, and closet influence. Ironically, Fox was to be the victim of the type of behaviour which whig mythology had long claimed was George III's stock-in-trade. Because of the controversy over the India bill and the anxiety expressed in many quarters about the sanctity of charter privileges, the king recognised that the moment had come when he could challenge the coalition with every prospect of success. If he could procure the defeat of the bill he could dismiss his ministers with due propriety. He would even be able to convince men that he was doing no more than his political duty.

George III used Lord Temple, the former lord-lieutenant of Ireland, as his chief agent, and by indicating to sufficient peers that they would incur the wrath of the king if they voted for the India bill it was hoped to ensure that the bill would be rejected in the house of lords. George III already had an alternative first minister in William Pitt, who cleverly insisted on an unmistakable sign of royal displeasure towards the Fox-North ministry being displayed while remaining free of any public association with the steps being taken to destroy the administration. The king gave Temple a letter which he was to show to all doubters; those voting the wrong way would not only be regarded as no friends of the king, rather they were told that they would be deemed one of their sovereign's enemies. Meanwhile John Robinson was making inquiries about the prospects of a new government winning a general election and about the likely shift in political loyalties in the house of commons. Unless the peers stood firm the fate of the coalition was sealed.

During December the signs became more ominous. The activities of the king and Temple became so notorious that Fitzpatrick told his brother of the gloomy outlook for the coalition on 15 December:

Lord Temple had a long audience on Thursday last, and is said to have come out declaring himself authorised to say that the king disapproved of the bill as unconstitutional, and subversive of the rights of the crown, and that he should consider all who voted for it as his enemies. Lord Temple has not dared to avow this, but continues to insinuate it. The bishops waver, and *the thanes fly from us*; in my opinion the bill will not pass; the lords are now sitting, and the debate will certainly be too late to send you an account of the division; the proxies of the king's friends are arrived against the bill. The public is full of alarm and astonishment at the treachery as well as the imprudence of this unconstitutional interference. Nobody guesses what will be the consequence of a conduct that is generally compared to that of Charles I in 1641.[17]

But Fitzpatrick could not refrain from adding, 'I consider the ministry as over'. On 15 December the ministry was defeated by eight votes in the lords; two days later the margin between the two sides was nineteen, again in the opposition's favour. In the early hours of 18 December George III unceremoniously dismissed his ministers. Fox and North were out, but Fox could not share North's phlegmatic resignation to his fate.

He had never really faced the probability of going out of office. Though the defeat of the India bill had become more probable as the debates in the lords approached, Fox had still hoped to ride out the storm. After the ministry's defeat in the lords on 15 December he had clung desperately to the possibility of a recovery. To one friend he complained that the ministry had been beaten by 'such treachery on the part of the king, and such meanness on the part of his *friends* in the house of lords, as one could not expect either from him or them'. 'We are not out yet,' he defiantly wrote, 'but I suppose we shall be tomorrow.' He took heart from the fact that he and North were still so strong in the commons that no one could long survive without coming to terms with them. Anyone seeking to form a government without them was mad: 'I think we shall destroy them almost as soon as they are formed.' Outraged and perplexed as he was by the turn of events Fox was by no means pessimistic. His fierce indignation buoyed up his spirits for the fray. Like most of his friends he saw little chance of Pitt's ministry lasting for long. When Temple resigned as secretary of state only three days after receiving the seals Fox thought he saw the writing on the wall. He hoped to turn Pitt out and to condemn the king's actions as unconstitutional. Bitterness was inflamed with self-righteous anger. So, for a time, depression was kept at a distance, and over Christmas the prospect of vengeance soothed his troubles.

George III's intervention was unfortunate for Fox in more than one sense. Not only did it ensure his fall, it enabled him to evade all responsibility for what had happened. Instead of seeing the king's actions as indissolubly linked with a chain of events which the ministers themselves had initiated, Fox took the more superficial view that he had fallen victim to the arbitrary exercise of sinister royal influence. He had been unlucky, but though he was punished beyond his deserts he had not been blameless. Had he been more patient in sounding out opinion, more respectful of either the king's viewpoint or the legitimate interests of the East India company, and more willing to humour the house of commons, he would have been able to improve Indian administration without risking political defeat or personal humiliation. His fall has often been depicted as retributive judgment upon his coalition with North. It is more just to explain it in terms of errors of political judgment and deficiencies of political insight more closely related to the passage of a highly controversial piece of legislation. Fox might well have survived his alliance with North, for such a realignment was explicable and acceptable within the contemporary political framework. But he could not escape unscathed after provoking the king, antagonising a major interest group, and arousing the hostility of independent opinion in the commons and in the country. Within any political system such behaviour was offering hostages to fortune; in eighteenth-century England it was courting disaster.

5 The Triumph of William Pitt

Christmas 1783 was a fretful season. Festivity and good cheer were clouded by political calculation. Uncertainty stimulated soaring hopes and gnawing anxiety. Few expected William Pitt's administration to survive the rigours of the new year. Cheerfully men talked of the mincepie government, anticipating that as soon as families had exhausted their stocks of mincepies Fox and North would enjoy the satisfying experience of completing their revenge upon the king and his young accomplice. Fox's own mood was one of feverish expectancy. Everything pointed to a victory in the new year. Intuition and reason confirmed the bright prophecies of his friends. Yet even in the midst of much complacent optimism he was on edge, nervously contemplating the wreck of the past and the more attractive future with a bright confidence that seemed forced and artificial. Having suffered one stern shock he seemed anxious even when he was outwardly sanguine.

Yet there were times when he was as hopeful as any of his companions. Three days before Christmas he assured Northington that there could be little doubt but that the Fox-North administration would be re-established. The confusion among the king's friends was 'beyond all description', and he was beginning to be sorry that things had not after all been pushed to a dissolution and an election; it would have been best to have exposed the folly of the king and Pitt in the most unquestionable and most public manner possible. Now there was a danger that the ministry would collapse so quickly that Temple's 'cowardice' would provide them all with a convenient alibi. On Boxing Day Fox wrote to Northington again, assuring him that in January the opposition would certainly inflict a decisive defeat upon the government. In the circumstances it would be foolish to have any unnecessary change in the Irish administration; he advised Northington to hang on. Fox also detected improved morale among the coalitionists and this heartened him tremendously. Even those who had previously disapproved of the alliance were now reconciled to it, having been impressed by the disinterested way in which North had conducted himself and by the close cooperation between the two groups making up the coalition.

Fox was especially bitter about Pitt's willingness to respond to the king's request to form a new government. He was shocked and angry over Pitt's conduct and yet he had no cause to be surprised. Pitt had served under Shelburne and had proved loyal to him throughout the abortive negotiations to strengthen the Shelburne government by a reconciliation with the Foxites. Pitt had defended the king's right to choose his ministers, and had associated himself with Shelburne's affirmation that the king of England was and ought to remain more than a king of the Mahrattas. In opposition Pitt had criticised Fox's India bill. The only surprise therefore was that Pitt should have been sufficiently convinced that his ministry had a good enough chance of surviving to make it worth his while to take on the job of leading it. Fox's attitude to Pitt had never been other than ambivalent. He was impressed by Pitt's abilities, but he was suspicious of Pitt's motives from an early date. Possibly this sprang from an understandable dislike of Pitt's determination never to accept a merely subordinate situation. It may have stemmed, too, from a growing realisation that, despite their common opposition to the American war, and their common sympathy for parliamentary and administrative reform, Pitt was no Rockinghamite, obsessed by fears of the influence of the crown. Fox was irritated by Pitt's ostentatious independence. He may have been jealous of his reputation for disinterested patriotism, a reputation which Fox thought had been too easily won. He was resentful because he believed Pitt's longing for power to be as insatiable as any man's. He took an uncharitable view of Pitt's actions. In negotiation he often suspected him of doing no more than encompassing the humiliation of the whigs. To Fox Pitt was a sinister Machiavellian figure, a master of guile and duplicity without a spark of decent feeling. Consequently, however powerful the theoretical arguments were for an understanding between them, an irreconcilable divergence in temperament, and a mutual aversion to each other's personality, combined to ensure that they remained apart. The obstacle to any effective negotiation was simple: Fox avowed that he was willing to serve with Pitt but not under him. Pitt was prepared to admit Fox and a number of his friends to places in the government, but saw no reason why he should step down as first lord of the treasury. Fox never forgave Pitt for his part in the defeat of the coalition; only by yielding the chief place in administration to another could he atone for his misdeeds. To Pitt this was further proof of Fox's disregard for the king's freedom to choose his first minister. In such a situation no fruitful negotiation was possible.

Pitt's position was stronger than it seemed at the close of 1783. Fox persistently underrated the independence of the country gentlemen, and their willingness to give any ministry which had the confidence of the king the chance to prove itself in office. He also overlooked the intense suspicions which the India bill had aroused on the backbenches. He saw Pitt's deficiency in first-rate colleagues and assumed that the ministry was doomed. He did not anticipate the impression which Pitt made upon the commons by his cool defence of the government throughout a gruelling series of debates. Fox had hoped for a speedy resolution of the crisis. After several defeats in the house Pitt would resign, much as Shelburne had resigned before him. But when Pitt obstinately hung on, and the government's supporters in the commons rallied, Fox was left without a political strategy. Even the notion of a dissolution and a general election (which had so briefly been attractive) was now fraught with danger. The knowledge that Robinson was doggedly working his way through all the preliminaries to a general election was disturbing, while a steady stream of addresses voted from boroughs up and down the country was further evidence of the unpopularity of the coalition and the extent of approval for Pitt and the king. Fox was therefore compelled to denounce a dissolution as unconstitutional and an attack on the status and independence of the house of commons. This was itself an indication of the scale on which the situation was transformed between December 1783 and March 1784, as well as a tribute to the skill and courage of William Pitt.

The struggle for power was fought out within the house. Here both Pitt and Fox sought to justify their past conduct and establish their claim to the confidence of the commons. Naturally Fox made great play with Temple's contribution to his discomfiture. Even before his dismissal Fox had argued that Temple's behaviour was tantamount to maintaining that the house of commons was unequal to the trust reposed in it. Temple's actions, which had been condoned by the king, undermined the privileges of the house and violated the canons of parliamentary conduct, through which the lords and commons fulfilled their constitutional obligations. It was particularly significant that Temple's unconstitutional intervention had occurred during the discussion of a measure of considerable importance. No bill had ever been so violently and so systematically opposed as the India bill; its provisions had been thoroughly investigated, nothing had been left unexamined. Yet it had passed the commons by a respectable and convincing majority. Precisely because the India bill had been vindicated in the house it had been necessary for its opponents to resort to tactics based on influence and treachery. Fox confessed his misgivings:

> It is a public and a crying grievance that we are not the first who have
> felt this secret influence. It seems to be a habit against which no change
> of men or measures can operate with success.... To this infernal spirit
> of intrigue we owe that incessant fluctuation in his majesty's councils,
> by which the spirit of government is so much relaxed, and all its min-
> utest objects so fatally arranged.[1]

Once they were dismissed Fox and his friends became anxious about the
possibility of a dissolution. The hope of routing Temple and his associates
at the polls was exposed as an empty day-dream. In any case Pitt was a
more formidable opponent than Temple, and everyone knew how usual
it was for governments to win elections. As long as Pitt could be defeated
in the house of commons Fox had to maintain the existing house as the
arena in which the struggle for power would be fought out and the
authority by which it would be decided. It was necessary to stigmatise any
thought of a dissolution as a sinister assault on the privileges and constitutional procedures of the house of commons. Since he had been taunted
with excessive ambition Fox retorted by affirming that Pitt's ambition
would be served by dissolving parliament, since this would allow the influence of the crown to prevent the electorate freely exercising its franchises. Fox was in a difficult situation here. Everyone knew that the
chances of the government—any government—winning an election were
considerable, yet to say so publicly was tantamount either to conceding defeat in advance, and thereby helping to bring it about, or to confessing that
the public were averse to the Foxites, or to contending that the public were
gullible and corruptible. Fox had to take the gamble; his hope of victory
lay within the commons, not outside it. His appeal had to be to the
susceptibilities of the members of the house. He had to take the risk of
appearing to shrink from electoral combat, and of doubting the public's
probity. This was the only way of regaining the support of those independents who were more sensitive to any disrespect for their own privileges
than to any other political pressure or argument. Above everything else,
he had to avert a dissolution.

    This is a stark reminder that Fox was an eighteenth-century politician,
working in a political context which was radically different from that of
the twentieth century and far from approximating to the world which
Gladstone and Disraeli knew. Because Fox has too often been discussed
as if he were a Victorian liberal his behaviour has often been unfairly
condemned, just as his ideas have been inaccurately admired. The thought
of an appeal to the people as against the king did not seriously enter

his head. He did not conceive of politics in those terms. Like his contemporaries he could think of his constituents giving him a vote of confidence; he did not project such an assumption on to a national scale, for he was fully aware of the wide divergencies over the country and the primary significance of local and regional issues and family loyalties. In the cold December dawn, when he realised that he had been humiliatingly dismissed by the king, he soberly recognised that the only real hope of victory lay within the house of commons. On this he was driven to stake everything. If he failed consistently and overwhelmingly to defeat Pitt in the commons, on a scale sufficient to break the young minister's nerve, he knew that he had little to hope for from an election.

When Fox moved for a committee to inquire into the state of the nation on 12 January 1784 he sought to clarify his attitude towards the prerogatives of the crown. He did not deny that the crown had the right to appoint and dismiss ministers and to dissolve parliament, but rights were not to be exercised simply because they were rights. Consideration had to be given to the special circumstances governing each case. The commons had the right to refuse supplies but this did not mean that they should do so without regard to the ensuing confusion. The constitution consisted of a series of checks and balances, but this could work only if constitutional privileges were exercised temperately and sensibly. The situation was made all the more complicated when the government was dependent upon secret influence. This was itself a stimulus to jealousy and suspicion. The question was not simply who was to be the crown's chief minister, but rather what principles were to guide the government in its relations with the king and its handling of the nation's affairs. Fox maintained that party brought stability to the system, allowing the preservation of 'that happy practicable equilibrium which has all the efficacy of monarchy, and all the liberty of republicanism, moderating the despotism of the one and the licentiousness of the other'. This language was chosen to appeal to the backbenchers, and to refute allegations that the India bill had been motivated by a desire to destroy the just prerogatives of the crown. It was also meant to shift the responsibility for any constitutional crisis on to the shoulders of the new ministers. But although the Foxites had a comfortable majority in a large division, defeating the government by 232 votes to 193, the margin between Fox and his opponents had narrowed since early December. Already support for Pitt's government was growing, possibly because he was, before everything else, the king's choice as first minister.

Furthermore, while every initiative taken by the opposition was backward-looking, in that it was intended to condemn the way in which the coalition had been dismissed or the means taken to defeat the India bill in the lords, Pitt was able to show that he was interested in securing effective reform. His India bill was an attempt to improve governmental control over the East India company and the administration of the company's territories in India, while avoiding offending contemporary sensibilities about charter and property rights. In the most convincing fashion possible Pitt was demonstrating that he was not the mute tool of reaction, and that practicable improvements could be achieved without resorting to the more dubious tactics which had so discredited Fox and Burke. In India the governor-general in Bengal was to be vested with more definite powers of scrutiny over the conduct and policies of the other governors-general, while, instead of Fox's ill-fated board of seven commissioners, a board of control was to be set up, comprising ministers who were appointed by the crown in the normal way, and, what was more important, who were removable in the normal way. Nor was the board of control to get its hands on the patronage of the company, which remained the responsibility of the East India company's directors. Fox denounced Pitt's bill as a shady compromise, which would produce the greatest confusion in the management of company business. Compared with his own bill, Fox insisted, Pitt's was superficial and piecemeal. It was toying with the problems of British India, not solving them. Even the plea that Pitt's was a better measure because it had the consent of the company was bogus, although Fox brought himself to admit that his own bill had 'violated the company's charter to a certain degree'. Pitt's proposals were the deplorable results of allowing shallow expediency to have primacy over principle. But though the government was worsted in a division by 222 votes to 214, Fox could take little comfort from the vote. In a comparatively well attended house only eight votes separated the opposition and the government. In so far as one can ever talk of a swing in eighteenth-century politics, the trend was moving in favour of Pitt.

A motion calling for the removal of the king's ministers on 16 January fared rather better, being carried by 205 votes to 184. Perhaps this was a sign that Pitt's Indian proposals had picked up a measure of support from those who were sufficiently doubtful about the government's origins or its future to hold aloof on a direct motion of confidence, but there was no indication that an outright attempt to force George III to dismiss his ministers was either specially attractive or even particularly interesting to many members. There was no irresistible surge of anger by which the government was to be buried in the house of commons. As long as Pitt's nerve held Fox knew that victories by such narrow margins were inconclusive triumphs. It was always possible for the government to plead that it needed more time, and to gain more time by throwing out suggestions of a possible negotiation to soothe the hostility of its opponents in parliament and to broaden the ministry's bottom. During the debate on Lord Charles Spencer's resolution calling for the dismissal of Pitt and his colleagues Fox had tried to explain his constitutional standpoint, and to meet the suggestion that negotiations between the leading groups was the best means of ending the political stalemate. He was sadly conscious that a negotiation was favoured by many of the independents, and instead of inspiring an assault which would sweep his enemies into oblivion he began to look more like a politician seeking to insure himself against disaster.

He argued that traditional distinctions between whig and tory had nothing to do with the constitutional question facing the house. No one denied the right of the king to choose his own ministers, but it was essential to vindicate the privileges of the house of commons 'to decide on the conduct of the administration, on the peculiarity of their introduction into office, and on those circumstances which either entitle them to the confidence or the reprobation of the house'. Though the king had the right to appoint his ministers it was worth asking if it was wise or politic for a monarch to continue a set of ministers in office when the commons had declared them to have been installed by unconstitutional means and to be unworthy of the house's confidence. But however forcefully Fox defended the rights of parliament, and however vigorously he condemned 'conspiracies' against the constitution, he claimed that he had no wish 'to diminish those rights which are legally invested in his majesty':

> The prerogative of the negative is a maxim which I have always admitted, always asserted, always defended.... And had this prerogative on a late occasion been exerted, not in the dark and under the baleful shade of a secret influence, but in an honest, open, and avowed manner, I should have applauded the measure.[2]

This was hardly convincing, since it was commonly recognised that, though Fox conceded that the crown had a right to veto legislation and that this would have been the best way for George III to have indicated his disapproval of the India bill, he also believed that the veto should not normally be exercised without the consent of the cabinet, which made nonsense of the suggestion that the king either should or could have successfully vetoed the India bill.

On the issue of negotiation Fox seemed more inclined to justify his past conduct than to be very clear about the future. He was possibly right to confine himself to a discussion of broad principles, for he could not afford wantonly to condemn any suggested reconciliation between Pitt and the opposition; to do so would antagonise those backbenchers who thought coalition was the answer to every difficulty, and whatever their intellectual shortcomings Fox needed their support. He was, therefore, unusually guarded in his remarks:

> A coalition has been the subject of recommendation during the course of debate. I neither court nor avoid union with any party. Such coalition, however, must be established on a broad and consistent basis. Every well-constituted administration must be one with itself. This is absolutely indispensable.[3]

But inevitably any discussion on the principle of coalition brought him back to his own alliance with North:

> The noble lord with whom I formed a coalition, differed from me on various grounds previous to the establishment of this connexion. We differed on the subject of the American war. This difference, however, was obviated when that war came to a period. I thought the influence of the crown too great. On this subject the noble lord also differed from me. This ground of contrariety of opinion was likewise, in some measure, taken away. A third thing, in which the noble lord and myself entertained a variety of sentiment, was his connecting himself with an administration of whose measures he did not perfectly approve. This point the noble lord may still defend, whilst I entertain my former opinions. These were the material grounds on which, in our political conduct, we differed, and which being done away, every objection to connect myself with persons of any description, with whom I can form a permanent union on sound and general principles, with men who enjoy the confidence of this house and of the public.[4]

The sting lay in the reference to the confidence of the commons; this could be interpreted as a dutiful gesture of deference to the opinion of those members whose goodwill Fox was desperately seeking to cultivate, but it was also a hint of intransigence towards ministers who clearly did not have the confidence of the house and who had come to power by means of an intrigue of dubious constitutionality. It was by no means clear how Pitt was to atone for his misdeeds or what issues of public concern kept Pitt and Fox apart. To many men the dispute seemed no more than a clash of personalities not of principle. In the struggle to impress the public with one's integrity it was Fox who eventually appeared the more vindictive and the more preoccupied with personal reputation.

Yet it was understandable that Fox should be cautious about embarking on any prolonged negotiation or entering upon any new coalition. He had suffered so much abuse because of the alliance with North that he was apprehensive about the impression which any new negotiation would make upon the public. He was genuinely doubtful about the possibility as well as the desirability of any union with Pitt. Rhetorical exaggeration heightened his denunciations of the influence of the crown but he nevertheless fiercely resented what he considered Pitt's selfish willingness to defer to the king's whims in order to advance his own career. To accept Pitt as the head of any ministry would be to condone the underhand stratagem which had brought about the coalition's downfall. Fox was also mindful of the arguments which he had used to denounce Shelburne's succession to the premiership on the death of Rockingham and the claims which he had then made for a greater degree of cabinet initiative in the selection of a chief minister. Mutely to acquiesce in Pitt's continuation as first lord of the treasury would by implication deny his own words and lay him open to the accusation that his resignation in 1782 had been motivated by personal pique. He was in such a frustrating plight that vague talk of a negotiation between the government and opposition only added to his worries. If he acted rashly he was risking any chorus of unrestrained invective and vicious misrepresentation.

Fox did his best to damp down irresponsible speculation about a possible coalition. On 20 January he denied that there was any foundation for what was little more than idle gossip. He went on to remind the commons that the political contest which was taking place was more than a squabble over place. It was a 'contest between privilege and prerogative, or rather between prerogative and the constitution'. Was a secret and unconstitutional influence to be allowed to maintain in office a group of ministers in whom the house of commons had declared they had no confidence? Yet Fox had to admit, when Lord Frederick Campbell and others equally respectable recommended 'union' to both sides of the house, that he had no objection in principle to a coalition, although he felt in honour bound to add a word of warning. It was much easier to recommend a union than to carry it into effect, and it was important for gentlemen not to be hurried away by 'too sanguine hopes'. A union could not be as quickly accomplished as it could be wished for. To be of any service to the public it would have to be based on principle. 'How can these two parties,' Fox asked, 'ever agree in measures when they disagree in principles, with respect to the very foundation on which a ministry ought to stand?'[5]

But the pressures in favour of some negotiation were building up in ways which made it difficult for Fox and friends to resist them. At the beginning of February the commons agreed to a motion calling for 'an efficient, extended and unified administration' without a division, and however pious such resolutions were they represented a body of opinion which the leading politicians on both sides of the house had to humour. More important still, George III was eager to broaden the basis of his ministry if possible. It was not that the king wished Fox to return to office; rather he sensed that if a negotiation would be successfully managed it might be possible to detach a number of Northites and some of the more moderate Rockinghamites from Fox. The king knew how unattractive and unrewarding opposition was to those who saw themselves as potential servants of the state, and since Pitt and Robinson were making their preparations for a general election a negotiation would prove an invaluable preliminary to the dissolution of parliament. If it succeeded the ministry would be placed on a thoroughly firm foundation; if it failed its sterility could be cited as further evidence of the factious spirit of Fox and the whigs.

On 15 February George III wrote to the duke of Portland, telling him of a wish to heal 'present divisions' by placing a new administration on 'a wide basis' and on 'a fair and equal footing'. He sent Lord Sydney to ask Portland to meet Pitt to confer on the subject, assuring Portland of his readiness to consider any proposals which might be put before him. The king was scrupulously correct in making his approach to Portland, who was the nominal leader of the whigs and the former head of what was usually thought of as the Fox-North ministry. Portland's response was stiffly polite. While expressing his appreciation of the king's wish to end present divisions, and his willingness to do anything in his power towards forming a broader ministry on a wide and solid basis, he informed Sydney of the impossibility of his conferring with Pitt on any proposal to extend the administration. Portland asserted his unalterable opinion that the confidence of the house of commons was indispensable to any arrangement which promised stable and energetic government. The first requirement was for Pitt to give some indication to the commons that he intended to comply with their wishes. This could only mean that Pitt should indicate his readiness to step down as first lord of the treasury, the new ministry being wholly new and free from any connexion with the events of December 1783. Who would then head a new ministry? If Portland were chosen this would be widely interpreted as a victory for Fox, the victory which he had failed to win in July 1782. Part of the confusion stemmed from a misunderstanding of what equal and fair meant. For Pitt this amounted to a generous allocation of government places to members of the Foxite and Rockinghamite groups, but it did not imply that he should ask forgiveness for taking office after the dismissal of the coalition or do anything which suggested that his critics had been right all along. Pitt was in the fortunate position of knowing that opinion was shifting towards him, and that the prospects of the government doing well in an early general election were promising. He had good reason to wish to avert unnecessary political strife by broadening his ministry, but he was under no necessity to concede victory, in everything but name, to his opponents. He was willing to admit Portland and Fox to the government and to let bygones be bygones, but he was adamantly opposed to yielding the post which he had bravely filled when few others wanted it, and however charitable he was to Fox and the whigs he obstinately refused to allow North to fill any place in his administration.

Despite Portland's formal response to the approach made by the king and Sydney negotiations were carried on by resorting to third and fourth parties. Fox heard of the unofficial discussions from Portland. Thurlow, Gower, and Richmond were regarded by the ministerialists as having a prior right to a cabinet place, in addition to Pitt. Thurlow, the lord chancellor, was the king's own favourite, and George III's insistence upon him was awkward for Fox, who had Loughborough's claims to the lord chancellorship to consider. Richmond, who acted for the government throughout the discussions, took great care to tell Portland of the ministry's determination not to resign, either collectively or individually. As Portland wistfully wrote to Fox, concerning the resignation of any or all of the ministers, 'it would be an avowal on their part of the charge alleged against them by the house of commons'. Portland was excessively sensitive about the honour of the house of commons during the negotiations; he was wary of dealing directly with Pitt or Richmond, perhaps because he feared that he would be outmanoeuvred. He was also embarrassed by Fox's absence at St Anne's Hill. Fox was sceptical throughout. He suspected that Pitt's own position was being safeguarded whatever suggestions were being made to soothe Portland's anxieties. There was no point in Portland having an audience with the king, if he knew all along that the king would simply repeat proposals which had already been communicated in writing. Instead of the king asking Portland to act as his agent in forming a new comprehensive ministry George III was, in effect, acting as Pitt's agent. Even Fox was incapable of devising any solution to the teasing question of how the honour of the house of commons was to be met. All he could do was to assure Portland, 'I own I think that part of the difficulty which relates to the honour of the house of commons will be in great degree got over whenever the king shall have sent to you to assist *him* (not Pitt) in forming a new administration.'[6] Fox was displaying a tendency, which became stronger as the years passed, to retire to the country at moments of crisis, leaving others to shoulder the responsibility for unpleasant decisions.

Pitt reasserted his own conviction that the best means of securing a full and mutually satisfactory explanation of all measures and arrangements pertaining to the formation of a new ministry would be by 'personal and confidential intercourse', so Portland informed Fox on 29 February. But though he reiterated his adherence to the principle of equality Pitt shrewdly refrained from stating precisely what it entailed. By doing this he cleverly thrust the chief responsibility for the success or failure of the negotiations on to the whigs, and since he was by now doubtful that there was any possibility of an equal union with Fox and Portland he had exploited the situation intelligently. It was not that he was primarily concerned with embarrassing the whigs; it was rather that he had clear guidelines in his own mind as to the most sensible method of conducting the negotiations. He outwitted Fox, not because he was more unscrupulous or more devious, but because the whole business of negotiation posed fewer and simpler problems for him than it did for Fox. Pitt had a dissolution to fall back on; Fox had already exhausted his resources; he had virtually nothing in reserve. He had banked heavily on winning a decisive victory in the commons; his depression reflected a growing suspicion that he was a beaten man. Perhaps he would have cut his losses by accepting office under Pitt, but emotionally this was more than he could bring himself to do. At least when he had come to terms with North Fox could pride himself that he had had the best of the bargain; whatever the formalities the dominant position in the coalition had been his. If he agreed to serve under Pitt no similar assurance would be operative. After what he had said about the behaviour of the king, and what he regarded as Pitt's collusion with George III, he needed some gesture which went some way towards justifying his words and deeds to the house of commons and to the public. But such a gesture Pitt was determined not to give. At a more primitive level than political calculation Fox had not recovered from the humiliations of December; the wound inflicted by George III's shabby intrigue and curt, heartless dismissal still festered. In one sense Fox was no longer interested in office if it involved paying the only price which, in the circumstances, would ensure a place in the government. He was physically and emotionally exhausted by the sustained crisis of the previous six months. He longed for vindication; he yearned even more intensely for ease and quiet. In some ways he was past caring about the tortuous inanities of negotiation. He was going through one of his temporary moods of escapism tinged with defeatism. The only thing that remained to him was his reputation as the uncompromising foe of the influence of the crown. He could not risk losing that solitary vestige of consistency. He therefore turned aside from serving under Pitt because to do so would mean sacrificing what was left of his integrity. He was under no illusions; there was no likelihood of George III or Pitt submitting to the preconditions which he and Portland had laid down for the commencement of meaningful negotiations. Fox was therefore driven further into the barren wastes of opposition. There was only bitter remorse in reflecting that he had been outgeneralled. In 1784 Fox was the tormented, though not the innocent, victim of circumstances. At a time when flexibility might have brought him the office for which he craved he chose to remain obstinately, even hopelessly, faithful to what he conceived as constitutional principle and political integrity.

With the failure of negotiation Fox and Portland were driven to consider their tactics. There was no alternative but to resume the struggle in the house of commons, heightening tension whenever possible, seeking to throw into greater relief than ever before the contrast between government and opposition, and threatening to withhold the supplies if the expressed wishes of the commons continued to be so persistently ignored by the government. Yet this threat was little more than bluff. Its chief purpose was to weaken the resolve and shatter the nerves of the king's ministers. But Pitt showed himself to be singularly indifferent to bluff and bluster. He moved with feline certainty among the complexities of politics. Fox knew that to refuse the supplies would bring the constitutional crisis down from the heights of theory and speculation to the sour bitter world of conflicting interests, where emotions would be raw and inflamed and passions fierce. To threaten to refuse supplies was to impose some measure of strain upon the ministers, but the possibility was more of an anxiety than the actuality, for if Fox and his friends refused to vote supplies they would lay themselves open to accusations of selfish ambition and questionable judgment. They would most probably antagonise moderate opinion and far from provoking the government's resignation they would merely bring forward the dissolution of parliament, which they were anxious to avoid above everything else. Every report from the constituencies was fraught with ominous stories of a groundswell of opinion in favour of the king and of Pitt, and in addition to the free play of opinion Fox had to contend against the influence of the crown and the monumental patronage of the East India company.

It would seem, therefore, that Fox's tactics were determined as much by a desire for self-justification as by any real hope of persuading independent-minded men to come over to him. When his allegations of unconstitutional conduct on the part of Pitt and the king failed to bring the much-needed upsurge of parliamentary hostility towards George III and his ministers, Fox could only repeat his accusations. The controversy was futile, stalely predictable, and, for the majority of MPs, irrelevant to the immediate business of politics. When Fox moved an address on 1 March 1784 asking the king to dismiss his ministers he sought to convince the commons of the gravity of the constitutional crisis, and with the shadow of a dissolution hanging over him he attempted to pose as the defender of the house of commons as the greatest security for the rights of the people; but there was little new in his arguments and members were conscious of going through the postures appropriate to what was being depicted as a major political upheaval. It was ironic that Fox should be so devoted to a house of commons which had originally been returned to support North in 1780, and which had given varying degrees of support to ministries of varied political character. Even by Foxite standards the house was not distinguished by the consistency with which it had supported Foxite principles. But any house of commons in which Fox discerned signs that he had his clutches on a majority was preferable to all the uncertainties of a general election.

Fox claimed to be taking the commons into his confidence, making no secret of his ideas concerning the prerogatives of the crown, which he ever had, and would ever, avow.

> No prerogative of the crown was, in his opinion, distinct or unconnected with the whole of that free and liberal system in which our government chiefly consisted. The people were the great source of all power, and their welfare the sole object for which it was to be exerted; but who in this case were to be the judges? The house of commons undoubtedly were competent to protect the rights of the people, to pronounce on whatever they deemed an encroachment on their privileges; and the moment they could not prevent everything which struck them as such, they were not equal to the design of such an institution. This he called a due seasoning of modification of that enormous power devolved by the constitution on the executive government of the country. The house of commons consequently were possessed of the power of putting a negative on the choice of ministers; they were stationed as sentinels by the people, to watch over whatever could more or less remotely or nearly affect their interest; so that whenever they discovered in those nominated by his majesty to the several and great offices of state, want of ability, want of weight to render their situations respectable, or want of such principles as were necessary to give effect to the wishes of the House; in any or all of such cases they

were entitled to advise his majesty against employing such persons as his faithful commons could not trust. . . .[7]

Many MPs went along with general reasoning such as this; what worried them was the failure on Fox's part to observe what they considered to be the corollary to what he was saying: the need to allow a ministry possessing the confidence of the king a real opportunity to prove itself in office. Fox's opposition to Pitt's India bill seemed wilful and capricious and to talk of withholding supplies introduced a perverse and eccentric element into the atmosphere which ensured that politics would not settle down in the way MPs hoped. They were tiring of permanent crisis. Many of them sympathised with Fox and North over Temple's intrigue, but they still found the coalition and India bill hard to forgive, and since the king had made it plain in whom he had confidence, a good many members were beginning to feel that it was time to give the new administration the chance to get on with the tasks of government, rather than endlessly bickering over points of constitutional theory and procedural nicety. It also seemed puzzling that Fox had shrunk from refusing supplies when, if the constitutional crisis was as grave as he had claimed, such a step was the only feasible method of compelling the king to accede to the demands of the commons. Fox's explanation of his failure to carry his threats into effect was lame:

> Why, it had been asked, were the supplies not withheld? The reason, at least on which he, for one, had hitherto voted for the supplies, might strike the house as a paradox. It was nevertheless real. He had not sufficient confidence in the ministers of the day to withhold supplies ... The ministers' love for the constitution was not sufficiently visible to make them willing to risk the experiment.[8]

It was feeble to argue that there was a major constitutional crisis, and that the only possible retort by the commons to the imposition of unacceptable ministers upon the country was to refuse to vote supplies, only to argue that this was too risky because it might provoke the ministers to further unconstitutional excesses. Such logic was essentially the logic of defeat. Fox knew that by formally refusing supplies the opposition would make a dissolution certain, and all the signs were pointing to a victory for the king and Pitt at a general election. It was as appropriate for the government to appeal from a factious house of commons to the people as it was for Fox to appeal to the house of commons to vindicate its privileges against the prerogatives of the crown. Fox did not want an election, yet he had rendered a negotiation for a broadening of the ministry futile by insisting on conditions which he knew were abhorrent to Pitt and impossible of fulfilment. Though in December his hopes of frightening Pitt into resignation by defeating him time after time in the commons had been high these had been blighted by Pitt's tenacity and the shifting loyalties of many backbenchers. Fox's political strategy had collapsed. He was caught in the toils of a rhetoric which was every day becoming more contorted and more purposeless. Even within the house Pitt's position was becoming stronger. Fox's resolution of 1 March was carried by only twelve votes; when another motion deploring the king's choice of ministers and lamenting the nation's plight was carried by a single vote the total failure of Fox's conduct of opposition was manifest to all. Even within the commons he had managed to lose ground to Pitt. When Pitt brought forward the mutiny bill the confidence of the Foxites was so badly shaken that they allowed it to pass, knowing as they did that even if they had mounted a sustained campaign they might well have seen it go through just the same. As it was Pitt could now appeal to the people for confirmation of that steadily growing confidence which he had so arduously won from the commons by his fortitude and devotion to duty. While Pitt appealed to the country as the king's minister, the embodiment of a patriotic and non-party attitude to politics, and the herald of tranquillity after two crisis-riven years, Fox appeared more dubiously as the representative of a shallow partisan spirit, arrogant and wilful in office, obstinate and spiteful in defeat. Fox had staked everything on winning an indisputable and decisive victory within the house of commons; he was unprepared for a general election, and the methods with which he had chosen to attack Pitt unfitted him for the peculiar rigours of an electoral contest. When the king dissolved parliament on 25 March 1784 Fox's worst fears were realised.

Although the 1784 election excited a great deal of passionate interest at the time, and although it has been the subject of much historical controversy since, it is important to resist the temptation of seeing it in deceptively modern terms. The conflict between the two major political figures, Fox and Pitt, should not be taken as implying that the election was a national contest in the sense which is so familiar today. The overall picture emerged from a multitude of local returns, and in many seats what mattered was not the replacement of one MP by another but the persuasion of the sitting member that it was in the interests of his patron or his constituents that he should in future give regular support to the king's government, rather than involving himself with the partisan practices encouraged and fomented by Fox. In many constituencies there was no poll, a natural accompaniment of eighteenth-century politics, but where there was no open contest there was sometimes a bitter wrangle among the body of electors or the dominant interest or family groups about the assurances which it was deemed proper to extort from a candidate who would be formally unopposed. It was not always easy to synchronise the needs of local industries, or the security of regional interests, or the continued pre-eminence of a distinguished country family, with guarantees of good behaviour concerning the king's government or particular attitudes towards the struggle between Pitt and Fox in parliament. There was no equivalent of a modern general election campaign: throughout the days of the poll Fox was preoccupied with his own contest at Westminster, not with any generalised national electoral strategy.

But in certain constituencies there was undoubtedly a genuine and fierce conflict of opinion. Westminster, Yorkshire, Middlesex, Southwark, Norwich, Bristol, Liverpool, Canterbury and Leicester were constituencies in which 'the sense of the people' played a significant, even a decisive, part in determining the outcome. In the majority of the open constituencies victory went to candidates either favourable to Pitt or careful to separate themselves from the Foxite interest. Even in seats where coalitionists gained memorable victories they were often the less well supported of the two successful candidates. Fox himself came second to Hood in Westminster after a remarkable and exciting struggle. There was never any probability of Fox beating Hood, the question was whether he would be able to fend off the challenge from the third candidate, Wray. At Norwich, though the Foxites rejoiced in Windham's success, he still came a poor second to a Pittite candidate. In a system of two-member seats it was possible for a good deal of cross voting to take place, and men were doing more than merely expressing an opinion on the merits of the coalition or the patronage provisions of Fox's India bill. They were judging the extent to which MPs had defended their interests. But although the influence of the crown and of the East India company was far from negligible it is clear that, within the limits set by the traditional electoral system, Pitt's victory reflected a significant expression of public opinion. The scale of his victory was exceptional, the government doing even better in the open constituencies than Robinson had expected, and George III joyfully congratulated Pitt on the results.

The pamphlet *Fox's Martyrs* listed 97 Foxites who failed to return to the house of commons after the 1784 election. This does not mean that every one of Fox's martyrs lost his seat in an open contest in the manner usual today. Many MPs withdrew from candidatures when negotiation with the dominant interests in their constituency revealed to them the impossibility of their retaining the seat. Others chose to retain their seats by defecting from Fox. When the contemporary prejudice against disturbing a sitting member is taken into account the revulsion of feeling against Fox, North, the coalition and their India bill, was astonishing. Fox could only brood on the final consequences of a unique combination of prejudice, honest and free opinion, influence and self-interest, and it was especially galling for him to realise George III's insight into the minds and feelings of his subjects. The public resented Fox's coalition with North, but if the outcome had been good government they would have forgiven him. But he antagonised moderate and respectable opinion by his disregard for the legitimate wishes of the king, the avarice and ambition represented by the patronage clauses of his India bill, and by his arrogant refusal to enter into responsible negotiations with Pitt to secure a stable ministry and end two years of political confusion. There can be no doubt about Fox's unpopularity at this period. As good a whig as Dr Richard Watson, the Bishop of Llandaff, summed it up admirably:

> The numberless addresses ... against the coalition ministry sufficiently showed the voice of the people to be with Mr Pitt. ... It was not so much the prerogative of the crown that kept Mr Pitt in his place, and set the house of commons at defiance, as it was the sense of the nation, which on this occasion was in direct contradiction to the sense of the house of commons.[9]

The cartoon showing Fox entering Leadenhall Street in triumph as Carlo Khan, bestriding an elephant with the features of Lord North, and accompanied by a herald with a marked resemblance to Burke in his most Jesuitical guise, is familiar, but compared with other attacks on Fox it was noteworthy for its mildness. He was credited with every sordid motive, and he was likened to Satan, Beelzebub, Belial and sinister tyrants and republicans such as Cataline and Cromwell. Every charge that could damage his reputation was hurled at him with venomous fury and a disregard for any restraint. Fox sadly confessed that Sayers' caricatures had done him more harm than the debates in parliament or the printed pamphlets, and however regretful he was at their impact on the popular mind he appreciated the vividness of the Carlo Khan print and others showing him running off with India House or fleeing paradise (when turned out of office) with a convenient burden of ill-gotten loot.

Fox's own contest at Westminster was noisy, uninhibited, and almost unbearably exciting. The issue was fought out entirely on the basis of personalities, and since Admiral Lord Hood was a popular and highly respected figure the struggle soon resolved itself into one between Fox and Sir Cecil Wray. It was all the more bitter because Wray was a renegade whig. During the earlier part of the long forty-day polling period Fox did disappointingly, and at the end of the tenth day he was trailing Wray by 318 votes. Only in the last ten days did he push convincingly ahead. The final figures were: Lord Hood–6694; Mr Fox–6234; Sir Cecil Wray–5998. Though Fox beat Wray by 236 votes he was 760 votes behind Hood: this in an election which was hailed by Fox's supporters at the time and by many historians since as a remarkable triumph for Fox. During the protracted struggle Fox's feelings had fluctuated wildly, especially in the first week in April when things looked black indeed. Though he claimed on 3 April that 'misfortunes, when they come thick, have the effect rather of rousing my spirits than sinking them', these cheerful assertions of indefatigable optimism were not borne out during the next week. He became depressed, almost listlessly resigned to defeat. On 5 April he thought that being defeated on two successive days looked ugly, although 'the thing is far from over, and I have still hopes'. Two days later he was plunged in gloom: 'Worse and worse, but I am afraid I must not give it up, though there is very little chance indeed.' On 8 April he was even more downcast, wearily commenting, 'I must not give it up, though I wish it. Indeed, I feel I ought not, while there is a bare possibility. Bad news from York, and alarms about poor Andrew St John in Bedfordshire. I have serious thoughts, if I am beaten here, of not coming into parliament at all.' He became slightly more optimistic when he found himself leading Wray by six votes at the close of the poll on 8 April, but he still did not rate his chances highly. Only after 20 April did he become brimful of confidence and display his usual high spirits. At the same time his friends took the precaution of returning him for Orkney and Shetland. He doubted whether this was necessary, but deferred to advice, wistfully commenting, 'I always think their judgment better than my own, with respect to what regards *myself* in political matters.'[10]

The voters of Westminster were subjected to every ruse contemporary electioneering expertise could devise. Intimidation, bribery and corruption, even murder, as well as noisy processions and permitted riot kept feelings high and tempers hot. There was no time for reflection or temperate debate. The countess of Salisbury canvassed for Wray; the dazzling duchess of Devonshire for Fox. A butcher thought a kiss an appropriate price for a vote, and though it was the duchess' sister who obliged, popular rumour preferred to credit the duchess with the favour. It was said that she visited brothels in Long Acre in order to win votes for Fox, and highly as her beauty was prized she had to endure gross abuse and filthy rumour. Fox's victory was celebrated by his friends with the frantic relief of men who had feared the worst and who sensed that Westminster would have to con-

sole them for much bad news. The prince of Wales joined the procession
of triumph as one of Fox's partisans; Carlton House echoed with the
sound of revelry and the whig toast of 'Buff and blue and Mrs Crewe';
but the celebrations were set against a wider background of defeat. The
tumult of chairing the member could not drown the rumbling murmurs
of disaffection and desertion which told Fox of the convincing vindication
which the electorate up and down the country had given to the king and
Pitt. Thomas Coke boasted of being one of Fox's martyrs, but the whigs
could not console themselves with artificial sentiment. The ultimate conclusion of the political strategy which had governed their parliamentary
conduct for the past twelve months was nothing less than catastrophe.
Contemporaries were taken aback by the overwhelming nature of Fox's
defeat. Even the legends which soon gathered around the 1784 election
were a tribute to the scale of Pitt's achievement and the depths of Fox's
decline.

Further humiliations were in store for him. The streak of cold, remorseless logic which was one of Pitt's less endearing characteristics found expression in the sorry affair of the Westminster scrutiny. There was nothing
unusual in the house of commons vetting election returns; to do so was a
familiar method by which the ministry of the day reinforced its majority.
Defeated candidates often avenged themselves for their failure at the polls
by unseating a victorious rival on charges of bribery or corruption, of the
manufacture of illegal franchises, or the exploitation of impersonation and
intimidation. The Westminster election had been so noisy and so close
that Wray was understandably loath to let even the remotest chance of
replacing Fox slip without attempting to win from the house of commons
the confidence he had failed to extort from the Westminster electors. The
scale of the government's victory and the evident unpopularity of the
Foxites proved a temptation which it was impossible to resist. It was almost unthinkable for Pitt to refuse a scrutiny, but men were disturbed
by the keenness with which he pressed the affair. Sympathy flowed back
to Fox, the more so since having taken his seat for Orkney and Shetland
he was able to defend himself in the house of commons. Earlier, during
the Westminster election, Pitt had expressed the hope that even if Fox
were elected it would be possible to regain the ground lost by a scrutiny;
now he expected Fox to be thrown out so far as sitting for Westminster was
concerned. If Fox could be unseated from Westminster it would be a fitting
climax to the triumph which the king and his minister had achieved at
the polls, and a counter-weight to any lingering suggestions that Fox was
in any sense the people's darling. There was a lurid poetic justice in the

formal unseating of Fox on charges of improper conduct during the election campaign which Pitt found irresistible.

Fox impressed the commons with the vigour with which he fought his own defence. On the technical issues connected with the scrutiny he was a match for Pitt and the government lawyers, and his plea that he was the victim of a vindictive political and personal persecution carried conviction for most backbenchers. He stood forth as an individual who could not hope to compete with the government in the financial resources necessary to investigate fully and satisfactorily all the allegations which had been made against him. He accused the government of attempting to overawe the commons in the relentless pursuit of a private vendetta, and he warned Pitt of the dangers of such arrogance. 'Though he may exert all the influence of his situation to harass and persecute, he shall find that we are incapable of unbecoming submissions. There is a principle of resistance in mankind which will not brook such injuries; and a good cause and a good heart will animate men to struggle in proportion to the size of their wrongs.'[11] During the long wearisome process of examining the Westminster electors opinion rallied behind Fox. By February 1785 only thirty-nine votes separated the two sides; a month later the commons decided that Hood and Fox had been legally returned. Pitt had suffered a humiliating and merited reverse. Fox had the special satisfaction of a victory within the commons to compensate him for his other disappointments. Ironically, when the scrutiny was terminated, about the same number of invalid votes had been deducted from each of the three candidates. Fox argued that he was no more the beneficiary of electoral malpractice than either of his rivals. The episode is a reminder of the independence of the eighteenth-century house of commons in any matter relating to its own privileges and membership. Pitt's massive electoral victory did not mean that he could impose his will upon the commons or ignore the feelings of the country gentlemen. Men who had vehemently objected to the Fox-North coalition and the India bill still had a fond regard for Fox as a fellow member of the house. He had been ousted from office; he and his companions had suffered the additional mortification of a uniquely severe trouncing in the 1784 election. There seemed little reason to thrust Fox even further into the slime. Members found Pitt's remorselessness repulsive and unnecessary; their sense of fair play was outraged. They saw Fox as the champion of the ordinary member against the administration. Fox's eloquence played effectively upon their emotions; they responded once more to the familiar verbal inventiveness, the sharp invective, the virtuosity of his wit. That irrecoverable and intangible characteristic to which all contemporaries paid tribute, Fox's charm, won over the most hostile of critics on an issue so fraught with notions of private honour and political dignity.

Yet Fox had good cause to be bitter after the scrutiny. Previously his suspicions of Pitt had been frequently ill-founded, the reflection of his own uneasy conscience rather than any objective considerations. Unhappily the scrutiny saw Pitt at his worst; for once all Fox's misgivings were confirmed. For the rest of their long rivalry Fox never forgot or forgave what he regarded as Pitt's malignant unscrupulousness. He was always likely to explain away every unwelcome experience by invoking fears of Pitt's vindictive cunning. Whenever offers of negotiation were tendered Fox never trusted Pitt's good faith. A streak of personal dislike added its baleful influence to their political confrontation. Fox was often magnanimous towards political opponents, but he was never generous or warm-hearted—or even wholly fair—towards Pitt. He could never forget the 1784 election and its aftermath, nor could he forgive the unyielding spirit which had sought to add personal degradation to political mortification. The events of 1782-4 were never far from Fox's mind. They were the yardstick by which he judged much in later politics; and too often the obsessive memory of those years led him seriously astray, luring him into making false analogies and drawing misleading parallels with the years in which he had challenged George III and lost.

The general election had been more than a vindication of George III and Pitt; it was also a vote of no confidence in the ideas relating to the appointment of ministers, the conduct of government, and the virtues of opposition which Fox had expounded so vigorously since the death of Rockingham. Men were still distrustful of anything which tended to limit the legitimate powers of the king; party was stigmatised as faction, and the notion of a systematic opposition, though it had by now escaped from the taint of treason, was still associated with conspiracy. When men refused to discuss Fox's constitutional ideas purely in the abstract they were showing a wise awareness of the way in which Fox's theories were inextricably mingled with political calculations. Fox himself was always unresponsive to, and ill at ease with, theoretical speculation. His constitutional ideas were very much related to particular political situations. He held them sincerely; they were not intended to deceive or to confuse. He was convinced of their utility and he was confident that if applied they would lead to more effective government and the smoother working of the constitution. But they were, in one sense, rationalisations of attitudes upon which he had already decided; they were attempts to justify his own political behaviour and to convince men of the acceptability of his own conduct. Perceptive though Fox's constitutional doctrines were and however much they were prophetic of later developments relating to collective responsibility and party politics, they were always subordinate in Fox's mind to the demands of the current political situation. Sometimes Fox has been depicted as the protagonist of progressive ideals in a hostile and uncomprehending environment, a martyr in the cause of a more democratic notion of politics. This is fundamentally to misunderstand Fox's personality and the political context in which he was placed. In many ways Fox accepted the principles which his contemporaries took for granted in politics; he never formulated a comprehensive interpretation of the meaning of representation or the relationship between government and society or the scope and nature of administration. Even when supporting the reform of parliament he did so in language which all too clearly reflected an essentially traditional cast of mind. Fox's radicalism was provoked by the unique pressures imposed upon him by the frustrations of eighteenth-century politics. The vocabulary of political innovation was subordinate to the practice of opposition, but because of the special importance of rhetoric in a political system dominated by the house of commons, Fox's oratory had a real influence on the course of events, though frequently in a sense other than that which he desired or anticipated. Ideas were tools exploited by the debater; they were not transcendent inspirations determining the whole tendency of politics. Personal vindication was as significant in their evolution as any far-sighted concern for a transformed pattern of political behaviour. Rather than initiating a completely new concept of politics Fox's ideas were meant to secure significant shifts of emphasis within the traditional system while leaving the fundamentals untouched. He was less radical in intention than many later apologists assumed.

The frustrations of Fox's career sprang as much from his own failure adequately to manage the complexities of opposition politics as from a foolish inability on the part of his contemporaries to appreciate the wisdom of new ideas. Fox suffered from a series of misjudgments which were all comprehensible or even permissible in the circumstances of the time, but which taken together combined to exclude him from office for a generation. He could have recovered from his resignation after the death of Rockingham (though many of his later misjudgments sprang from this foolhardy action); he might possibly have recovered from the obloquy of the coalition with North or, less convincingly, from the India bill; but taken in sequence these blunders added up to an indictment which was all the more telling because Fox's unusual ideas about the future working of the constitution were interpreted as the motivating force behind the most forbidding of his political activities, instead of an attempt to give some coherence to actions which owed more to the exigencies of politics than to any articulate political theory. Fox knew that the old style of opposition was doomed to failure unless he was willing to compromise himself by coming to terms with the government of the day, but however eloquently he pleaded the case for party politics and systematic opposition his own application of these ideas was insufficiently consistent for the depth of his own commitment to them and the likelihood of their being widely practised to be generally accepted.

Since the fall of North English politics had been blighted by a sequence of unstable and short-lived ministries. The explanation did not lie in any unconstitutional conduct on the part of the king, despite George III's tactics over the India bill, any more than the ministerial crises of the 1760s were the result of a determined attack by George III on the constitutional conventions of the day. Nor did anything approximating to the twentieth-century conception of party politics adversely prevent the collaboration of diverse associations of politicians. Though the members of every administration were divided about the merits of particular policies or obsessed by different aspects of current problems, none of these disagreements was insuperable. Dissension, or at least an agreement to differ except on the most fundamental issues of finance and foreign policy, was an inescapable accompaniment to government. The clash of personality was more important than ideological differences; within the enclosed world of high politics an incompatibility of temperament or an unforgiven personal affront were more difficult for a cabinet to surmount than a difference of opinion, however violent, on one of the transient problems which from time to time obtruded themselves on the attention of the government. Without the confidence which sprang from mutual respect, if not from affection or friendship, no administration could survive. Fox's behaviour had called his loyalty in question, and his impatience with what most men regarded as the normal and intelligent way to manage matters such as the appointment of ministers seemed a reflection of vaulting political ambition, rather than evidence of constitutional insight. By his alliance with North, Fox had made many men doubt his integrity, for his attacks on North over the influence of the crown (rather than the American war) had gone far beyond what was generally accepted as permissible. Even after the virtual abandonment of the policy of coercion in America Fox had been denouncing North as one of the chief agents of corruption in politics, yet if Fox was prepared to ally himself with North, instead of reaching a reconciliation with Shelburne, how valid had his original accusations been and how seriously had they been meant? Most men were sceptical about the threats of impeachment which coloured Fox's more extravagant statements; they were also dubious about the genuineness of some of Fox's other sweeping assaults on North. Could anyone, some members asked themselves, who behaved in such a fashion be worthy of the king's confidence? The patronage clauses of the India bill sapped Fox's credibility still further. There seemed to be one law for Fox in opposition, and another when he and his friends were in office.

Fox outraged his contemporaries more because he offended their susceptibilities as to the way they expected a politician to behave than because he gave expression to ideas which they did not understand. They distrusted his ideas, but they saw them as affording further proof that what they had thought of Fox all along was true, that he was temperamentally unfitted for the confidence of the house and unreliable in the stresses of political conflict. They did not see his ideas as clues to an understanding of his actions but as a confirmation of his feckless irresponsibility. That Fox was prepared to force himself on the king by allying with North, that he was willing to rob the East India company in order to maintain himself in office, were more decisive in antagonising backbenchers and country gentlemen in the house of commons and respectable dissenters outside it, than any of Fox's eloquent defences of party politics and a formed opposition. That such a theory could be held to condone conduct such as Fox's made it all the more untenable, and Fox himself all the more reprehensible as a raffish politician of immense gifts and dubious character who would stoop to anything in order to seize power. Worst of all was the feeling that he wanted power on his own terms, which amounted to demanding virtual dictatorial status for himself by denying the legitimate freedom of opinion and action which was thought indispensable within any administration which respected the intelligence and integrity of its members. Fox's practice was often as much in conflict with his theories as the expression of them, but it was his practice which antagonised his contemporaries and which discredited his constitutional innovations in their eyes, partly because his shady behaviour was widely believed to be the inevitable consequence of holding such outlandish notions in the first place. For Fox the tragedy was that however eloquently he might argue the advantages of party and the benefits of formed opposition his own behaviour was held to discredit such ideas, while the circumstances of the 1780s made it impossible to practise coherent party politics and a systematic opposition except in a fragmentary and intermittent sense.

6 *The Peacetime Opposition*

After the 1784 election Fox and his friends were under no illusions about the situation in which they found themselves. The recognition of their defeat and the unpopularity which accompanied it remained a vivid and painful memory for many years. Despite all their talk of a formed opposition they knew that for the foreseeable future there was little hope of their replacing Pitt. As long as the king's support continued unabated and as long as Pitt did nothing to offend the independent country gentlemen on any issue connected with the survival of his administration, the opposition could only trust that some wholly unexpected crisis, some freak of fortune, would arise to discredit the first minister. For all their sneers about a kingdom trusted to a schoolboy's care they had already experienced the bitter consequences of underestimating Pitt's abilities and courage. They hated Pitt as the author of their woes, as a renegade whig who, they fancifully told themselves, had made the king's triumph possible by deigning to become the tool of an intriguing monarch; but they could not deny, except at their own peril, his power over the house of commons and his judgment as a politician. They were rawly sensitive to the dire consequences of offending a major political interest, and although Fox took comfort in the thought that he had been wilfully misrepresented and abused by his enemies he was always careful throughout the 1780s to cultivate any interest which gave any indication of being antagonised by the policies of Pitt and his government.

Fox's own spirits fell during the summer and autumn of 1784. Bravely though he bore himself during the wrangles in the house of commons over the Westminster scrutiny he was despondent about the future and sceptical of the value of parliamentary opposition. Whenever Portland and his colleagues pleaded with him to attend the commons he took refuge in excuses about the hopelessness of the parliamentary situation, arguing that the majority of the house of commons were motivated by a dislike for himself and his friends rather than by any positive fondness for Pitt's administration. It would be better to stay away from the house at a time when he had only to open his mouth to make the ministry's proposals more palatable to many members regardless of their merits. He believed there was much to be gained by allowing MPs to become sick of their own folly, and although he applauded the skill which some of his colleagues, such as Sheridan, showed in exposing weaknesses in the government's case at every available opportunity he was often happy to let them carry the burden of opposing Pitt. When he was so reluctant to attend the house himself he did not wish to put any pressure upon his friends to go to the debates. He was not, so he explained to Portland on 27 July, arguing the case for anything amounting to a complete secession from the commons: he was prepared to attend on particular business if Portland thought it desirable for him to do so. Nevertheless,

I must say it will be as much against my opinion as my inclination. With respect to my inclination I know it ought to give way, but yet if anyone else had done all I have for the past eight months, and was as completely tired out with it body and mind as I am I believe he would think he had some right to consult it. I cannot express to you how fatigued I was with the last day's attendance, and how totally unequal I feel myself in point of spirits to acquit myself as I ought to do either for the good of the party or for my own reputation. However, I must submit to your judgment and to theirs if you persist in your opinion but I am sure you will not repent it if you will so far trust me as to believe that I know the house of commons as well and myself something better than those who differ from me. I am sure you will do me the justice to believe that, if it were nothing more than caprice or laziness that kept me here, your letter would have produced my immediate attendance in town instead of this long answer. Great injustice indeed is done to me if I am suspected of any want of zeal for the cause, but I *know* that, both on my own account and in consideration of the present state of the house, I can serve it better by lying by for a little while. . . .[1]

Fox was torn by a sense of loyalty to his colleagues and an anxious awareness of what the practice of party politics entailed. He was also deeply worried by a gloomy conviction of the hopelessness of the parliamentary outlook and offended by what he considered a lack of sympathy and understanding on the part of his political associates. They seemed to have little comprehension of the weight of responsibility which he had borne, the emotional exhaustion which the strain of the Westminster election and the enervating humiliation of defeat in the struggle for power had combined to produce. He sadly reflected that they expected him to soldier

on, month after month, year after year, regardless of the weariness of
spirit which afflicted him. After the depressing events of the spring he
had looked for more compassion and a greater patience on the part of
his friends, but few realised the toll which the political struggle had taken
of him. His friends were so used to his energy and brilliance in debate that
they took it all for granted. In his misery he resented their apparent expectation that he should continue to indulge in all the stratagems of
parliamentary warfare regardless of his physical tiredness, his mental
fatigue, and his agonised longing for a period of rest and relaxation. They
seemed to have no appreciation of all he had suffered, lightly assuming as
they did that he should throw off all the disappointments of the past eight
months to expose himself once more to the rigours of political campaigning. Fox was too shrewd not to grasp the full enormity of the predicament
in which the party found itself and too sensitive not to feel anguish and
frustration at the thought of an indefinite period of wearisome and futile
opposition. At least during the American war he had been sustained by
the thought that he was the champion of a free people and even during
the struggle with Pitt it was only towards the end that he had been
sickened by a growing realisation that defeat not victory might crown his
efforts. But now there seemed no great cause to fight for and Pitt was so
soundly entrenched in office that desperately to oppose him would only
add to the feeling of misery and purposeless endeavour.

Despite the theory of a formed opposition which Fox had so lucidly
expounded over a period of two or three years he knew that the theory
alone was insufficient to meet the demands of the contemporary situation.
A doctrine of systematic opposition implied some principle or attitude of
mind relevant to current political issues which could bind the opposition
together; it also implied that there was some possibility of the opposition
ousting the government, more or less comprehensively, and taking their
place collectively. Neither of these conditions was present in 1784. The
American war had created an apparent ideological unity among the
opposition groups, giving a common purpose to what was really a diverse
association of varied political factions; from time to time, such as in the
winter of 1779-80, and the months after the surrender at Yorktown, the
whigs could reasonably hope that North's nerve would break and a far-
reaching change of government implemented. Rockingham had been able
to insist on a virtually complete change of ministers. But the war had
been an exceptional instance, and such circumstances were unlikely to be
repeated. The vocabulary of party was certain to prove sterile in peacetime conditions. Though it clothed opposition with some semblance of
dignity and though it soothed the feelings and kept up the spirits of the

more naïve of those engaged in opposition, it would also revive fears of storming the closet, of wilfully perpetuating a purely factious opposition for reasons of personal ambition, and of conspiring to deny to the government that fair hearing, and that chance to justify itself in practice, which were so fundamental to the proper working of the constitution. Fox was all too conscious of these disturbing considerations. He was impatient with the failures of his colleagues to perceive the extent to which the political situation had been transformed and the significance which this carried for the conduct of parliamentary opposition.

His depression of spirit was temporary but the problem of how he and his friends were to act in opposition to Pitt remained throughout the 1780s, and it was never adequately solved. Once the French revolution had broken out the means by which Fox and his friends were to challenge Pitt were more obvious, though still beset with frustration. In any case the resemblance which Fox's opposition to the French war bore to his opposition to the American war was deceptive, and the greater consistency of opposition in the 1790s was gained at the price of losing the more conservative whigs who followed Burke, Portland and Fitzwilliam in giving varying degrees of support to Pitt in the struggle against the French republic. Ironically, throughout Pitt's peacetime ministry, Fox's direction of the parliamentary opposition was reminiscent of the old techniques of opposition going back to the days of Walpole and Chatham. Yet to be fully effective the traditional notion of opposition depended on a willingness among the opposition leaders to come to terms with the ministry, and on the ministry being equally prepared to admit at least some of the opposition leaders to office. If both of these attitudes were conspicuously absent old-style opposition was destined to be as futile as new-style opposition. Pitt was always willing to give a fair share of cabinet posts to those whigs who were prepared to join the administration, but he would never step down as first minister, and this was, for Fox, the first requirement of any significant negotiation.

Fox's leadership was often casual; he neglected to consult his colleagues, and his enthusiasm for the job was always fitful. Sometimes he would burst forth in a moment of excessive optimism, at other times he sank to the depths of bored pessimism and exasperated disgust. He left the organisational side of political activity to Portland (later this was William Adam's major responsibility), but though his friends criticised his bouts of lethargy and indifference they nevertheless still regarded him as the spiritual leader of the party. Fox was even driven to rely on a revival of the old reversionary interest. Knowing as he did that George III's hostility was absolute and immovable, Fox came to rely more and more upon the favour of the prince of Wales as holding out the most likely hope of any entry into office in the foreseeable future. This depended on the death of George III but by the mid-1780s the king had already been on the throne for a quarter of a century and though he was only in middle age no one expected him to survive for almost another forty years. It might do some good and it seemed unlikely to do much harm for Fox to make sure that the future George IV would be well disposed towards the opposition whigs. Yet the influence of the prince was often disruptive and during the incapacity of the king in 1788-9 the opposition's reliance on the heir apparent tempted them into making political misjudgments of the first magnitude.

The prince of Wales and Fox shared their pleasures as well as their politics. Both enjoyed gambling and horse-racing, the company of witty and beautiful women, glittering banquets in the ostentatious luxury of Carlton House. George III's hatred of Fox owed as much to his conviction that he had led his eldest son astray by pandering to his feckless delight in all the colourful excesses of high living, as to his loathing for Fox on political grounds. But it is important not to exaggerate the intimacy of Fox's friendship with the prince or the intensity of the emotional bond between them. They were closest during the early 1780s. Once Fox had settled down to enjoy the domestic peace of St Anne's Hill with Mrs Armistead he became less interested in being one of the prince's boon companions. Nor was the prince always honest and open with Fox. He deceived Fox with as much impunity as he outraged his father. That political circumstances compelled him to seek the approval of the prince was often galling for Fox. He knew that his political future, as well as his private reputation, was at the mercy of the prince, who himself was often swayed by violent emotions and passionate whims.

The secret and doubly illegal marriage of the prince of Wales to Mrs Fitzherbert was an example of the way in which the prince deceived Fox with a selfish indifference to the consequences for Fox's political prospects and disregarded Fox's advice whenever it suited him to do so. Fox was angry over the affair for he was made to appear foolish and ignorant, if not a downright liar, in the commons. The Fitzherbert episode afforded ample opportunities for Fox's enemies to embarrass him by probing into the dubious recesses of the prince's private life.

Mrs Fitzherbert was an attractive and intelligent widow, with whom the prince of Wales had fallen head over heels in love. But she was also a woman of character and integrity and she had no wish to become another of the prince's mistresses. If he wished to enjoy her favours she insisted that he should marry her. This George Augustus was willing to do, but there were several obstacles to the union. The royal marriages act (which Fox had always steadily opposed as a thoroughly obnoxious measure) made it impossible for the prince to contract a legal marriage without his father's consent, and since it was assumed that the prince would, in the fullness of time, marry some princess whom convention deemed as appropriate, there was no hope that the king would condone his son's marriage with a woman who was a commoner and a widow, no matter how respectable. Nor was this all. Mrs Fitzherbert was a devout catholic and under the terms of the act of settlement the prince was forbidden to marry a catholic under the penalty of losing his right to the crown and of becoming legally dead so far as his status as a member of the royal family was concerned. George III would have been so infuriated at the thought that his son could consider abandoning his duties in order to marry a catholic that even the merest whisper of such a possibility had to be kept from him. But Mrs Fitzherbert refused to cohabit with the prince unless the union was blessed by the church. The prince protested his undying affection and fidelity; he even sought to commit suicide by the not very effective application of a penknife to his ample person, trying to convince Mrs Fitzherbert of the intensity of his devotion as he writhed on the floor. She sought to escape from these embarrassing attentions by leaving the country. But she was attracted to the prince and however determined she was not to become his mistress she longed to prove her own love for him by becoming his wife. She was motivated throughout by more than mere convention. She was prepared to defy the slanders of respectable society if she could be united with the prince in a fashion which would be valid in the sight of heaven if not of the law. She learned that a religious form of marriage would be held binding in the eyes of the church whatever its status in the law of the land. Meanwhile the prince's infatuation was unabated and rumours about his relationship with Mrs Fitzherbert were eagerly spread abroad by those whose sense of morality fed gleefully on the lapses of others. Was the prince married to Mrs Fitzherbert? Was she his mistress? What would be the position of any children born to them? Would parliament invoke the terms of the act of settlement? Would exceptional legislation cover the prince's case? These were the questions which were bandied to and fro at all levels of society. Rumours stimulated a prurient interest in the affairs of the prince of Wales.

Fox could not ignore them; he had hoped that the prince would be a political asset but in a situation such as this he was a liability. Though Fox knew that Pitt was as reluctant as himself to take any formal action with respect to the prince he fully appreciated that if the prince behaved in a sufficiently outrageous manner the government might be compelled to take some legal action against him, possibly against its own inclinations. It was pointless for the opposition to identify itself with the heir to the throne if the prince persisted in behaving in such a way as to court personal catastrophe for himself and political disaster for his friends. On 10 December 1785 Fox felt compelled to write to the prince warning him of the dangers he was risking. He did so with considerable reluctance, particularly since he knew that what he had to say would not be agreeable to the prince. But he showed considerable sympathy for the prince in dealing with the persistent rumours that he intended to marry Mrs Fitzherbert:

> I was told just before I left town yesterday that Mrs Fitzherbert was arrived, and if I had heard only this, I should have felt most unfeigned joy at an event which I knew would contribute so much to your royal highness's satisfaction: but I was told at the same time, that from a variety of circumstances ... there was reason to suppose that you were going to take the very desperate step (pardon the expression) of marrying her at this moment. If such an idea be really in your mind, and it is not too late, for God's sake let me call your attention to some considerations, which my attachment to your royal highness, and the real concern that I take in whatever relates to your interest, have suggested to me, and which may possibly have the more weight with you when you perceive that Mrs Fitzherbert is equally interested in most of them with yourself.

Fox reminded the Prince that marriage with a catholic would eliminate him from succeeding to the throne. He drew his attention to the king's feelings of antagonism towards him, to George III's well-known preference for the duke of York as his favourite son, and to the nation's long-standing prejudice against catholics. There was a widespread anxiety about any dispute over the succession to the crown. In such circumstances the prince's enemies would take such advantages that Fox shuddered to think of them. Nor should the prince overlook Mrs Fitzherbert's feelings if a marriage took place and precipitated a political crisis: 'though your generosity might think no sacrifice too great to be made to the person whom you love so entirely, consider what her reflections must be in such an event, and how impossible it would be for her ever to forgive herself.' Fox was not closely acquainted with Mrs Fitzherbert but he knew her character to be irreproachable and her manners amiable.

The marriage could not be recognised in law but Fox begged the prince to remember what a source of uneasiness it would be to have constant discussion and dispute as to whether the prince of Wales was married or not.

If men's minds were in a state of perpetual agitation a greater ferment would be provoked than in any other situation. If there were children from an illegal marriage speculation and anxiety would be aggravated and once they came about these mischiefs could not be remedied. The prince would never be able to undo the damage; he would have to live with the consequences of a single thoughtless or hasty action for the rest of his life.

Furthermore, Fox asked, what would be the position when the prince came to marry—as the nation expected him to do—some designated princess in order to provide for the succession to the throne?

> For, if your royal highness should think proper, when you are twenty-five years old, to testify to parliament your intention to marry (by which means alone a legal marriage can be contracted) in what manner can it be notified? If the previous marriage is sanctioned or owned, will it not be said that you have set at defiance the laws of your country, and that you now come to parliament for a sanction to what you have already done in contempt of it? If there are children, will it not be said that we must look for future applications to legitimate them, and consequently be liable to disputes for the succession between the eldest son, and the eldest son after legal marriage? And will not the entire annulling of the whole marriage be suggested as the most secure way of preventing all such disputes? If the marriage is not mentioned to parliament, but yet is known to have been solemnised ... these are the consequences: *first*, that any child born in the interim is immediately illegitimated; and *next*, that arguments will be drawn from the circumstance of the concealed marriage against the public one.

Fox argued that the complications flowing from an illegal marriage were endless, and he confined himself to the discussion of only the more important aspects of the problem. He was conscious of the freedom with which he had written to the prince. On any other occasion he would have felt it unbecoming, but he was compelled to write as he had done by his deep sense of duty to the prince, who would have had but an ill return for all his goodness to Fox had he avoided speaking the truth to him, however disagreeable this might seem at so critical a juncture. The sum of Fox's advice and earnest entreaties was that the prince should not think of marrying until he could do so legally: 'Under the present circumstances marriage appears to me to be the most desperate measure for all the parties concerned that their worst enemies could have suggested.'[2] He had written as a man who did not share many of the conventional prejudices of the day against princes marrying commoners, but he believed it the height of folly to defy the law and play into the hands of the prince's political enemies.

The prince's reply was prompt and engaging. He dashed off a brief note in the early hours of Sunday morning, 11 December 1785, addressing himself in apparently cordial fashion to his 'dear Charles':

> Your letter of last night afforded me more true satisfaction than I can find words to express, as it is an additional proof to me, which I assure you I did not want, of your having that true regard and affection for me, which is not only the wish but the ambition of my life to inherit. Make yourself easy, my dear friend; believe me the world will now soon be convinced that there not only is, but never was, any ground for these reports which of late have so malevolently been circulated.[3]

After this bright reassurance he went on to refer in passing to Eden's desertion to the ministry, possibly in a naïve attempt to divert Fox's attention from the principal matter under discussion. On the face of things all was well. Fox had been given the most direct disavowal of the rumoured marriage that it was possible for him to desire. Of course, with hindsight, he could later see a deliberate ambiguity in the prince's words, but in the circumstances there was no doubt what the prince intended Fox to believe. He could hardly have been expected to read the prince's letter with his eyes open for excessive subtlety, deducing the worst from the absence of any reference to future intent as distinct from past behaviour and present conduct. Fox was left in the dark about the prince's intentions and he was to remain ignorant of the prince's secret marriage to Mrs Fitzherbert for some considerable time. Within ten days of his letter to Fox the prince married Mrs Fitzherbert according to the Anglican rite. Later, when Rolle raised the prince's marital state in the commons, Fox was confident enough firmly to deny the Fitzherbert marriage. This earned him the undying dislike of Mrs Fitzherbert, who deeply resented what she interpreted as a deliberate and heartless slur on her reputation. It also helped to ingratiate Sheridan with the prince, since Sheridan undertook the thankless task of saying something in the commons to mollify Mrs Fitzherbert's outraged feelings without actually confirming the rumours which had prodded Rolle into action. For a year after this incident Fox and the prince were on distant terms. Fox was justifiably indignant at being deceived by one whom he had tried to save from the consequences of his own folly. He had sought to put the prince's confidence to a worthy public purpose; he had been rewarded for his thoughtfulness and sympathy by duplicity and treachery.

It was an embarrassing reminder of the weaknesses inherent in any political dependence on the prince of Wales. Yet such were the relentless pressures of politics that Fox was driven to make up his quarrel with the prince. They were never again as close as they had been in the early 1780s, however, and sadly for Fox his political reliance upon the prince contributed to his discomfiture during the regency crisis of 1788. That Fox was compelled to revive the reversionary interest as a factor in politics is an indication of how inadequate his theories of party were in the creation of a systematic opposition to Pitt's peacetime administration. When the crude realities demanded it Fox's attitude approximated to more conventional approaches to the problems of conducting opposition with some shadow of purpose and credibility. Fox was imprisoned in a situation in which the conditions for the successful application of old techniques were absent (though had he been more open to the possibility of accepting office under Pitt this might not have been so) and which still militated against the application of new ideas of a formed opposition. Fox's intermittent regard for party consistency and his stubborn fidelity to what he had persuaded himself was the Rockinghamite ideal only contributed towards his continuing frustration within the old pattern of politics without bringing him any nearer to the creation of a new pattern.

The issues on which opinion within the house of commons was divided during Pitt's peacetime ministry were not those on which a neo-ideological opposition could successfully be built. Divided counsels were as prevalent on the opposition side of the house as within the cabinet and with the possible exception of free trade with Ireland the subjects on which Pitt was thwarted in the commons were not ones which brought collective comfort to the opposition.

Pitt had pledged himself both as a man and a minister to honour his promises to the Reverend Christopher Wyvill and the other reformers by introducing a measure of parliamentary reform. But opinion within the cabinet was divided and it was therefore impossible for Pitt to put forward his proposals as a government bill. At one stage Pitt had been encouraged by the knowledge that the king would not give any public indication of his opposition to a measure of reform, and the prospect of a silent neutrality on the part of George III had buoyed up Pitt's spirits, possibly excessively so, since he found opposition among the more conservative members of his government unrelenting and immovable. Pitt was also conscious of the need to allay the fears and suspicions of the independents within the commons. The controversy over Fox's India bill had alerted men to the issue of charter rights and the security of property. For many backbenchers the disfranchisement of even the worst rotten boroughs looked ominously like an invasion of property and charter rights. With the furore over the India bill in his mind Pitt carefully framed his resolutions so as to respect property. He wanted to disfranchise thirty-six of the most decayed boroughs, redistributing the seats to the more populous counties and boroughs such as London. A million pounds were to be set aside to compensate the boroughmongers, and by allowing boroughs to be disfranchised on a petition signed by two-thirds of their electors Pitt was hoping to establish a precedent which would make regular purification of the electoral system possible with the least fuss and controversy. He also favoured adding copyholders to the electorates in the counties, arguing that the acquisition of these new voters would give fresh energy and conviction to the traditional pattern of representation.

Fox favoured reform in principle, but he was sceptical of anything emanating from Pitt, while certain aspects of Pitt's proposals filled him with misgiving. Because his own side of the house was as divided as the government on the issue of parliamentary reform he could afford to examine Pitt's proposals on their merits. Nothing could shake his fidelity to the principle of reform, however hesitant he was about the particular means being adopted to put the principle into effect. In spite of his doubts he gave general support to Pitt's proposals, but he was careful to make clear where he differed from him. He even took the opportunity of defending the cohesion of parties—which had been criticised by some of the speakers in the debate—claiming that the country had derived too many benefits from party for him to be an enemy to it. He could not refrain from alleging that Pitt's present resolutions marked a retreat from some of his earlier statements on parliamentary reform. Pitt was too anxious to meet the charge of innovation by moderating his proposals; far from being ashamed of innovation Fox gloried in it, though his own use of the term was not entirely free from a subtle ambivalence:

From the earliest periods of our government, the principle of innovation, but which should more properly be called amendment, was neither more nor less than the practice of the constitution. In every species of government (putting absolute monarchy out of the question, as one which ought never to exist in any country) democracy and aristocracy were always in a state of gradual improvement, when experience came to the aid of theory and speculation. In all these, the voice of the people, when deliberately and generally collected, was invariably sure to succeed. There were moments of periodical impulse and delusion, in which they should not be gratified, but when the views of a people had been formed and determined on the attainment of any object, they must ultimately succeed. On this subject the people of this country had petitioned from time to time, and their applications were made to their parliament. For every reason, therefore, they should be gratified, lest they should be inclined to sue for redress in another quarter, where their application would have every possibility of success, from the experience of the last year. Failing in their representatives, they might have recourse to prerogative.

Fox's reference to prerogative was more in the nature of an allegation about the origins of Pitt's elevation to the head of government and the explanation of his success in the general election than a contribution to debate. He knew that there was little chance of George III personally exerting himself to ensure the passage of a measure of reform. The warning not to ignore legitimate requests from the people for timely reforms was a familiar argument which Fox had made good use of before when pleading for the reform of parliament. Ironically he was doubtful of the wisdom of allowing the present parliament to run its course before any reforms in the constituencies took effect. He approved of the proposal to purify the borough representation and to increase the number of county MPs but despite his respect for the house of commons he could find no good reason in either the 'superlative excellence' or the 'just superiority' of the present house for postponing the operation of the proposed reforms. Many MPs must have smiled at this; obviously Fox had hoped to do rather better in new elections with the worst of the rotten boroughs abolished than he had done in 1784. There was little basis for this optimism, since he and his friends had fared very badly in the open constituencies. Furthermore, when members recalled Fox's warnings against a premature dissolution of parliament only a year before they sensed that he had preferred the dubious advantage of making a debating point to preserving any semblance of consistency. Had he forgotten his warnings against the influence of the crown in a general election? Or was the prospect of fighting on in the current house of commons so dismal that he was willing to clutch at any straw in order to resolve his difficulties?

His support for the principle of reform meant that he would not vote against Pitt's resolutions but Fox severely criticised the details of Pitt's proposals, which were sufficiently objectionable for him to hope that they would be modified and amended in committee. He objected to the proposal to compensate the boroughmongers; he could not agree that it was right to purchase from a majority of electors those privileges which were the property of the whole. In this he saw so much injustice and so much that was repugnant to the spirit of the constitution that he refused to

entertain the idea for a moment. Where the franchises in a particular
borough had been acquired by one man he did not think that the compensation offered would be effective in reconciling the individual to the
justice of being deprived of his property. Of course Fox was having it
both ways: it was easy to argue that Pitt's proposals were wrong in principle and unworkable in practice. Fox made no suggestion as to how the
most objectionable boroughs could be disfranchised while respecting the
convictions of those who believed that such a step was an unfair interference with their property rights or charter privileges. Instead of coming
down to practicalities he was content to talk in generalities:

> There was something injurious in holding out pecuniary temptations to
> an Englishman to relinquish his franchise on the one hand, and a
> political principle which equally forbade it on another. He was uni-
> formly of an opinion, which, though not a popular one, he was ready
> to aver, that the right of governing was not a property, but a trust; and
> that whatever was given for constitutional purposes, should be resumed
> when those purposes should no longer be carried into effect.

He could not resist a particular gibe at those supporters of the government
who were aiding the king's first minister in his attempts, however fumbling and confused, to reform the system of representation. He claimed to
be surprised that none of the administration's boroughmongers had come
forward, offering to make a personal sacrifice for the public good. With
some sarcasm he referred to those whom the government had 'loaded with
honours' and whose connexion with the ministry had excited 'an expectation of something more liberal than a procedure by mere bargain and sale'.
He was averse to limiting parliamentary ambitions to men of large fortunes, or to those who had distinguished themselves in public professions.
If this should come about 'there was scarcely any man so little acquainted
with the history of parliament as not to know that the house would
lose half its force. It was not from men of large and easy fortunes, that
attention, vigilance, energy, and enterprise were to be expected.'[4]

Pitt's motion was defeated by 248 votes to 174, a respectably large, possibly surprisingly good, vote for the minority but still a comfortable victory
for those opposed to reform. Fox probably realised that there was little
hope for the resolutions to pass; perhaps he was therefore content to limit
his response to criticisms of Pitt's proposals and affirmations of general
principle. But there was nothing in Fox's speech to convince doubters of
the wisdom or urgency of supporting Pitt's reforms, and in the state of
current opinion there was every possibility that if Pitt's attempt at reform
failed there would be no serious opportunity for the reformers to renew

their efforts with any chance of success within the lifetime of the existing parliament. Had opinion among the opposition whigs been more united perhaps there would have been greater interest in supporting Pitt's proposals, in order to ensure that at least some degree of reform was achieved, with every effort being made to amend them in committee where this was thought necessary. But Fox spoke as a man who was more concerned with the preservation of his reputation than with the passage of an effective piece of reform, however limited in scope. Fox could not stomach the thought of Pitt gaining the credit for reforming parliament. He could not bring himself to believe in Pitt's sincerity or to concede the practical necessity for Pitt to make some attempt to come to terms with contemporary prejudices if any measure of reform was to get through parliament. Fox sometimes talked as if it was possible to ignore the house of lords; Pitt never made the same mistake. Fox assumed that the king could always be browbeaten into submission; Pitt was never forgetful of the king's attitude towards government bills. Fox's language may have had more in common with that of later reformers, though it was still more traditional in inspiration than many men realised, but Pitt was the more seriously engaged in the problem of attaining parliamentary reform as an exercise in practical politics. But since rhetoric has a more glamorous appeal than the intricate negotiations of politics Fox's reputation as a reformer has been less tarnished than Pitt's. Since Fox was more preoccupied than Pitt with reputation the outcome is not without a certain bizarre logic, though it has hardly been just. All too often Fox has been glibly misrepresented as a Victorian reformer born half a century too soon, which in the light of any close study of Fox's career is not a little ridiculous.

Because parliamentary reform proved to be one of the major legislative interests of the nineteenth century it was assumed that late eighteenth-century politicians should have made it one of their dominant concerns. But this is to impose a false set of values upon the evaluation of the earlier period. Pitt and Fox were much less ideological in their approach to the reform of parliament than Victorian radicals or many historians. They were content to work within the pattern of political attitudes which they had inherited, and though they were convinced of the wisdom and utility of reforming parliament they did not give priority to any legislative project in their assessment of political objectives. They wanted to purify the system of representation and to ensure that all interests within the community were adequately represented; they wished to strengthen the people's confidence in their political institutions. But nothing was further from their minds than to challenge the supremacy of the landed interest or to suggest that the dominance of mere numbers was either desirable or practicable. When Fox disclaimed that 'theoretical speculation' formed any part of his advocacy of reform he meant his words to be taken literally. It was not that he was devoid of ideas or that he had no overall comprehension of the issues involved; it was simply that his primary concerns were those of a politician not a theorist. He knew which improvements were beneficial but he never lost sight of the circumstances limiting the range of any reforms and far from wanting to destroy the traditional representative system he sincerely believed that the reforms which he advocated were faithful to the spirit and helpful to the practice of the constitution. Fox was never prepared to subordinate the legitimate aims of a practising politician to the visionary abstractions of an ideologue. He saw the reform of parliament as an intelligent adjustment of the balance of interests within the traditional system, not a rejection of the pattern of representation which had evolved throughout the country's history and which, whatever its imperfections, had been proved by experience. Fox was too good a house of commons man not to be at home in the familiar parliamentary atmosphere; he found the parliamentary climate too congenial to be attracted to anything which would undermine the prestige or weaken the predominance of the house of commons.

The conventional cast of much of Fox's thinking was fully revealed during the controversy over Pitt's attempt to secure a measure of free trade with Ireland in 1785. Pitt was anxious to find some way of ameliorating the tense and ominous situation in Ireland and since the recent concession of legislative independence had not of itself healed the bitter divisions in Irish society Pitt became increasingly interested in seeking to win the confidence of the Irish by stimulating trade between Britain and Ireland. Influenced as he was by the free trade ideas of Adam Smith and possibly also by the way in which the commercial benefits which had been so much in evidence in Scotland since the union of 1707 had contributed to better Anglo-Scottish relations Pitt sought to generate Irish prosperity by freeing Anglo-Irish trade from some of the old-fashioned restrictions which still cramped it. The policy was doubly attractive: it would fit in nicely with his general economic and fiscal reforms and it would probably contribute to that reconciliation with Ireland on which he had set his heart. But when Pitt brought forward his proposals he was met with a storm of abuse and criticism. Old fears of Irish competition and anxieties at the prospect of the Irish sharing more fully in the commercial advantages of empire, inspired a wave of fierce and ill-informed invective. Pitt had wanted to allow foreign and colonial products to pass between Britain and Ireland without any increase in duty; he also recommended that British and Irish produce and manufactures should be imported either at the lower of the customs duties already in force, or in some cases free of duty altogether, and that obsolete prohibitions on commerce between Britain and Ireland should be scrapped. He was conscious that some compensation and security would be demanded, and he therefore suggested that whenever Irish revenue exceeded £656,000 a year the surplus should be used for the maintenance of the navy, though this latter proposal was very unpopular in Dublin.

Fox avidly seized the opportunity to embarrass the government. The prospect of gaining support from the commercial and business community was particularly satisfying after his own experience of what the hostility of the East India company could mean. The thought that Pitt might well have committed an act of folly comparable in its political consequences with his own India bill flickered in Fox's mind. Ill-equipped as he was to grasp the more subtle aspects of the government's economic policy Fox knew that the majority of backbenchers shared his own distaste for new-fangled economic theories. He dreamed of a double attack on the government: the one mounted by his friends in Dublin, the other by himself at Westminster. There was a certain paradox here, if not a deliberate hypocrisy, for while Irish critics argued that the proposed commercial concessions did not go far enough in accepting full equality between Britain and Ireland, the government's opponents in England maintained that Pitt was giving too much away. Fox shamelessly exploited every prejudice in his attack on Pitt's proposals, using language about Irish competition which was calculated to appeal to the most extreme advocates of a monopolistic view of trade. He was even prepared to do his best to stimulate renewed fears for the security of charter rights and to step boldly forward as the defender of the navigation acts. Every available argument, logical or illogical, fair or unfair, rational or irrational, was pressed into service. Fox sought throughout, not merely to whip up opposition to the government's policy within the commons, but also to place himself at the head of the growing movement of agitation and protest in the country.

His speech in the commons on 12 May was a typical example of the arguments which he used and the emotions which he was determined to arouse. He claimed that Pitt's original resolutions (for Pitt was already modifying his proposals because of the hostility which they had provoked) would have meant that Britain would lose forever her monopoly of the East India trade. He even went so far as to assert that the charter of the East India company would depend on Irish whims and fancies for its renewal. If Pitt had his way the duty raised from imported spirits would probably vanish completely, while the navigation laws, described by Fox as 'the great source of our commercial opulence, the prime origin of our maritime strength', would be 'delivered up in trust to Ireland, leaving us forever after totally dependent on her policy, and on her bounty, for the future guardianship of our dearest interests'. He was incapable of realising or admitting that Britain and Ireland might have a common interest in stimulating trade to their mutual benefit; for partisan political purposes he fanned the flames of jealousy, suspicion, and fear. He claimed that Pitt was about to open 'the door to a more extensive contraband trade than ever yet was known to exist in this country, for not a shadow of protection was provided against every species of smuggling, not even the means which we think it necessary to use in our own traffic from port to port—that of requiring bonds, cockets, and other instruments on goods sent coastwise'. Fox foresaw a danger that the colonial market would be lost to the manufacturers of Great Britain; no care had been taken to prevent the Irish from giving bounties on goods exported to the colonies. The Irish were to be left with the power to give such decisive 'advantages' to their own manufacturers as would either ensure their domination of the colonial market or force Britain to compete by similar inducements on such a scale as would bankrupt the British exchequer and ruin the British economy. Fox argued that these dangers threatened the colonies just as much as they did Britain for the securities normally afforded by the levying of customs duties were being taken away. Unlike Britain Ireland had no obligations towards the overseas dependencies of the British crown:

> Not a single provision was stipulated for laying permanent high duties on the produce of foreign colonies imported into Ireland; so that, at any future time, Ireland might have taken off the annual high duties and given admission to the produce of foreign colonies on terms which must completely have ruined our West Indian islands. I need not state ... a fact as universally known as that the produce of our colonies is dearer than that of the foreign islands. But we have nevertheless preferred the home market, on account of the natural interest which we have in them: and undoubtedly we must continue to do so. Ireland has no such obligation: on the contrary her interest would as forcibly lead her to the foreign colonies.[5]

Fox saw the government's proposals as 'irretrievably' binding Britain to keep her part of the bargain, whereas Ireland would not be similarly bound to keep hers. It was even possible that the Irish would lay an internal duty on goods before they were exported to Britain for British consumption, and the effect of this would be for the Irish to exploit the domestic market in an unfair way. Fox gave an example of the possibility he had in mind: while Britain was bound to send oak bark to Ireland duty-free, the Irish were not bound to prohibit the exportation of raw hides to Great Britain, thus laying the British leather trade open to dangerous competition.

Reasoning such as this was often confused and perverse. It wilfully linked diverse aspects of the government's proposals in a highly misleading way and its forecasts of the likely consequences of free trade with Ireland were more symptomatic of Fox's own difficulties in understanding commercial matters than related to any objective examination of what Pitt was putting forward. Fox knew that many men feared free trade, preferring to rely on monopolies to give them a secure profit. He knew that the notion of commerce as something akin to war died hard and he fully appreciated the unique degree of distrust which any suggestion of commercial parity between Britain and Ireland aroused. Most important of all he sensed the opportunity of humiliating Pitt, possibly even of driving him from office if a sufficient crisis of confidence could be precipitated inside the house of commons and throughout the country, and this political objective took precedence over any regard for the merits of commercial reciprocity. But although Fox was grossly unfair to what Pitt was seeking to achieve he did not violate his own assumptions concerning the control of trade. The fondness which he revealed for the navigation acts might have been little more than a colourful piece of exaggeration, but he was nevertheless fundamentally conservative in his thinking about the management of the colonial system. Whatever he might have said during the American war he had never denied the right of the British government to control the trade of the empire in the interests of the whole. Pitt's Irish proposals seemed to Fox to be an abandonment of this primary duty. In the heat of the controversy and inspired by the opportunity to wreak some degree of vengeance upon Pitt Fox forgot the liberality of sentiment which had once characterised his attitude towards Ireland. Despite his avowal, 'I will not barter English commerce for Irish slavery!', Fox ruthlessly and irresponsibly exploited anti-Irish prejudice in England and instead of exorcising old hatreds he made political capital out of them.

Tactically the campaign against Pitt's Irish propositions was a success. In towns such as Bristol, Manchester, Paisley, and Glasgow addresses were voted against the government's proposals. Although Pitt made concessions to protect the monopoly of the East India company, to apply the navigation acts in Ireland, and to ensure that the Irish parliament would enact all legislation passed at Westminster regulating trade between the two countries, he failed to meet his critics' requirements. The concessions he made only heightened hopes among his opponents that a determined continuation of the struggle would bring about the abandonment of the free trade resolutions, while in Ireland the Dublin parliament saw in the provision concerning commercial legislation an ominous invasion of its recently won legislative independence. With mounting opposition in London, and increasing misgivings in Dublin, adding weight to the arguments of those ministers counselling the tactful dropping of the commercial resolutions, Pitt finally allowed the matter to rest when it was clear that his modified proposals had outraged Irish susceptibilities without soothing English anxieties.

Fox took pride in his undeniable success. He had the satisfaction of forcing Pitt to climb down and he had the pleasant experience of renewed popularity, even among those who had previously been antagonistic towards him. It was with considerable gratification that he told Mrs Armistead of a great meeting of opponents of the Irish resolutions at Manchester. Writing to his mistress on 10 September he cheerfully commented:

> Our reception at Manchester was the finest thing imaginable, and handsome in all respects. All the principal people came out to meet us, and attended us into the town with blue and buff cockades, and a procession as fine, and not unlike, that upon my chairing at Westminster. We dined with 150 people; and Mr Walker (one of their principal men, who was in London last year on their business), before he gave me as a toast, made them a speech, in which he told them, they knew how prejudiced he had been for Pitt and against the India bill; but that in the course of his business in town he had occasion to know both Pitt and me, and found how much he had been mistaken in both; that it was the part of honest men, when they found they had been wrong, to set themselves right as soon as possible ... ; all which was echoed by the whole room in the most cordial manner. You must allow this was very handsome. The concourse of people to see us was immense; and I never saw more apparent unanimity than seemed to be in our favour; and all this in the town of Manchester, which used to be reckoned the worst place for us in the whole country.[6]

Nevertheless, although one of Pitt's most far-sighted policies had been thwarted, the ministry was as firmly entrenched in office as ever. Whatever Mr Walker of Manchester might say few of those who worked for the defeat of free trade with Ireland were eager to transfer their political allegiance to Fox. Despite their misgivings about Pitt's Irish policy the business community had no wish to see a change of government. Furthermore Pitt's political touch had not left him. Bitterly though he regretted it, he saw the need first to try to meet the charges of his critics by modifying his proposals, in the hope that by doing so he would be able to commend them to that broad combination of interests on which he depended for his support, and secondly to abandon the proposals altogether when he failed to achieve this objective. Because Pitt was able to isolate the discussion of his Irish propositions from the wider issue of confidence in his government it was impossible for Fox to gain any strategic advantage from his tactical victory. In general Pitt's policy of administrative and economic reform, the pruning of customs duties and the simplification of taxation, commended itself to the majority of his contemporaries. They therefore saw the Irish controversy as evidence only of a temporary aberration, a passing error of judgment, which did not in any sense justify withdrawing their support from Pitt's government. It was no surprise that Fox made entertaining and lively speeches denouncing free trade with Ireland; his verbal dexterity was sufficiently well known for this to cause no undue concern. But it was one thing to accept Fox's assistance in parliament if only to obstruct one reprehensible piece of government policy; it was quite another to allow one controversy to tempt one into risking a new government dominated by Fox. Many businessmen preferred to utilise Fox for their own purposes, rather than permitting him to exploit them for his. However much they admired his gifts and valued his cooperation they were cautious of anything savouring of a permanent alliance. They could not perceive any sufficiently stable bond of interest between Fox and themselves to make a change of political allegiance worthwhile.

Consequently a real though limited victory reminded Fox of the limitations of opposition. He was striving to blend old and new techniques of opposition into a harmonious whole, but with little success. It was traditional for an opposition leader to challenge the government on controversial policies, especially where trade and finance were involved, and where a significant interest believed itself to be seriously threatened. It was not unusual for governments to concede defeat over such issues, but it was rare for such an episode to lead to a change of government. The most that could be hoped for in such circumstances was a political negotiation by which the opposition leaders could be accommodated within the ministry. But the conditions for such a broadening of the ministry were conspicuously absent in 1785. To wring any tangible political advantage out of the reverse which he had inflicted upon the government Fox had to be willing to accept office under Pitt. This he was manifestly unprepared to do, yet this was the most he could reasonably hope for, since there was never any possibility of Pitt losing his nerve and offering his own resignation to the king. By looking for the impossible Fox threw away any chance of emerging from the shadows of opposition. He could hardly hope to achieve anything as dramatic as the collapse of the government by falling back on traditional methods of opposition which depended for their complete success on the acceptance of conventions which he claimed to have rejected. Yet he had been driven to adopt old-fashioned styles of opposition because most men abhorred his newer concept of opposition based on party as a departure from the spirit of the constitution. This ebb and flow on Fox's part, this tendency to oscillate bewilderingly between incompatible ideas of how to conduct a parliamentary opposition, were recurrent themes throughout the long years he spent vainly seeking for a means of discrediting Pitt and entering office on his own terms. Although Fox often reverted, in theory at least, to the cult of party and the advocacy of a formed opposition, he was incapable of getting these ideas fully and consistently accepted even within his own party, and he was certainly guilty, whenever the political situation prompted him to do so, of abandoning the practice of those ideas he so often praised, attempting instead to salvage his political fortunes by desperately exploiting devices which directly conflicted with the theory and the practice of a formed opposition based on the stability of party. The Irish controversy was especially tempting in this respect, for it was bound up with the sort of interests which Fox believed he could successfully exploit in order to inflict a reverse upon the government and with the financial and economic complexities with which Fox felt least at ease. To compensate for his inability to master the intricacies of Pitt's fiscal policies by a dazzling collaboration with those commercial interests which had formerly staunchly supported Pitt was an irresistible temptation which Fox succumbed to with alacrity.

Despite his boredom with fiscal theories and the baffling speculations of economists Fox's opposition to Pitt's free trade treaty with France was inspired as much by a preoccupation with foreign policy as by his dislike for new methods of stimulating commerce. He became more distrustful of France in the years after the treaty of Versailles. In November 1785 he confessed to Fitzpatrick that he thought France had gained more since the peace than during the war. Unless the drift of events could be corrected he feared that the British government might be tempted to throw in their lot with France:

In short ... there seems to be little left for England but to join the train and become one of the followers of the house of Bourbon, which would be almost as dangerous as it would be disgraceful. I am sure this was Shelburne's system. I had been persuaded by Sir James Harris that it was not Pitt's, but there are several circumstances that look like it, and indeed it may be a doubt whether the German league leaves him the choice of any other. The worst of all is, that I am far from sure whether the country in general would not like a good understanding with France (from the vain hopes of a durable peace) better than anything. I am sure that any minister who can like it must not only be insensible for the interests of his country, but to any feelings of personal pride; for, depend upon it, whenever you are in such a situation the French will make you feel it enough. . . .[7]

Fox remained convinced that the policy of Louis XVI was unchanged from that of his predecessors: the French were committed, by any means, fair or foul, open or secret, peaceful or warlike, to securing their hegemony in Europe. Fox therefore followed the commercial negotiations which Pitt conducted with the French government with anxiety. That the initiative for following up the articles of the treaty of Versailles came from the French seemed further confirmation that their aims were sinister. Fox saw the government as falling into a trap; he was oblivious to the commercial advantages for Britain which Pitt and Eden had gained by their careful preparations for the complex negotiations and the skill with which they had gained every major point upon which the British manufacturers had insisted. Fox was also sceptical of any suggestion that it was possible for Britain and France to forget their own quarrels and be reconciled. He did not disguise his conviction that the two countries were natural enemies, and although this earned him a rebuke from Pitt in the latter's most icy style, such a supposition being decried as 'weak and childish', Fox's opposition to the commercial treaty was obstinate and unyielding.

In the commons' debates he preferred to criticise the treaty because of what he claimed was its ominous significance in foreign policy, rather than concentrating upon its detailed provisions. He did from time to time seek to expose its limitations more precisely, arguing that it would bring hardship and unemployment to particular British industries, but he soon realised that there was no similar pool of discontent to that which had made Pitt's Irish proposals so unpopular. This, combined with Fox's awareness that he was usually at his weakest when discussing economics and finance, led him to argue his case against the treaty largely in diplomatic terms, the commercial aspect being carefully subordinated to overall considerations of foreign policy.

On 23 January 1787 he warned the house of commons against taking

French assurances of friendship at their face value:

> He desired it to be remembered that France had only changed her means—not her end. Her object had uniformly been the same, though her system of acting was different. In the reign of Louis XIV the aim of France was open and avowed: the means she employed to attain the end, offensive, arrogant and shameless. She had seen her error, and acted upon principles of a wiser policy.... What was the engine with which France operated her wished-for end at this time? Influence! that secret and almost resistless power; that power with which ambition gains its purpose, almost imperceptibly, but much more effectually than with any other.[8]

Louis XVI, Fox told his audience, possessed 'abundantly more power' than Louis XIV had been able to boast of. In all probability it would be heightened 'very shortly': at such a moment was it right to enter into a connexion by treaty with the king of France? Fox continued:

> Past experience proved that whenever France saw this country weak, and thought her incapable of effectually resisting, she seized the opportunity, and aimed at effecting her long desired destruction.... A similar opportunity would doubtless produce similar circumstances. It was idle, therefore, to suppose that France, who had really had such frequent reason to consider Great Britain as her most powerful rival, and who had received so many checks from her, that she had long wished to annihilate her as a state whose enmity was to be dreaded, would all of a sudden forget her resentment, and, just at that moment when there appeared to be the least rational motive to prompt her, abandon a purpose she had long and uniformly endeavoured to achieve.

This was to assume that the destruction of Britain as a major power took precedence in the mind of the French government over all other considerations of foreign policy. Had Fox contented himself with saying that the French were motivated, just as the British were, by a due regard for the protection and preservation of their own interests, and not by any more altruistic motives, he would have made a valid point, though it would not have rendered the commercial understanding null and void. But Fox insisted on discussing the free trade treaty largely from a diplomatic viewpoint. He claimed that it would have disastrous consequences for Britain's relations with other powers: it was possible for the 'present connexion' with France to 'operate to the destruction of all our former connexions with other powers, so far that when, at a future period, France might think it worth her while to break with us, we should find ourselves destitute of friends, and universally abandoned'.

Fox was conscious that he would be misrepresented as a man 'so far possessed by illiberal and vulgar prejudices against France, as to wish never to enter into any connexion with her'. His defiance against these accusations was idiosyncratic:

> Be that as it might, he should not easily forget that those prejudices against France, and that jealousy, which had for years prevailed, of her ambition, had been productive of no bad consequences to this country; on the contrary, that the wars grounded on our alarms at her stretches after inordinate power, and the jealousy which he had entertained of her desire to overturn the balance of power in Europe, had made this country great and glorious.[9]

Fox was trying to appeal to the patriotic feelings of the country gentlemen. He was conscious of the need to avoid any suspicion of pursuing a factious opposition, contrary to the national interest. He also claimed that he was on firm ground in defending the need to give due regard to the preservation of the balance of power in Europe. His suspicions of France were deep-rooted, even if they were not always well-founded. Yet his reading of the situation was above all else an intuitive one. He was grossly ignorant of the state of affairs in France and incapable of standing up to Pitt in any systematic debate on what the treaty actually said. He was arguing from inference, but there was in truth no evidence that Pitt's willingness to come to a trading agreement with France had sapped his vigilance in foreign policy or tempted him to attach Britain diplomatically to France. In this, as in other matters, Pitt liked to go one step at a time. He favoured the commercial treaty because he was convinced of the mutual benefits which would follow a freeing of trade, and because he knew from his consultations with the commercial interest that there were dazzling opportunities for English manufacturers once the French market was opened up to them. Neither of these considerations diminished his determination to preserve the balance of power on the continent or to prevent the rise of excessive French influence in the Low Countries. It is unnecessary to follow contemporary French critics, such as Robespierre, who saw the Eden treaty as a subtle plot by which Pitt undermined French industry in order to combine increased profits for British factory owners with a weakening of France's ability to sustain herself as a great power. But Pitt undoubtedly believed in the advantages of freer trade, in the folly of treating France in every respect as a permanent enemy, and in the immediate commercial benefits which the treaty would bring to British industry. He never lost sight of British interests and Eden, as the chief British negotiator, was outstandingly successful in outmanoeuvering the French in almost every respect. Fox was sceptical about Pitt's sincerity, incredulous about his diplomatic realism, and disdainful about his economic insight, in both theory and practice.

Fox expressed his misgivings in private as well as in public. He was very much afraid that the treaty would be popular and he remained convinced that 'in a *political* view it is the commencement of a most mischievous system'. Even if commercially advantageous in the short term he thought that the example of Holland ought to 'teach the world that it is not in the long run good policy to be always sacrificing political importance to gain and peace'. No country had had more years of peace during the previous half-century than Holland; no country had 'so much declined in its importance, or is more in danger of complete ruin'. The so-called benefits of the treaty were immediate, but its mischiefs and dangers were all 'more or less remote'. Fox had, therefore, little hope of any considerable section of the public forming a 'right' judgment upon it. He was even prepared to argue that in the purely commercial context the long-term benefits lay with France: 'where France had the advantage (as in wines, brandies, vinegars, etc.) the advantage is permanent and certain; where we have it (as in cutlery, cotton, etc.) it is accidental and temporary: they may gain our skill, but we can never gain their soil and climate'.[10]

With his usual obstinacy Fox was reluctant to move an inch from his opposition to the treaty. Even when Pitt was able to make great play with the stupidity of regarding France as the natural and eternal enemy of England Fox was unwilling to withdraw. He took refuge in verbal qualifications, hedging his original statement around with a prolific stream of subtle conditions, but in principle he remained immovable. Perhaps he sincerely believed that what he was saying was both right and, in the long run, likely to be justified by events. Perhaps he flattered himself that he would gain popularity by appealing to the prejudices of the country gentlemen. His speech in the commons on 12 February 1787 was emphatic in its renewed warnings against any commercial connexion with France; he still concentrated on the imagined duplicity of the French and the diplomatic consequences of the treaty, stubbornly seeking to justify his original attitude.

He undoubtedly ... would not go to the length of asserting that France was, and must remain, the unalterable enemy of Great Britain, and that there was not a possibility for any circumstances to occur, under which France might not secretly feel a wish to act amicably with respect to this kingdom. It was possible; but it was scarcely probable. That she, however, felt in that manner at present, he not only doubted but disbelieved. France was the natural political enemy of Great Britain. What made her so? Not the memory of Cressy and of Agincourt. . . . It was the overweening pride and boundless ambition of France; her invariable and ardent desire to hold the sway of Europe.[11]

He was scornful of Pitt's naïvety in believing French assurances of sincerity and he reminded the house of the deceptions practised by the French government shortly before France entered the American war on the side of the colonists. He repeated his assertion that France was 'the natural foe of Great Britain', arguing that she sought by entering into the commercial treaty 'to tie our hands, and prevent us from engaging in any alliances with other powers'. In the past Anglo-French relations had been amicable only when the two countries were bound together by a common hostility towards Spain. Nor was Fox persuaded by the argument that individual British citizens would reap great benefits from the treaty. He took a lofty patriotic line, affirming that 'connexions of such great political importance ought not to rest on the advantage that would accrue from them to interested individuals, but on the good effect they were likely to produce to the public and to the state'.

Pitt made much of the absence of any popular outcry against the treaty; Fox retorted by saying that Pitt had not been borne out by the facts when making similar claims during the controversy over the Irish commercial proposals. The truth of the matter was that the minister was being bluffed, Fox argued. The French were seeking to draw Britain within their sphere of influence in order to tip the balance of power in France's favour. The cooperative attitude manifested by the French during the negotiations was further evidence of their sinister motives. They were concerned with their own interests not with the good of Great Britain. Anxious 'to grasp at more than a due influence over the other powers of Europe', France was endeavouring to attain her objective by more subtle and sophisticated tactics.

There were, Fox went on, insuperable differences of interest separating Britain and France:

This country ought not by any means, in point of policy, to connect itself too closely with France. Her true situation was that . . . of a great maritime power looked up to by the other powers of Europe, as that to which the distressed should fly for assistance, whenever France unjustly attacked them with a view to the attainment of her favourite object. Two things it behoved a wise ministry of this country to aim at, with respect to France, the one was to divert her attention from her marine, and turn it to land connexions and fortifications; the other, to procure an alliance for Great Britain with some maritime power that could assist her whenever France thought it a fit moment to attack her.[12]

He remained sceptical about the commercial advantages which had been claimed for the treaty, particularly with respect to the wool industry and the importation of French wines, and while Pitt was fond of arguing that Britain and France were bound together by geographical proximity, commercial intercourse, and a common interest in growing prosperity, Fox rigorously maintained that the treaty was 'a tempting bait, which none but gudgeons the most simple would have bitten at'.

Fox was wrong on almost every count. The Eden treaty did not mean that Britain succumbed to French domination in foreign affairs, as the Dutch crisis soon showed. By entering into alliance with Holland and Prussia Pitt demonstrated that he was conscious of Britain's diplomatic isolation and that he was eager to end it. At no time did Pitt neglect the defence of British interests out of deference to France. Though he valued improved relations with France he had no illusions about the scope or nature of the treaty which Eden had so deftly negotiated. He took sensible precautions to limit French influence in the Low Countries, and he was just as sensitive to the need to maintain the balance of power in Europe as Fox. Pitt was capable of appreciating the benefits of commercial intercourse with France without putting aside the considerations which inevitably influenced the conduct of British foreign policy. He did not confuse common economic interests with a common foreign policy. He preferred friendly relations with France to traditional hostility, but though he firmly rejected any suggestion that France was Britain's natural enemy he did not make the mistake of thinking that she was Britain's natural friend. He did not overlook areas of possible conflict or the likelihood that there would be clashes of diplomatic interest between the two countries. On a more limited scale the Eden treaty was a triumphant success. Fox's apprehensions about the commercial consequences of the agreement were misplaced. British manufacturers thrived on the new markets which the treaty allowed them to exploit. It was the French who felt the pinch of competing in an open market with a neighbour more advanced industrially than themselves. Far from envisaging the free trade treaty as an opportunity to weaken Britain and subvert her status as an independent power many Frenchmen came bitterly to accuse the British of having outwitted them in order to exploit them.

In many ways Fox's stance over the Eden treaty was the product of the unenviable situation in which he was placed and the agonising pressures to which he was subjected. For all his eloquent pleas in favour of party and a formed opposition he was acutely conscious of the difficulties of keeping his followers together. North's health was declining and the fidelity of many of the old Northites was crumbling fast. It was one thing to oppose Pitt when hopes of speedily regaining office were high; it was another to commit oneself to years of fruitless and factious opposition with no prospect of either turning the government out or being assimilated to it. Even some of those who liked to cheer Fox's glowing apologies for party to the echo had little appreciation of their wider implications. Although Fox sought to maintain some semblance of consistency by seeking wherever possible to differentiate himself and his friends from the government, to many contemporaries this seemed wilfully irresponsible, a cult of opposition for opposition's sake. The knowledge that on many issues Pitt was proved right and Fox wrong contributed still further to the demoralisation of the opposition. So much depended on friendship, on a personal confidence between the persons leading the party in the lords and the commons, that a misunderstanding or a crisis in personal relations could shatter an opposition's chances of making any impact in either of the two houses or upon the public. Ideology was irrelevant and organisation virtually non-existent, yet without some bond of principle or some modicum of party discipline, the type of opposition which Fox's speeches delineated was an impossibility. Caught in a series of frustrating cross-currents Fox and his colleagues frequently resorted to makeshift tactics which were inconsistent with their declared ideals and all too reminiscent of the traditional techniques of opposition which they claimed to have left behind. Too much depended on sheer luck; if Pitt's judgment and expectations over the Eden treaty had been shown to be faulty then Fox might have reaped a splendid harvest, especially among the more independent sections of the house of commons, but in the 1780s Fox's luck had all but completely run out.

He had no alternative, therefore, but to reiterate the concepts of party and of systematic opposition even if he could apply them only spasmodically in practice. The more humiliating the realities of politics, the more he took refuge in a world of imagination which lent dignity and purpose to the squalid perplexities of controversy. But the fragility of the unity which the whig opposition simulated was all too evident in the embarrassments which relentlessly haunted Fox throughout the peaceful decade in which Pitt's supremacy blossomed with success.

Although Fox experienced little but humiliation in matters germane to the central themes of politics he was at his best on subjects which evoked broad humanitarian principles and straddled conventional loyalties. Free from the need to exaggerate his differences from Pitt, and from the necessity of conciliating the prejudices of the house, he stood forth uncompromisingly in favour of repealing the test and corporation acts and abolishing the slave trade.

Fox was consistently in favour of abolishing the seventeenth-century restrictions on dissenters, whether protestant or catholic, and he supported parliamentary resolutions to this effect whenever they came before the commons. Whereas Burke was sympathetic to catholic claims for relief but disposed to oppose those of the protestant dissenters, Fox denounced the principle of using religion as a test for political office or as a guide to political reliability. 'Religion', he told the house of commons during the debate on Beaufoy's motion to repeal the test and corporation acts on 28 March 1787, 'was not a proper test for political institutions'. To claim that it was unnecessary to repeal the Clarendon code because the dissenters were not really penalised in practice was merely to reveal the nonsensical situation for the absurdity that it was. It was impossible to argue that the dissenters were any danger to the security of church or state. The general conduct of dissenters was praiseworthy: 'in all former times they had been actuated by principles of liberty not inconsistent with the well-being of the state'. Conscious as he was that the sense of the house was against him Fox warned members that in the past the dissenters had been persevering and active for the redress of their grievances: 'if they used the same perseverance now, they could not fail of success'. Those who wished for a quiet life ought above everything else to agree to the repeal of the penal laws. He advised the dissenters to repeat their applications for relief until parliament deferred to their wishes.[13] But Beaufoy's motion was defeated by 176 votes to 98, and though Fox had the satisfaction of speaking boldly on behalf of what he believed was common justice he was in the familiar position of voting in the minority.

Just over two years later Beaufoy renewed his efforts to repeal the test and corporation acts and on this occasion the reformers fell only twenty votes short of success. In the debate on 8 May 1789 Fox expounded the case for repeal eloquently and comprehensively. He affirmed his belief that religion should always be distinct from civil government: 'it was not otherwise connected with it, than as it tended to promote morality among the people, and thus conduced to good order in the state.' Fox found any suggestion of enforcing the profession of belief by external or legal means repulsive and abhorrent. No government had the right to impose any set of religious convictions upon its subjects. Liberty of conscience and freedom of thought were inviolate in any civilised society:

> No human government had a right to enquire into private opinions, to presume that it knew them, or to act on that presumption. Men were the best judges of the consequences of their own opinions, and how far they were likely to influence their actions; and it was most unnatural and tyrannical to say, 'As you think, so must you act. I will collect the evidence of your future conduct from what I know to be your opinions'. The very reverse of this was the rule of conduct which ought to be pursued. The one could be fixed and ascertained, the other could only be a matter of speculation.[14]

Fox was so firmly convinced of the rightness of this opinion that he avowed that no man should be punished for disseminating heterodox political or constitutional ideas. Only if he carried his 'detestable opinions' into practice should such a man be disabled from filling any civil or military office, suffering whatever legal penalties were deemed appropriate as a deterrent to prevent others from acting in the same 'dangerous and absurd' manner. Nothing was more consonant with common sense, reason, and justice than that men should be tried by their actions and not by their opinions, and what was undeniable with respect to political opinions was even more applicable in matters of religion. Fox argued that he was supported in his contention by the 'general tenour' of the laws of the land. But there was one glaring exception, the case of Roman catholics. Even here historical factors and political considerations had played as great a part in influencing legislation as matters of religious belief:

> The Roman catholics ... had been supposed by our ancestors to entertain opinions which might lead to mischief against the state. But was it their religious opinions that were feared? Quite the contrary. Their acknowledging a foreign authority paramount to that of the legislature; their acknowledging a title to the crown superior to that conferred by the voice of the people; their political opinions, which they were supposed to attach to their religious creed, were dreaded, and justly dreaded, as inimical to the constitution. Laws, therefore, were enacted to guard against the pernicious tendency of their political, but not of their religious opinions, and the principle thus adopted, if not founded on justice, was at least followed up with consistency.[15]

Nevertheless, Fox observed, the legislature ought not to have acted against the catholics until, by carrying into practice some of the dangerous doctrines which they were thought to entertain, they had rendered themselves liable to the penalties of the law. 'Disability and punishment ought to have followed, but not to have anticipated, offence.'

In the case of the dissenters, those who attempted to justify the disabilities under which they laboured ought to contend, not that their religious opinions were inimical to the established church, but that their political opinions were inimical to the constitution. Even so, Fox maintained, it was wrong to victimise a particular group of citizens merely for holding a set of opinions which were deemed unconstitutional, or which were simply unpopular with the authorities or misunderstood by the populace.

Fox was not, in the strict sense, an advocate of disestablishing the church of England. With a sentimental affection, not altogether surprising in one who bore the formalities of religious belief and practice so lightly, he liked to think of the Anglican church as the national church, comprehensive in its membership, liberal in its doctrines, and charitable and tolerant to those who could not conscientiously find peace of mind within its extensive borders. But he was vehemently opposed to the use of the coercive power of the state to support the church:

> It was an irreverent and impious opinion to maintain, that the church must depend for support as an engine or ally of the state, and not on the evidence of its doctrines, to be found by searching the scriptures, and the moral effects which it produced on the minds of those whom it was its duty to instruct.[16]

It was common to hear men defend the disabilities technically enforcable upon dissenters and catholics by referring to the moderation of the church of England, but Fox reminded the house that there had been times when moderation had not been the distinguishing characteristic of the establishment. In the reign of Charles II the church's fortitude had been greater than her moderation, and in the reign of James II 'her servility had been greater than either'. Since the Hanoverian succession the church had merited every praise for tolerant and temperate behaviour, and by its refusal to indulge either its whims or its apprehensions. The church had become moderate because it had been forced to answer the claims of the dissenters argument by argument instead of imposing silence by the coercive powers of the law. The church's confidence in her own doctrines, and her charity towards those of others, were the product of open liberal discussion, among men living under the same government and equally protected by it. 'Moderation ... and indulgence to other sects were equally conducive to the happiness of mankind and the safety of the church.'

Fox argued that the willingness to take communion according to the Anglican rite did not demonstrate any change in a man's political or religious opinions. It did not even ensure any fundamental loyalty to the state or to the constitution. An unscrupulous opponent of the church or a fanatical enemy of the state would not be deterred by the provisions of the test act. On the other hand there were men who were not of the established church to whose services the nation had a claim, but however eager they were to render public service their sincerity prevented them from abusing a religious sacrament in order to qualify for political office. 'Ought any such man,' Fox asked, 'to be examined before he came into office touching his private opinions? Was it not sufficient that he did his duty as a good citizen?'

Fox reminded his audience that there were two established churches in the United Kingdom, one in England, the other in Scotland. Yet the members of one of these establishments enjoyed privileges denied to the members of the other, equally established.

> According to this doctrine of protecting the church of England, if the practice had kept pace with the principle, the country must have been deprived of all those gallant characters of the kirk of Scotland, who had so eminently distinguished themselves in the army and navy; and of all those celebrated legislators and senators who added learning and dignity to the courts of justice, and wisdom to his majesty's councils. If tests were right, the present was clearly a wrong test, because it shunned all the purposes for which tests were originally introduced.[17]

The fact that the test and corporation acts had lasted for over a century was no argument for their retention; they had survived by 'repeated suspensions', for indemnity bills had become annual acts. The church of England had a glorious opportunity to stand forth as the champion of tolerance; if it did so it would be true to all that was best in its heritage:

> Surely the church of England ought, if possible, more than any other ecclesiastical establishment upon earth, practically to inculcate the glorious idea that indulgence to other sects, the most candid allowance for diversity of their opinions, and a sincere zeal for the advancement of mutual charity and benevolence, were the truest and happiest testimonies which she could give to the divine origin of her religion.[18]

In advocating the repeal of religious tests Fox did not see himself as initiating startling revolutionary developments. He was happy to think that all that was best in the country's political and religious traditions pointed to the abandonment of pieces of penal legislation whose only possible justification had been rendered obsolete by the passage of time. The acceptance of dissenters and catholics as full citizens, on equal terms with Anglicans, was for Fox the inevitable fulfilment of the constitutional principles of the glorious revolution. He was not pleading for a completely fresh start in church-state relations; he was simply asking that the measure of toleration which had been achieved under the Hanoverian kings should be unequivocally recognised and secured by law. What was conceded through charity and expediency should be granted of right. The experience of a hundred years confirmed the rightness and political benefits of toleration; it was now time to expunge obsolete relics of old antagonisms from the statute book. Without the irritant of religious tests dissenters and catholics would be more likely to give their full and uncompromising loyalty to the constitution; a motive for giving fuller service to the nation would be created; ancient bitterness would die. Far from plunging into untried waters Fox was convinced that religious toleration confirmed the policies successfully applied for seventy years. He was persuaded that no shock would be given to the church of England and that no tremor would disrupt the morality of the people. Fox's advocacy of repeal was a striking testimony to the depth of his commitment to the English way of life and to what he believed to be noblest in the traditions of his country. His faith in religious and political liberty was the fruit of experience, the expression of an appreciation of a rich and varied pattern of behaviour, rather than the consequence of an ordered series of abstract speculations. When men turned their backs on toleration they were, in Fox's eyes, untrue to all that was best in their country's history. He spoke as a patriot not a philosopher. With that unerring preference for the concrete rather than the speculative which governed virtually all his actions Fox tested the demand for repeal by the dominant themes of constitutional development and judged that it was the defenders of religious discrimination who were denying the wisdom of the past, clinging instead to its prejudices and shibboleths. It was possible to cleanse public life from the errors of outmoded hostilities and to reaffirm in convincing fashion the justice of the principles of 1689, freed from the conditioning circumstances of a bygone age.

It was, therefore, completely consistent for Fox to be a friend to religious toleration and a supporter of the establishment. The church of England was the church of the vast majority of Englishmen and the greatest single security for the moral welfare of the nation; but it did not speak for all Englishmen and therefore it ought not to be perverted by abusing a religious rite to establish political acceptability. If religious belief and ecclesiastical allegiance were no obstacle to full citizenship, both the church of England and the dissenters (whether protestant or catholic) would contribute more fully to the well-being of the nation. The principle of religious freedom was the proven ally of civil and political liberty. The English experience, compromised though it was by unjustifiable laws, was living proof that the two flourished together.

Although the reformers seemed on the brink of victory in May 1789 they suffered a sharp reverse in March 1790. Fox's motion calling for the repeal of the test and corporation acts was defeated by 294 votes to 105. There was no falling off in the numbers favouring repeal, but there was a dramatic rise in those who feared any change in the laws of the land. Possibly many of those who had been absent the previous year had been jolted out of their complacency by the smallness of the majority; possibly events in France fortified the determination of many backbenchers to maintain the constitution inviolate, without any dabbling in innovation. The sympathy for the French revolution which many prominent dissenters had displayed had raised doubts about their political soundness. When Price and Priestley talked enthusiastically of the course of events in France they did their co-religionists no small disservice. Fox's own identification with the cause of reform in France did not commend him to the country gentlemen. They suspected him of rashness and with his anti-French speeches at the time of the Eden treaty in their minds they were inclined to add hypocrisy to his other failings. But there was no falling off in Fox's eloquence; his speech calling for the repeal of the test and corporation acts was vigorously argued and skilfully phrased to mollify some of the anxieties which Fox knew to be pressing heavily on members' minds.

Fox reaffirmed his detestation of any species of persecution, whether political or religious, and condemned the spirit of intolerance which had inspired the acts when they were originally passed. He praised the attempts of the French national assembly to abolish the spirit of persecution and intolerance which had for so long disgraced public life in France. He even went so far as to praise the French declaration of the rights of man and the efforts being made to apply its principles in legislation. But he also pointed out that if members of the house of commons were willing to revert to first principles they would find that in the first stages of Christianity 'no vice, evil, or detriment had ever sprung from toleration'. It was persecution which had been a fertile source of evil: 'perfidy, cruelty, and murder had often been the consequence of intolerant principles'. He descanted with considerable passion on the evils of persecution and the motives which had inspired it.

Morality was thought to be most effectually enforced and propagated by insisting on a general unity of religious sentiments; the dogmas of men in power were to be substituted in the room of every other religious opinion, as it might best answer the ends of policy and ambition: it proceeded entirely on this grand fundamental error—that one man could better judge of the religious opinion of another than the man himself could.[19]

Toleration proceeded on the contrary principle, yet its doctrines, he was sorry to say, were, even in an enlightened age, 'but of a modern date in any part of the world'. Before the reign of William III toleration had not had a footing in England. Persecution always reasoned from cause to effect, 'from opinion to action', and generally speaking this had proved to be erroneous. By judging men from their actions, not from their opinions, toleration invariably led to the formulation of just conclusions. Every political and religious test was absurd; the only test which ought to be adopted was a man's actions.

Fox reminded the house that the character of catholic citizens had been much misrepresented and abused on account of the supposed tendency of their religious tenets to encourage 'murder, treason and every other species of horrid crimes, from a principle of conscience'. This deplorable practice stemmed from 'a base imputation of evil intentions from the uncharitable opinions entertained of that profession as a sect'. The dissenters, Fox argued, had always conducted themselves meritoriously; they had cheerfully taken part in the defence of the country, especially during the rebellions of 1715 and 1745, and their loyalty to the house of Hanover was undeniable. To those who maintained that while the dissenters strenuously advocated toleration they were themselves capable of great intolerance when in authority, Fox held up the example of America to prove that the dissenting sects were not necessarily intolerant when they were themselves the establishment.

Two other anxieties had to be set at rest: the concern which most members shared for the security and well-being of the church of England, and the fear that the critical situation in France made all reforms dangerous. Fox took care to state his own approval for the church's doctrine and discipline. 'It had wisely avoided all that was superstitious and retained what appeared to him to be essential.' He both admired and revered the Anglican church, declaring that he was himself firmly attached to it. So far as the state of affairs in France was concerned he pointed out that the hopes of the dissenters were not the outcome of a wish to imitate the French example; their request for the repeal of the discriminatory laws had been made long before events in France had taken their dramatic turn. Both church and state had benefited in the past from timely reform: 'the church had owed its existence to a rational innovation, and the constitution had derived much of its excellence and beauty from the same source.' Fox could not resist the temptation of allowing his incipient anti-clericalism expression, complaining that the clergy had 'uniformly acted with great artifice and duplicity down from the time of the reformation, when they made their own chimerical fears ... the ground of unprovoked and unmerited persecution'. But for the most part his speech was conciliatory in tone; even when he criticised Burke's contribution to the debate he sought to avoid antagonising members by not making a violent personal attack on him. Though he thought Burke's opposition to repeal was lamentable he carefully paid tribute to Burke's intellectual powers and claimed that, different though their conclusions were on this particular issue, they still shared the same fundamental principles and convictions.

With the wisdom of hindsight it is difficult to appreciate the force of opposition which Fox's desire to repeal the religious laws encountered. The notion that liberty in church and state was in any significant sense secured by the test and corporation acts seems ludicrously inappropriate in the circumstances of 1789 and 1790. Fears that the dissenters were fired by enthusiasm for French ideas were exaggerated. Advanced modernists such as Price and Priestley represented the unitarian minority among English dissenters; the majority, though initially inclined to view the French revolution in the light of the English Revolution of 1688, were more judicious. They approved of constitutional monarchy, whether in France or England; they admired the abolition of religious discrimination in France; but they were sceptical of republicanism and deplored secularism. As the French revolution became more violent they rallied round the English constitution. But to many country gentlemen dissent was synonymous with republicanism and the ghost of Cromwell could always be invoked to revive hereditary anxieties and aged antagonisms. It was still common for most men to believe that to tamper with the establishment in one respect was to open the door to wholesale alteration. The constitution's much vaunted stability was itself the product of history; to question the validity of what history had produced was to put the country's institutions at the mercy of the disruptive inroads of speculation. Men preferred to live with the pattern of life which they knew, whatever its theoretical shortcomings, than to venture along the hazardous paths of abstract wisdom. Because he appreciated this point of view Fox was careful to argue that the repeal of the test and corporation acts was in harmony with the overall constitutional development of the previous century. He was prepared to allow for contemporary misgivings in his presentation of his case but he was unable fully to satisfy them and he could not fully overcome them. Yet the appeal to the historicity of toleration was more than a debater's trick; it reflected a deep-seated love of the English way of life which was a fundamental part of Fox's nature.

The abolition of the slave trade was another issue which brought out the best in Fox. Unhampered by mundane political considerations—there was no political advantage to be gained by attacking the commerce in slaves—Fox's artless humanitarianism was allowed free play. He was always opposed to the compromise suggestion that the slave trade ought to be regulated rather than destroyed. But though he expressed his detestation of the traffic in vehement language he never neglected to justify his position on grounds of political expediency as well as of principle. He assured the house of commons on 9 May 1788 that he did not see how any political question could be considered in the abstract without referring to the circumstances in which the country was placed. He believed that the slave trade should be abolished, not only because it offended the principles of justice and humanity, but because it was inimical to the best interests of the country. In the commons' debate on Wilberforce's resolution calling for the abolition of the slave trade on 12 May 1789 Fox repeated his belief that total abolition was not only more desirable than a stricter regulation of the trade but that it would also be easier to apply. The slave trade was an example of how much more practicable a remedy was than a palliative. He was especially eager to refute the argument, which was popular with those who were seeking to thwart the abolitionists, that if Britain ceased to take part in the slave trade other countries would exploit the opportunity to bring more of the traffic under their own control, supplying the West Indian islands with slaves in an illicit manner. Fox urged that the best way of dealing with this problem was to make sure that foreign nations understood that when Britain thought it proper to abolish the slave trade she was also possessed of the resources to prevent the trade being carried on in any manner with her colonies. The most efficacious method of dealing with the problem was by international cooperation and in this respect Fox held out the prospect of Anglo-French collaboration to suppress the slave trade:

> If there was any great and enlightened nation now existing in Europe it was France, which was as likely as any nation on the face of the globe, to act on the present subject with warmth and with enthusiasm; to catch a spark from the light of our fire, and run a race with us in promoting the ends of humanity. France had been often improperly stimulated by her ambition; he had no doubt but that she would, in

the present instance, readily follow its honourable dictates.[20]

In the closing stages of the debate on 21 May Fox repeated his preference for going to the root of the problem:

He felt no difficulty in saying, that without having seen one tittle of evidence he should have been for abolition. With respect to a regulation of the trade, a detestation of its existence must naturally lead him to remark, that he knew of no such thing as regulation of robbery or a restriction of murder. There was no medium; the legislature must either abolish the trade or avow their own criminality.[21]

Possibly he was seeking to combine an appeal to the idealistic impulses which he hoped flickered even in the stodgiest backbencher's brain; more probably he was trying to meet one of the most prevalent of arguments against abolition, that for Britain to act alone would simply consign a profitable trade to her French competitors. Despite the high-flown protestations of devotion to the spirit of liberty and the universal rights of man which were so familiar an accompaniment to the proceedings of the French national assembly there was very little prospect of any real cooperation to stamp out the slave trade. It was one of the attractive figments of Fox's imagination, inspired by a longing to bring about collaboration between Britain and the new constitutional monarchy in France in a field in which high principle could serve enlightened self-interest. If it was meant to soothe growing apprehensiveness about the future state of affairs in France it failed; and it was hardly deemed convincing, or even relevant, by those who feared that a premature abolition of the slave trade would strike a mortal blow at British prosperity.

Frustrated as they were Fox's efforts to abolish the slave trade sprang from a deep commitment to the cause. He combined a dedication to a lofty principle with a thoughtful approach to the political problems which the controversy involved. He did not act hastily, confessing on one occasion, 'I am very much inclined to undertake the business, but I must both read and hear more before I engage. I should like very much to put down so vile a thing if it is possible.'[22] Perhaps the issue supplied a deep need within his personality. It was satisfying to feel that the subject transcended the limitations of conventional politics, and that whatever the outcome a great principle was being justified to the world. Fox felt that obloquy for the continuation of an inhuman and monstrous abuse lay with others. However saddened he was by defeat, the slave trade never brought him the sour bitterness of spirit that less reputable failures inflicted upon him. He told Mrs Armistead of it all in April 1791, prefacing his serious confidences by confessions of a more trivial nature:

> I had led a sad life sitting up late, always either at the house of commons, or gaming and losing my money every night that I have played. Getting up late, of course, and finding people in my room so that I have had no morning time to myself, and have gone out as soon as I could, though generally very late, to get rid of them, so that I have scarce ever had a moment to write. You have heard how poor a figure we made in numbers on the slave trade, but I spoke I believe very well and indeed it is the thing that has given me the most pleasure since I saw Liz, for I do think it a cause in which one ought to be an enthusiast and in which one cannot help being pleased with oneself for having done right.[23]

For many years self-respect was the only reward Fox gained for all his sterling efforts to better the lot of the negroes. A measure of regulation, to avert the worst horrors and the most appalling cruelties of the traffic, was all that the combined devotion and talents of Wilberforce, Fox, Pitt and Burke could wring out of a cautious and suspicious house of commons. It was not that the MPs who repudiated so much eloquence were exceptionally callous men. They were simply baffled and puzzled by a problem which was beyond their comprehension and which they lacked the imagination to visualise or to understand. They were ill-equipped by education or experience to sort the nonsense from the conflicting jumble of arguments which descended upon their heads every time the slave trade was debated within the house. They were swamped by statistics, by irreconcilable allegations of unspeakable atrocities and claims of the diminution of suffering. For some a vested interest in a commerce which brought prosperity to Bristol and Liverpool clinched the argument; for others a state of bewilderment seemed best resolved by following the most cautious line of action. Only towards the end of his life was Fox's fidelity to the abolition of the slave trade to earn a thoroughly deserved and universally acclaimed triumph.

The impeachment of Warren Hastings for alleged misconduct as governor-general in Bengal was one of the most colourful episodes of the 1780s. That Hastings had to endure the long agony of his trial in Westminster Hall was a tribute to the idealism, untiring application, and ruthlessness of Edmund Burke. But though Fox shared Burke's desire to ensure that the government of India was responsibly conducted he never allied himself with the most vindictive aspects of the affair. Burke pursued Hastings with the self-righteous indignation of an outraged moralist; Fox thought it right that Hastings should answer the charges which had been made against him, but had he known that the impeachment would drag on for seven weary years he would have been more sceptical about initiating it. Fox and Sheridan were aware of the advantages of the case in embarrassing Pitt and his government. Anything which underlined the deficiencies of governmental control over the Indian administration or which brought to light the abuses perpetrated by the officials and representatives of the East India company could be exploited to give retrospective conviction to Fox's ill-fated India bill. To suggest that Pitt was lukewarm in eliminating corruption and malpractice in Indian affairs was a welcome tactic in a contest in which so many of the trumps lay with the government.

But the complexity of the charges confused the public and eliminated the initial political advantages which Fox believed he had discerned in the case. Though Fox made a three-hour speech on the Benares accusation as late as 20 May 1795 his interest had waned long before. Even the most devoted advocate of better government in India could be forgiven for losing his enthusiasm for such a lengthy campaign. Only Burke remained obstinately and obsessively dedicated to hounding Hastings down. The protracted nature of the trial divested it of any substantial political impact. By the time Hastings was acquitted the French revolution and the war with France had made the whole affair an echo from a more leisurely and peaceful era, when the happiness of remote millions could command the interest, and occupy the time, of the most active and prominent statesmen. In 1795 more immediate and more terrifying problems monopolised attention. That bleak February day in 1788 when amid pomp and pageantry Burke had begun to plead the prosecution's case in a series of weighty and learned speeches made all the more impressive by his sonorous and theatrical delivery seemed centuries away from an England at bay against revolutionary France. In the long run Hastings' impeachment made a bigger impression upon historians than upon contemporaries. After the first fine careless rapture the opposition became bored with the affair; in November 1788 Sheridan confided to the duchess of Devonshire that he was heartily sick of the Hastings trial and that he wished Hastings would run away, 'and Burke after him'. Idealism and opportunism were often strongly mingled in the behaviour of Fox and his friends during the 1780s and nowhere was this more in evidence than in their attitude to the Hastings impeachment.

Throughout Pitt's peacetime administration the opposition were in an impossible position. Everything favoured Pitt. He possessed the confidence of the king, the support of parliament and the goodwill of the country. Whatever the shortcomings of many of his ministerial colleagues, and the limitations imposed upon him by the need to defer to the prejudices of the king and the feelings of the house of commons, Pitt's handling of financial and administrative matters was outstandingly successful. Time after time Fox's opposition seemed perverse and wilful, the outcome of personal hostility or factious opportunism. Even in the sphere of foreign policy, where Fox always claimed to be more at home than Pitt, there was little scope for effective criticism of the government. Indeed, during the Dutch crisis in 1787, Fox found himself in favour of Pitt's tough anti-French line. He had the satisfaction of reminding the house of commons that the crisis in Holland confirmed all his warnings against trusting the French, warnings which had been so lightly set aside during the debates on the Eden treaty.

The struggle for power in the Netherlands was complex. The Stadtholder and his wife looked to England and Prussia for support in their struggle with the republican party, which, although comprised as it was of conservative oligarchs and some more radically minded opponents of the prince of Orange, looked to France for help. The British government was chiefly concerned with the dangers of increased French influence in the Netherlands and with the diplomatic consequences which would follow the installation of a Dutch régime dependent on the support of the Bourbons. No British government could tolerate the prospect of a French puppet state in the Low Countries and this traditional preoccupation with Dutch independence dominated Pitt's conduct throughout the crisis. He had no desire to jeopardise the country's prosperity and the possibility of armed conflict depressed him. Determined though he was to secure Britain's essential interests he acted throughout with deliberate caution. Subsidies were sent to the Stadtholder and forty ships of the line were put in readiness to meet any emergency. The government considered the possibility of mediation by the powers, but the crisis was speedily resolved when in September 1787 Prussian troops crossed the Dutch border in order to secure the persons of the Dutch royal family. Republican resistance collapsed, and the French, who were uncertain of the extent to which they could risk war and increasingly worried by events in eastern Europe, where Austria and Russia were contemplating an attack upon Turkey, had no choice but to accept defeat.

Fox had throughout advocated a strongly anti-French policy. He criticised the government for exhibiting excessive caution at a time when speed was essential for success. He claimed that the government's policy was a confirmation of those principles of foreign policy which he had always expounded, but which had all too often been disregarded. He might also have been influenced by the fact that the British ambassador at the Hague, Sir James Harris, was something of a whig, and Harris had consistently urged the government to act promptly and effectively to curtail French influence in Holland. There was no ambiguity about Fox's own position. He made it perfectly clear where he stood when speaking in the debate on the address to the king's speech on 27 November 1787.

> Mr Fox ... observed that he should contradict every political principle and sentiment that he had acted upon through life, were he not to give his most hearty concurrence to the sum and substance of the speech from the throne, and the address ... because he took the substance of both to be a public avowal from the throne, and as public an acknow-ledgement on the part of the house, that those systems of politics, which had on former occasions been called romantic, were serious systems, and such as it was the true interest of this country to be governed by; namely, systems established on that sound and solid political maxim, that Great Britain ought to look to the situation of affairs on the continent, and to take such measures upon every change of circumstances abroad, as should tend best to preserve the balance of power in Europe. Upon that principle he had founded all his political conduct, and convinced as he was of its justness, he should continue to adhere to it, and consequently could not withhold his ready and sincere assent to an address admitting the maxim completely....[24]

He had repeatedly warned the house of the perfidy and treachery of France in exerting her influence in foreign states. He had sought to per-suade members of the futility of hoping that a commercial treaty would bring about a transformation of French foreign policy. Now the govern-ment were themselves telling the house of the way in which the French had attempted to corrupt the government of Holland and to aid those who were plotting the downfall of the legally constituted government. This made his own former criticisms of French policy seem too mild and too weak when compared with the brutal reality.

Fox was careful to avoid being caught up in the internal wrangles which had brought about the Dutch crisis. It was neither wise nor becom-ing for the house of commons to inquire into the constitutional propriety of forms of government in foreign states. 'It was sufficient for him and for the house to consider which party in the republic of the United Provinces was most inclined to be friendly to Great Britain, and to renew a natural alliance with us, in preference to an unnatural alliance

with France.'[25] He was of the opinion that the word 'lawful' as applied
to the Dutch government in the address was redundant. He also had
misgivings about the precise meaning of the mutual undertakings to dis-
arm which the British and French governments had given at the close
of the crisis. He was concerned lest naval armaments should be reduced
without corresponding limitations being made effective with respect to
land forces, and he affirmed that no agreed level of disarmament pre-
cluded any increase in the armed services should future circumstances
justify it. Nevertheless he

> expressed his satisfaction at the system of measures lately adopted. He
> said that whether government had adopted those measures ... suffici-
> ently soon, or whether they ought to have adopted them earlier, were
> matters of opinion; but he was extremely glad to find that they had
> at length embraced them, and he hoped when we should have con-
> nected ourselves with the United Provinces by a solid and substantial
> treaty, to which he could not but with reasonable expectation look
> forward, since the interest of each power was one and the same, that
> the government would pursue the idea of taking the most effectual
> steps to preserve the balance of power, and carry it into execution with
> regard to other European states and countries.[26]

He argued that the British government should counteract every species
of interference, open or concealed, on the part of France in the internal
affairs of other countries, especially Holland. Vigilance and preparedness
were the two essential conditions for the prosecution of a vigorous and
successful foreign policy:

> The best means to insure the continuance of peace was to add to our
> strength rather than trust to the weakness of our oldest and most
> inveterate rival. Let us enlarge the number of our alliances, insure the
> cooperation of other powers in the hour of attack, improve our marine,
> cherish and preserve it, and all that belonged to that favourite service,
> and we might then consider the ambition of the house of Bourbon, its
> imbecility or its power, as matters of equally trifling consideration.[27]

Fox could justifiably argue that his conduct during the Dutch crisis had
conformed to the type held to be appropriate to notions of patriotic opposition. He had consistently pleaded for the firm defence of British interests,
and far from dabbling in isolationism he had forcefully defended the
concept of the balance of power. Like so many of Fox's pronouncements
on foreign policy his speeches in 1787 reflected traditional assumptions.
Fox's dislike of any intervention in the domestic affairs of sovereign states

antedated his anxiety to protect the constitutional monarchy in France between 1789 and 1792 from Austrian or Prussian intervention. The alteration in Fox's attitudes after 1789 did not mean that he had abandoned either the notion of the balance of power or the security of British interests as the primary objective of British foreign policy. The change of régime in France led to a greater willingness to envisage a French alliance as a means of preserving the balance of power and protecting British interests, but it did not imply any conversion to a vague internationalism. In many ways Fox saw politics primarily in terms of the practice of diplomacy. However bravely he championed unpopular causes and the reform of established institutions he did not interpret these as the areas within which a government either could or should exercise its powers as a first priority.

Foreign policy was the dominant political enthusiasm of his life. However much he was tempted to play politics with other issues he was always more scrupulous in his regard for the protection of Britain's vital interests. The whole of his career was a tribute to the wisdom and sanity of traditional eighteenth-century diplomacy; the frustrations of the revolutionary war were evidence of the deficiencies of traditional diplomatic theory when confronted with a wholly novel situation. But throughout Pitt's peacetime ministry Fox tried to act as a protector of the country's status in the world. Whenever he believed Pitt to be erring on the side of restraint he sought to act as a goad. This is not to say that Fox's judgment of particular situations was exempt from faults; he undoubtedly exaggerated the potential evils of the commercial treaty with France and he was apt to overlook the undemonstrative firmness underlying Pitt's foreign policy. But however eager Fox was to exploit any opportunity to embarrass or confuse the government he subordinated the ambitions of party to what he considered to be the demands of national security. Above all else, he believed that the biggest threat to international peace and order sprang from the restless ambitions of France. Like many others he failed to grasp the essential weakness of the French position in the 1780s. He did not appreciate the full meaning of France's exhaustion after the war of American independence. When the French government attempted to be conciliatory Fox was apt to discern guile and conspiracy behind smooth words, and he was completely bemused by the financial and economic considerations which explained so many of the twists of French policy after the peace of Versailles. Fox still thought of the French monarchy as a powerful, centralised absolutism; he credited Louis XVI with the ambitions and industry of Louis XIV.

At the same time there was little to lose by appealing to the anti-French instincts of the house of commons. Fox was under no illusions about the possibility of luring the independent gentry from their general loyalty to the king and Pitt, but if the government made a serious misjudgment about foreign affairs this was more likely to provoke a governmental crisis, with all the possibilities of a change of ministry, than any domestic issue could possibly do. Fox's staunch defence of British interests in the Low Countries was politically astute as well as perfectly genuine. Conviction and expediency happily coincided. The posture of stimulating the government to the more energetic defence of national interests was also consistent with Fox's previous criticisms of Pitt's policy of a commercial understanding with France, although whereas Fox was ill-informed about the technicalities of the Eden treaty he had a much better understanding of the Dutch problem. There was nothing mealy-mouthed about Fox's approach to foreign affairs; he never doubted that the government should seriously attend to foreign politics and that it should 'mix' in them.

Just as Fox criticised Pitt for being too hesitant in his treatment of the Dutch crisis, so during the Nootka Sound dispute he urged the government to the boldest possible assertion of British rights. He accepted all that this implied by way of rearmament and the risk of war. If there was one power which competed with France for Fox's distaste it was Spain. He detected the malignant influence of the family compact at work during the crisis and he favoured any policy which would strike at the power of France by diminishing that of Spain. When the Spaniards apprehended several British vessels off Vancouver Island old antagonisms flared up with astonishing intensity. The Spaniards repeated their old claim of sovereignty over the whole of the western coast of America, and argued that the small British settlement at Nootka Sound was a violation of Spanish rights. The Spaniards resented the exploitation of fishing and hunting grounds by British interlopers, while the British, sensitive as they were to opportunities for trade, whaling, fishing and settlement, refuted the obsolete Spanish claim and resented high-handed Spanish action. Pitt demanded satisfaction, and successfully asked parliament to vote a million pounds for the fleet, but he was more concerned with securing the enjoyment of commercial advantages and the redress of specific grievances than in becoming involved in controversies over speculative rights and disputes over sovereignty. The situation was made all the more uncertain by the ambivalent attitude of the French. Fortunately for Britain the national assembly chose to seize the opportunity to weaken the traditional control of the French king over foreign policy by denouncing the family compact as a principle of French foreign policy. French divisions prevented a firm French policy from being followed, while Holland and Prussia both gave every indication of remaining faithful to their commitments under the triple alliance. Eventually the Spaniards gave way; the prospect of facing British naval power without an ally was more than they could contemplate. But Pitt skilfully avoided discussions on the theoretical rights and wrongs of Spanish sovereignty. The British diplomatic victory was all the more remarkable for respecting Spanish susceptibilities. The British were allowed to set up commercial stations on the west coast of America, but they agreed to keep outside a limit of ten leagues round every Spanish settlement, to carry on their business peacefully, and to refrain from indulging in any illegal commerce with the Spanish colonies.

Fox watched all this with mixed feelings. He was convinced of the necessity of taking steps to put the British fleet in a state of preparedness, for he deeply resented an instance of unprovoked aggression on the part of the Spanish authorities. It was probable that immediate and vigorous armament would compel the Spaniards to come to terms without incurring the outbreak of hostilities, but the Spaniards had acted in a fashion which amply justified energetic military and naval preparations by the British government. It was high time, in Fox's view, to put an end to the absurd claim of the Spanish crown to the whole of the western coastline of north America. He claimed that any talk of agreed disarmament with France was unrealistic as long as the two branches of the house of Bourbon behaved as allies. He was unflinching and vehement in his denunciation of the Spanish claim and he pressed for the renunciation of this claim by the Spaniards as well as satisfaction for the specific outrages which had been inflicted upon British merchants and sailors:

> He conceived the exploded claim of the pope's demarcation to be wholly set aside, and that the discovery of any place, and making it the possession of this or that king by setting up a cross, or any other token of having been there, was equally exploded. In fact, occupancy and possession should be considered as the only right and title.[28]

He continued by expressing the hope

> that we should not rest contented merely with a satisfaction for the injury, but obtain a renunciation of the claim set up with so little ground of reason; that he conceived to be the intent and meaning of his majesty's message; and on that idea he heartily gave his vote for the address. As to the other topic, the disappointment of this country as to its situation, he hoped that it would prove a lesson to his majesty's ministers for the future, not to be too sanguine in their expectations of the permanency of peace when they were, in fact, on the eve of war.[29]

However frequently Fox avowed the intensity of his conviction that peace was to be preferred to war, he had no illusions as to the ease with which peace might be secured. Though he warned the government in the autumn of 1790 that it would be wise to seize every opportunity which changing circumstances allowed to adjust its choice of allies to the realities of a developing situation, he argued the case for a thorough going review of foreign policy on a basis of realism not altruism. Throughout the Nootka Sound dispute Fox criticised Pitt for a lack of toughness, and a willingness to defer to Spanish anxieties; characteristically Fox was inclined to elevate the issue of principle to major significance, while Pitt was concerned with tangible concessions and practicable objectives. Fox bewailed the limited nature of the British diplomatic triumph, but he erred in accusing Pitt of weakness. The Nootka Sound affair seemed to the majority of Englishmen to be yet another proof of Pitt's ability to command events, and to impose his will upon circumstances which were beset with difficulties. Despite Fox's misgivings Pitt's foreign policy had been consistently successful. The Eden treaty had been commercially advantageous without blinding the government to the dangers of French policy in the Low Countries. The Dutch crisis had firmly checked French designs and the triple alliance had survived the test of the dispute with Spain. Only when Pitt attempted to take a firm stand in the less familiar complexities of eastern European diplomacy did he experience diplomatic embarrassment and Fox come near to breaking the hold of the government on the loyalties of the house of commons.

But in domestic politics Pitt remained supreme. He brushed aside every attempt Fox made to expose weaknesses in his command of finance and administration. However mediocre many of his colleagues were this seemed merely to heighten the dominance wielded by Pitt over all branches of government. Even in foreign policy his was the decisive voice. Fox could only look to some stroke of unexpected fortune to rescue him from indefinite frustration. In the autumn of 1788 the illness of George III threw the political world into confusion. For the whigs it seemed as if a miracle was about to rescue them from the depths of defeat and despair. In the dubious company of the prince of Wales they anticipated returning to the delights of office. No one foresaw that the outcome of the regency crisis would see Fox and friends humiliated, divided, and even more distant from office than before.

During the summer of 1788 George III's health gave cause for anxiety and in October the king took a marked turn for the worse. He was incapable of performing his official duties and his behaviour was an acute embarrassment to his family and to his ministers. His conduct was unpredictable, periods of lucidity alternating with spasms of intense physical distress and mental confusion. He shook hands with a tree in Windsor Great Park, under the delusion that it was the king of Prussia; he attacked one of his pages, babbled incoherently about London being under water, and insulted and assaulted the prince of Wales at dinner. The king was out of his mind, but while for many years it has been usual to diagnose his affliction as recurrent manic depression, recent research has made out a strong case for a rare disease of the bodily metabolism, porphyria, which is consistent with the physical symptoms recorded by the king's doctors and with the mental breakdown which accompanied his illness. The diagnosis is interesting in that it would mean that the root cause of the king's incapacity was physical rather than mental, and this would do something to exonerate those of the king's doctors who were pessimistic in their prognosis, though they could not hope correctly to diagnose the king's illness, in the state of medical knowledge at the time.

The doctors differed widely in their views of what should be done; only when Willis arrived on the scene did some measure of optimism counterbalance the prevailing gloom. But for Pitt an insane or permanently incapacitated George III meant political extinction. If the king died the young George IV was bound to bring in Fox and the whigs; if the king survived as an invalid then the prince would become regent, and this too boded ill for Pitt, Fox and Portland undoubtedly being the prince's choice as his chief ministers. The situation was made all the more confusing by the constitutional issues raised by the king's incapacity. Did the prince have a right to the regency? If so, how was he to be invested with the office? Or did parliament have the initiating role in deciding who should be regent and what were his powers? Did parliament have the right to limit the prerogatives of the crown when these were to be exercised by a regent? These were the questions which formulated themselves in Pitt's mind as he studied both the precedents involved in providing for previous regencies and the political realities governing the struggle for power. A study of precedents proved more complicated than many men had anticipated, for was the king's illness to be held analogous to previous minorities of the crown or to royal absences from the country? The closest precedents were those providing for the carrying on of government during Henry VI's bouts of madness in 1454 and 1455, but even here the remoteness in time and the wholly different political and constitutional context made the correct interpretation of precedent exceedingly difficult.

Pitt shrewdly assessed the various alternatives. He prepared to resume his practice at the bar, but he was determined not to give in without a fight. He genuinely wished to do all in his power to safeguard the legitimate rights of the sick king, and once the doctors held out some hope of a recovery this became more urgent a priority. Pitt and Grenville gradually came to the conclusion that parliament had the right to choose the person of the regent, since no hereditary right to the regency could be held to reside in the heir to the throne, though apart from a brief consideration of the queen's claims it was unthinkable that anyone other than the prince of Wales should be nominated. They also decided that parliament could restrict the powers of a regent, and by limiting the regent's patronage they hoped to safeguard the rights of the king and their own chance of resuming office should George III's recovery be not too long delayed. Amid all the speculation, the flurry of conspiracy and intrigue, and the severest political pressures, Pitt remained cool and collected. He came to decisions which were constitutionally defensible and politically shrewd, and though he could not have anticipated the extent to which Fox was to make his task so much easier he kept his head in a situation of exceptional difficulty.

Fox was out of the country when the crisis broke, holidaying (as the newspapers said) 'no man knew where in the arms of faded beauty'. He was, in fact, enjoying the delights of Italy in the company of Mrs Armistead. His absence in the early days of the crisis had serious consequences for the whig party. Without Fox to seize the initiative and to determine the direction of party policy and the allocation of posts in the ministry the disruptive tendencies and personal rivalries which constantly threatened the credibility of the party had full sway. Sheridan exploited his friendship with the prince of Wales in order to push the opposition into a realistic assessment of the situation, which involved negotiating with Thurlow, the lord chancellor being eager to continue if possible in the new administration. This in turn offended Loughborough, who felt that he was being sacrificed to Thurlow's selfishness as much as in the interests of the party. Burke brooded on the constitutional issues raised by the crisis in virtual isolation. Since Rockingham's death he had lost the influence he had once had over the opposition leaders, and while most of his colleagues assumed that the king's illness would inevitably restore the party's fortunes Burke detected a lack of serious regard among the whigs for the constitutional principles involved in the regency, and most particularly for the principle of hereditary right. Where others were content to exploit the situation in the spirit of party advantage and political expediency Burke discerned in the principle of hereditary succession the clue to an understanding of the fundamentals of the case. Portland, the nominal leader of the party, foundered helplessly, seeking for a time to evade the burdens of responsibility by refusing to come to town or to discuss the crisis with his colleagues. Meanwhile the behaviour of the prince of Wales and the duke of York shocked respectable opinion; the public eagerly devoured rumours purporting to describe the king's state of mind and the unfilial and heart-less excesses of the prince and his brother. Though many men expected a change of ministry few contemplated it with equanimity. Fox, Burke and North were still distrusted, while Sheridan and Grey and the younger element in the opposition were despised as feckless adventurers.

As soon as Fox heard of the king's illness he abandoned his vacation and hurried home, neglecting his own comfort and convenience in a furious six-day gallop across Italy and France. The information which he picked up on his journey was fragmentary and bewildering and at one stage Fox expected George IV to have been declared king before he him-self arrived back in England. Worst of all Fox contracted dystentery on his homeward dash. He arrived in London physically exhausted, mentally tired and wracked by pain. He found confusion all about him, and he disapproved of much that had been done in his absence. But although he hated submitting to the possibility of Thurlow continuing as lord chan-cellor in a new government he reluctantly recognised that he had no alternative but to honour the undertakings which had been given by the prince and Sheridan, however vigorously he warned his friends against trusting Thurlow. If the lord chancellor was willing to betray confidential cabinet discussions to the opposition there was every reason for thinking that he would desert the opposition with as little impunity should it be to his own advantage to do so. It was small wonder that Fox found it diffi-cult to explain himself to Loughborough:

I am so perfectly ashamed of the letter I am writing that I scarce know how to begin.... When I first came over I found a very general anxiety among all our friends, and in the prince still more than others, to have the [lord] chancellor make a part of our new administration, and (ex-cepting only the duke of Portland) they all seemed to carry their wishes so far as to think his friendship worth buying, even at the expense of the great seal. This idea seemed so strange to me ... that I took all sorts of means to discourage it, and have actually prevented the prince ... from saying anything to Thurlow which might commit him.... The difficulties which have arisen within these last few days ... have had the effect of increasing the anxiety of our friends for Thurlow's support ... I feel the part I am acting to be contrary to every principle of con-duct I ever laid down for myself and that I can bring myself to act at all I strongly suspect to be more owing to my weakness than my judgment....[30]

By the time he wrote to Loughborough Fox had already committed his biggest error of judgment in the whole of the crisis. During the debate in the house of commons on 10 December Pitt had moved for the appointment of a committee 'to examine into, search for, and report precedents', arguing that although the doctors' report suggested that it was possible that the king would recover from his incapacity it was important to move towards settling the constitutional problems which the king's illness raised without further delay. Fox sensed the skill with which Pitt was playing for time. After so many years of frustration even a delay of a week was more than he could bear. It seemed obvious that the prince of Wales should be regent; Fox saw no reason to allow Pitt to stay in office for a day longer than was necessary. He was impatient with arid technicalities and contemptuous of procrastination. He had not discussed the constitutional aspects of the crisis with his friends; their discussions had been devoted to considerations of political tactics and the conflicting claims of various personalities to posts in the new administration. Fox's fluency as a debater misled him, his ability to manufacture arguments on the spur of the moment luring him into a disastrous miscalculation. His eagerness to seize power, and his loathing for Pitt's obstinate refusal to accept the inevitable, led him to affirm that Pitt's motion was irrelevant to the primary task of providing for the current exigency:

> What were they going to search for? ... Not parliamentary precedents, but precedents in the history of England. He would be bold to say ... that the doing so would prove a loss of time, for there existed no precedent whatever that could bear upon the present case.... There was a person in the kingdom different from any other person that any existing precedents could refer to—an heir apparent of full age and capacity to exercise the royal power. It behoved them, therefore, to waste not a moment unnecessarily, but to proceed with all becoming diligence to restore the sovereign power, and the exercise of the royal authority.[31]

Fox ignored the genuine constitutional predicament; the question was not the person of the regent, but rather how he was to be appointed and whether or not his powers were to be restricted in certain respects. There would undoubtedly be difficulties and controversy over the interpretation of precedents; but this did not mean that an examination of precedents was pointless. Even those who sympathised with Fox's desire to settle the problem of the regency as quickly as possible were hardly prepared for what followed.

> The prince of Wales had as clear, as express a right to assume the reins of government, and exercise the power of sovereignty during the continuance of the illness and incapacity with which it had pleased God to

afflict his majesty, as in the case of his majesty's having undergone a perfect and natural demise; and, as to this right which he conceived the prince of Wales had he was himself to judge when he was entitled to exercise it, but the two houses of parliament as the organs of the nation, were alone qualified to pronounce when the prince ought to take possession of and exercise his right.... But ought he to wait unnecessarily? ... while precedents were searched for, when it was known that none that bore on the case which so nearly concerned him existed? ... He should not oppose the motion, but he thought it his duty to say, that it was incumbent upon the house to lose no time in restoring the third estate.[32]

In his anxiety to discount the search for precedents Fox thoughtlessly brought the constitutional aspects of the crisis to the centre of the struggle for power. By defining the right of the prince of Wales to the regency in a style which seemed to reduce the lords and the commons to the ambiguous status of mere ratifiers of what the prince had already decided for himself Fox offended those members of the house who were especially sensitive to any attack on the privileges of parliament. By suggesting that the temporary incapacity of the king was analogous to the death of the monarch Fox played into the hands of those who were anxious to study precedents in order to satisfy themselves about the complexities of the situation. Most seriously of all, Fox's unguarded and imprecise language allowed Pitt to stand forth as the defender of parliament against what many men interpreted as a shameless assertion of royal prerogative. As Fox was speaking Pitt slapped his thigh, whispering to his neighbour that he would unwhig the gentleman for life, and for the rest of the crisis Fox and his friends were fighting a protracted rearguard action against the dismal consequences of the debate of 10 December.

It was easy for Pitt to remind the commons that the wild assertions which Fox had made were themselves convincing reasons for appointing a committee of the type which he had proposed. Pitt stressed the responsibility of the lords and commons for providing for the due exercise of executive powers when the personal exercise of the prerogatives of the crown was interrupted by illness. Pitt conceded that the prince of Wales had an 'irresistible claim' to the regency, but he denied that this was synonymous with the notion of inherent right.

> However strong the arguments might be ... in favour of the prince of Wales ... it did not affect the question of right; because neither the whole, nor any part, of the royal authority could belong to him in the present circumstances, unless conferred by the two houses of parliament.

As to the right honourable gentleman's repeated enforcement of the prince of Wales's claim, he admitted that it was a claim entitled to their most serious consideration; and thence ... it was more necessary to learn how the house had acted in cases of similar exigency, and what had been the opinion of parliament on such occasions. He would not allow that no precedent analogous to an interruption of the personal exercise of the royal authority could be found, although there might possibly not exist a precedent of an heir apparent in a state of majority during such an occurrence, and in that case ... it devolved on the part of the people of England, to exercise their discretion in providing a substitute.... The question now was, the question of their own rights.[33]

No amount of skilful sophistry by Fox could effectively counteract the impact of Pitt's speech. To many backbenchers the primary issue became the defence of the privileges of parliament. It seemed pedantic for Fox to argue that because of the incapacity of the king parliament could not be said to be complete. This was taken as further evidence of Fox's baffling anxiety to affirm the prerogative power in language offensive to the majority of MPs. His dependence on the prince was well known; it appeared as if he was willing to abandon every principle in order to ingratiate himself with the prince. The man who had made a political alliance with North, in defiance of prior assurances, who had wantonly attempted to exploit the East India company's patronage, in order to impose himself upon the king, and who had persistently posed as the unflinching critic of the influence of the crown, was now asserting the prince's right to the regency because this was the quickest way of installing himself in power. Within days handbills and posters were widely distributed, contrasting Fox's assertion of the prince's prerogative with Pitt's defence of the privileges of parliament, and the liberties of the nation. Grenville voiced the feelings of Fox's opponents when he confessed to his brother, 'Fox's declaration of the prince of Wales's right has been of no small service to us. Is it not wonderful that such great talents should be conducted with so little judgment?'[34]

Astonishment was not limited to the government benches. Grey and Sheridan rebuked Fox as they drove away together after the debate, and though they realised that in public they would have to try to save something from the wreck, in their hearts they bitterly regretted Fox's speech. Sheridan was particularly angry. He shared Fox's impatience and for public and private reasons he was itching to get into office. He had assiduously cultivated the prince, and he had no illusions about the realities on which all political calculations had to be based. But Fox had violated what to Sheridan was the fundamental principle guiding the conduct of the opposition: the need to sacrifice every speculative consideration to the urgent priority of getting into office as quickly as possible. Once installed in power the prince and his friends would be able to dispense with any restrictions at their convenience. Sheridan would have allowed Pitt's committee to have been approved without debate, but once the abstract issue had been raised it was impossible for the opposition to evade the controversy. Fox's blunder had enabled Pitt to dictate the terms of the debate and to select the ground on which the conflict was to be fought.

Possibly Fox's willingness to raise the prince's inherent right to the regency sprang from a desire to mollify Loughborough, who had been asked to sacrifice his hopes of the lord chancellorship in order to increase the opposition's chances of gaining Thurlow. Loughborough had outlined the doctrine of inherent right in a paper prepared for the prince; it was easy for Fox to take up this line of argument, hoping that it would convince Loughborough that his views were appreciated and that his opinions and expertise were valued within the party. But while Fox adopted the theory of inherent right as a gesture of confidence towards one disgruntled member of the opposition he committed the party—in ignorance and against its better judgment—to a constitutional principle which neither he nor the majority of his colleagues were competent to defend. Because he failed to take the constitutional aspects of the crisis with complete seriousness Fox blithely created a trap which enmeshed all the members of the opposition.

It was understandable that Fox's misjudgment should outrage his friends and raise doubts about the efficacy of his leadership. The duchess of Devonshire, who always retained a deep affection for Fox, nevertheless lamented in after life that Fox's foibles told against him during the regency crisis, citing in particular 'a contempt for even necessary expedients, a great imprudence in conversation; and a fear, which in him is superior to anything, of seeming to yield what he thinks right to the bias of public opinion'. Even this could be misread as indicating too severe a devotion to principle on Fox's part; if he had to set his face against public opinion this was because he had outraged popular sentiment by his provocative assertions in the house of commons, not because he had selflessly advocated lofty ideals in a spirit of disinterested patriotism.

Fox was too experienced a house of commons man not to sense the seriousness of his mistake but he was complacently confident of the possibility of avoiding the worst consequences of his misjudgment by some dazzling performance in the house. On 12 December he assured the commons that he had spoken two days earlier in an individual capacity; he had not been speaking on behalf of the prince of Wales. He then sought to win over the house by making a distinction between the right of the prince to be regent and the actual possession of that right, reinstating parliament with at least a deliberative role in the emergency:

> He conceived the exercise of the royal authority to be the right of the prince of Wales, but he had spoken of it as a right and not a possession. Before the prince could exercise that right he must appeal to the court competent to decide ... or must wait until that court ... made such a declaration. That court was composed of the two houses of parliament while they were sitting; the prince had the right, but the adjudication of that right belonged to the two houses.[35]

But instead of clarifying the point at issue this only added to the prevalent confusion. Many MPs found it difficult to grasp the distinction between a right which needed parliamentary adjudication and a claim which deserved the consideration of the two houses. Fox seemed to be striving to make his original statement mean something quite different from what it had been taken to mean; Pitt had put forward a consistent and lucid argument. The more Fox wriggled, the more he took refuge in allegations of misrepresentation and victimisation, the more dubious and bewildering his conduct appeared in the eyes of the majority of backbenchers. When Fox tried to turn the bafflement of MPs to his own advantage by arguing that the distinction between an inherent right and an irresistible claim was an irrelevant speculative point many men felt that if this was so why had he been so insistent on urging the prince's right in the first place. Every tactical inspiration only threw Fox's strategic blunder into greater relief. The means of installing the prince as regent, and the range of powers which was to be granted to him, were hardly irrelevant abstractions; they were the essentials of the controversy, for they would determine the duration of any new administration. If, for example, the prince was not to have the right to dissolve parliament, the regent would be deprived of a valuable method of strengthening his ministers' position in the house of commons. Fox was compelled, therefore, to plead the case for granting the full prerogatives of the crown to the regent, and this enabled Pitt to defend the privileges of parliament and the rights of the sick king. Such a combination of virtuous purposes was beyond the capacity of the opposition to refute or resist. Even Sheridan, in some ways the most irrepressible of Fox's colleagues, became depressed and sunk in gloomy lethargy. Fox's mistake had led to vociferous and vituperative controversy within the ranks of the opposition, and Pitt ruthlessly exploited every weakness in his opponent's case. The cheerful optimism which had buoyed up the opposition during November gave way in December to anxiety and fretful distrust, the frustrated Foxites venting their spite upon each other. Fox was in many ways the scapegoat; his intervention in the debate of 10 December was seen as the turning point, and try as he did to right the situation he became more embroiled in toils of his own making. His obstinacy did not help; when Sheridan urged that it would be expedient for the prince to accept the regency, even with restrictions on his right to create peers, Fox refused to make such a concession. Every defeat in the house of commons provoked further dissensions among the whigs.

Yet even in the midst of these tribulations Fox remained perversely optimistic. Perhaps he could not bring himself to admit the magnitude of his initial blunder, or the skill with which Pitt had exploited it. Fox refused to allow that Sheridan had been right and that he had been wrong. He had heard ugly stories of Sheridan's behaviour during the weeks when he had been absent on the continent; although he relied upon the prince to bring him and his friends into office he could never trust him as he had done before the scandal of the Fitzherbert marriage. He knew that he had made a mistake, that it had been embarrassing, perhaps unnecessary, but he could not accept that it had been decisive. He exerted all his charm upon his friends to win their forgiveness, and if Pitt had won the opening battle Fox still believed that Pitt would lose the war. So much turned on the king's health, and Fox, seeking to discern a silver lining behind every black cloud, found it comforting to accept Dr Warren's gloomiest forecasts about his royal patient. Despite the short-term disappointments which he had encountered Fox refused to give up hope. He was weak and physically exhausted and he needed the mental stimulus of the prospect of power; when he wrote to Mrs Armistead on 15 December he surveyed the political situation optimistically:

Though I am fatigued to death, and ought to go to bed it being near three, I cannot let go the opportunity ... to write a few lines to my Liz. ... We shall have several hard fights in the house of commons this week, and next, in some of which I fear we shall be beat, but whether we are or not, I think it certain that in about a fortnight we shall come in. If we carry our questions we shall come in in a more creditable and triumphant way, but at any rate the prince must be regent and of consequence the ministry must be changed. The manner in which the prince has behaved throughout the whole has been most steady, the most friendly, and the handsomest that can be conceived. You know when he sets his mind to a thing he can do it well, and in this instance he has done so most thoroughly. The duke of York who is steadiness itself has undoubtedly contributed to keep him to his good resolutions and seems as warmly our friend as the prince himself. In short with regard to the princes everything is easy and pleasant much beyond what I could form any idea of. In regard to other things I am rather afraid they will get some cry against the prince for grasping as they call it at too much power, but I am sure I cannot in consequence advise him to give up anything that is really necessary to his government, or to claim anything else as regent, but the full power of a king, to which he is certainly entitled. The king himself (notwithstanding the reports which you may possibly hear) is certainly worse and perfectly mad. I believe the chance of his recovery is very small indeed but I do not think there is any probability of his dying. Adieu, my dearest Liz. It is so late that I can only write here what I dare not by post. The sooner you come the better, but I own I think this next fortnight will be such a scene of hurry that I should have little time to enjoy what I most value in the world, my dearest Liz's company. I take for granted you want some money and will if I can send you some by next post, but I have hardly a minute to myself, either to get the money or to write, adieu my dear Liz, indeed, indeed, you are more than all the world to me.[36]

Fox's attitude was a strange mixture of brash self-confidence and uneasy doubt. Even when expressing his satisfaction at the prince's conduct he could not disguise the uncertainty lurking beneath the surface. He failed to analyse either the general political situation or the tensions within the opposition. He preferred to believe what was congenial, relying on events to rescue him from the consequences of his own folly. His own expectations were unpredictable, fluctuating with every mood and with every bulletin on the king's condition. On one day Fox was cheerfully boasting of the virtual certainty of defeating the government in the commons; on the next briskly reconciling himself to a sequence of reverses in the house. So long as he clutched desperately at every straw of comfort he was incapable of thinking through the constitutional problems posed by the crisis, and for as long as he shrank from the difficulties raised by the constitutional wrangle which he had so thoughtlessly provoked he could not provide his supporters with the consistent and coherent leadership they so urgently needed. As the debates dragged out their weary course Fox was compelled to utter contradiction after contradiction, denying the relevance of precedents in the same breath as he attempted to persuade the house of commons that the precedents drawn from the reign of Henry VI actually supported his side of the question. Above everything else the principle of inherent right dogged every step in the argument, embarrassing Fox yet compelling him to explain and justify himself at the same time, and preventing him from focusing his attention upon a realistic consideration of the more practical controversy over the limitations which Pitt proposed to impose upon the regent.

On 16 December the opposition was soundly trounced in the commons by 268 votes to 204, and thereafter Fox was unable to recover the initiative. Though he was eventually forced to yield to pressure to be more flexible in giving Sheridan a free hand in negotiation with Northumberland and Stormont, who were seeking to chart a middle course between the Pittite and Foxite positions with a keen eye for self-advancement, he had at least the satisfaction of seeing the negotiation with Thurlow collapse. It was with considerable relief and pleasure that Fox wrote to Loughborough on 26 December:

> The negotiation is off with an express desire on his part that no more may be said to him on the subject till the regency is settled. . . . It was the pleasantest conversation I have had with him for years. . . . In short I think the negotiation is fairly at an end; and if when the regency is settled the prince wishes to revive it, it must be considered as a proposition entirely new and treated upon that footing.[37]

But Fox's jubilation was clouded by the realisation that Thurlow's change of heart was more likely to have resulted from a shrewd calculation that the odds now favoured Pitt than from any profound concern with the issues of principle raised by the regency debates. Thurlow had a remarkable instinct for self-preservation; his judgment of what was in his own best interests rarely erred. Fox wondered whether the tide of events was now running steadily in Pitt's favour, but whatever his misgivings he had to shrug them off and present a cheerful face to the world.

Fox was still suffering from recurrent bouts of sickness and dysentery. His physical weakness was commented on during the debate in the commons on 16 December; though he spoke as well as he had ever done his supporters noticed that it was only with great difficulty that he was able to finish his speech. Three days later Sir John Eden remarked that he should not be surprised if Fox fell 'a martyr to his exertions, for he is very far from well'. Fox's health became a subject for newspaper speculation, and it was claimed that he was suffering from an obstruction in the bladder. Though the journalists overdramatised Fox's plight there was no doubt that he was very poorly indeed. It was doubly hard for him to bear political disappointment at the same time that his health collapsed and he must have deeply resented the way in which so many of his political associates blamed his speech of 10 December for delivering the opposition into the relentless hands of William Pitt. Grave though Fox's error had been he had little respect for those who eagerly made him into a scapegoat, as if he bore the sole responsibility for the misfortunes of the opposition.

It was not only within the house of commons that the opposition suffered disappointments, as the old year died. Public meetings in towns throughout the country were voting addresses in support of Pitt and condemning Fox's defence of the royal prerogative. Though it was possible for Fox to be philosophical over the resolutions of the merchants and bankers of the city of London and of the corporation of Cambridge approving Pitt's conduct he could not be so disdainful of the news from the provinces. The preponderant element in public activity was clearly Pittite. Fitzwilliam lamented the failure to revive the opposition interest in Yorkshire, where his agents counselled caution because of their reluctance to risk rekindling the popular passions which had proved so injurious to their interests in the 1784 general election. As information came in from various areas the Foxites had to admit that prevailing opinion was decidedly with Pitt. To add to this humiliation the news came through that the king's health was improving, and that despite setbacks the doctors were confident of a recovery in the not too distant future. Fox and his friends had initially expected a quick end to the crisis. They had not anticipated having to fight a long campaign. Many men, including some who were wholly antipathetic to Fox, had shared the belief that the king's illness would bring about a speedy change of ministry, but once these expectations were proved false the protracted nature of the dispute became itself a factor working against the opposition. Those who had tried to reinsure themselves against an imminent reversal in government drew back from too hasty a commitment to Fox when his entry into office was delayed. It was one thing for Fox to be installed promptly by a regent without controversy; it was another for the opposition to become the government only after a lengthy period of complicated theoretical disputation and shady political intrigue. The longer the crisis lasted the more men realised what they risked losing if Pitt was turned out, and the more dubious they became about what would take his place. On Christmas Day George Cavendish expressed the disappointment of the opposition when writing to Mrs Ponsonby: Pitt had been supported by bigger majorities in the commons than anyone had thought possible. He continued: 'On our side was some misfortune and perhaps some mismanagement. We despise parliamentary craft too much, and are sadly deficient in it.'[38] It was a sad comment on Fox's leadership of the party.

The new year brought little consolation. On 2 January W. W. Cornwall, the speaker of the house of commons, died and on 5 January William

Wyndham Grenville was chosen as his successor by 215 votes to 144. This was another resounding triumph for Pitt, who saw his cousin elected at a time when the proposed restrictions on the powers of the regent were to be debated in the commons. Sir Gilbert Elliot, the opposition candidate, had been put forward only after a period of prolonged wrangling. Fox was doubtful about the wisdom of contesting the election and only gave his approval to Elliot's candidature the day before the vote. While the government had canvassed for Grenville as soon as the speakership was vacant the opposition had not canvassed on Elliot's behalf until the morning of the election.

Ironically, when the commons returned to discussing the regency on 6 January, Fox supported a call for a new inquiry into the precise state of the king's health. This could only delay the installation of the regent still further, but Fox was hoping to undermine the confidence of the house in the optimistic versions of the king's condition which the government were putting abroad. He hoped to expose Willis as an unscrupulous charlatan, but by lending his support to a new examination of the doctors he could cloak his objective with at least a degree of objectivity. Fox was also anxious to distract attention from the rivalries which were rife among the opposition over the allocation of posts in the new administration. But it was an indication of the extent to which Fox had lost ground in the conflict that he pressed for a re-examination of the doctors at a time when Pitt was eager to press on with his proposed restrictions.

On 10 January Fox was ill again; he was too exhausted to attend a party conference and in his absence new quarrels broke out between Sheridan and Grey, Sheridan being accused of currying favour with the prince and encouraging newspaper criticism of Fox. Not even the emergence of North from virtual retirement, to which his blindness had confined him, could restore the morale of the opposition, although North's contribution to the commons' debates showed that he had lost little of his gift for sensing the mood of the house and appealing to the members' sense of fairness and moderation.

Despite his physical debility Fox forced himself to play a major part in the debates over the Pitt's limitations. The new examination of the physicians proved a disappointment; far from discrediting the doctors who argued that the king was on the way to recovery it convinced many of the independents that the prospects for a recovery were good. Fox was cruelly dissatisfied with Warren's performance, but he could hardly expect the doctor to do the impossible. The stories which had leaked out about arguments between the king's doctors damaged Warren's reputation more than Willis'. Warren's known whig loyalties prevented men from accepting him as an impartial expert. But more time had been lost, and Fox was aware that his supporters were divided in their attitudes towards the restrictions; some wished to submit to Pitt's limitations in order to hasten the prince's investiture as regent; others wished to fight the government's proposals every inch of the way.

Pitt asked the commons on 16 January to approve his restrictions on the regency. The regent was not to possess the power of creating peers of the realm, except in the instance of members of the royal family, or of granting any office, salary or pension in reversion or for any other period than during his majesty's pleasure, except such offices as the law required to be granted for life or during good behaviour. The regent was not to dispose of any part of the king's personal or real estate, while the care of the king's person, and the control of the royal household, were to remain with the queen. Fox immediately recognised the seriousness of the limitations on the prince's patronage for any new administration striving to build up its support in the lords and commons. It would be impossible adequately to reward old friends, let alone entice waverers to cast in their lot with the government. Not surprisingly North warned the commons of the constitutional dangers involved in the policy of restriction, while Sheridan affirmed that the only motive behind the policy of restriction was Pitt's knowledge that the prince would take into his service a different set of ministers from those in office. On 19 January Fox made a forthright attack on the government's policy in general and the proposals affecting the royal household in particular. The wisdom of our ancestors, he argued, had invested all the prerogatives necessary for good government in the king, but the government's proposals would deprive government of the powers essential for its competence. He emphasized the seriousness of making such a change in the nature of the royal office, linking what was proposed with the evident obscurities of medical opinion:

> It might be for a short time; it might be for a long time; it was certainly for an indefinite time that they were to change the constitution of the country, and all this was to be done on the report of the physicians. Physicians had acknowledged that the science of physic was the most uncertain of all arts; and that of all branches of physics, this particular malady was the most uncertain. So then they were, for an unlimited time, to change the nature of the third estate, to impoverish and weaken the executive arm, to create a new estate in the country; and all this, on the report of the most uncertain case which can come within the view of the most uncertain of all sciences.[39]

But however inventive Fox was in argument, to many MPs his concern for the constitutional rights of the crown seemed hollow and false, inspired by a calculation of political advantage rather than by a disinterested regard for the balance of the constitution. Pitt's limitations were carried by comfortable majorities of 65 and 56.

Worse still for Fox was the embarrassment of seeing Rolle raise the question of the Fitzherbert marriage in the closing stages of the debate. The issue was fraught with danger for the opposition. Fortunately Pitt was as determined as his opponents to prevent the dispute over the regency from becoming embroiled with a sensational inquiry into the scandals of the prince's private life, and the issue did not take the turn that at one stage Fox feared it might. But though a formal investigation was refused the mere raising of the subject in the commons was a reminder of the vulnerability of the prince on this delicate matter.

Fox was finding the strain intolerable. Earlier in the crisis the conviction that he stood on the brink of office had buoyed him up. Now disappointment and vexation added their toll to the exactions of dysentery. He was caught up in trying to patch up troublesome quarrels between his followers over the allocation of places in the new government and in trying to find places for Northumberland and Stormont and others of the so-called armed neutrality, who had now thrown in their lot with the opposition. But a price had to be paid and Fox complained bitterly of the difficulties of dealing with 'these most unreasonable people'. Plans for an impressive public meeting in Westminster came to nothing, and it was a weary and frustrated Fox who left London on 28 January for Bath, where he intended to take a cure for his health.

His stay at Bath restored his health, but although he corresponded with Portland on political subjects and the distribution of posts in the new ministry, he could only watch events move still further in Pitt's favour. The final debates were enlivened by Burke's vehement defence of the principle of hereditary right and those fundamentals of the constitution which he thought were being threatened by the conduct of the government and betrayed by the opposition's fondness for expediency rather than principle. But however selfless Burke's devotion to what he conceived his duty to be was, he merely roused suspicions of his sanity and fortified the conviction of many members that Pitt's approach to the regency made sense. Fox remained optimistic, ignoring everything that was uncongenial and clinging desperately to the delusion that the favourable reports of the king's improvement were ill-founded. He was heartened by good news from Dublin of the Irish parliament's disdain for a policy of limitations, and he tried to stiffen the resolve of his friends in London. He bewailed the 'habitual spirit of despondency and fear' that characterised his party and however disgusted he was with Warren he obstinately argued that no change of policy should be agreed upon simply in response to rumours of the king's recovery. When a public meeting was finally held in Westminster on 14 February, after the breakdown of previous plans, Fox congratulated his constituents for voting an address of support for the prince, although only a fortnight earlier he had been relieved by the decision to drop such a meeting. Fox was retreating from reality: he had seemed so close to breaking out of the defeats of the post-coalition years that a victory for Pitt was too hideous to contemplate. But once the opposition found difficulties in their path there was no reason for thinking that any irresistible tendency would carry either themselves or the prince to the delights of office. On 17 February the official bulletin declared George III to be convalescent. Three days later the prince of Wales and the duke of York saw their father and on 24 February Pitt had an interview with the king at Kew. Fox had recovered his health, but that was small comfort when compared with the dire consequences which followed his monarch's restoration to his senses. It was pathetic to look for any sign of a relapse. Pitt had won—deservedly so, for he earned his good fortune by his consummate statecraft. Fox had had one amazing piece of luck; because of a combination of bad judgment and bad fortune he was incapable of exploiting his initial advantage.

His opportunism was much in evidence throughout the crisis. However deeply he became entangled in the complexities of the theory of inherent right he was paying for verbal dexterity rather than suffering on behalf of any profound idealism. His absence in the opening weeks of the political crisis compelled him to acquiesce in decisions which he might have avoided or deferred, and his illness removed him from the centre of power when the policy of the opposition was being hammered out (though the steady recovery of the king was already rendering those discussions meaningless). Had Fox been wholly unprincipled, had he followed the line so consistently urged by Sheridan of getting into office as quickly as possible even if this meant accepting Pitt's advocacy of a parliamentary initiative and his restrictions, it was probable that the prince might have become regent and Fox foreign secretary in a ministry headed by Portland two or three weeks before the king recovered towards the end of February. But the certainty of such a hold on office was highly questionable, and there were valid reasons for not allowing Pitt's handling of the situation to go unchallenged. Fox had no desire to take part in a ministerial reshuffle, by which the prince brought his friends into the government while leaving Pitt first lord of the treasury. It seemed expedient to refuse to follow Pitt's lead in meeting the exigency caused by the king's illness;

it also appeared unimportant in determining the outcome of events, for Fox was convinced that nothing could prevent a change of ministry: the king's incapacity was assumed to be irrevocable and decisive. There was nothing to lose, and perhaps there was something to gain, by heightening the impression that there was, after all, a real difference of approach separating Pitt from Fox. The error was in indulging in careless talk about the constitutional aspects of the crisis without fully analysing them first. Fox was not only seen as subordinating the examination of the technicalities of a regency to the pursuit of power, he was exposed as ignorant and impulsive, a shallow rhetorician who preferred the satisfactions of a temporary triumph to the long-term interests of the country. If this judgment seems harsh it is no harsher than the exasperated criticisms of Fox's disappointed colleagues, who were in no doubt of the degree of responsibility which Fox had to bear for their continued exclusion from office. Fox ought to have consulted his companions before raising the constitutional issue so provocatively in the house of commons; if an attempt were to be made to challenge Pitt's reading of what was procedurally correct it required much more careful preparation than either Fox or Loughborough had given to the problem. The only opposition spokesman who had probed deeply into the constitutional aspects of a regency was Burke, but he had little influence over the party as a whole and he was not close to Fox at this period.

Yet Fox's blunders were themselves reflections of the impossible contradictions created by the conditions of opposition in the 1780s. The loyalties within the whig party were fragile and personal, too dependent on the gratification of restless ambitions and too vulnerable to the erosions of frustrated aspiration to sustain the miseries of a defeat snatched from the jaws of victory. Fox knew that his only hope of office lay in the patronage of the prince of Wales and this blinded him to the complexities of the situation created by the illness of the king. Yet he ought to have been more sensitive to the obvious accusations which would follow too vehement an affirmation of the doctrine of inherent right; as the relentless opponent of anything savouring of the influence of the crown he ought to have been respectful of the privileges of parliament, despite the need to dissociate himself from Pitt and his understandable impatience to get into office with the least delay. Had Fox limited himself to arguing for the advisability of speed, without committing himself to any interpretation of precedent, he would have achieved his political objective without laying himself open to the Pittite counter-attack. He would also have avoided distressing his friends.

The crisis revealed weaknesses in the opposition which the controversy over the French revolution was to intensify and exacerbate. It is true that the dispute over the revolution did not follow the same lines as that over the regency and that the personal antagonisms which had been heightened by the earlier crisis were not synonymous with those which characterised the latter. Nevertheless the suspicions and resentments nursed by many members of the opposition after their failure to oust Pitt made it less easy for them to sustain the renewed strains upon their loyalties imposed by the French controversy. Fox's credibility as the spiritual leader of the whigs was significantly damaged by his folly during the regency debates. Those who believed that their prospects had been blighted by his thoughtlessness were reluctant to take his insight into the French situation on trust, the more so since his apparent enthusiasm clashed with their own misgivings. Burke's isolation during the winter of 1788-9 made him all the more inclined to throw party loyalty to the winds when another crisis broke which involved issues of fundamental principle and profound political conviction. Any ideological unity which the opposition possessed was an accidental legacy from the American war. It had been rendered irrelevant to the needs of political controversy by events since 1783; now it was fractured and fragmented by the regency crisis. The French revolution destroyed it utterly, and by so doing it destroyed the old Rockinghamite party for ever.

But before the full measure of the French revolution's significance for the opposition was generally appreciated Fox once again experienced the tantalising frustration of coming close to success, and this time, though Pitt fended off the challenge, Fox was the one whose reputation in the house rose, and who sustained his sense of political purpose throughout a complex controversy. As Fox had often said, the opportunity for embarrassing the government came in the field of foreign policy. Here he was invariably at his best; he had no factious past to live down, for he had supported Pitt's foreign policy on a number of occasions. His sense of what was practicable in the conduct of foreign affairs enabled him to criticise the ministry for over-extending themselves, for interfering in a part of the world which they did not understand and for adopting public postures which they lacked the military resources to sustain.

British policy over the Orchakov affair was a series of uncertain responses to a sequence of events in eastern Europe which the government could do little to control. The situation was made all the more perplexing because the attitudes of the other powers, including Britain's ally Prussia, was by no means easy to determine. There was nothing new about disputes between the Austrians and Russians and the Ottoman empire. Catherine II pursued a consistently hostile policy towards Turkey throughout the 1780s, while Joseph II had not been remiss in attacking the Turks. A Russian army pushed as far as Bucharest; an Austrian army occupied Belgrade. Frederick William of Prussia was already contemplating extending his sphere of influence in Poland, but though he was uneasy at the prospect of an increase of Russian power in the Balkans he could not make up his mind whether the continuation of the war between Russia and Turkey was a welcome distraction for a powerful rival or an ominous means of aggrandising a future opponent. The death of Joseph II meant that Austrian policy towards the Turks became less ambitious: Leopold II came to terms with the Sultan. But Catherine II saw no reason for making peace; her armies were still successful in the field, and there seemed nothing to be gained by halting their advance. The more territory she occupied the more favourable would be the peace she could wring out of a defeated and isolated foe. Moved neither by sentiment nor by any concern for the interests of other powers she was eager to take everything that the fortunes of war placed in her grasp.

The king of Prussia became frightened and turned to England for help. With the Austrians out of the war with Turkey it seemed sensible to try to induce the Russian empress to make peace. Frederick William reminded his British allies that if the Russians established too great a superiority over the Turks this could prejudice British interests. He proposed persuading the Russian empress to cede Orchakov to Turkey and he trusted that the Austrians would support an attempt to terminate the Russo-Turkish war.

The British cabinet was divided. The duke of Leeds, the foreign secretary, favoured a firm policy: above everything else the triple alliance must be preserved, and if Russia became too powerful in the eastern Mediterranean this could adversely affect British interests in an area which was vital to her commerce and to one route to her Indian empire. The duke of Richmond, on the other hand, vehemently opposed any commitment implying a willingness or intention to go to war with Russia. British naval power alone could not counter-balance Russian designs against Turkey, or her plans for expansion in the Balkans. Without the active support of the Prussians, to defy, outrage or provoke Russia was tantamount to inviting disaster. The ambivalent and indecisive behaviour of the king of Prussia, whose attitude was bellicose and pacific by turns, made it impossible fully to rely on Prussian support. It was by no means clear what would be gained by antagonising Catherine over a town on the Black Sea of which few people had ever heard. Nor was it easy to say exactly which British interests were directly threatened by the success of the Russian armies in their campaign against the Turks. The triple alliance owed its existence to an identity of interests in the Low Countries; it was essentially a defensive alliance, and it did not commit Britain to supporting Prussian policy in eastern Europe, any more than it involved Prussia in the defence of British interests in India. There was no common interest binding Prussia and Britain together in their attitudes towards events in Poland or the Balkans. Whatever opinions British statesmen might entertain about the partitioning of Poland there was nothing they could do to influence matters one way or the other.

The tensions within the cabinet were manifested in Pitt's behaviour throughout the crisis. Not surprisingly for a minister who favoured a strong, though by no means an aggressive or intransigent foreign policy, he sympathised with Leeds' point of view, but he was also conscious of the difficulties of convincing the commons of the need to challenge Russia over Orchakov in order to secure 'the most valuable interests of the country'. He was apprehensive about any risks to the willingness of the commons to vote supplies and he regarded the diminution of the government's majority with grave concern. He was so uncertain of what the Prussians would do that he refused to yield to demands in the house of commons for further information, and attempted to avoid speaking himself on the issue unless he was absolutely driven to do so.

This strengthened the opposition to an extent which shocked and surprised Pitt. On 12 April the government's majority slumped to 80, and although it would be foolish to exaggerate the possibility of resignation so far as Pitt was concerned the morale of the opposition was boosted. Fox was excited, but cautious: he had no exaggerated expectations of immediate success, gratifying though the reverses inflicted on the government were. Pitt moved towards a more moderate policy. The most provocative draft ultimatum had never been sent. Pitt sent a message to the Russian empress, conceding her right to keep Orchakov, and the duke of Leeds resigned in protest. Within four months Russia and Turkey made peace (August 1791). Nevertheless, though the outcome had been neither his own departure from office nor the collapse of Turkey, Pitt confessed that the Orchakov affair was the greatest mortification he had ever experienced.

Fox could boast that the final result was ample justification for the policy which he urged all along. He had consistently argued the folly of risking a war for the recovery of a single town. But he had also taken care to relate the Orchakov affair to the ultimate aims of British foreign policy. He thought it wrong to discuss the crisis in isolation, and he was at pains to refute accusations of partisanship or opportunism which were levelled at the opposition. In the debate of 29 March 1791 he reminded the house of commons that he and friends had supported the government's firm policies during the Dutch crisis and the Nootka Sound dispute, and whatever criticisms they had made in detail the triple alliance had had their uncompromising support. But it was not enough for the government to mouth generalities:

> When gentlemen talked of the balance of power as a reason for arming, they ought to show how it is endangered. When they called for supplies to prevent the aggrandisement of Russia, new as it was to a British house of commons to hear the greatness of Russia represented as an object of dread, they ought to state whom she meant to attack. Was it Prussia against whom her arms were to be directed?[40]

Fox pointed out that for at least twenty years Russia had been involved in clashes with Turkey and no British government had been alarmed by the way in which Russia was strengthening her position in the Black Sea. In 1782 Britain had actually refused to respond to suggestions by the French and Spanish governments that the western powers should object to the cession of the Crimea to Russia. More recently the British government had done nothing to prevent the Turks attacking the Russians; there were even stories that we had instigated the Turkish attack. It was incredible that we should presume to insist that the Russian empress should renounce all her conquests. The dispute was a very simple one, but Fox claimed that when examined in all its simplicity it exposed the obstinate stupidity of the British government. The Russian empress offered to cede all her conquests between the Neister and the Danube, while retaining only those between the Neister and the Bog; the British government was insisting that she should surrender all her conquests without exception:

> Our whole ground of quarrel with Russia was ... the tract of country he had mentioned, unprofitable and worthless to any power, except for a single place contained in it, and this place Orchakov. Now, had Orchakov been taken in the present year, as far as its value went, it might have been said to have produced a change of circumstances; but it was taken in 1788 and in 1789 his majesty again assured parliament, after mentioning the war as usual, that the situation of affairs was such as promised a continuance of peace. This was an explicit declaration ... that Orchakov was not thought of such importance then as to be deemed the object of an armament, and a strong presumption that it was not the real object of the present armament.

Some might argue that the previous attitudes shown by successive governments towards Russia were foolish and ill-founded, and that the attitude of the current administration was right, but he reminded the house of the immense change of policy which had taken place since 1782 and of the difficulties which the Russians would have in understanding it: 'With what surprise must she now hear that England, who had aided her in obtaining an establishment on the Black Sea, who had enabled her first to enter the Mediterranean, and who had refused to oppose her in seizing on the Crimea, was jealous of her power'.[41]

Fox maintained that the ministers had shown gross incapacity. They had failed to follow any policy of continental alliances with any consistency and they had been naïve and unrealistic in expecting Russia to yield the advantages she had gained when the fortunes of war turned in her favour. The government seemed spiteful and vindicative in its attitude towards Russia and Fox piously reminded the house that 'in all interferences with foreign nations, justice was the best foundation of policy, and moderation the surest pledge of peace'. He discerned a restless urge to interfere in the domestic affairs of other nations in much of the explanations of their conduct which the government put out. To glory in the internal dissensions of France because they were held to benefit Britain's prestige in Europe was cowardly and contemptible; it contrasted with previous claims made by the government that the country's improved situation was the result of Pitt's policies of reducing public expenditure, restoring the nation's finances, and securing several years of peace. Fox was uneasily conscious of the way in which the ominous state of things in France was weighing on men's minds. He feared that the ministry might be listening to those who favoured a measure of British intervention, or more probably tacit British approval for the actions taken by Austria and Prussia to restore the powers of the French monarchy. He wished therefore to exploit the Orchakov dispute to point the moral of how ill-advised intervention was, unless clearly justified by some specific threat to the country's recognisable interests. Since he had formerly approved of the joint Anglo-Prussian intervention in Holland he could not claim that he opposed all forms of intervention in the internal affairs of other countries, and though he tried to disguise the extent of his inconsistency he did not succeed in avoiding all suspicion of special pleading.

> By the absurd pride of interfering in the affairs of every foreign state, we had involved ourselves in expense, and obtained only the hazard of war. Neither had we been successful in any one instance, except that of Holland. . . . If our allies were attacked or threatened, then, indeed, the honour of the nation would be concerned to interfere. We had no alliance with Turkey, and were only called on to gratify the pride of our

own ministers, and to second the ill-judged policy of Prussia. How far ministers were pledged to support that policy he knew not; but he knew that the country was not pledged to support it.

Fox was wrong in suggesting that the government had either intervened in the domestic policies of other nations (with the exception of Holland) or that such a project was seriously contemplated. Already the controversy over the French revolution was casting its baleful influence over the conduct of the leadership of the opposition. But when Fox addressed himself to the diplomatic aspects of the crisis he was on stronger ground:

> The conquests of Russia towards the south could never interfere with the commerce of this country, nor give any reasonable ground of alarm to the king of Prussia, whose interest it rather was that her view should be directed in that quarter; and Orchakov could be no acquisition to Russia but for the purposes of defence. An alliance with Russia was the most natural and advantageous that we could enter into; and when he himself was in office the empress was well inclined to such an alliance; but the healing balm of all our errors, the hope that our first efforts would effect a peace, was delusive.[42]

Alliance with the northern powers had constantly fascinated and attracted Fox. Until the French revolution he had harboured a strong antipathy towards France, and because of the Austrian alliance, which had brought about the Seven Years war, and the marriage of Marie Antoinette to the future Louis XVI, he had some lingering hostility towards Austria. France was the chief threat to the stability of Europe, and she was the only one of the powers of major rank which rivalled Britain in her colonial territories. It was tempting to invoke an alliance with Russia and Prussia in order to check the pretensions of France. Wherever and whenever the peace of Europe was disturbed Fox saw French influences at work. This obsession with the ambitions of the French Bourbons paralleled Fox's preoccupation with the influence of the crown in domestic politics and it is interesting to note that in his speech in the commons on 15 April 1791 Fox linked the government's handling of the Orchakov affair with an apparent disregard for the normal conventions determining the relationship between crown and parliament. This intermingling of domestic politics and foreign affairs was a recurrent theme of Fox's criticisms of the administration during his opposition to the war against republican France; often domestic circumstances dictated his reading of the diplomatic situation. But to argue that the ministry's incompetence in foreign policy stemmed from their lack of respect for the traditional usages of the constitution was a tactic which Fox had indulged to the full during the American war and, however fancifully, the American war was now regarded as epitomising the judicious and successful conduct of a parliamentary opposition. Besides, Fox was compelled to utilise the Orchakov crisis in order to bring general discredit upon the government; he was obliged to spread dissatisfaction with their overall competence to govern as well as forcefully to denounce specific aspects of policy.

Fox argued that the ministry were undermining the mixed constitution by disturbing the balance between the crown and the house of commons. The government was so contemptuous of legitimate requests for information by members of the commons that they clearly wished to deprive the house of its traditional right to debate policy and to discuss the objectives of the nation's foreign policy.

> There was a clear distinction between the object of a negotiation and the means employed to obtain it. Of the former, they claimed an indisputable right to judge, and the latter they confided to the executive power. He was not fond of stating general propositions, without any exception; but he could hardly conceive a case in which the king might arm at the expense of the people, without informing them of the object. . . . It was the prerogative of the crown to make war, but a prerogative was not to be trusted for a moment without its corrective—the right of the commons to refuse supplies.[43]

There was little chance of Fox actually being in a position to refuse supplies. Though he sensed the ministry's weakness over the Orchakov episode and though he had won a temporary measure of support from the independent country gentlemen Fox knew how difficult it was to transform a deep-rooted misgiving about one aspect of policy into a willingness to contemplate a change of ministry. Yet in order to give greater credibility to his attack on the government he had to define the legitimate distinction of functions between crown and parliament before emphasizing the potential dangers to the balance of the constitution. If he did not do so his denunciations of the ministry would be branded as merely factious; more significantly, he had to appear as the defender of the privileges of parliament in terms which the majority of his audience could understand and with which they could identify themselves. He therefore drove home his allegation that Pitt had deceived the house and that no concern with general matters of confidence could weaken parliament's claim to play a positive role in the formulation of policy. If the nation were to put itself on something approaching a war footing the people had every right to know exactly what they were letting themselves in for. Nothing could justify rearming which could not justify war and if the country built up its military and naval forces out of bravado it would find that once its bluff had been called little regard would be paid to similar preparations in future. If the government was in earnest the commons should be convinced that the purposes for which a war was being risked were necessitated by the essential interests of the country.

Although Fox referred to the concept of the balance of power to justify his critique of government policy he defined it rather differently than on previous occasions. His references to France did little to commend him to those independents who shared his anxiety about Orchakov without sharing his enthusiasm for the new régime in France. Yet so divided was the opposition at this period over the French issue that Fox's praise for the new order could hardly be explained by a desire to unify his own supporters. Silence, not controversy, was the only means of preventing the dissensions on the opposition side of the house from becoming embarrassingly public. But silence would make nonsense of Fox's own appraisal of foreign policy. He owed a full explanation to the commons; he could hardly draw back from attempting to convince members of the wisdom of his approach when he had so vehemently accused Pitt of deception, secretiveness, and a lack of honesty. If, for Fox, honesty had become a political necessity, it was fraught with dangers to the continued existence of the whig party.

> He had been a strenuous advocate of the balance of power while France was that intriguing, restless nation which she had formerly proved. Now that the situation of France was altered, that she had erected a government, from which neither insult nor injustice was to be dreaded by her neighbours, he was extremely indifferent concerning the balance of power, and should continue so till he saw some other nations combine the same power with the same principles of government. His idea of this balance was, that every state was not to be kept in its precise old situation, but to prevent anyone from obtaining such an ascendancy as to be dangerous to the rest. No man could say that Russia was the successor of France in this respect. Her extent of territory, scanty revenue, and their population, made her power by no means formidable to us; a power whom we could neither attack, nor be attacked by; and this was the power against whom we were going to war![44]

Fox would have been wiser to have limited himself to delineating the errors of the government in asserting that Russian designs in the Balkans were a threat to the safety of Britain; by referring, not only to the changed situation in France but to the virtues and benefits of the new government, he was offering hostages to fortune and he and Burke clashed later in the debate. On the precise problem under discussion Fox was both intelligent and prescient:

> Overturning the Ottoman empire, he conceived to be an argument of no weight. The event was not probable, and if it should happen, it was more likely to be of an advantage than injurious to us.... But he believed there would be no war; the empress would either be compelled to give up Orchakov or, what was much more probable, the minister, after his bullying and blustering, would recede from all his arrogant demands, and we should have nothing in return for an expense of perhaps half a million, but the shame of having interfered where we had no right to interfere, and the disgrace of having completely failed.

He charged Pitt with insolence, arrogance, incapacity, and wilful imposition on the house of commons. Only the belief that there would be no war, that indeed Pitt dared not go to war, had kept the government's majority in the house at a safe level. Yet Fox threw away any advantage he had gained by comparing the present state of France with that country's former situation, specifically praising the new form of government because it aimed to make all Frenchmen happy, and he concluded with the provocative statement that the new French constitution was 'the most stupendous and glorious edifice of liberty which had been erected on the foundation of human integrity in any time or country'. Burke rose in anger, and in much visible distress, but he gave way to the sense of the house and sat down. It was ominous that discussion of the Orchakov affair, which had gone so well for Fox, should be involved, like so many other issues of the day, with attitudes towards the revolution in France.

Perhaps Fox was now resigned to the fact that there was little likelihood of his defeating the government on the Orchakov issue, and none of his overturning Pitt's administration. He knew to his cost just how bitter were the disagreements within the opposition on the French revolution; perhaps he recognised that he and some of his colleagues could never be reconciled on the points in dispute and that the party would have to choose between them. There could be no better ruse for condoning a sympathetic attitude towards the French than demonstrating the advantages which the change of régime in France had brought to Britain's diplomatic situation, and suggesting that if the French were deftly handled the potential benefits to Britain were virtually limitless. But no one was taken in: Burke's antipathy to Fox on the French issue was common knowledge, and far from uniting opposition sentiment every public reference to the condition of France divided it still further.

As late as 25 May Fox made capital out of the confusions of government policy but the political initiative was already moving back to Pitt. Fox took care to assert parliament's right to discover exactly how public money was being spent and for what purposes public treasure was being poured out on a vast scale. Was Pitt simply keeping up the pretence of arming in order to enable him to yield with greater dignity? He noted the danger that when parliament was prorogued the minister might plunge the country into a ruinous and senseless war. There was also the disturbing prospect of the government seeking to act as 'avowed bullies'; but if the ministry tried to force the Russian empress to give Orchakov to the Turks they would simply make themselves the laughing stock of Europe. Many continental statesmen believed that the recent disturbances in the Netherlands sprang from British intrigues; far from earning a reputation as peacemakers the ministry were earning a reputation as foolish meddlers, whose intrigues embroiled all Europe. Without the interference of the British government, Fox argued, peace would have been established between Russia and Turkey. Since the government sought to explain away its behaviour by referring to the responsibilities incurred by the defensive alliance with Prussia Fox commented on certain aspects of the situation, reprobating

> the new doctrine, that out of every defensive treaty grew a defensive system, which gave us a power to attack any one of our allies. Perpetual interference ... would ... occasion perpetual war. He spoke of the degree of power that the mere accident of the present situation of France had given us, and declared that had we used it rightly we might have done anything.[45]

Yet, however much Fox blamed Pitt for throwing away the opportunity of bringing about a diplomatic revolution in alliances he must have known that he was exaggerating the freedom of action which was open to the minister. By the time the Orchakov affair had passed its climax Fox's preoccupations had moved away from the Black Sea and the Balkans. He had enjoyed humiliating Pitt but he could happily indulge his taste for vengeance in the comfortable knowledge that there would be no war between Britain and Russia. He tried, therefore, to wring out of the Orchakov controversy lessons which could be applied to the wholly different problems raised by the régime in France and the increasing hostility shown towards that régime by Prussia and Austria. He never fully abandoned the notion of a balance of power, but he was concerned to give it a new elasticity, seeing it as capable of more than one application within a changing diplomatic context. Because he was apprehensive about Austrian and Prussian intervention in the internal affairs of France he sought to differentiate the maintenance of a balance of power in Europe from a permanently anti-French stance by Britain and from an habitual interference in the domestic politics of other countries. Non intervention did not mean the abandonment of a foreign policy; it implied a greater subtlety in the formulation and conduct of foreign policy, but in many ways Fox was advocating a policy which was positive and challenging, probably more disturbing and more provocative than anything contemplated by Pitt. Even when exposing the folly of antagonising Russia in an area where British sea power could not decisively influence events Fox had his eye on the possibilities of Prussia and Austria intervening in France and what this might mean for British policy in Europe. Though the Orchakov crisis marked the first serious check to Pitt's foreign policy it nevertheless failed to reunify the opposition. For a brief spell the government was embarrassed and Fox enjoyed the experience of winning over a section of uncommitted opinion to a critical stance on the Orchakov issue, but the dissensions within the opposition needed more than a psychological fillip to end them. It was impossible to consider the Orchakov episode without ranging over the whole field of foreign policy and to do this was to involve discussion of policy in the near east with speculation about the régime in France. Orchakov revealed that Pitt was vulnerable, but it could not disguise the stresses and strains which were disturbing the political coherence of the opposition. In some ways Orchakov was a welcome morale booster for Fox, but it could not save him from the hideous dilemma which the controversy over the French revolution had thrust him into. He had shown all his old gifts in debate; he had swooped upon the weaknesses in the government's case with dexterity and brilliance; he had demonstrated his sureness of touch and his quickness of wit in the congenial complexities of foreign policy. But he had neither defeated Pitt nor soothed the raw anxieties and bruised sensitivities of his colleagues. Only office could have restored the opposition leaders' faith in each other. Curbed by the responsibilities of power and disciplined by the decisions required of them in office, Fox and his friends might have recovered a sense of mutual trust and a willingness to subordinate private apprehensions to the needs of public service. In opposition their misgivings stimulated further disagreements and quarrels and added to the suspicions of treachery which were already making divergences in principle and policy all the more bitter and intransigent. Fox might have avoided some hostility if he had refrained from introducing the situation in France into the consideration of policy in eastern Europe, but he knew that once Orchakov failed to topple Pitt that western Europe would resume its position as the main theme of political debate.

It had been comforting and flattering to know of the Empress Catherine's admiration and to hear that she had placed his bust in a place of honour in her art gallery between Demosthenes and Cicero, but though it had been useful to correspond in cipher with Robert Adair in St Petersburg and to have confidential information about the reactions and ambitions of the Russian empress, Fox's friendship with Adair led to suspicions of duplicity and intrigue. Burke was convinced that Adair was acting as a sinister private agent, who fanned the flames of Russian aggressiveness by reminding the empress of Fox's opposition to Pitt's policy, while Fox acted as little more than the empress's mouthpiece in London, his hopes of displacing Pitt outweighing any considerations of patriotic duty. Though the imputation of base motives was unfounded the suspicion casts a lurid light on Fox's reputation at this time. There was no species of political chicanery which it was believed he was incapable of, while his ambition, frustrated as it was by Pitt's successes, was thought to be unrestrained by any sense of private honour or public obligation. Since the humiliation of Pitt was an indispensable preliminary to any prospect of Fox pushing himself into office men assumed that there was nothing which Fox would not contemplate in order to discredit Pitt, even if this meant the defeat or degradation of his country. Before the war with France broke out Fox's patriotism was suspect. He was generally regarded, not as a selfless idealist vainly challenging popular delusions, but as an egocentric and unscrupulous politician who subordinated everything to the dictates of embittered expediency. The accusation was unjust; though Fox never lost sight of the immediate demands of party politics he was always eager to place the intelligent conduct of foreign policy above every other consideration. It was unfortunate that his inability to divorce the Orchakov affair from the debate over the French revolution made men lose sight of his moderation on the former issue because of the emotion roused by the latter. There was always an element of opportunism in Fox's reactions to and comments upon events in France, but throughout the Orchakov crisis he spoke as one who deeply distrusted any over-ambitious British commitment in the Balkans and the near east. He never allowed the discussion of the principles of foreign policy to be become wholly separated from the sober assessment of the realities of power.

Nothing could compensate Fox for the disappointment which he had suffered in the political struggle. He was still out of office, embarrassingly dependent for any hope of advancement on the dubious favours of the prince of Wales. The wisdom of his arguments on behalf of a realistic and restrained foreign policy did not erase suspicions of his good faith and doubts about his integrity. The opposition was by now a frail and dejected assortment of ill-consorted individuals. The regency crisis had humiliated the party, destroying the personal confidence and harmony without which it could not survive. The French revolution was driving new wedges between old friends, sowing dissension instead of union and hatred instead of amity. If the Foxites owed the degree of ideological unity they possessed to the controversies associated with the American war, the French revolution was revealing how obsolete and irrelevant old platitudes were. Burke insisted on attacking the revolution as a denial of all that the whig party stood for. Fox was drawn, against his better judgment, into a dispute which he was unprepared for, and which was personally distressing and politically disastrous. It was hardly surprising that he was already feeling the pull of domestic happiness and ordinary comforts enjoyed far from the turmoil of politics. With Elizabeth Armistead he had found stability and peace. Soothed by her sympathy and affection and enriched by her companionship he discovered a new happiness when the bottom was falling out of his political world. The heightened appreciation of simple pleasures, a renewed sense of the beauties of nature, and a deep refreshment drawn from literature and intellectual relaxation, threw into greater relief the boisterous anxieties and frustrations of public life and the agonising rifts which were separating old friends.

Ironically, although the opposition was sorely battered in the years before the revolutionary war broke out and destroyed the old whig party forever, and although Fox was alienated from a number of faithful companions, the late 1780s had seen an improvement in the party's organisation. Portland and William Adam carefully cultivated all those electoral contacts which were favourably disposed to the opposition, corresponding with every individual or interest whose support might retrieve the electoral débâcle of 1784 at the next election. Fox was not personally involved in the management of the party; the routine business of party politics bored him, and he was happy to leave the initiative in such matters to Portland. The ideological development of the party became repetitive and listless and soon new controversies recast the whole mould of British politics. But the other aspect of party—the organisational—was moving forward despite the ideological stalemate. In the long run this bore little fruit for Fox, for the improvements in organisation were most marked among those who identified themselves with the Portland interest rather than the Foxite (though Adam himself remained faithful to Fox).

Even in the short run the practical consequences of the devoted efforts of Portland and Adam were limited: there was no sensational opposition recovery in the general election of 1790, but at least the opposition held their own and whig support was more firmly based, being closely related to the cultivation of important and stable constituency interests. So much attention has been focussed on Fox's advocacy of the ideological justification for party and a systematic opposition that the significance of improvements in party organisation has all too often been ignored.

But for the Foxites personal devotion to Fox and to the ideas which he was thought to represent took precedence over organisation. With Portland's adherence to the ministry in 1794 Fox was bereft of one of his most important electoral organisers. Portland could not challenge Fox in intellect, debating skill, or political acumen, but he was more than the nominal head of the party. He represented aristocratic influence, social status, political respectability, and parliamentary management, and many backbenchers found Portland's stolidity more appealing than Fox's brilliance. Fox's grief at the prospect of losing Portland and Fitzwilliam was intense and sincere; he knew how much they meant to the party. Similarly neither Burke nor Pitt underestimated the importance of assimilating Portland and his friends to the government interest. Although the fortunes of the party in the years immediately preceding the war with France were not wholly dismal the more promising aspects of the state of the opposition were not associated closely with Fox; to a large extent they had come about independently of him and it was easy for men to contrast Portland's sober common sense with Fox's unruly temperament. It was also understandable that Fox should from time to time feel that he was forgotten or thrust to one side, that circumstances were isolating him even within his own party, and that only some astonishing catastrophe or the death of George III could restore him to place and power.

It was a lonely and disheartened Fox who braced himself to face the severest test of his career as the worsening situation in France dragged a reluctant government into war and imposed strains which proved too intense for the opposition to bear. The crisis was all the more grievous for Fox in that he was uncertain in his own mind of what was best for the country and for the party. Despite the public image of him as an extreme French sympathiser his feelings were mixed and his understanding of what was happening in France confused and partial. After almost a decade of political frustration he shrank back from the unyielding pressure of events. Yearning for peace he was drawn into conflict, and worse than the tribulations of controversy was 'the loss of friends'. When judged against the background of misfortune, miscalculation and defeat which Pitt's sequence of triumphs had created Fox's bewildered and contradictory attitudes towards the French revolution become more comprehensible. He had exhausted almost every trick of the politician's trade; he seemed to have little to lose, and less to hope for. Victory seemed impossibly far away; defeat and further humiliation desperately close at hand. The French controversy allowed him no respite from vain and fruitless labour. If he became ever more unpredictable in his conduct of affairs this was a natural response to the situation in which he was placed, and which the craft of eighteenth-century politics could do little to change.

7 *The Impact of the French Revolution*

'How much the greatest event it is that ever happened in the world! And how much the best!' wrote Fox to his friend Fitzpatrick on 30 July 1789. The news of the fall of the Bastille filled him with enthusiasm. As a lifelong foe of Bourbon absolutism he was heartened by the spectacle of an ancient tyranny being overthrown. He found it easy and congenial to identify himself with the reformers in France, confessing that if the revolution in France had the results he expected his 'prepossessions' against 'French connexions' would be at an end. His conception of the European political system was also altered; sensing the possibilities latent in the situation he could not refrain from hoping for the best. The rejection of traditional authority by the French held out the most stirring prospect for human improvement. Fox was so caught up in the dizzy passions of the moment that he became indifferent to calculations of political advantage. There seemed little to fear: once the French had cast off the yoke of Bourbon repression enlightenment would transform both the character of French politics and the practice of French diplomacy. As yet there was no threat to other countries. Like so many Englishmen Fox saw events in France as parallel to those of 1688 in England. Instead of absolutism representative government would be established; instead of arbitrary justice the rule of law; instead of censorship freedom of speech; instead of superstition, freedom of thought. These were the expectations which led Fox from the start to express openly and unrestrainedly his sympathy for and personal commitment to the ideals of the French reformers. A victory for constitutionalism was the most precious expectation nurtured by Fox in these early days. Even if he was troubled by the revolution's tendency to violence he was indulgent and forgiving in the first heady rush of reckless inspiration. It was all the more wonderful because it was almost incredible that the French should so love liberty as to rise against traditional despotism in order to achieve it.

But although Fox never abandoned his enthusiasm for the ideals of 1789 (or for what he imagined those ideals to be) he went through periods of intense doubt about the worthiness of the men who were charged with the solemn duty of giving those principles effect. Like many Englishmen he was essentially ignorant of the state of affairs in France; he did not grasp the fundamental differences between government and politics in France and in England. The complexities of the structure of French society were beyond him, and he had little comprehension of the detailed constitutional struggles within the national assembly. He drew false analogies between the French revolution and the English and American revolutions. He did not understand the personalities involved in the French crisis and all too often he believed acceptable rumours without bothering to check or analyse his facts. Once he had affirmed his broad support for the revolution Fox was determined not to go back on his word or to give the impression that he was unfaithful to his principles. There were occasions when he went to great lengths to excuse or condone the behaviour of the national assembly and the convention and though his private misgivings often conflicted with his public confidence his critics were in no position to be aware of his innermost doubts.

The exigencies of party politics contributed to Fox's determination to defend the French revolution at all costs. Almost from the start the reactions of the members of the whig opposition to the situation in France reflected the wide diversity of feeling among Englishmen as a whole. In some ways the greatest controversy raged not so much over the actual course of events in France as over the contentious views of Edmund Burke. Burke determined the broad lines of debate, and because he was deeply conscious that the issues raised by the revolution were fundamental to the continued existence of everything worthy of the name of civilisation he was unflinching in his resolve to bring the subject to the attention of the government, of the house of commons, and of his own colleagues, in order to compel them to make a decision in the interests of stability, order, and constitutional government. It was in response to Burke's preoccupation with French affairs that Fox committed himself more fully to the advocacy of the French revolution and the French constitution. Every new manifestation of pessimism on the part of Burke provoked a new affirmation of optimism on the part of Fox. Where Burke discerned lawlessness, destructiveness and atheism, Fox perceived impartial justice, a free society, and the happy progress of reason and toleration. Whatever the country gentlemen in the commons made of it all Fox and Burke were fighting for the soul of the old whig party; ironically both appealed to the spirit of Rockingham and to the principles on which they had opposed the influence of the crown and the policy of coercion in America. Both claimed consistency, but while Burke saw the French revolution as the denial of everything for which he had fought during his political life, Fox argued that it was in the fortunate tradition of the English and American revolutions and that all good whigs should bless it as 'a good stout blow at the influence of the crown'.

Despite the legend of Fox as a lonely apologist for progress amid the gathering gloom of black reaction, his attitude to the revolution in France was closer to that of the majority of thinking Englishmen during the first two years of the new order in France than was Burke's. Most men who bothered their heads about the matter at all were mildly favourable or at least inclined to applaud the fact that the French were too pre-occupied with internal discord to cause much trouble to the other nations of Europe. Some Englishmen thought of the French as following the English example; others simply despised the unnecessary fuss which the French were making about putting their own house in order. The last thing anyone wanted (except for the small circle of Burke and his disciples) was to become involved in the internal affairs of France. Pitt thought that France had become the object of pity even to a rival, but he was not sorry to see her traditional strength in diplomacy reduced in consequence. He thought it likely that after a period of confusion the French would settle down to some form of constitutional monarchy and as late as February 1792 he anticipated fifteen years of peace in Europe, cheerfully making economies in defence expenditure. Pitt's reluctance to take any active stance towards the situation in France infuriated Burke, but in order to put Fox's early reactions in perspective it is necessary to remember that though his enthusiasm for the French revolution was thought excessive by some it was by no means as unusual as it afterwards seemed, or as some wished to make it appear. Until the revolution entered its violent phase there was not a massive revulsion of feeling in England, although there was always suspicion of what the French were up to. The greatest antagonism was reserved for those who suggested that England could learn from the French example; the introduction of French ideas was always received with more distaste than generalised expressions of sympathy for the way the French chose to look after their own concerns. However inspiring or however appalling men felt it to be, the fall of the Bastille could be regarded as a uniquely French event, not the precursor of international upheaval. Fox welcomed it as a sign that the French were seeing the error of their traditional habits of government and of deference, and he had no need to expound the need for English imitation. Since 1789 was the anniversary of the bill of rights and the settlement which gave legal form to the revolution of 1688 it was inevitable that Englishmen should be ready to commemorate their own deliverance from absolutism and to draw encouragement from the evidence that in France the spirit of constitutionalism, humanitarianism, and improvement should be stirring to active life. The expectation of gloom was not abroad in the summer of 1789; the symbolism of the fall of the Bastille condoned violence in the service of liberty, but it could be argued that a willingness to dare all in the cause of freedom was what was new in France, not a taste for blood, vengeance, or a propensity to take the law into one's own hands.

Fox's sympathy for the revolution stemmed from his devotion to civil and religious liberty. The ancient régime typified everything which offended his ideals of political and social freedom and he was sufficiently ignorant of the situation in France to miss the point of Pitt's remark that though the French had not possessed political liberty under the old order they enjoyed more civil liberty than many people in England realised. It was only in the most general terms that Fox praised the revolution; he never troubled to inform himself closely of the precise state of events in France, and his understanding of the political rivalries within the national assembly and convention were muddled and inaccurate. But Burke, however deficient he was in his own comprehension of the realities of French society and politics, was incapable of lazily interpreting the revolution in the light of a few general principles and leaving the matter there. Once he was convinced of the full significance of the French revolution he devoted all his energies to the study of French affairs and to the education of English opinion. From Fox's point of view this spelt trouble, both for their personal and political relationship and for the opposition in both houses of parliament. Their disagreements over the regency crisis and the different approaches which had marked their behaviour over the impeachment of Hastings, meant that dissensions over the French revolution came after a period of growing estrangement, no matter how desperately they tried to avert a complete breach. Burke regretted that Fox was ever more influenced by men such as Sheridan and Grey; Fox suspected Burke of seeking to convert Portland, Fitzwilliam and Windham to his own extremist views on the French crisis. Despite affection, sentiment and a common regard for the pious memories of the opposition to the American war and the distant and shadowy glories of the Rockingham administration, this gnawing sense of distrust and betrayal heightened the confrontation between the two old friends. Neither was moved to heat and passion simply by contemplating events in Paris. Fox's defence of the revolution was inspired as much by the need to refute Burke as by any consideration of the French situation. It was unfortunate that the debate was fought out on the floor of the house of commons, where the necessity of rallying friends and humiliating enemies brought an additional incentive to the intensification of passion, to the encouragement of opportunism in debate, and to the neglect of restrained common sense and cool logic. In private discussion differences of opinion might have been more fully understood, even if they could not be reconciled, but in parliamentary debate the constant temptation was to exaggerate and distort disagreements in order to seize transient advantages. This was not conducive to the preservation of harmonious personal relations, and in Burke's case it strengthened the attractiveness of making a clean, though nonetheless painful, break with the opposition in order to follow his own line without deferring to the wishes of his old associates.

For Fox the problem was made all the more intractable by the disconcerting tendency for comment and opinion on France to be introduced into any debate which could be seen as involving any general consideration of constitutional principles. France was too obvious a comparison for the purposes of praising the inherent worth of British institutions or of rejoicing in the apparently invincible march of progress. Even those who found Burke's preoccupation with the French revolution tiresome often provoked a new outburst by referring to the situation in France during parliamentary debates. Since the first indications were that continual debate involving even the most oblique reference to French affairs would split the opposition it was convenient for Pitt to allow events to take their course. The ministry had no particular desire to initiate discussion of the French crisis, for their own attitudes were as hesitant and as ill-defined as anyone else's, but when their opponents attacked each other the ministers could hardly have done other than what they did. Pitt breathed a sigh of relief, and watched his enemies embarrassing themselves.

Even before the high drama of the fall of the Bastille Fox had publicly expressed his sympathy for those seeking reform in France. On 12 May 1789 during a debate on the slave trade he had paid generous tribute to the progress of enlightenment in France, expressing the hope that where the abolition of the slave trade was concerned the French would follow any lead given by Britain in the cause of humanity. In February 1790, in a debate on the army estimates, he went out of his way to give retrospective approval to the behaviour which had caused so much heart-searching among British observers the previous summer: the willingness of the French soldiers to identify themselves with the mob rather than obeying orders. It was legitimate for Fox to argue that the state of France made it unnecessary to worry over much about defence since the country had little to fear from its traditional rival, but some of his remarks went far beyond what was called for in debate. Burke could be forgiven for regarding them as wilfully provocative. Their implications were far-reaching, and they could easily be interpreted in a more sinister light than Fox had intended. Fox used events in France as a text for moral exhortation. Though he was admitting that in certain circumstances the traditional distrust of standing armies as a threat to liberty was inapplicable his choice of language was unhappy:

> He had never thought it expedient to make the internal circumstances of other nations the subject of much conversation in that house; but if there ever could be a period in which he should be less jealous of an increase of the army, from any danger to be apprehended to the constitution, the present was that precise period. The example of a neighbouring nation had proved that former imputations on armies were unfounded calumnies; and it was now universally known throughout all Europe, *that a man, by becoming a soldier, did not cease to be a citizen.*[1]

This could be interpreted as condoning mutiny or at least indiscipline providing some political extenuation could be pleaded for the actions of the troops. To most of his hearers Fox's remarks were ominous; they implied that only the outbursts of mutiny and riot in France had reconciled him to the constitutional validity of a standing army, and because it seemed that Fox was encouraging British soldiers to follow the example of the French he was thought to be inciting the British army to disobedience. The potential use to which Fox's words might be put in England worried men more than what they signified within the French context. Fox's advice to pursue a generous policy of disarmament and goodwill to persuade France of Britain's good intentions made little impression. It was little more than a pious platitude and was much less significant than his approval of the seditious and disloyal conduct of the French army which had so distressed British opinion. In an age when the army was still valued for its utility in maintaining law and order, anything which tampered with military discipline was deeply resented by the respectable and propertied sections of society. Memories of the Gordon riots were vivid and to many upright Londoners the fall of the Bastille seemed more like those horrific experiences than the dawn of a new enlightenment.

On 9 February Fox made further references to the French situation.

He believed that the state of France was such as ought neither to fill people with alarm nor excite them to indignation. Wracked as France was by internal divisions and calamities she could not suddenly overcome these difficulties. But Fox's reference to what had happened in France seemed too exultant for Burke, who, although attributing Fox's enthusiasm to his known zeal for 'the best of all causes, liberty', rebuked the tenor of Fox's speech and warned the house against the wild and foolish conduct of the French.

Inevitably Fox was compelled to reply. He did so with considerable reluctance, for he hated challenging Burke in public on such a controversial subject. He paid a warm tribute to Burke at the beginning of his reply:

> He must ... declare that such was his sense of the judgment of his right honourable friend, such his knowledge of his principles, such the value which he had set upon him, and such the estimation in which he held his friendship, that if he were to put all the political information which he had learnt from books, all which he had gained from science, and all which any knowledge of the world and its affairs had taught him, into one scale, and the improvement which he had derived from his right honourable friend's instruction and conversation were placed in the other, he should be at a loss to decide to give the preference. He had learnt more from his right honourable friend than from all the men with whom he had ever conversed.[2]

But he nevertheless dissociated himself from the viewpoint which Burke represented and he took particular care to challenge Burke's interpretation of the English revolution and to argue that there was a much greater parallel between 1688 and 1789 than Burke was willing to admit. Yet Fox was also scrupulous to dissociate himself from those who described themselves as democrats. Even when defending the behaviour of the French troops Fox appealed to traditional theories of balanced and limited government. He declared himself to the enemy of all forms of absolute government whether absolute monarchy, absolute aristocracy, or absolute democracy:

> He was averse to all extremes, and a friend only to a mixed government, like our own, in which, if the aristocracy, or indeed either of the three branches of the constitution, were destroyed, the good effect of the whole, and the happiness derived under it, would, in his mind, be at an end. When he described himself as exulting over the success of some of the late attempts in France, he certainly meant to pay a just

tribute of applause to those who, feeling alive to a sense of the oppressions under which their countrymen had groaned, disobeyed the despotic commands of their leaders, and gallantly espoused the cause of their fellow citizens in a struggle for the acquisition of that liberty the sweets of which we all enjoyed.

Because he had been so widely misunderstood Fox was careful to explain what he had in mind. Liberty could only exist when there was unforced and harmonious cooperation between the executive and legislative powers. He made a clear distinction between dangerous innovation, to which he was an enemy, and necessary development, to which he was a friend. The perfection of the constitution was itself the product of innovation, experience being the true test of any constitution, however admirable the theory underlying it. Here Fox made a plea for Burke to tolerate differences of opinion over French affairs in the same way as the whigs had previously tolerated differences over parliamentary reform. He reminded Burke that in the past their differences had sprung, not from a disagreement in principle, but from varying appreciations of how their principles were to be applied. It was in this context that he sought to place consideration of the situation in France, and here Fox was unrepentant.

> The scenes of bloodshed and cruelty which had been acted in France no man can have heard of without lamenting; but still, when the severe tyranny under which the people had so long groaned was considered, the excesses which they had committed, in their endeavour to shake off the yoke of despotism, might ... be spoken of with some degree of compassion; and he was persuaded that, unsettled as their present state appeared, it would be preferable to their former condition, and that ultimately it would be for the advantage of this country that France had regained her freedom.[3]

France was taking a long time to settle her constitution because there was 'so much despotism to destroy'. Britain had been lucky, for there had been little which called for destruction when the revolution of 1688 took place. Burke had emphasized the violence of events in France and the threat which they posed to stability and order throughout Europe, but Fox believed that he had no choice but to draw attention to the constitutionalism of the revolution. Burke argued that disorder and savagery were essentially involved in the revolution and that they were the most significant clues to its character as well as its most terrifying symptoms. Fox maintained that the bloodshed which had occurred was incidental to the revolution, an aberration to be explained by the degrading effects of despotism and the magnitude of the obstacles to the establishment of constitutional government in a country which had languished under absolutism for so long.

The differences between Burke and many of his old colleagues could not be lightly overlooked. Although neither Fox nor Burke was in the position of a modern politician appealing to the ill-defined mass of public opinion for support, both recognised the significance of the dispute over French affairs for the future of the whig party. Fox genuinely believed that his optimism was well founded and that it would be justified by events, but whereas Fox was prepared to tolerate differences of opinion until developments in France removed the issue from political debate, Burke was so inflamed by the blindness of his countrymen that he sought every opportunity to jolt them out of their complacency. Fox found Burke's obsessive vehemence distressing and bewildering. He could not understand why his reiterated optimism spurred Burke to new outbursts of indignation. To the casual observer the pattern of events in France seemed to be encouraging until the spring of 1791. Fox could therefore feel confident that his cheerfulness would be justified by the establishment of a constitutional monarchy in France and that Burke's extremism would be forgotten as circumstances rendered it the more incredible. There was nothing to be gained politically by trying to meet Burke halfway; the younger members of the opposition were as baffled as Fox by Burke's unbalanced fanaticism. Even those who were anxious about what was happening in France found it impossible to share Burke's ideological frenzy; they were more disturbed by the practicalities of the French situation than by any philosophical considerations. Pitt and the government were just as inclined as Fox to wait upon events. Burke's loneliness heightened his disgust, and when the final breach with Fox came it was agonising in its intensity. Fox regretted the tendency of Sheridan and some of the younger whigs to indulge in the questionable pastime of baiting Burke, but he could not control his more irresponsible colleagues. He discovered all too late that the disagreement was so fundamental and so bitter that friendship and affection could not withstand the disruptive strains imposed by the controversy.

Pitt's government was compelled to make new provisions for the government of Canada. The problems of administering that territory were complex, especially since an influx of protestant loyalists from the United States had added to the tensions between the English- and French-speaking sections of the colony's population. Differences of religion and culture, as well as differences of economic interest, made it expedient for the province to be divided into Upper and Lower Canada, so that the desire of the English-speaking protestants for a greater share in government could be met without injustice to French-speaking catholics. There was a deliberate attempt to reproduce the familiar pattern of a mixed constitution for the Canadian provinces. In Upper and Lower Canada there were to be legislative assemblies, elected on a property franchise every seven years, with the power to vote supplies; the other legislative chamber was to be composed of life appointments and some hereditary members, in an effort to create something approximating to the house of lords; an executive council was to be nominated by the lieutenant-governor in each province. The proposals reflected the government's confidence that the 'constitution of Great Britain is sufficient to pervade the whole world'. Though there were important amendments during the Canada bill's passage through parliament there was general agreement on the basic principles underlying the proposals. Although the property qualification was lowered, triennial elections substituted for septennial ones, and the granting of 'hereditary' peerages dropped, the bill went through both houses without serious difficulty. Unhappily for Fox the general discussion of constitutional principles involved some comparison with the new constitution in France; even dutiful compliments paid to the English constitution had some bearing on what men thought of the French arrangements.

Fox accepted the principles underlying the government's proposals but he had serious reservations in detail. He thought it absurd to try to introduce hereditary honours into Canada; he believed that the original £5 property qualification was too high; and he wanted the legislative councils to be as independent of the lieutenant-governors as the practicalities of the situation permitted. He was aware of the embarrassment felt by Burke whenever he sought to illustrate his argument by referring to the way in which the French were solving their constitutional problems, yet he hoped that no irreparable disagreement would sever him from Burke for ever. On 21 April 1791 Fox called on Burke on his way to the house of commons; he was anxious to allay his friend's suspicions that he was being victimised by some members of the opposition and to show that the affection built up during the years when they had fought the king and North on the American issue was as strong as ever, despite the way in which they had drifted apart in recent years. The discussion was sufficiently amicable for them to walk arm in arm to the house. This was the last occasion when Fox visited Burke and the last time they went together to the commons. On 6 May a debate on the Canada bill precipitated a scene of such distress that it was indelibly imprinted on the mind of the house. The familiar partnership of Burke and Fox was shattered for ever.

Burke spoke at length on the atrocities committed in the French West Indies, on 'the deplorable condition of France itself', and on the misfortunes of Louis XVI, in the course of a speech ostensibly devoted to the Canada bill. Calls to order provoked a long and extraordinary altercation, in the course of which Fox tried to soothe inflamed and angry feelings by referring to Burke's speech in ironic terms: 'it seemed that this was a day of privilege when any gentleman might stand up, select his mark, and abuse any government he pleased whether it had any reference or not to the point in question'. But this only provoked Burke still further and eventually Fox seconded a motion proposed by Lord Sheffield stating that 'dissertations' on affairs in France were irregular and that the Canada bill should be read a second time. Fox was sorry that Burke's behaviour had compelled him to support the motion, and he particularly regretted Burke's insinuation that in former debates on the bill he had put forward republican principles as applicable to the English constitution. No such argument had been urged by him, and instead of seeking for differences of opinion on topics which were matters of 'speculation' Fox stated that the house should devote itself to matters of fact and of practical application.

Burke's response was more heated than ever. He had had differences with Fox before, but no difference of opinion had for a single moment interrupted their friendship. Though it was indiscreet at his time of life to provoke enemies or to give his friends occasion to desert him if his adherence to the British constitution placed him in such a dilemma he would risk everything. Public duty and public prudence taught him, with his last breath, to exclaim 'Fly from the French constitution!' At this point Fox leaned over and whispered that there was, he hoped, no loss of friendship. Burke replied that there was: he knew the price of his conduct. He had done his duty at the price of his friend; their friendship was at an end.

Fox was stunned: he had not been prepared for this. He had not recognised Burke's growing sense of isolation and his bitterness at the fashion in which he had been tormented and abused in the house. That Fox should associate himself with a motion of personal censure was more than Burke could bear, but the intensity of Burke's interjection wounded Fox deeply. He rose to reply but he was so overwrought by what Burke had said that it was some time before he could speak. As the *Parliamentary History* recorded the scene, 'Tears trickled down his cheeks and he strove in vain to give utterance to feelings that dignified and exalted his nature'. The members of the commons were deeply moved; they sensed the tragedy in what they had witnessed. Once Fox had recovered sufficiently to express himself coherently he paid a generous tribute to Burke:

> He said, that however events might have altered the mind of his right honourable friend, for so he must call him, notwithstanding what had passed—because, grating as it was to any man to be unkindly treated by those to whom they felt the greatest obligations, and whom notwithstanding their harshness and severity, they found they must still love and esteem—he could not forget, that when a boy almost, he had been in the habit of receiving favours from his right honourable friend, that their friendship had grown with their years, and that it had continued for upwards of five and twenty years, for the last twenty of which they had acted together, and lived on terms of the most familiar intimacy. He hoped, therefore, that notwithstanding what had happened that day, his right honourable friend would think on past times, and however imprudent words or intemperance of his might have offended him, it would show that it had not been at least intentionally his fault.[4]

Fox appealed to Burke to recognise that their difference of opinion over the French revolution, although substantial, was no more serious than some of their former disagreements. He had never disguised his own sentiments, nor had he shrunk from stating his disapproval of Burke's *Reflections on the Revolution in France*. Even when appealing for patience and forbearance on Burke's part Fox could not resist suggesting that Burke's conduct earlier in the debate had sprung from an intention of injuring him: by crediting him with advocating republican principles in the new constitution of Canada Burke was wilfully misrepresenting him, for he well knew that his principles were very far from being republican.

It was significant that in trying to explain his position after Burke's public dissociation from him Fox reverted to theories of mixed government. He was determined to justify a reformist stance, but he was all the more eager to do so in language which made Burke's accusations all the more outrageous. Characteristically Fox stressed the contrast between constitutional theorising and constitutional practice:

> He had ever thought that the British constitution in theory was imperfect and defective; but that in practice it was excellently adapted to this country. He had often publicly said this; but because he had

admired the British constitution, was it to be concluded that there was no part of the constitution that was not still capable of improvement? He, therefore, could neither consent to abuse every other constitution; nor to extol our own so extravagantly as the right honourable gentleman seemed to think it merited.

He defended his support for a reform in parliamentary representation and for a strict examination of public spending; he had done so to improve the house of commons and to retrench the influence of the crown. Would Burke be prepared to say that he was a bad man for having voted for either? It was especially misleading for Burke to describe Fox's friends as a phalanx: he ought to have been more thoroughly acquainted with the manner in which the opposition conducted themselves; such a charge was completely false. It was true that no friendship could stand in the way of public duty, but if Burke thought that he served his country by denouncing the French revolution he must allow others, who thought differently, to behave differently from himself. He reminded Burke of the reasons which had induced them to enter into a systematic opposition. They had done so, not to obtain power and emolument by the exploitation of faction, but in order to maintain the true principles of the constitution and to keep watch on the prerogatives of the crown. If Burke claimed the liberty to expound his own opinions, Fox cried, 'Let him not blame me for having mine!'

By this stage Fox had warmed to his subject. A combination of wounded pride and growing indignation convinced him that he had been used harshly and cruelly by Burke. Fox's latent self-pity came to the surface and he spoke of the pain which Burke's words had inflicted upon him. There was only one proper course for him to pursue: he would keep out of Burke's way until time and reflection fitted him to think differently on the subject. Perhaps it would be possible for their mutual friends to bring them together again. Should Burke bring forward the question of the French revolution on a future occasion he would try to discuss it as temperately as he could; for the moment there was no more that he could usefully say.

Important as the clash with Burke was, it did not of itself mark the end of the old whig party. Distressing though it had been for Fox to break with Burke so violently and so publicly, it was nevertheless true that Burke carried little weight in the counsels of the party at this period. He had no significant following and even those who shared many of his anxieties over the French revolution could not follow the higher flights of his imagination or the wilder excesses of his rhetoric. Most members of the opposition regretted the loss of Burke, but they were moved by sentiment about the past rather than by insight into the realities of the current political situation. They knew that Burke was no longer a key figure in the party's high command, and though they were sorry to part with a familiar friend they were not disposed to see his departure as a disaster from which the party stood no chance of recovering. Only after the opposition had gone to pieces in 1794 did Burke's quarrel with Fox take on a symbolic significance. At the time it was regarded with sadness, nostalgia and compassion. For Fox it was an excruciating experience, marking as it did the end of a long association; but it was not a catastrophe. More serious was the growing anxiety with which Portland and Fitzwilliam and their friends contemplated the deteriorating state of affairs in France. The opposition would remain a credible political force without Burke but it could not survive without the stability and reputation afforded it by its aristocratic wing.

The debates over the Canada bill threw into greater relief Fox's unrepentant sympathy with the French revolution, but they also revealed the essentially conservative and non-democratic cast of his thinking. Hesitant though he was over some aspects of the government's proposals, his speeches were eloquent expositions of conventional constitutional wisdom. He criticised Pitt and Grenville for the methods by which they hoped to create an aristocratic element in the government of Canada, but he did not criticise their desire to do so. Because discussion of the Canada bill became so inextricably bound up with attitudes towards the French revolution Fox found it convenient to use the debates on the bill to clear himself of charges of republicanism which had been cast in his face because of his avowed fondness for the French constitution. To make his sympathy for the French constitution more respectable he engaged in lengthy discussions on the principles underlying the reform of government in Canada. This did not conflict with his repeated distaste for continued controversy on purely speculative points. Everything he said was a necessary preliminary to his criticisms of the ministry's proposals, and a valuable explanation of his constitutional position in general. He was engaged in refuting misrepresentations imputed to him by Burke and in commending himself to the country gentlemen as a sound constitutionalist instead of a dangerous innovator. He had to show that his reformist ideas were rooted in the English past; that British constitutional theory and practice counted for more with him than anything said or done in Paris, and that he sympathised with the French reformers in so far as their ideas and behaviour coincided with the British example.

It was therefore entirely justifiable that Fox should preface his remarks by substantial excursions into constitutional theory. On 11 May he told the commons of his fundamental convictions about the principles underlying the reform of the government of Canada:

> First he laid it down as a principle never to be departed from that every part of the British dominions ought to possess a government in the constitution of which monarchy, aristocracy, and democracy were mutually blended and united; nor could any government be a fit one for British subjects to live under, which did not contain its due weight of aristocracy, because that he considered to be the proper poise of the constitution, the balance that equalised and meliorated the powers of the two other extreme branches, and gave stability and firmness to the whole.[5]

Encouraged by loud cries of 'Hear! Hear!' he went on to say that aristocracy was founded on rank and property and that the British house of lords formed the aristocracy, uniting as it did noble families of ancient origin and newly created peers, possessing extensive landed property and therefore manifesting the qualities of status and ownership. A respect for the established nobility was valid and valuable in a country such as England, but it was just as important to cultivate a deep regard for those who had best served the state.

But so far as Canada was concerned Fox believed that very careful thought should go into deciding the best means of expressing the aristocratic principle in a new country. Essential though it was to combine the aristocratic principle with the monarchic and the popular it would be foolish to attempt to set up in Canada 'a servile imitation' of the British aristocracy. It was impossible to give the Canadians a house of lords like the British. He therefore objected to the suggestion of introducing the hereditary principle into the Canadian legislative councils, and he argued that these should be independent both of the governor and the people. In this he was reiterating the familiar whig warning against the influence of the crown and the ascendancy of the people. But he emphatically defended property as the necessary foundation of aristocracy, disclaiming any desire to use the word aristocracy in any 'odious' sense. He was concerned with its true meaning: an indispensable part of a mixed government under a free constitution.

However eloquent his exposition of general principles Fox was careful to allow that particular circumstances should determine their application:

> Mr Fox observed it might possibly be said to him, if you are decidedly in favour of an elective aristocracy why do you not follow up your own

principle and propose to abolish the house of lords and make them elective? For this plain reason, because the British house of lords stood on the hereditary, known, and acknowledged respect of the country for particular institutions, and it was impossible to put an infant constitution upon the same footing.

He was also quick to make nonsense of the commonly-repeated charge of republicanism:

> From what he had said Mr Fox remarked that he might possibly be deemed an advocate for aristocracy singly; he might undoubtedly, with as much reason as he had been called republican. Those who pretended that he was in favour of democratical principles, had surely read very little, and little understood the subject.

It was with some pleasure that he singled out the Americans for praise:

> He mentioned the American governments, and said, he thought they had acted wisely, when upon finding themselves reduced to the melancholy and unfortunate situation of being obliged to change their governments, they had preserved as much as they possibly could of the old form of their governments, and thus made that form of government which was best for themselves; most of which consisted of the powers of monarchy, aristocracy, and democracy blended, though under a different name.[6]

Even when he repeated his distaste for any attempt to introduce a hereditary nobility into Canada Fox was eloquent in praising the value of the aristocratic element in any free constitution, and he skilfully reminded the house of the dangers when the stabilising factor of aristocracy was absent.

> Mr Fox ... remarked that so necessary was aristocracy to all governments that, in his opinion, the destruction of all that had been destroyed, could be proved to have arisen from the neglect of a true aristocracy, upon which it depended whether a constitution should be great, energetic and powerful. He explained that he was so far a republican that he approved all governments where the *respublica* was the universal principle, and the people, as under our constitution, had considerable weight in the government. Mr Fox concluded with declaring emphatically that true aristocracy gave a country that sort of energy, that sort of spirit, and that sort of enterprise which always made a country great and happy.[7]

Fox was determined to establish his claim to speak as an admirer of the

British constitution; every Englishman was bound to love a constitution under which the nation had lived so happily and whenever it was attacked he would be active in its defence. Even when Burke denounced the democratic nature of his proposals Fox replied by assuring him that once he repented of separating himself from his friends they would be happy to receive him, respecting and loving him as warmly as before. He also argued that according to the principles which he had explained to the house Pitt was as much a republican as he was. He reiterated the Rocking-hamite belief that it was desirable to reduce the influence of the crown and he emphasized that it was in the interests of England to give as much liberty to her dependencies as would contribute to their happiness and prosperity. It was impossible to foresee what would happen to colonies in the distant future, but there could be no harm in allowing the people a greater share in the running of their affairs. It was still true that the greatest threat to stable constitutional government came from an increase in the influence of the crown, rather than an increase in the power of the people.

He was eager to defend freedom of speech, although he was by no means unaware of its dangers. He commented on Burke's warnings against the distribution of inflammatory literature.

> If any dangerous doctrines were disseminated in pamphlets ... it behoved the government to look to them, and in case the law-officers of the crown failed in doing so, it was then the duty of that house to remind the ministers of their neglect. He owned, however, that for his part, he was of the opinion that free discussions of the principles of the constitution ought to be suffered. If the constitution had opposers, it would also have advocates, and the more it was discussed the better.[8]

He could not resist a skilful thrust at Burke, stating that it was abuse of the privileges of the house of commons for any member to indulge in long discourses, personal to himself and relative to imaginary plots, which prevented the house from getting on with the business in hand. Such irrelevances disrupted the performance by the commons of their essential duties of scrutinising the executive, examining the measures put forward by the ministry, and controlling public expenditure.

The debates over the Canada bill revealed the interrelationship between domestic politics and attitudes towards the French revolution. This interaction was to prevail throughout the 1790s, ultimately to the discredit and confusion of the Foxite opposition. No discussion of French affairs could ignore the consideration of general constitutional principles; no exposition of fundamental constitutional principles was complete without references to the situation in France. Throughout 1791 Fox had cleverly sought to reconcile a sympathy for the French reformers with an orthodox whig view of the English constitution; only by doing so could he retain the support of Portland, Fitzwilliam and the more conservative whigs. It was important for him to dissociate himself from Burke, but it was equally important to remind men of his belief in mixed government, a balanced constitution, and the indispensability of property as a security for free and stable government. His conviction that the French constitution was admirable in so far as it demonstrated the welcome desire of the French to remodel their forms of government in the light of the British example was used to appeal to the middle-of-the-road men in the house of commons. For as long as constitutional monarchy had any chance of permanence in France Fox's attitude was politically justifiable, and no mean attempt to reconcile divergent opinions and a variety of political judgments, but when the French monarchy became more exposed to criticisms because of the distrust roused by Louis XVI's ambivalence and the desire of many of those surrounding the king to restore the old order by invoking foreign intervention, Fox found it more difficult to maintain his shrewdly-chosen middle ground. The more violent and the more republican the French revolution became the greater was the pressure to revert to a more conservative position, which had the distasteful connotation of giving at least retrospective approval to Burke, or to try to align oneself with those who openly embraced the more advanced of French doctrines and the more extreme of the French factions. Fox was by temperament sympathetic to the thinking of Montesquieu and Voltaire; it was flattering and reassuring to patronise the anglophiles among the French reformers. But when Rousseau was taken up and cited as the more plausible exponent of the republic one and indivisible and when familiar arguments justifying classical ideas of the separation of powers were rejected as mere reflections of an outmoded prejudice in favour of aristocratic privilege, it was difficult for whigs such as Fox to make sense of what was happening in Paris.

He could not abandon the cheerful hopes which the summer of 1789 had so vividly stimulated. The descent into terror and violence was incomprehensible to him. The exigencies of British policies made it unthinkable for him to follow those of his friends who discerned a sinister link between disorder at home and the pernicious influence of French ideas and of the French example. Fox had always disapproved of Burke's propagandist activities. He thought Burke's warnings that the French revolution threatened the foundations of civilisation 'mere madness' and he particularly deplored any suggestion of a general war for the purpose of restoring legitimate (and therefore Bourbon) government in France. It was tempting to argue that Burke's prophecies had helped to pervert the true course of the revolution; that even when they were fulfilled they proved not the perspicacity of Burke but the determination of the kings of Europe to stamp out liberty in France. Burke's forecasts of disorder were fulfilled because he provided repression with an ideology, not because of the innate character of the revolution. Fox was also aware of the avaricious designs of Russia, Prussia and Austria towards Poland. If Burke saw a revolutionary plot to destroy established governments at the root of the ills afflicting Europe Fox responded by arguing that the real conspiracy was on the part of the central powers to eliminate freedom throughout Europe.

But however fiercely Fox denounced Burke he was no friend to the more advanced radicals. He read only the first part of Paine's *Rights of Man* and he loathed it. He sensed the contrast between his own traditional reformist views and Paine's more forthright advocacy of something akin to democracy. Although Paine heartily approved of the provision in the French constitution of 1791 limiting the franchise to those who paid a certain level in taxes he went out of his way to ridicule theories of a balanced constitution, comparing the English constitution unflatteringly with the French. To Fox this was embarrassing and unnecessary. Though both Fox and Paine were fond of drawing parallels between the American and French revolutions this was virtually all that they had in common. Significantly this propensity to interpret the French situation in the light of the American war led them both astray in their reading of French affairs.

Fox was always conscious of the folly and irresponsibility of many of his colleagues. He lamented that they seemed insensitive towards the necessary regard for popular feeling which no politician could safely dispense with. Fox knew from his own experience how big a price could be extorted for one thoughtless act or speech, and whatever his misgivings about Burke or about the policy of Pitt and the ministry he knew that it would be foolish to ignore the widespread suspicion of the French which was ascertainable throughout all sections of English society. In May 1791 he counselled Sheridan against attending a meeting which was being planned for the second anniversary of the fall of the Bastille on 14 July. It was important to avoid giving the impression that Sheridan was being frightened out of repeating his conduct of the previous year, and Fox was far from thinking that it was always right to give way to unfounded prejudices, but it was only common sense to make some allowance for changes in prevailing opinion, and for the likely response in some quarters to actions which might be held to be unduly provocative. Even when giving general approval to Mackintosh's reply to Burke's *Reflections*—his *Vindiciae Gallicae*—Fox confided to Holland that he had heard that good though it was it went too far in some respects. The truth was that Fox felt threatened and betrayed on all sides. Some of his friends were so appalled by the flight to Varennes and the increasing evidence that the constitutional monarchy in France was doomed that they began to see virtue in Burke's extremism after all; others seemed too willing to indulge in thoughtless gestures which, however satisfying as proofs of devotion to the cause of liberty, played into the hands of that growing body of Englishmen who were having very serious second thoughts about the French revolution and all that it implied. Fox was striving desperately, amid mounting political confusion, to avoid either the total abandonment of the revolution, or the feckless acceptance of those levelling ideas which would destroy society.

It was this preoccupation which led Fox to advise Grey against involving himself with the advanced reformers by founding the society of the Friends of the People. Many years later Grey admitted that the society meant that he had to deal with people whose opinions differed widely from his own, and with whom he finally realised it had been foolish, even dangerous, for him to have any communication. He was making full use of the advantages of hindsight, and in his anxiety to purge himself from contamination by those whose principles filled him with revulsion he maintained that one word from Fox would have saved him from becoming entangled 'in all that mess of the Friends of the People'. He conveniently forgot that Fox had advised caution. At the time Fox lamented that his young colleagues were determined not to take any advice and in particular not to follow his. He refrained from condemning the Friends of the People and was probably responsible for a gradual moderation in the tone of the association's statements, but he was too anxious to preserve the whig opposition as a credible parliamentary force to be attracted to what his enemies could all too convincingly denounce as a dangerous and immature instance of political exhibitionism.

Nor could Fox ignore the potential dangers of invoking extra-parliamentary agitation without deliberation and thoughtful preparation. He never forgot that in the summer of 1791 it had been the loyalist faction which had exploited popular prejudice in Birmingham in order to terrorise dissenters and sack Priestley's library. Much as Fox appreciated the plaudits of the Westminster mob he was too experienced a campaigner not to have grave reservations about appealing to mass support outside parliament. Even when he was most downhearted he never abandoned his pristine whig faith in the primacy of the house of commons. His repeated affirmations of the need to preserve the independence of the house of commons from the encroachments of the crown and the domination of the people were more than habitual repetitions of a jaded debating trick; they represented a fundamental conviction without which his advocacy of parliamentary government would have been meaningless. During the debate on the king's speech on 31 January 1792 Fox drew the attention of the commons to the riots in Birmingham the previous summer. It was expedient for a friend of the French revolution to defend law and order and to affirm his own detestation of mob licence, but it was also entirely fitting that Fox should give uncompromising expression to a primary article of his political faith. He did so with abundant parliamentary skill:

It must have been owing to the unwillingness of ministers to damp the pleasure arising from so many topics of satisfaction as the speech from the throne contained, that with the mention of the inestimable blessings of liberty and order, they had introduced no expressions of regret and concern at the violent interruption of order that had occurred in the course of the summer. Nothing, surely, but extreme reluctance to cast the least shade over so many subjects of rejoicing could account for such an omission.[9]

After this telling opening Fox fully exploited the opportunity for satire at the ministry's expense. He savagely criticised the incapacity of the magistrates and he emphasized the apparent reluctance of the Birmingham magistrates to do what was their public duty:

But whether or not they, and those who acted under them, had exerted themselves, as they ought in repressing the devastation of a mob, at all times mischievous, but doubly so when it assumed the pretext of supporting government or religion, was it not melancholy to see that mob reigning triumphant for near a week in a rich and populous part of the country, and those, whose duty it was to have denounced the rigour of the law, addressing them in terms of approbation than rebuke?

Such behaviour was all too obviously calculated to convey the impression that the principles on which the mob had claimed to act were congenial to the government, and that therefore the mob's actions were to be tacitly condoned, though a few scapegoats were punished to preserve a semblance of regularity. Fox did not make the mistake of accusing the ministers of holding such opinions; he sensibly contented himself with arguing that when such misleading allegations were in circulation it was all the more imperative for the government publicly to refute them by expressing their horror at the riots and their thorough approval of every means being taken to suppress them and to bring the ringleaders and their henchmen to justice.

Fox warned the commons of the sinister implications of political riots, especially those associated (however deceptively) with the defence of established institutions.

> These were not riots for the want of bread—such, every feeling heart must pity while it condemned: neither were they riots in the cause of liberty, which, though highly blameable, and highly to be reprobated by every good man and every friend to liberty, had yet some excuse in their principle. No, they were riots of men neither aggrieved nor complaining, but who, pretending to be the executors of government, did not select individual objects of party animosity, or private hatred, but by personal insult, violence and fire, set on foot an indiscriminate persecution of an entire description of their fellow citizens, that had furnished persons as eminent, as good subjects, and as zealous supporters of the family on the throne, as any other in the kingdom could boast. Instead of passing over such acts in silence, ought not his majesty's sentiments have gone forth as a manifesto, applying to them every epithet expressive of abomination, which the language could furnish?[10]

He singled out for special condemnation, and as a particularly deplorable example of the evils which flowed from weakness and indolence among those responsible for the maintenance of law and order, the wanton destruction of Priestley's library, together with the accumulated labours of a lifetime. Fox was rightly indignant at this act of wanton spite: nothing, neither money nor industry nor time could replace what Priestley had lost. But he was also making sure that no one could accuse him of approving mob violence, or the destruction of property, or of threats against individual citizens. It was ironic that those who were so vigorous in their denunciation of disorder in France should be so reluctant to condemn a ferocious instance of mob-rule at home. Fox knew the mixed motives which explained this hesitancy, and for himself principle and expediency united to prompt his conduct. He realised that should law and order break down it would be the liberals who would be the first casualties in any appeal from reason to the exploitation of brute force. Furthermore, though he sensed the extent to which public opinion still fell short of embracing Burke's interpretation of the French revolution, he had a shrewd appreciation that popular feeling was becoming increasingly anti-French and more hostile towards those who were suspected, rightly or wrongly, of harbouring subversive or republican ideas. Fox was conscious of the wide interpretation which popular passion would give to crypto-revolutionary sentiments. Everything therefore pointed to caution in anything involving public reactions to the course of events in France. He deeply regretted that this elementary consideration weighed so little in the minds of his younger followers.

The French revolution was rarely absent from Fox's thoughts from the spring of 1791 onwards. He realised that events in Paris would have grave repercussions on English politics. But he did not allow it to push everything else out of his mind. The Orchakov crisis demonstrated his abiding concern with foreign policy, and his ability to come to terms with a changing balance of power upon the continent. But one of his most satisfying achievements in the last two years of peace was to persuade the commons to carry his libel bill. It was not approved immediately; though introduced in May 1791 it did not become law until the following year. But its importance became all the more evident during the years of the anti-Jacobin frenzy. Its provisions made it more difficult to gain convictions in cases of alleged libel by extending the jury's competence to cover the whole matter under trial, not merely the fact of publication. Fox's bill still allowed the judge considerable scope in directing a jury, but it also allowed juries a much wider measure of discretion, the jury being permitted to bring in a 'special verdict' if they thought fit, just as they could in other criminal cases.

In presenting his bill to the commons Fox argued that if a jury was deemed competent to assess the fact of publication it ought to be competent to assess the issue under dispute, the innuendoes and inferences contained in the alleged libel as well as the simple matter of the defendant's responsibility for its publication. He was anxious to rectify a situation in which it seemed that the onus of proving his innocence lay on the accused rather than the need to prove his guilt resting with the prosecution. Especially when discussing matters of government policy it was essential that men should be free to discuss them without incurring a greater risk to their persons and property than would otherwise be the case. He was satisfied that in anything affecting the personal reputation of ministers or members of the house of commons the law afforded ample security against libel, slander and defamation, but it was important to ensure that in political controversies a legitimate freedom of debate was guaranteed by law. He was anxious to protect the individual from the bad effects of unbridled free speech, as his comments on the relevance of the truth to the issue of libel showed:

Mr Fox proceeded to observe that there was, on the subject of libels, one great and popular topic.... It was ... the doctrine that truth was not only not a justification, but that a libel was the more a libel because it was true.... To say that truth was not sometimes a justification would be very extraordinary indeed; and yet there certainly were cases in which truth would not be a justification but an aggravation. Suppose, for instance, a man had any personal defect or misfortune, anything disagreeable about his body, or was unfortunate in any of his relations, and that any person went about exposing him on these accounts, for the purpose of malice, and that all these evils were one day brought forward, to make a man's life unhappy to himself and tending to hold him out as the object of undeserved contempt and ridicule to the world, which was apt to consider individuals as contemptible for their misfortunes, rather than odious for their crimes and vices; would any man tell him, that in cases of that sort, the truth was not rather an aggravation?[11]

Fox was eager to relate his provisions for the trial of libel cases to the wider issues of constitutional practice in general. In his view the constitution turned on two mainsprings: the representation of the people through the house of commons, and the judicial power of the people through the medium of juries. The privileges of the commons ought always to be vigilantly guarded by MPs but the right of trial by jury was of 'infinite importance' and it could not be complete unless in every criminal case, 'where law and fact were mixed, the juries were the judges; and unless the intention was to be decided by the jury, and not by men who could judge by means of books, and many subtleties and distinctions, but could never find out the heart of man and distinguish between his actions'. Throughout the treason trials of the 1790s Fox was anxious that the law should remain a security for free speech instead of being perverted as an instrument of repression. The rule of law was fundamental to the enjoyment of traditional liberties, as were the balanced constitution and the independence of the house of commons.

It seemed as if freedom of speech would be the first casualty of heightened anxiety over the situation in France. As the French monarchy collapsed under the conflicting pressures of those who sought the restoration of absolutism and those who desired the establishment of a republic, the internationalist flavour in French propaganda, discerned by Burke three years earlier, became more pronounced. Fox saw with loathing the emergence of an Austro-Prussian alliance pledged to intervention in France. The flight to Varennes had been ominous enough; the declaration of Pillnitz was worse. All Fox's worst suspicions were confirmed, and much as he would have liked to have seen Britain and France draw closer together in a common front against the absolutist powers of central and eastern Europe he was disheartened by the folly of the French. No matter how much he sought to exonerate the French from bearing the sole responsibility for the outbreak of war in April 1792 he was anxious about the outcome of a war. He feared the consequences of French defeat, yet he could not ignore French designs in the Austrian Netherlands. He believed that the longer the war lasted the more far-reaching and more uncontrollable both its scope and its effects would be. Convinced as he was that peace was more faithful to the essential nature of the revolution he was apprehensive about the impact of war upon the new régime in France. Even if war was an inescapable necessity to save the liberal revolution from being crushed by foreign reactionaries Fox recognised the risk that the cruel expedients of war would jeopardise those vulnerable freedoms which had so recently been won. A traditional war for attainable ends was sufficiently depressing, but an ideological war would be reminiscent of the wars of religion: common humanity, a sense of tolerance, and a recognition that the truth was often complex and many-sided would be the first casualties. Amid the fury of competing righteousnesses, freedom of thought and freedom of speech would be buried in a welter of savage controversy. Fox felt compelled, therefore, to keep a watchful eye on any tendency in England to curtail traditional freedoms, particularly with reference to the freedom of the press. He was distrustful of the government, believing that Pitt was capable of fanning the flames of public panic in order to clamp down on his critics. He was always willing to discern the influence of George III and the selfish ambition he always credited to Pitt behind everything smacking of intolerance or repression, just as when his friends expressed their misgivings about the state of affairs in France he saw the malignant influence of Burke at work. But it was easy to denounce any limitation of the freedom of speech as an infringement of the rule of law and a preliminary to the subversion of the independence of the house of commons and the destruction of the constitution. In a fundamental sense, therefore, Fox saw himself as a great conservative force throughout his opposition to the government in the 1790s: Pitt and Burke were the aggressors, the frightened men who were threatening the English constitution, while Fox was the defender of traditional liberties and the guardian of established constitutional values.

But when the government gave way to mounting anxiety over the propagation of subversive ideas by issuing a proclamation against seditious writings in May 1792, Fox was in a position of considerable embarrassment. He was deeply suspicious of the ministry's motives, believing the proclamation to be alarmist without being effective in curbing the dissemination of dangerous ideas. But he was uneasy about the activities of some of his friends in becoming associated with some of the more advanced radicals. He had warned Grey against the possible repercussions of forming the association of the Friends of the People, and he had taken care to stand aloof from what he regarded as dubious and futile machinations. He would have preferred to have remained silent; in many ways his primary task was the maintenance of the unity of the opposition and any heightening of political tension would make this task all the more difficult. He was aware that some of the more conservative whigs were prepared to support the proclamation and although he explained their conduct by describing them as dupes of the government this was hardly likely to commend them to the house or himself to his former friends. He admitted that his friends, on all sides, had got themselves into strange company and he strove to dissociate himself from extremism on either right or left. It was a measure of his desperation that he was forced to appeal to the familiar loyalties of old associates by claiming that the government's principle objective was the destruction of the whig party:

> The plain intention of this proclamation was to strive to make a division between that great body of united patriots, known by the name of the whig interest; a party, the firm union of which he considered as one of the utmost consequences, as, indeed, essential to the maintenance of the constitution. He knew of no plan so good, no object so desirable, as their firm union; and he was proud to say that to divide them was impossible. They might think differently on particular subjects; but, united on principles so salutary for the nation, no acts, however insidious, could prevail in dividing them.[12]

This was a brave gesture, and it emphasised that whatever his hopes or fears about the course of events in France, Fox's first preoccupation was the preservation of the whig party; but the sad truth was that the opposition was already crumbling, as Fox's concluding words all too unhappily revealed, consisting as they did of what was described as 'a warm and feeling allusion' to the friends of his political life, 'from whose side he would never separate, to whose opinion he had often yielded fair objects of personal ambition, but whose union he considered as essential to the public good'.

Fox was trying to accomplish in public what he had already sought and failed to do in private. On 16 March 1792 he had unburdened himself to Fitzwilliam, complaining of the behaviour of the former Northites over the religious tests, and confessing his own doubts about the advisability of pressing for a measure of parliamentary reform,

> I am more bound by former declarations and consistency, than by any strong opinion I entertain in its favour. I am far from being sanguine that any new scheme would produce better parliaments than the present mode of election has furnished; but perhaps the house of commons in the present reign has been so dragged through the dirt and bespattered, in the early times by the whigs, and in later by the king and Pitt and the tories that one constructed on a new plan might be better from the mere circumstance of its novelty.[13]

Disturbed by the possibility that reaction might yet triumph in France Fox was deeply alarmed by 'the present *state* of the country': the prospect seemed black and bitter in every direction. Though Fox supported Grey's motions in the commons calling for a reform of parliament he did so out of a sense of loyalty and friendship; he thought the move politically unwise and certain to fail. Yet personal relationships within the opposition were now so warped by suspicions of betrayal and duplicity that Fox could not risk offending his younger and less experienced supporters. Should any irreconcilable breach take place it was to the younger members of the party that Fox looked for support. He was publicly pledged to a reform of parliament; any change of front would provoke a storm of criticism and lead to old accusations of opportunism being renewed. Besides, if Fox abandoned the cause the leadership would pass all the more quickly to the wilder spirits among the reformers.

The summer of 1792 saw the situation in France take a marked turn for the worse. The failure of the French armies, the duke of Brunswick's declaration, the apparently irresistible advance of the Prussians towards Paris, provoked the revolution of 10 August, the downfall of the constitutional monarchy and the establishment of a republic. For Fox the problems posed by this sequence of events were excruciating. He could not abandon the cause of the revolution, for that would be tantamount to admitting that Burke had been right in the beginning, yet he had no wish to condone the violence and bloodshed with which the monarchy had been overthrown. He resented the policies of Austria, Prussia and Russia, both in western Europe and in Poland, yet he sensed Britain's inability to do much to change the pattern of developments on the continent. Worst of all he was ignorant of the real situation in France. He was ill-informed about the various French factions, about the personalities and principles of the leaders of the convention, and about the struggle for power between the Girondins and the Jacobins. All too often he allowed his vivid imagination to play around the events which so outraged British opinion; all too often the needs of the English political situation seduced him into accepting interpretations of the French crisis which were consoling or encouraging but rarely accurate. Far from possessing any consistent insight into the revolution Fox's opinions were at the mercy not only of every exaggerated rumour from Paris but of the changing pressures imposed by a complex political situation in London. His letters at this period fully reveal the extent of his confusion and his perplexity

On 20 August he wrote to his nephew Lord Holland, in language which reflected his anxiety. Exasperation, despair, and wishful thinking were all intermingled.

> It is over as you have already heard, with poor Poland, and what has happened at Paris seems to make the chance of the poor French being settled worse than ever. It seems as if the Jacobins had determined to do something as revolting to the feelings of mankind as the duke of Brunswick's proclamation; but though it must be owned that they have done their utmost for this purpose, yet with respect to mine they have not succeeded, for the proclamation in my judgment still remains unrivalled.[14]

But on 3 September Fox's spirits had rallied somewhat:

> I do not think near so ill of the business of the 10th of August as I did upon first hearing it. If the king and his ministers were really determined not to act in concert with the assembly, and still more if they secretly favoured the invasion of the barbarians, it was necessary at any rate to begin by getting rid of him and them. Indeed you know that from the moment of the dismission of the Jacobin ministry I have thought that it was absolutely necessary, either that the assembly should come round to the Feuillants or, which seemed most according to our whig ideas, that the king should be forced to have ministers of the same complexion with the assembly. However, it is impossible not to look with disgust at the bloody means which have been taken even supposing the end to be good, and I cannot help fearing that we are not yet near the end of these trials and executions.[15]

His premonitions of disaster conflicted with his innate optimism, and however much he tried to discern some signs of encouragement, his sense of decency and humanity was offended by so much that was happening at Paris that he found it impossible not to fear the worst even when he was desperately hoping for the best. However severely he condemned the political behaviour of Marie Antoinette he was deeply concerned for her personal safety, confiding to Holland that he felt great uneasiness about the queen and that he regretted that she had not been either shut up or sent away after the flight to Varennes.

There were times, too, when his old antipathy to the French broke out anew. Despite his advocacy of the revolution he never lost his initial distrust of the French national character; whenever he believed that noble ideals had been sadly betrayed by ignoble deeds his prejudices got the better of his judgment. When so much was at stake he found the contradictions of the French character intolerable, stoutly though he strove to master his feelings.

> There is a want of propriety and dignity in everything they do. When the enemy is in a manner at their door, to be amusing themselves with funerals and inscriptions and demotions of statues and creations of honorary citizens is quite intolerable, and to talk so pompously of dying for liberty and their country before one single gallant action has been performed by any part of their army against the enemy is worse than ridiculous. And yet with all their faults and all their nonsense I do interest myself for their success to the greatest degree. It is a great crisis for the real cause of liberty whatever we may think of the particular people who are to fight the present battle. I wish they were like our friends the Americans and I should scarcely be afraid for them.[16]

The lingering desire to link the French revolution with the American war of independence, and the fond hope to see both as springing from the English revolution of 1688, were symptomatic of Fox's recurrent tendency to explain all the complexities of the French situation not by thoroughly studying the circumstances from which it had emerged but by an over-easy appeal to false analogies and dubious parallels. To wish that the French were like the Americans was more than an idle fancy; it reflected one of Fox's deepest convictions about the French revolution, which he constantly sought to confine within the limits of the American example. Preoccupied with conventional whig platitudes about the influence of the crown he misunderstood the real nature of the struggle for power in France. He placed too much emphasis on the purely constitutional aspects of the crisis; he was ignorant—even disdainful—of the social and economic background; and he was deceived by superficial similarities of language into confusing the French *parlements* with the British parliament. He saw the ideals of 1789 in a narrowly whig light; it was not, therefore, surprising that the more cataclysmic aspects of the revolution should fill him with bewildered anguish and baffled distress. Even when he had come to terms with one piece of dreadful news further atrocities disturbed his hard-won peace of mind. He told his nephew how deeply shocked he was by the events of September 1792:

> I had just made up my mind to the events of the 10th of August when the horrid accounts of the second of this month arrived, and I really consider the horrors of that day and night as the most heartbreaking event that ever happened to those who like me are fundamentally and unalterably attached to the true cause. There is not in my opinion a shadow of excuse for this horrid massacre, not even a possibility of extenuating it in the smallest degree.[17]

But his misgivings about the Prussians got the better of his doubts about the French. Stained though it was by civil strife and wanton bloodshed the revolution held out possibilities of free government, religious toleration, a free press, perhaps even a pacific foreign policy; a victory for the duke of Brunswick would mean the undoing of any good that had been achieved since 1789 and massacres as bad as anything the revolutionaries had perpetrated. Fox was overjoyed by the news of the battle of Valmy: not even Saratoga or Yorktown had given him such delight: 'I would not allow myself to believe it for some days for fear of disappointment,' he gleefully confessed, once the initial reports were confirmed beyond all reasonable doubt. He was excited and cheerful when breaking the news to Mrs Armistead:

> The duke of Brunswick has made a most precipitate retreat and there is reason to think that France will be entirely free from its invaders in a short time. As far as I can collect from circumstances I believe this is true, and it is almost foolish to be so much rejoiced at it as I own I am. Anything that proves that it is not in the power of kings and princes by their great armies to have everything their own way is of such good example that without any goodwill to the French one cannot help being delighted with it, and you know I have a natural partiality to what some people call rebels.[18]

With a victory in the field to cheer him up Fox began to be more hopeful about the state of affairs in Paris. He was foolish enough to flatter himself with the thought that Roland, whose conduct he thought admirable, and whose political significance he grotesquely exaggerated, was gaining the ascendancy as against Robespierre 'and that vile crew'. Although he feared that the authors of the September massacres would never be properly punished he nevertheless thought that they would be 'almost universally condemned and execrated' and he was deeply shocked by reports that a village had been taken and sacked and razed to the ground by a body of émigré soldiers. 'I hope to God it is not true; it exceeds even what has passed at Paris.' One certain good would follow from the retreat of the German armies: extreme horrors would cease, though Fox was apprehensive that 'pretendedly legal' executions would continue.

The heartening news of Valmy encouraged him to explain the fall of the ministry in August in terms appropriate to the British house of commons, but it was strangely irrelevant to the situation in Paris. Fox was doing his best to bring some semblance of order out of chaos, and to preserve something approximating to ideological consistency, but what he wrote was a greater testimony to his ingenuity than evidence of his understanding of French politics. He expressed his feelings, at some length, to Holland on 12 October:

> If you admit that the Jacobins, having the confidence of the assembly and the country, ought to be ministers, what can be said for the Feuillants who encouraged and supported the king in maintaining an administration of an adverse faction, and in using his veto and other prerogatives in opposition to the will of the assembly and the nation? He who defends this cannot be a whig. But further I think there is not *now* a shadow of doubt but the ministers who preceded and succeeded the Jacobins not only did this, but intentionally weakened the defence of the kingdom, for the purpose of maintaining the king and themselves against the Jacobins by the Austrian arms. That Lafayette and Larochefoucault were in this part of the guilt I cannot bring myself to believe, but well meaning men may be deceived, and when so are to be pitied; but that they gave in to the idea of availing themselves of the letter of the constitution ... is what they themselves would not deny and what I must disapprove unless I abandon every political principle of my life.[19]

He even rebuked his nephew for admitting to a preference for the Feuillant party as against the Jacobins.

> Partiality to persons out of the question, an English whig must disapprove of the Feuillant party or quit his English principles. But it may be said that there is something in the argument *against* the Feuillants but not *for* the Jacobins. I own I think that it goes a great way to justify the greater part of their conduct and to palliate even the worst. For what people would not be driven to madness at seeing a ministry acting notoriously against the nation that employed them, abusing the royal prerogative for the purpose of preventing the country from defending itself ... giving a veto to the raising of an army voted by the assembly,

and dismissing the only ministers who were *not* suspected of wishing success to the invading armies?

But Fox was eager to qualify his approval of the Jacobins in order to avoid any likelihood of being misunderstood. He only meant to defend the Jacobins as far as 10 August for there was no excuse for the base cruelties practised on 2 September. He was even hopeful that there was now some prospect of bringing the perpetrators of the September massacres to justice, admitting that so long as they were at large their impunity threw 'a slur upon the present brilliant administration of France which gives pain to all true friends of liberty'. It was not, in Fox's opinion, enough merely to express horror at the September massacres; no man of 'proper feelings' could bear to be a member of a government which was unable to punish those who were responsible for them.

From the fall of the French monarchy until the establishment of the Directory, Fox's attitudes towards the endless complexities of French politics lacked any consistency of insight or purpose. A vague fondness for what he assumed to be the ideas of 1789 was of little assistance in comprehending the sudden and savage twists of fortune so frequent in Paris. When considering Fox's opposition to the war with republican France and his attacks on the domestic policies of Pitt's government, it is worth remembering that however warmly Fox defended the French revolution he did so without any overall grasp of the way in which the political situation was developing in France. His comprehension of French affairs was fragmentary, marred by confusions of thought and failures of judgment and vulnerable to rude jolts with every piece of surprising news that came over from Paris. In defending the revolution he was defending his own version of what it had meant in its early days, those distant summer days of humanitarian sentiment and expansive benevolence; even when he urged that the British government should come to terms with reality by making peace with the French republic he did not imply approval for everything with which the republic was associated in the minds of Englishmen. Contemporaries found it difficult to make this distinction, partly because Fox's exposition of his own viewpoint frequently lacked clarity, however passionate and full-throated his invective. Fox's explanation of French politics was usually inspired by the exigencies of English politics, the overriding need of defining a 'whig' position, in the hope that this would contribute to the survival of the whig party. Only when this is borne in mind does Fox's constantly fluctuating response to the brutal realities of French politics become comprehensible, not as a logical, harmoniously developing appreciation of a complex historical event, but as the reflection of a quick mind's desire to piece together something resembling a coherent standpoint without sacrificing political opportunism to the abstractions of ideology.

The familiar pattern of optimism, doubt, wishful thinking, and renewed pessimism remained through all the agonies of every political upheaval. In June 1793, for example, Fox was bewailing the possibility that the Brissotin party would probably be guillotined after a sham trial, but while he complained that things in Paris had gone from bad to worse he marvelled that the French armies fought 'like heroes'. Torn by conflicting sentiments he could not decide whether the revolutionaries or the despots were the more guilty of crimes against humanity. The war itself seemed to lead to the perversion of much that the revolution stood for. In December 1792 he had told Fitzpatrick that he did not believe that there would be war but that if it should break out he anticipated 'dangers innumerable and no chance of good'.[20] He confided to his nephew all his misgivings, and his conviction that life was very trying for a friend of constitutional government:

> I do not know whether there is not some comfort in seeing that, while the French are doing all in their power to make the name of liberty odious to the world the despots are conducting themselves so as to show that tyranny is worse. I believe the love of political liberty is not an error, but if it is one I am sure I never shall be converted from it, and I hope you never will. If it be an illusion it is one that has brought forth more of the best qualities and exertions of the human mind than all other causes put together, and it serves to give an interest in the affairs of the world which without it would be insipid; but it is unnecessary to preach to you upon this subject.[21]

Fox took comfort from the fact that, hideous though the crimes committed by the French revolutionaries were, those of their adversaries were worse. He had vehemently disapproved of the execution of Louis XVI and he hoped vainly and desperately that the republicans would refrain from executing Marie Antoinette, an act, in Fox's eyes, of sheer butchery. Wherever he looked on the continent he saw the triumph of crime and rapine.In August 1793 he was particularly depressed, sadly confessing to his nephew:

> Everything in the world seems to be taking a wrong turn, and strange as it sounds I think the success of the wretches who now govern Paris is like to be the least evil of any that can happen.... We live in a time

when everything is so extraordinary that it is in vain to conjecture what will happen of any political kind.[22]

When the news arrived of the execution of Marie Antoinette Fox thought the act 'more disgusting and detestable than any other murder recorded in history' and as the terror moved to its climax he sighed, 'What a pity that a people capable of such incredible energy should be guilty or rather be governed by those who are guilty of such unheard-of crimes and cruelties.' He was puzzled by the course of events in France. At one time he believed St Just to be Robespierre's chief rival, only to admit his mistake when the two fell together. But though he welcomed the news of Robespierre's death he was plunged into gloom by the thought of its likely consequences.

> I own I think it a very good event in one view that it will serve to destroy an opinion that was gaining ground that extreme severity and cruelty are the means of safety and success to those who practise them. Whoever comes in Robespierre's place cannot be worse than he was in these repects and I am afraid too they are not like to be much better.[23]

Yet by Christmas he was consoling himself with the thought that the general conduct of the French since the fall of Robespierre had been 'extremely good' and that it had reconciled him to them 'wonderfully'. He still thought the French régime could go further towards winning the goodwill of those who, while supporting the principles of the revolution, had been antagonised and even victimised by the terror. Fox hoped that the more liberal elements in France would draw closer together, re-establishing the freedoms secured in the early days of the revolution, and making peace with England and their other enemies in order to concentrate on the tasks of conciliation and indemnity at home. He was anxious lest the revolutionary régimes let the opportunity to make a just peace slip by; he never forgot that an intransigent attitude on the part of republican France would make a Bourbon restoration more probable in the long run, and this he believed the worst possible thing that could happen. Even Robespierre was preferable to the Bourbons.

The sad truth was that in point of ability and energy the 'moderate' governments of France were inferior to the tyrannical ones. Fox was deeply distressed by this unpalatable fact for he feared that the admirers of tyranny and violence, of whom there were more in the world than many people imagined, would draw encouragement from the French experience. Even in English history the precedents were more powerful in favour of tyranny than was generally supposed. It was a perplexing and depressing time for those who loved liberty and constitutional government. However deeply he was committed to defending the ideals of 1789 and the cause of liberty and humanitarian principles Fox was acutely sensitive to the way in which the practices of the revolutionaries contradicted the ideas they were pledged to serve. Though in popular mythology he was depicted merely as a French sympathiser—the secret worshipper of Robespierre and Marat and other alien divinities, the reckless admirer of savage foreign foes—his attitude was much less easily defined and far less consistent. In public he often seemed to argue the French case more persuasively than they could argue it themselves; in private his changes of mood, revisions of opinion, and fluctuations between bright optimism and black despair were so common and so unpredictable as to defy any simple chronology or any regular pattern.

It was true that Fox often played into the hands of his critics. His anxiety to subject the policies of the government to searching scrutiny could easily be mistaken for a superficial determination to do anything and everything necessary to excuse or indemnify the French. Men re-membered his rejoicings at British defeats during the American war; and his enthusiasm for the fall of the Bastille, for the French victory at Valmy and later for the young Bonaparte, was frequently confused with a desire to see his own country defeated. Fox's well-known fondness for drawing parallels with the American war reminded men that defeat had been the indispensable preliminary to the fall of North and the entry of the Rock-inghamites into office, and they were ready to draw the obvious inference (which was not without foundation) that Fox saw defeat at the hands of the French, or at the very least the termination of the war with France on something less than a victorious note, as the prelude to his return to power in succession to a discredited Pitt. Nor was it only in public that Fox acted in ways which stimulated this type of speculation. He did suffer from a tendency to exult exceedingly over military reverses which he thought politically advantageous, and he was not above anticipating those failures which he most desired politically. On 10 September 1795 he wrote to Holland:

An expedition is after all gone to France under General Doyle con-sisting of 4,000 British besides emigrants.... Violent as the wish may sound I had much rather hear they were all cut to pieces than that they gained any considerable success, for in the latter case the war may be prolonged to the utter destruction of both countries and to the total ex-tinction of all principles of liberty and humanity in Europe. I think nothing can shew the complete infatuation of the government so much as this desperate expedition which I believe as well as hope has not the smallest chance of success.[24]

Contemporaries were right in seeing Fox, not as a far-sighted visionary elevated far above the desperate confusions of politics, but as a resourceful and ambitious politician, closely involved in every twist of the political conflict and prepared to countenance any stratagem which held out the possibility of success.

While Fox's comprehension of the French revolution was as deficient as that shown by the majority of Englishmen, he was also subjected during 1792 to the stresses of a protracted and yet faltering negotiation which was intended to broaden the ministry by bringing in not only the aristocratic wing of the whig opposition, which Burke was hoping to detach from Fox, but also Fox himself. Fox's own priorities throughout the discussions were simple: he wished at all costs to preserve the unity and the existence of the whig party. The chief danger was that Pitt would be able to enlist some members of the opposition and thus destroy the old Rockinghamite party forever. Tempting though the prospect of office was the conditions which Fox laid down throughout the negotiation were impossible of fulfilment. He stated his willingness to serve with Pitt, and his determination never to serve under him. Though this attitude gave some measure of encouragement to those who hoped to see Pitt replaced as first lord of the treasury by some figure—perhaps Portland, perhaps Leeds— who would have Pitt and Fox serving under him, it was really Fox's method of keeping the negotiation alive for a time while ensuring that it would fail. Fox was deeply suspicious of Pitt's motives throughout the confused discussions about possible changes in the ministry, and it is probable that Pitt was himself equally sceptical of the chances of bringing Fox into the ministry but willing to see what could be done to broaden the ministry by winning over Portland and Fitzwilliam and the other conservative whigs. Pitt was eager to put the loyalties holding the opposition together to the test even though he was hesitant about the wisdom of broadening the government by bringing in too many whigs. There was a difference between a fair allocation of posts, which would give the ministry much-needed reinforcement, and allowing the administration to be swamped by erstwhile opponents who happened to have adopted a conservative attitude towards the French revolution. Pitt was never prepared to give up his own position as head of the government, and although he appreciated the utility of winning over a number of whigs and the wisdom of taking serious soundings of opinion, he did not take as grave a view of the government's alleged weakness as did some of his colleagues, and as did the more conservative whigs, who doubted whether the ministry would be tough enough in dealing with potential disorders at home.

Every participant in the negotiations had different objectives and conflicting motives. Some, such as the duke of Leeds, saw the premiership as their own reward. Others were less ambitious but more determined in pressing for their coveted place. Loughborough, who had realised that the lord chancellorship was within his grasp after Thurlow's resignation, wished to cloak his own defection from the opposition by bringing with him a number of aristocratic companions, thereby adding strength to the government and building up his own prestige and influence within it. He was prepared to come in alone, for his own ambition counted for more than anything else and he was deeply resentful of the way in which Fox had twice allowed his claims to the lord chancellorship to be set aside in the interests of the unity of the whig party. Subtle in negotiation, but inclined to allow his own virtuosity to tempt him into over-complex sophistications, Loughborough was distrusted on all sides. His abilities were appreciated and his adherence was tenaciously sought, but there was little love for him among those who knew how deep a game he was playing. It suited Loughborough to exaggerate the chances of a substantial reshaping of the ministry, and many historians have followed him in heightening the possibility of a real coalition ministry in 1792. Portland and Fitzwilliam were more disturbed by radical agitations in the northern industrial towns, particularly Sheffield, where the artisans were especially well organised and active, than by generalised fears of the French, and they were doubtful of the government's competence to deal with what was a perplexing new factor in English political life. Because of the deterioration of the situation in France they began to look more kindly on the interpretation of the revolution identified with Burke. Certainly the conservative whigs took a more alarmist view than Pitt of the dangers of violent political upheaval in Britain, and for this reason they hankered for places in the government from which they could galvanise their colleagues into more effective action. But they were also torn by powerful ties of friendship and affection binding them to Fox. They had no wish to abandon their old friend and they feared any close association with Pitt without the security which Fox's presence in the ministry would give. They remembered how Pitt had thwarted them in 1783, humiliated them in 1784, and outwitted them in 1788, and they regarded him as vindictive and relentless in the pursuit of power: they had no wish to expose themselves to the ruthless deceptions practised, so they imagined, by his cold and lofty intellect. They therefore tried desperately to bring Fox into the ministry with them, hoping that they would thereby preserve their own reputations for loyalty, while conveniently dissociating Fox from Grey, Sheridan and the younger whigs, who had so embarrassed their elders by founding the society of the Friends of the People, and pressing on, despite all the warning signs and Fox's own misgivings, with rapid and provocative motions calling for parliamentary reform. Burke was also intimately concerned with the fate of his old party and his former friends. Despite his own trenchant opposition to the French revolution he had not given up hope of bringing over Portland and Fitzwilliam to the ministry, and there were even times when he believed that it might be possible to convert Fox to a more reasonable point of view.

Amid this confused turmoil, with men putting different interpretations on events and seeking similar ends for irreconcilable reasons, it was not surprising that intrigue and suspicion should flourish and that honest differences of opinion should be mistaken for treacherous betrayals. Some of the politicians genuinely wanted a coalition government; others thought it desirable but unlikely; others saw it as possible but undesirable; others regarded it as almost impossible but worth trying. Pitt saw the advantages in sounding out the opposition; by doing so he might divide them still further, driving their temporary recovery during the Orchakov affair into oblivion. Fox was anxious to maintain the whig opposition as a credible political party; in order to achieve this he embarked on the negotiation with a shrewd sense of what was practicable uppermost in his mind. Yet his motives were not without confusion and his feelings fluctuated with every ebb and flow of rumour and second-hand allegation. He saw other men as the dupes of Pitt or the victims of Burke. As his own hopes were dashed, as the whig party fractured against the immovable realities of controversy and conflict, he saw conspiracy and treachery everywhere, controlled and directed by the remorseless Pitt and inflamed by Burke's obsessive passion. He forgot that his own motives were as mixed and as earthy as any man's and that his own conduct was as open to abuse or misrepresentation as that of Pitt or Burke, Portland or Fitzwilliam, Loughborough or Leeds. Most significantly, the essential difference between Pitt and Fox was political not ideological.

Both were sympathetic to certain aspects of the French revolution, yet worried by its descent into violence; both favoured parliamentary reform, but thought the summer of 1792 unpropitious; both were worried by radical extremism; and both desired peace. Their conflict at this period was a clash of personalities, not of ideals, and their failure to reach any agreement enabling them to work together owed more to the legacy of previous political conflicts than to any ideological divergence on the issues of the day. Fox liked to clothe his growing alienation from the Portland whigs with some vestige of political principle: no such explanation can be held to be valid for his continued antagonism towards Pitt. Ironically both set their faces against the men in their own parties who were seeking to lure them into extreme postures. The chief difference was that while Pitt was under pressure only from those seeking to compel him to take a more hostile attitude towards the French revolution abroad and the radical societies at home, Fox was seeking to resist both those who wanted him to abandon the cause of reform and to renounce his earlier sympathy with the French, and those who wished him to be more outspoken in advocating reformist ideas, in encouraging radical agitation and in defending the new order in France.

As the year 1792 drew to its close Fox became more pessimistic about the possibility of preserving the whig party. He tried to keep up his spirits, and some of his friends found him outwardly cheerful, but all the signs pointed to disaster and made a deep and painful impression upon his mind. In November he confessed to Adair that he was growing very doubtful about the preservation of 'those connexions which I love and esteem as much as ever, and without which I do not feel that I ever can act in political matters with any satisfaction to myself'.[25] Portland and Fitzwilliam were too eager to make concessions to the government and though Fox was reluctant to believe this he felt himself threatened by those who were seeking to 'pervert' Portland and Fitzwilliam and their friends. There were rascals on the democratic side too, but to the best of his knowledge they had not indulged in the dubious type of persuasion which had been so much in evidence on the other side. But optimism was easily dashed. On 29 November Fox unburdened himself to Adair:

> It is good not to despair, but I do assure you I am forced to use considerable exertion with myself to avoid it. I still am blind as to any disposition to what I call conciliation. The very word *forgive*, if it were mentioned, which I hope it never will, would put an end to all hopes of it. But what is worse than this is that I do not see any express renunciation of the plan of suspending opposition for the purpose of giving strength to government. This with *me* is the most real cause of separation of any that has been stated.[26]

He had heard rumours that the duke of Portland intended to give up active opposition and although he did not believe that this was the duke's real intention it seemed that the ministers thought it was unlikely that Portland would continue in formed opposition. Fox was in no position to deny these reports, but he was anxious to show that the responsibility for the break up of the party was not his, being particularly sensitive to suggestions that he had made innovations in theories of parliamentary reform. He had said nothing which he had not said months ago to Portland and Fitzwilliam and years before to Rockingham. Grey could be forgiven for being surprised at the violent storm which the issue of parliamentary reform had raised. He had tried to do nothing which Richmond had not approved of when he was on cordial terms with the whig party and which Sir George Savile and other Rockinghamites had lent their support to in public. It was especially cruel to see old friends taking fright on such an issue and running off to Pitt on such a pretext. Fox emphasized that reform was most necessary in Scotland and that it was more desirable in the boroughs than in the counties but even when striving to formulate some moderate reform programme Fox could not forget that the deliberations on the subject within the whig party were not confidential, and that it was likely that waverers such as Loughborough were passing on information to Pitt. In any event it was an awkward fact that parliamentary reform had never been an issue on which the whigs had been in full agreement, and this made it all the more galling that it should be cited as an excuse for desertion to the government. Even after the breach in 1794 about half of those whigs who remained loyal to Fox on the issue of the war were opposed to parliamentary reform. The Foxite whigs were a party of peace and civil and religious liberty: they could only agree to differ on the vexed topic of parliamentary reform.

Fox had no wish to make his friends recant their former opinions on parliamentary reform; he was more worried by the fact that Portland was suspect on the repeal of the penal laws affecting catholics and dissenters. Portland had not formally committed himself against repeal, but Fox knew that there was nothing to be hoped for from the duke on parliamentary reform. He had not the slightest desire to make this issue the test of any man's allegiance to the opposition.

> Now, as to the question of parliamentary reform, I never had even a wish that the duke of Portland should recede from his former opinion upon the subject. He and Lord Fitzwilliam were always against it; but what I want them to do is to adhere to their former line of conduct, and to oppose it without any *hostility* to the supporters of it, or any friendship with those who resist it. If this is said to be a difficult line, I answer it was theirs in '82, '83, '84, and '85. Indeed, indeed, instead of my making strides towards new opinions, or even leaning to them, they are adopting systems of conduct entirely *new*, and in so doing are, I am convinced, the dupes of those who have the worst intentions.[27]

It was tempting to argue that the dissident whigs were the real innovators and that they have gone far beyond any novelties in mere theory by indulging in conduct which violated the conventions governing their former behaviour. Actions spoke louder than words, and while Fox was remaining loyal in public (whatever his private misgivings) to those ideals for which he had stood in the days of the American war and the Rockingham ministry, Portland and Fitzwilliam were using old differences of viewpoint upon a familiar subject as a pretext for dissociating themselves from the whig opposition and allying themselves more closely with the government. Behind all this Fox discerned the malignant influence of Burke. It was Burke who was the chief instigator of every act of treachery and every instance of apostasy. Burke had given reactionaries a vocabulary for their prejudices and a justification for their fears; he had seduced former Rockinghamites from their allegiance, destroying the very party to which, in earlier days, he had devoted so much of his energies and abilities. This was a bitter blow for Fox to bear. Although Burke and he had never been as close as legend suggested, the breach with Burke in the commons had been a harrowing experience. But the thought that Burke was the principal negotiator on behalf of Pitt and the government was especially hard to contemplate without rancour. Fox remembered Pitt's triumph in 1784. He recalled the way in which the whigs had been outmanoeuvred over the India bill and trounced in the election. He could not forget that Pitt had won his victory as the nominee of the king, and to see Burke, the former enemy of the influence of the crown, coming to the aid of George III's chief accomplice, was repugnant. This was the worst betrayal of all. Burke had never been a parliamentary reformer, but he had always advocated limiting and destroying the secret influence of the crown, and now he was prepared to condone every dark deed because of his obsession with the French revolution and the need to inspire the government to take up a missionary stance in its attitude towards French affairs.

Fox shuddered at the inroads which were being made into the traditional right of free speech. He opposed every piece of legislation which the government introduced limiting the right to agitate or to publish material of a political nature. In defending the rights and liberties of the subject he was being faithful to the whig tradition. Yet even here old friends were slinking over to the government. He could condone misgivings about the French revolution but he could not forgive any act which deprived Englishmen of their familiar right to say or do what they thought was best. Fox believed that much of what the government was doing was intended to disrupt the whig party by exploiting temporary differences of opinion within the opposition. Pitt's cold and calculating vindictiveness was at work again, but Burke was providing a passion and a fury which the minister could not simulate. It was the Westminster scrutiny all over again, but this time the commons in their anti-French panic would not curb the arrogance of the minister. Fox was doing Pitt an injustice, but this did not alter the way in which he felt about things.

Brave though his defence of the rights of free speech and free assembly were at the height of the anti-Jacobin scare, Fox believed that by resisting the government's policies he was securing the old whig tradition, and possibly defending the old whig party in the only possible way in which this could be done. But he did not fully conceive of the intensity with which some of his old friends feared the French and their ideas, and how seriously they took any sign, however flimsy, that French ideas were abroad in England, luring the working classes into dangerous acts of sedition and riot. It was doubly disappointing for Fox to find that his re-affirmation of familiar whig principles produced only a faint or negative response. But he had no choice but to carry on the fight. Once his decision was made there could be no turning back. Idealism and self-interest coincided. When Fox denounced the treason trials, the aliens bill, the seditious meetings and treasonable practices bills, he was thinking, not of future tributes to his idealism, but of the pressing exigencies of parliamentary politics. He had to clarify his differences with the government and the gulf separating himself and Burke. He had to make some appeal on recognisable whig principles for the support of Portland, Fitzwilliam and the other waverers. And he had the persistent hope that if the government were sufficiently discredited by either the course of the war or by their domestic policies it might be possible to come into office in much the same way that Rockingham had succeeded North in 1782. In his conduct of party politics, in the only way which seemed possible in the circumstances, Fox provided future whigs with a memorable historical mythology and whatever the disappointments of foreign policy, civil and religious liberties were consistently defended and became an integral part of essential whiggery. Though Cobden's famous tribute to Fox in the 1790s—'The annals of parliament do not record a nobler struggle in a nobler cause'—was really paid to Fox's critique of the war against France and the foreign policy of Pitt and Grenville, its general tone of reverential adulation was also true of the attitude of many Victorian liberals towards Fox's record in domestic policies, and though this is a singular instance of the powerful spell cast by one historical legend, it is also a sign of the later impact of Fox's conduct of the whig opposition on another generation of English whigs.

Fox argued that the government exaggerated the extent of the danger of insurrection or rebellion. He believed that anxieties were whipped up for sinister political purposes. For himself he could never see why men got themselves into a state about the propagation of political or religious ideas. He did not believe that the discussion of any principles (no matter how outrageous they were generally thought to be) constituted a threat to public order and civil peace. He was convinced that the constitution was strong enough to withstand theoretical assaults, depending as it did on the confidence of the people, a confidence which was the fruit of historical and contemporary experience. It was not that he had any sympathy with advanced democrats. The reverse was the case. He read only the first part of Tom Paine's *Rights of Man* and he disliked it so much that he could not bring himself to read the second part. Such a devastating assault on theories of a balanced constitution was bound to be distasteful to someone like Fox, whose constitutional ideas were so bound up with doctrines of mixed government. Even when he defended parliamentary reform in the house of commons Fox was careful to remind MPs that he was opposed to universal manhood suffrage; he had always considered it to be a wild and ridiculous idea. But this did not give him the right to curb those who argued that manhood suffrage was right and desirable; they had every right to try to persuade their fellow countrymen that they ought to think again about the issue. The expression of opinion ought to be free and it should be restrained only when there was clear evidence that the propagation of certain ideas was linked with violence, crime, and breaches of the peace. Fox maintained that the government never produced convincing evidence that such a link existed between the ideas of the English radicals and the sort of activities which threatened public order. Throughout all his speeches on civil liberties Fox stoutly took up this line and never departed from it.

The chief embarrassment was that the deterioration of the situation in France made life difficult for reformers in England. In many men's minds English liberties and French liberty were bound up together; in some ways justifiably so, but it was easy to exploit French excesses to discredit English reformers, especially when some of the reformers derived their political vocabulary and styles of behaviour from French models. Fox regarded the cause of liberty as indivisible. But he was compelled to dissociate himself from the wildest extravagances perpetrated in Paris as long as he hoped to persuade his colleagues in the house of commons to take a more reasonable attitude towards those of their fellow countrymen who were pressing through legal channels for a reform of parliament.

Panic was the chief characteristic of the time and panic, in Fox's eyes, was being aided and abetted, possibly even inspired, by the government. He found it hard to believe that the ministry took their own allegations seriously. On 13 December 1792, in the debate on the king's speech in the commons he made great play with the failure of the government to prove its claim that there was a real danger of insurrection in the country. Fox maintained that the government was libelling the majority of Englishmen and he defied the ministers to reveal the evidence on which their sweeping charges were based:

> The next assertion is, that there exists at this moment an insurrection in this kingdom. An insurrection! Where is it? Where has it reared its head? Good God! An insurrection in Great Britain! No wonder that the militia were called out and parliament assembled in the extraordinary way in which they have been. But where is it?

All that the government would say was that insurrections were too notorious to be described; Fox preferred to argue that it was not the notoriety of the insurrections which prevented particulars from being given to the house, but their non-existence. The government was exploiting a few minor disorders in order to make a fundamental change in the law of the land. Fox conceded that there had been a few riots in different parts of the country, but these were being used to cover an attempt to destroy 'our happy constitution'.

> I have heard of a tumult at Shields, of another at Leith, of some riot at Yarmouth, and of something of the same nature at Perth and Dundee. I ask gentlemen if they believe that in each of these places the avowed object of the complaint of the people was not the real one—that the sailors at Shields, Yarmouth, etc. did not really want some increase of their wages, but were actuated by a design of overthrowing the constitution?[28]

The government was not content to judge events; they preferred to impute motives which were politically convenient to themselves but which had no real foundation in the attitudes and behaviour of the men who had taken part in the various disturbances. It was easy for the ministers to argue that even if constitutional reform was the stated objective of a number of popular movements their real purpose was the subversion of the constitution. This presumption was part of a system of intellectual oppression. 'So, then, by this new scheme of tyranny, we are not to judge of the conduct of men by their overt acts, but are to arrogate to ourselves at once the province and the power of the deity: we are to arraign a man for his secret thoughts, and to punish him because we choose to believe him guilty.'

There were genuine causes for grievances which were too lightly overlooked by the ministers. If the dissenters were discontented the surest remedy was to repeal the test and corporation acts, thus removing all reasons for denominational unrest. Similarly if it were argued that too many dissenters were sympathetic to republican ideas the best remedy would be to amend the representation of the house of commons and to show that the house of commons, though not chosen by all, should have no other interest than to prove itself the representative of all.

Fox closed by reaffirming his own devotion to the constitution. He spoke as the defender of English liberties, not as an advocate for new and foreign doctrines. He pleaded eloquently for the constitution to be respected but at the same time improved by returning to the first principles on which it was based. In the agony of trying to retain the loyalty of old friends and to expound, in all faithfulness, the familiar whig doctrine of the constitution Fox's eloquence reached great heights.

Sir, I love the constitution as it is established. It has grown up with me as a prejudice and a habit, as well as from conviction. I know that it is calculated for the happiness of man, and that its constituent branches of king, lords and commons could not be altered or impaired without entailing on this country the most dreadful miseries. It was the best adapted to England. . . . Heartily convinced, however, as I am, that to secure the peace, strength and happiness of the country we must maintain the constitution against all innovation yet I do not think so superstitiously of any human institution as to imagine that it is incapable of being perverted: on the contrary I believe that it requires an increasing vigilance on the part of the people to prevent the decay and dilapidations to which every edifice is subject. I think also, that we may be led asleep to our real danger by these perpetual alarms to loyalty, which, in my opinion, are daily sapping the constitution. Under the pretext of guarding it from the assaults of republicans and levellers, we run the hazard of leaving it open on the other and more feeble side. We are led insensibly to the opposite danger; that of increasing the power of the crown, and of degrading the influence of the commons house of parliament. It is in such moments as the present that the most dangerous, because unsuspected, attacks may be made on our dearest rights; for let us only look back to the whole course of the present administration and we shall see that, from their outset to the present day, it has been their invariable object to degrade the house of commons in the eyes of the people, and to diminish its power and influence in every possible way.[29]

Although Fox was seeking to put himself forward as the defender of the traditional constitution his closing remarks jarred on many members. It seemed too much like an attempt to reap party advantage from national emergency, and men who had faithfully supported Pitt's ministry, even when they had voted against Pitt's more far-sighted proposals, were hardly inclined to go along with Fox's claim that the government had always been active in undermining the house of commons and its place in the constitution. From Fox's own standpoint the appeal to the past was understandable, possibly inescapable. He had to do something to appeal to old friends and by reminding men of bygone struggles against Pitt and George III he hoped to revive their fading sense of loyalty to the opposition. It was significant that he revived bitter memories of the means by which Pitt had defeated the whigs, first by defying the house of commons and then by winning the general election of 1784. Fox could not afford to ignore any opportunity of appealing to familiar party loyalties, and a hatred of Pitt because of the events of 1783-4 was a fundamental principle with many Foxite whigs. Even when he was most anxious to defend his record as a defender of the constitution Fox had to evoke memories of the long struggle against George III and North and the departed but still cherished glories of the Rockinghamite era. Perhaps because he had never himself been an orthodox Rockinghamite Fox was all the more eager to establish his claim to the Rockinghamite succession. Yet even when doing this Fox knew that he would be accused of playing party politics. The mixture of sentiment, idealism, and political cunning which marked Fox's speeches during the 1790s was the consequence of the situation in which he was placed. His only hope of entering office (barring some understanding with Pitt, which became all the more unlikely as Fox heard of Burke's efforts to win the Portland group over to the government) was to establish the differences between Pitt and himself and trust that events would justify his reading of the political prospects. He was taking a gamble: the gamble that events would prove Pitt dramatically wrong, just as the surrender at Yorktown had shattered the assumptions on which North's policy in America had been based. This was no less marked in Fox's critique of the government's conduct of the war as it was in his criticisms of their domestic policies.

The fate of the whig party was decided both in debate in the two houses of parliament, and in private negotiations behind the scenes. A party which was so evidently parliamentary in character, and which owed its existence to a particular way of looking at the requirements of parliamentary politics, and to a complex web of personal friendships, was abnormally sensitive to the ebb and flow of parliamentary debate. The fortunes of the party had been made in the house of commons; this was why Fox's own activities as a debater had been so important in the past and why they were so crucial in the years leading up to Portland's final defection to the government in 1794. Fox hoped to shame some of his old colleagues out of their dallyings with Pitt and Burke by his conduct of debate. Unhappily for him the shift in political attitudes had gone much further than what could be retrieved by a tactical change of emphasis. The issues raised by the French revolution, and even more by the war, were too great for any display of parliamentary ingenuity, however brilliant, to solve them. Fears of agitation in England, and anxieties about the chances, however remote, of an eruption of violence on a major scale, rendered the confused manoeuvres in the house of commons redundant to the transformation of the deepest instincts in the hearts of men. Fox's own error in interpreting the events of the 1790s too much in terms of the 1770s, and his tendency constantly to recur to the crisis of 1782-4 in order to explain his attitude towards Pitt, the government and the conservative whigs, made it difficult for him to appreciate fully how drastically the political situation had changed. In some ways Fox failed to grasp the magnitude of the change which had been wrought by the French revolution; in this, as in other things, he was the opposite of Burke.

From an early date the lobbies reflected the extent to which Fox was losing the support of men who had remained faithful even after the débâcle of 1784. In December 1792 only 50 MPs followed Fox into the opposition lobby and men who were worried by the dangers to property manifested by the ideas of the French revolutionaries and the English radicals alike needed more than eloquence to woo them back to their old allegiance. Yet Fox had little alternative—once he had rejected any suggestion that he should serve under Pitt—but to do what he did, and within the limits imposed upon him by the general political situation he practised his policy with amazing parliamentary skill. He miscalculated, for he exaggerated the extent to which the government's policies would be exposed and overtaken by events. Far from making men feel that Pitt was repressive the worsening situation made them urge the government to be more active in its opposition to levelling ideas whether at home or abroad. The strains on the whig opposition were so severe that Fox had to identify his interpretation of the constitution and of the current crisis with the party's record in the past. By reviving old memories of the influence of the crown he hoped to challenge the dominance of Burke and secure something of a future for a party which was already too much under the spell of the past.

Throughout the long conflict, which lasted for almost two years before the fate of the whig opposition was finally sealed, Fox attempted to divorce political differences from private friendships. In the intense atmosphere of the months following the outbreak of the war with France it was difficult to maintain this distinction, however valuable it had been in the past, and Fox was pained by every onslaught made by old friends. During the debate on the aliens bill on 28 December 1792 he was hurt by the comments of Sir Gilbert Elliot, arguing that if their political dis-agreements had lasted for as long as Elliot had claimed then he ought to have stated them much earlier. Behind every desertion Fox detected influence and corruption; he was loath to believe that any honest differ-ence of opinion could take so many friends over to the government side. He became increasingly incapable of appreciating that there was a credible alternative viewpoint to his own. The loss of friends seemed to confirm the sinister malevolence which he now associated with Burke and Pitt. Even when deploring Elliot's conduct Fox claimed that the difference of opinion among the whigs over French affairs and foreign policy was not of itself sufficient to justify a complete break with former colleagues. He could understand the strength of Windham's feelings on the French issue, but even here he maintained that there was no difference of opinion sufficiently deep-rooted to make it impossible for men to preserve those political connexions with which they had always acted. Possibly Fox thought that the crisis would disappear as quickly as it had emerged. It was folly to wreck the whig party when a change of fortunes on the continent might end the war between France and the central powers, and when such a peace might enable some reconciliation to take place between France and England. Without the threat of a restoration of the Bourbons by force of foreign intervention the French would lose that irritating tendency to interfere in English domestic politics which had contributed to making their cause so unpopular in Britain.

Fox therefore devoted all his energies to advising those of his friends who differed from him on the subject of the French revolution to wait and see. Prudence and patience were better than precipitate haste. The existence of the whig party was at stake and if it were to be saved for-bearance and tolerance were necessary. Fox boasted of his pride in party in the commons:

He said ... that it was the pride of his heart to think, that the union and exertions of that connexion had kept alive everything that deserved the name of the spirit of liberty.... He wished not to call to mind particular expressions; but he could not but recollect that the difference between those with whom he had acted and the present ministry was formerly called fundamental and irreconcilable: and he did believe that this sentiment still pervaded the majority of them. Whether his opinion was or was not consonant with the opinion of that majority he did not know; but this he did know, that the cause of his country would not suffer him to say that he could support an administration which stood upon grounds not warranted by the constitution. He had heard ... that the present administration ought to be systematically supported at all events in the present state of affairs. He blamed not those who said so; but, with regard to himself and those who entertained that opinion, union and cooperation were at an end.[30]

It was significant that the decisive difference was not thought to be over French affairs, or even over the measures which the government were putting forward for the greater security of the country. It was whether general and consistent support ought to be given to the ministry in their efforts to tackle the dangers of internal disorder and foreign infiltration. Only when his friends gave overall support to Pitt did Fox consider his friendship and association with them to be at an end. It was usual for considerable freedom to be given to the party on particular issues: members were allowed ample scope for private conviction and conscientious objections to the dominant party line. Important though the controversies connected with the French revolution were Fox was prepared to be generous. He was appealing to a familiar eighteenth-century convention, one which both he and Pitt had to accept when in office, and one which held up the implementation of Fox's ideas on the conduct of opposition and the growth of cabinet responsibility. It was ironic that Fox had to shift his ground, appealing for a broad tolerance of conflicting viewpoints, even though this conflicted with the primary concern for the creation of a consistent and party-based opposition in the commons. But faced as he was by the rumour of so many desertions, this was all he could do to try to stem the tide.

Most distressing of all were the allegations that the duke of Portland was considering giving general support to the government. The issue came to a head over the aliens bill which Portland approved of. Fox had been on terms of friendship with the duke for sixteen or seventeen years. He could not believe that Portland was moving over to the administration. Despite his support for the aliens bill, however, Portland could not forget the means by which Pitt had come into office in 1783 and he made this widely known. Obviously, whatever Portland's misgivings about national security, he was trying to differentiate between general support for the ministry in a state of emergency and adherence to Pitt and the ministerial party. Portland felt that greater degree of control over the entry of aliens into the country was necessary, but if Fox understood him rightly he also believed that many of the difficulties facing the nation were the consequences of the weakness and misconduct of Pitt and the other ministers of the crown. Fox and Portland disagreed on the necessity for an aliens bill, but Fox claimed that this did not constitute a fundamental difference between the duke and himself and that it would not justify the end of their habitual political association.

Yet as the MPs listened to Fox arguing that there was little difference on fundamentals between himself and his friends, whatever might be said about the aliens bill, they could not resist feeling that Fox was indulging in a form of special pleading. His affirmations of loyalty and his clear wish that nothing should intensify the divisions already separating him from his friends any further seemed to smack of wishful thinking rather than political insight or personal confidence.

However resourceful Fox was in criticising the government he was seen in the guise of a man striving to salvage something from the wreck rather than the leader of a viable political party. It was almost as if he was refusing to accept what had already happened, his energies being expended in a fruitless attempt to prevent something that had already passed beyond his control.

In private Fox did his best to mend the breach with Portland. He told the duke that he thought Elliot's speech, unpleasant as it had been, nothing less than an attempt to force him into making a public statement which would widen the divisions within the whig party and push Portland further towards making his peace with the government. Fox reminded Portland that he was still the head of the whig opposition. If further questions continued to be asked about Portland's relations with his followers the state of the party would continue to deteriorate, with unpleasant consequences for everyone. Anxiety and distress would accompany further speculation about the future of the opposition. Fox warned Portland of the dangers of falling for the tactic of lessening the stringency of opposition. In practice this could mean nothing other than what Burke had called 'neutralisation' and which would consummate the destruction of the whigs. Fox went on:

Surely, then, though it may be necessary to support particular measures

which the safety of the country may require, it is a time with regard
to the men rather to redouble your vigilance and jealousy, rather than
to relax in your severity. The other expression which I heard of with
alarm, was a hope that we (meaning you and me) might soon *meet
again.* If anything of this sort is said, it will give great credit to those
who give out with so much industry that we are separated, and great
discredit to me who maintain everywhere the contrary.[31]

Fox was reiterating in private what he had already stated in public, that
to support individual measures of the administration, while acting in
general opposition to the ministry, was no new conduct for the opposition,
though he had to admit that if such measures became more important
and more frequent the union of those who differed on them would
become more lax, and the opposition to those with whom one concurred
more feeble. Fox asked Portland to be clear and explicit in his disavowal
of any intention of giving general support to the administration. He did
so for reasons of friendship, out of regard for Portland personally, and
most of all because of his desire to preserve the whig party.

Portland was uncomfortable under pressure. He was torn by his
friendship for Fox and his growing anxiety about the propagation of
revolutionary principles in England. He was just as anxious as Fox to
preserve the whig party. In matters of organisation he had played a
bigger part than Fox in keeping the party in being and in preparing it
to fight the general election of 1790. He had no wish to destroy his own
creation, fragile as it was, and no desire to break with Fox. But the
issues seemed to become more immense and more inescapable as time went
by. Mere party loyalties and considerations of friendship were dwarfed
by the magnitude of what was at stake. All Portland did, however, was
to wriggle, and this was less than satisfactory to Fox. It was impossible
for Portland to dissociate himself from those acts of government of which
he approved; indeed, he was more eager for effective measures of repression than Pitt himself. Yet Portland could not overlook the irrevocable
nature of an accession to the ministry, and his friendship for Fox and
fondness for familiar political ties, held him back from taking the steps
which followed logically from his response to events.

Fox hoped that by sticking to his guns in public he would win back
the confidence and affection of friends whose anxieties over the international situation might be eroded by events. So far as the aliens bill
was concerned, Fox emphasized the distinction between the repression of
acts of violence and the suppression of mere opinions. He did not deny
that in many people's minds the propagation of French opinions and the

fear of the progress of French arms could not be distinguished from each other, but nevertheless he believed that it was wise for such a distinction to be made. He did not believe that there was any great danger from the spread of French opinions in England, certainly not on a scale sufficient to merit serious alarm. Whatever appeal the ideas of the French made in other countries, he preferred to think that they would make slight progress in England, where rational liberty was enjoyed and understood. He was convinced that the people were deeply attached to the constitution and that this, not the steps taken by the government, explained the quiet state of the country. He could not accept that calling out the militia was an effective way of repressing opinions or of repelling ideas:

> Opinions were never yet driven out of a country by pikes, and swords, and guns. Against them the militia was no defence. How, then, were they to be met if they existed? By contempt, if they were absurd; by argument, if specious; by prosecutions, if they were seditious.... If ... any danger did exist, it was not to be repelled by calling out the militia, and under the pretence of waging war with obnoxious political principles, bringing bodies of them nearer to the metropolis.... He knew not how to fight an opinion, nor did history furnish him with instruction. The opinions of Luther and Calvin had been combated with arms; there was no want of war, no want of blood.... But were they extirpated? No; they had spread and flourished through bloodshed and persecution. The comparison of these with opinions of another description might seem invidious; but it was so only if they were attacked by reason, not if attacked by war. By force and power, no opinion, good or bad, had ever been subdued.[32]

He once again affirmed his loyalty to the constitution, declaring that its virtues called for vigilance if they were to be preserved. He was saddened at the spectacle of those who had acted with him on former occasions now giving their support to the government. It seemed as if their chief motive was the feeling that there was little hope of turning the ministry out. It was ironic that, when the ministers had so misconducted affairs as to create an unprecedented situation, they should have the support of those who had formerly opposed them. Yet, despite all Fox's efforts, his amendment calling for the postponement of further consideration of the bill was defeated without a division and the aliens act became law.

With the outbreak of war between England and France in January 1793 much of Fox's energies were turned to criticising the government's conduct of the war and their failure to negotiate a peace with the French republic. But throughout the war years the issue of free speech and the defence of civil liberties continued. Fox opposed the seditious meetings bill and the treasonable practices act; he supported motions calling for the reform of parliament and the repeal of the test act; and he denounced the suspension of habeas corpus. He also vigorously criticised the treason trials, both in London and Scotland, and the transportation of Muir and Palmer moved him to outraged scorn and eloquent anger.

The government was seeking to curb the activities of those radicals who were agitating for the reform of parliament, more especially those who were industriously distributing books such as Paine's *Rights of Man* and expounding ideas thought to be similar to those of the French republicans. Most historians are agreed that there was little real danger of revolution breaking out in England in these years, but the resources available to the authorities for the maintenance of law and order were minimal, and used as they were to reliance on the local magistrates for the policing of the country Pitt and his colleagues were baffled by a situation which was without precedent, and which seemed to transcend the traditional deference to the importance of the locality even where keeping the peace was involved. There were tales of planned insurrection and stocks of arms, and of French agents plotting violent outbreaks against the government. Partly because some of the radicals talked of holding conventions, making great play with grandiose phrases about the sovereignty of the people, the property-owning classes took fright. Yet the ministers were unhappily aware that they could not afford to take risks.

Most of them were content to follow events, not to anticipate them. Far from leading a systematic reign of terror Pitt and his colleagues merely responded to pressures put upon them; they did not take the initiative. Their ideas were traditional; they sought merely to strengthen the powers of the local JPs, while using the laws of sedition and libel to restrain and silence questionable publications. They had no wish to open windows into men's souls. As long as Paine's writings were read only by respectable members of society Pitt saw no danger in them. Only when working men began to read Paine's book in large numbers did the government become alarmed. It was the audience for Paine's ideas which worried the government, not Paine's ideas themselves. With the formation of societies such as the London Corresponding Society the ministers felt that the time for action had come. Reluctantly they tried to clamp down on radical activity. It was thought that a few examples would do the trick. But the treason trials were unfortunate for the government.

Chiefly because of the brilliance of Erskine, Horne Tooke, Hardy and Thelwall were acquittted, and it was noted that Pitt was taking action against men who were seeking to achieve by peaceful association and propaganda moderate parliamentary reforms which he had himself supported a decade earlier. Pitt in the witness box was a spectacle which reminded men that the English reformers had not needed to look to France for inspiration, despite the tendency to regard every demand for reform as echoing the extremism of the French Jacobins. But while in England the trials were conducted fairly, and were in one sense a remarkable tribute to the respect for the rule of law inculcated by constitutional theorists, in Scotland the trials were disgraceful. Lord Braxfield harangued the prisoners brutally and in a fashion which dispelled any illusions of his impartiality. Muir and Palmer were both given savage sentences of transportation, and on hearing the news Fox could not help exclaiming, 'God help the nation that has such judges!'

But—ruthless though Braxfield had been—it would be misleading to call the government's policy a reign of terror, a counterpart to the rule of the committee of public safety in Paris, or evidence of Pitt giving the lead to what might be fancifully described as a European counter-revolution. Disturbed as the government was by allegations of planned violence it simply invoked those methods for keeping the peace which were available to it. Though spies were used this was inevitable in the circumstances of the time. Possibly they were little different in practice from modern special branch detectives; the authorities had to use every possible method of attempting to procure reliable information about what was going on, and this was no easy matter when seeking to delve into the contemporary underworld of politics. Secret oaths could only be countered by secret agents. Without an effective police force the government was forced to use informers, and, although agents provocateurs have always had a bad reputation, the government was not always duped by the wild tales put about by informers eager to provoke actions which would give credence to their more dramatic revelations. The army was always used with restraint and almost invariably behaved well. The troops were sensibly led and usually impartial in the way in which they carried out difficult and unpopular assignments. Pitt and Dundas knew the widespread prejudice against the use of the soldiery in civil disturbances: it seemed an affront to the liberties of freeborn Englishmen. Consequently, the most efficient arm available for the control of mass meetings was used with discretion and restraint. Nevertheless, the government appeared to be taking excessive steps to cope with an exaggerated danger. It was not that extremists who talked of violent revolution were wholly absent;

it was rather that they had little support from the artisans who, for the most part, preferred peaceful methods of making their ideas known.

In this confused and confusing situation Fox was at his best in defending the rights of free speech and free political association. He had nothing to gain from this stance, other than the knowledge that he was defending traditional liberties. He knew that Portland was more alarmist than Pitt about the dangers and likelihood of disorder, and he was familiar with Fitzwilliam's anxieties about the corresponding society in Sheffield. The old whigs were more vehement than Pitt in demanding that the government should take action to thwart radical agitators and forestall any insurrection. The breach between Portland and Fitzwilliam and Fox finally owed more to their differences of opinion on domestic issues and on the maintenance of law and order than to any disagreement over the French revolution and the conduct of the war. Fox was bitterly distressed and acutely pained by the breach with these old friends. It was all the more depressing because he remembered how much he had owed to them in the past.

Although the government was fond of claiming that severe measures were justified by the necessity of preventing any repetition in England of what had happened in France Fox regarded the sentences on Muir and Palmer as a worthy imitation of the worst of the French excesses. In March 1794 he supported Adam's motion on the trials of Muir and Palmer, taking the opportunity to condemn the policies of which such trials were the expression. He was also quick to remind members that the ministers of the crown had themselves supported similar activities to those which were being singled out for condemnation.

It cannot have escaped gentlemen, that not many years ago associations were formed in this country, exactly on the same principles that Mr Muir and his friends formed their associations. Sir, it is precisely for those very offences which were committed by those very associations in England, that Mr Muir and Mr Palmer are now condemned to transportation for fourteen years. But it will be said that the French revolution has changed the nature of the case. It may be so; but I wish never to believe that what was once meritorious, what was once fit, and what was considered as the only means of preserving the liberties of this country, can all of a sudden have so changed its complexion, can have become so black and atrocious a crime, as to call down on the head of him who so far reveres the constitution of England as to wish to restore it to its primitive perfection, the unrelenting vengeance of persecution.... Yes, sir, these unfortunate gentlemen have done what the right honourable the chancellor of the exchequer, what the duke of Richmond have done before them. They have done no more. . . . Why are these very men now exalted to the most envied stations, while poor Muir and Palmer are doomed to waste out the remainder of their lives in a foreign climate, the companions of outcasts, felons, the most degraded of the human species! . . . Have we not all of us been guilty of crimes which might drive us to Botany Bay?[33]

But Fox was concerned to do more than plead the case on the basis of common humanity. He blamed the government for destroying the constitution which it was supposed to be defending. He was convinced that the radicals had acted within the law and that the law was being changed in order to prevent types of agitation which had previously been accepted as legal and permissible. Conventions were not in themselves seditious or treasonable. At Edinburgh the reformers had stated that they were interested in the redress of grievances, not merely in opposing the government. Fox reminded the house of the behaviour of the Yorkshire association and the Westminster committee in the early 1780s and he maintained that it was proper for men to meet together to formulate and present their requests and petitions to parliament. Nor was he impressed by arguments that such meetings constituted a threat to public order. The conventions which the government was proceeding against were not marked by the attendance of men of influence. Ordinary members of society could hardly be deemed a threat to the community. Nor was there anything to fear from working men. The weight of opinion in the country was so heavily in favour of the constitution that there was little to worry about because a handful of artisans became active in political agitation and in propagating ideas for the reform of parliament.

Fox wanted to keep the whole business in perspective. He had no time for democratic ideas, loathing Paine's principles as much as he despised Rousseau's. He thought attempts to model British agitations on the French convention ridiculous. But this made the extremism of the government's reaction all the more absurd. No popular movement stood the slightest chance of success without the support of a substantial section of the propertied classes. Fox thought it inconceivable that the radicals would succeed in doing this and he was therefore convinced that all their wild plans would remain no more than dreams and the delusions of naïve imaginations. He could not believe that Pitt and the other ministers really thought it likely that sufficient support would be given to radical movements for these to constitute a dangerous threat to the stability of the state. Nor did he think it likely that the French would seduce large numbers of Englishmen from their allegiance either by the attractiveness of their ideas or the lure of their gold.

The greatest danger was that, between anarchy on the one hand and the increase of the executive power on the other, true liberty—the liberty with which Englishmen were habitually familiar from birth—would be destroyed. The seditious meetings bill, the treasonable practices act and the suspension of habeas corpus represented a move towards the denial of elementary constitutional freedoms. Where would the government stop? Fox was worried at the prospect of a constant abandonment of every constitutional principle:

After suspending the habeas corpus act what would he do more? Would he prohibit all meetings of the people so as to debar them from all discussions on political subjects, and prevent all intercourse between man and man? And when this would be found ineffectual, would he give to ministers the power of making arbitrary imprisonment perpetual? Would he still further go in the exact and horrid imitation of the men who now held France in anarchy, and establish a revolutionary tribunal, or what, perhaps, he could call an anti-revolutionary tribunal? Where would he stop?[34]

Fox exaggerated the objectives of the government's actions. He was deceiving himself when he claimed to detect a deliberate attempt to increase the power of the executive and the influence of the crown at the expense of the house of commons. He overlooked the way in which so much of the ministerial reaction was an uncertain response to a strange and perplexing set of circumstances. There were good reasons, however, for seeking to revive memories of the struggle against the influence of the crown: only if these were kept bright would some of the Portland whigs hesitate to throw in their lot with Pitt and the administration. Yet it was nonsense to talk as if Pitt was striving to destroy the constitution; he and his colleagues were following opinion in the country and trying to tide themselves over a difficult period until the situation improved. Fox was right in claiming that there was an element of hysteria in the prevalent attitude towards anything smacking of reform, but he was wrong in seeing Pitt as the victim of this hysteria. As usual Pitt was trying to ascertain exactly what was happening, in order to meet pressing problems with practicable policies.

Fox was impatient to demonstrate that the government was making bad cases the basis of bad law. Because a legitimate constitutional privilege was occasionally abused this was no reason for abolishing the privilege:

> To deny to the people the right of discussion because upon some occasions that right had been exercised by indiscreet or bad men was what he could not subscribe to. The right of popular discussion was a salutary and an essential privilege of the subject.... In his opinion the best security for the due maintenance of the constitution was in the strict and incessant vigilance of the people over parliament itself. Meetings of the people, therefore, for the discussion of public objects were not merely legal but laudable; and unless it was to be contended that there was some magic in the word convention which brought with it disorder, anarchy and ruin, he could perceive no just ground for demolishing the constitution of England merely because it was intended to hold a meeting for the purpose of obtaining a parliamentary reform.[35]

He took care to make clear the extent to which he differed from the advanced radicals, reminding the house that he had always had one opinion and one only on the subject of universal suffrage: he had constantly and uniformly considered it to be 'a wild and ridiculous idea'.

Fox was speaking, therefore, not as the advocate of a new and more democratic type of politics but as the defender of the traditional system, suitably amended to remove reprehensible and troublesome abuses. He had no wish to be seen as going beyond the familiar whig position, and he was always scrupulous to put forward moderate reform as the alternative to revolution, not the prelude to violent change. He was incapable of appreciating the extent to which the right of free speech can break down under the stresses imposed by those who are willing to exploit it in order to destroy it. But he was profoundly distressed by an unparalleled sequence of events. Governments had never hesitated to put down disruptive elements in society but Fox believed that the menace of the radical clubs and societies was grossly and maliciously exaggerated and that the constitutionally minded majority were paying for the actions of a derisory and impotent minority. There were old shadows lurking in the back of his mind. He could not throw off his distrust of George III and his fear of royal influence or his hostility towards Pitt, whom he had never forgiven for playing such a critical part in the downfall of the coalition and the king's triumph in 1784.

At the same time as he took the lead in rallying his small band of followers in the commons Fox was undergoing the excruciating torment of seeing old friends move over to the government side. It was a sad time for him; much of his bravery in public was won at the cost of private suffering. It was small comfort to have Portland, Fitzwilliam and Thomas Grenville assuring him of their undying personal regard as they prepared to make their peace with Pitt and leave Fox ever more isolated, with only Sheridan, Grey, Erskine and a few others in faithful support. All the respectability and most of the wealth in the whig party followed Portland. Fox knew the seriousness of what was happening; it was nothing less than the destruction of the old whig opposition. That this should take place in circumstances in which George III and Pitt were the chief beneficiaries made it all the harder to bear.

The writing had been on the wall for a considerable time before Portland took the decisive step of joining the ministry. In December 1793 Thomas Grenville had written a long letter to Fox in which he had tried to define their differences of opinion more precisely than was possible in public and to explain his own position to his old friend. Grenville was aware of the painful nature of what he was about; he wrote in great distress, with manifest signs of strain. It was not that any new event had led him to change his opinions; rather he was becoming daily more convinced that he could not change his opinions, and that these were radically different from those entertained by Fox. On most of the issues likely to arise in public these differences would become ever more obvious and more decisive. Grenville saw two main points of disagreement between himself and Fox:

the one is respecting the war with France, which you condemn and oppose, while I think it the greatest of all duties to support and maintain it to the utmost; the other respects an apprehension which I entertain of those principles and designs in this country adverse to the constitution of it, which makes me feel it to be my duty to resist whatever can give to such designs either strength, opportunity, or countenance; while you, on the other hand, believe in no such designs, and believe the danger to arise from there being too little spirit of free inquiry and resistance in the minds of the people of this country. Either of these subjects of difference existing between us would tell much in public conduct, but both united extend very widely indeed, and must in their direct course, or at least in their bearings and consequences, pervade almost all measures of public discussion. I do not write to go on into the arguments of these questions; there is nothing new to be stated about them; nor to any detail of new measures which would seem to call for any explanation; I have none in view, other than a more direct and manifest assertion of those opinions which the pressure of the time seems to make necessary, and which it would be

neither manly nor honourable nor useful in me to disguise or suppress;
if I write to you at this moment it is rather to anticipate the pain which
I am to feel out of this miserable shape of things. . . .[36]

Grenville was saddened that he could only make his thoughts more clear
to Fox. There was no chance of reconciling their points of view; they
differed too widely for any easy resolution of their differences to take
place. It had been an unpleasant task to write to Fox in language such
as this but Grenville wished to give Fox prior notice of those public clashes
of opinion which would be all the more bitter if they erupted without
warning. Within the first few months of 1794 the final breach had taken
place. Fox told Holland about the state of affairs on 9 March. The duke
of Portland, Fitzwilliam and Grenville had all either called on him or
written to him some days before the meeting of parliament to let him
know that, despite their feelings of personal friendship and esteem, they
would have to take a more decided line than previously in support of
the ministry. Fox was under no illusions about what this meant: 'the
separation or rather the dissolution of the whig party'. He did not anticipate that his former friends would immediately take office under Pitt,
but they had all voted for the address and persuaded the duke of Devonshire to do the same. The Cavendishes had stayed away from parliament,
for although they had misgivings about the domestic situation they
could not bring themselves to vote for Pitt's war policy. Fox was downcast by the news. For months he had known that the outcome was
inevitable, but the emotional impact of what had happened was great.
He toyed with thoughts of retirement; his sense of isolation and frustration was complete.

You will easily imagine how much I felt the separation from persons
with whom I had so long been in the habit of agreeing. It seemed some
way as if I had the world to begin anew, and if I could have done it
with honour what I should best have liked would have been to retire
from politics altogether, but this could not be done, and therefore
there remains nothing but to get together the remains of our party
and begin like Sisyphus to roll up the stone again which long before
it reaches the summit may probably roll down again. Even in our small
party all is not quite in harmony, but I rather think that the necessity
of concert begins to be more felt and that we may soon become something like a party. In the house of commons we are weak in numbers
but not in argument nor I think in credit, for notwithstanding Pitt's
great majorities it is evident that the house is very far from sanguine

14 William Pitt addressing the House of Commons, 1793. Fox is seated on the
opposing front bench, fifth from the right *From a painting by K. A. Hickel*

15 'The Solicitor General for the French Republic' *Cartoon by Isaac Cruikshank, 18 February 1793*

about the war, if not altogether disgusted with it. . . .[37]

For much of the time Fox was clutching at straws. He was too experienced a campaigner to believe that moral victories were a substitute for inflicting actual defeats upon the enemy. He did not object to his party being small, but he realised that unless there was a dramatic change in the overall situation—perhaps a decisive French victory in the continental war which would bring about a general peace settlement discrediting Pitt—there was little to which to look forward. He was prepared to face the prospect of overwhelming defeats in the divisions in the commons, but there was a limit to the length of time for which this enervating type of warfare could be tolerated. He suspected that his fate depended on factors which were outside his control, and that was especially galling.

He consoled himself with the thought that men were tired and unhappy about the war but that they were frightened to show it. He saw himself as speaking for what men thought but dared not avow, guarding the conscience of the nation and preventing total submission to the spirit of panic and intolerance. In private he drew more parallels between the British government and the French Jacobins; both were the foes of liberty and the enemies of free speech. But to most of his contemporaries this comparison was far-fetched and unconvincing. They saw Fox as a dangerous crypto-traitor, oversympathetic to French ideas and less than enthusiastic about winning a war for self-preservation. The argument that in waging the war the government was risking the values for which the war was being fought was too sophisticated for the majority of MPs. They could not forget that the Rockinghamites had come into office in 1782 as the result of national defeat and they were aware that Fox saw the struggles of the 1790s as parallel to those of the 1770s and 1780s. Even when opinion turned against the war and when the mob rioted because of the high price of bread and the shortage of food, there was little benefit to Fox. He had little to say about the economic aspects of the war (he understood little about them). The subtleties of Foxite diplomacy were remote from the pressing needs of the nation and the masses cared little for abstract notions of mixed government and the constitutional significance of free speech.

Fox's attitude towards his old associates was mixed. He could not believe that the breach, however serious, was final. A sense of burning injustice almost amounting to a conviction of victimisation conflicted with sentiment and a deep sense of gratitude for all that he had owed his friends in the past. Even when his opinion of the political conduct of Portland, Fitzwilliam, Carlisle, and Grenville was harsh and bitter he still retained a genuine fondness for them personally. The complexities of politics were entwined with private feelings which were too intense for public display. In August 1794 he confessed his innermost feelings to Holland in a letter of great sensibility and charm:

> I have nothing to say for my old friends, nor indeed as *politicians* have they any right to any tenderness from me, but I cannot forget how long I have lived in friendship with them, nor can I avoid feeling the most severe mortification when I recollect the certainty I used to entertain that they never would disgrace themselves as I think they have done. I cannot forget that ever since I was a child Fitzwilliam has been in all situations my warmest and most affectionate friend and the person in the world of whom decidedly I had the best opinion, and so in most respects I have still, but as a politician I cannot reconcile his conduct with what I who have known him for more than five and thirty years have always thought to be his character. There is a sentiment in a writer from whom one would not expect much sentiment, I mean Lord Rochester, that I have always much admired and which I feel the truth of very forcibly upon this occasion; it is this: 'To be ill used by those on whom we have bestowed favours is so much in the course of things and ingratitude is so common that a wise man can feel neither much surprise or pain when he experiences it; but to be ill used by those to whom we owe obligations which we never can forget, and towards whom we must continue to feel affection and gratitude is indeed a most painful sensation.' I do not believe these are the words but I know they are the sense of the passage I allude to.[38]

He thought that his friends had treated him very badly, and for most of them—those who owed more to him than he to them—he felt nothing but contempt. He went so far as to assert that he did not trouble himself at all about them. But to all this Fitzwilliam was an exception, and for him his feelings were precisely described in the passage quoted from Rochester.

By August 1794 he was heartily sick of politics. Only a sense of duty ensured his attendance at the house of commons. He contrasted his public frustration with private bliss. At St Anne's Hill he was perfectly happy. He relaxed in the company of Mrs Armistead and lightheartedly enjoyed his literary pursuits. 'Idleness, fine weather, Ariosto, a little Spanish, and the constant company of a person whom I love I think more and more every day and every hour, make me as happy as I am capable of being and much more so than I could hope to be if politics took a different turn.'[39]

There were times when depression left him, even politics firing him with his old energy. In October he vigorously defended the idea of party in correspondence with his nephew, and for all the frustrations of his lot Fox's enthusiasms could still burn brightly. When Holland doubted the efficacy of party his uncle leaped to its defence. Although recent events had shaken the confidence of many of the old whigs, in Fox's view they revealed not the folly of a political system based on party, but the imperfections of party as the term was generally understood. Fox was bitterly aware of the extent to which the whig party had fallen short of the ideal, but he was unrepentant in thinking that party was the best means of securing the liberty of the country. The virtues of party were all the more apparent when the mischiefs following the demise of the whig party became obvious.

Fox told Holland that only the system of party—typified by the behaviour of the whig opposition during the American war—had saved the country from falling into the 'euthenasia' of absolute monarchy. It was his duty to preserve what was left of an opposition based on a party tie, and to work for the revival of a style of politics which too many men believed to be extinct. The exposition of the benefits of party brought back some of his old confidence and optimism: he even discerned hopeful signs in the state of affairs although it was significant that he relied on the experience of opposition to the American war to give him comfort and inspiration. He told his nephew that the party had had more famous names in its ranks at the beginning of the American troubles, but in numbers it had not been much bigger than the opposition to the French war. The sheer course of events had enabled the party to grow and the same thing might happen again. The French war, like the American, was bound to become more unpopular; perhaps it would become more unpopular than the American war had ever been: 'we may profit as a party by such an opinion becoming prevalent'.

There was one other crucial point. In what situations were men likely to act corruptly—as members of a party, or as individuals? Fox thought that there was no doubt that party was a security against corruption; it was easier to bribe one man than to bribe several and party was thus a check on both the ambition and the cupidity of individuals. Men learned to put the fortunes of the party above their own ambitions. In this way a degree of consistency was brought into political conduct. Party ensured public virtue, for to gain the confidence of a party a man had to have qualities of character as well as ability. The quality of public life would be sustained by consistent and honourable party connexions. This, Fox claimed, was the chief purpose for which he carried on what seemed like a hopeless political fight. He never lost the habit of calculating his own chances of benefiting from any military reverse which would discredit Pitt and the government and the policy of making war upon the French republic, but he came close to steadfastly nailing his colours to the party mast. The reality was still far different from the dream. He and his followers were too distrusted, too identified with defeatism, for their conduct to be seen as anything other than factious by most members of parliament. It was easy for men to say that Fox's new consistency was merely a reflection of his isolation, of his perverse refusal to recognise that he was wrong, and that he had made a political miscalculation of the first magnitude when he decided to oppose the government tooth and nail. It was true that initially his response had been one of anger; he could not bear the thought that there were moves afoot to persuade whigs to unite with Pitt along the lines advocated by Burke. But if the element of personal pique, of the familiar gambler's instinct, has to be recognised, Fox undoubtedly believed that by the mid-1790s he was defending not only a particular policy towards France but a system of politics which alone could ensure the future harmonious development of responsible and representative government.

There were also times when he sought to console himself with the thought that the people supported him, whatever the size of the majorities supporting Pitt in the commons. He was proud of his connexion with Westminster and the politics of London. He could not bear the idea that his thankless and exhausting task was unappreciated outside the house of commons. As he and his friends filed into the division lobbies their awareness that they were a tiny, almost a derisory, minority was soothed by the thought that they represented the true feelings and expressed the deepest longings of the people of England. Pitt talked of defending English liberties against French aggression; Fox believed that the real threat to traditional liberties lay nearer at home, as the actions of the government curtailed familiar rights of speech and association. It would have been unbearable if the people were themselves indifferent towards the efforts being made on their behalf. Even if the propertied classes took Pitt's part Fox became convinced that he was the more popular among the lower classes. In October 1795 he was convinced that he and his friends were more popular than Pitt in and around London, although he was forced to admit that in the north the ministry seemed to carry the day.

It was, therefore, all the more necessary for Fox to believe that Pitt's supporters in the commons were the craven dupes of craft and corruption; the influence of the crown remained the gravest threat to liberty and this was the one issue which for Fox bound the English and French situations together. His domestic anxieties sustained his foreign hopes and sympathies.

Yet Fox could not argue that the crown should be without political influence or significance. In December 1794 he cautioned Holland against thinking that the influence of the crown was 'all abuse'. In certain circumstances royal influence was an unavoidable element in political life and since it was always liable to be improperly exploited it was all the more necessary for party to be maintained in order to counteract its evil consequences. The defence of extensive possessions and the collection of a large revenue ensured a substantial crown influence; the same principle applied to the heads of government in republics. Far from weakening the case for party Fox was convinced that a due regard for the proper role of monarchs made it all the more necessary.

Political calculation, private ambition, and fundamental convictions about the nature of British politics contributed to those attitudes and actions which Fox steadfastly maintained in order to defend traditional liberties against the dangerous and fear-ridden aggressions of the government. He argued that the government grotesquely and perversely exaggerated the danger of revolution and insurrection in England. He thought anxieties over French ideas and the links between the English reform societies and the French revolutionaries baseless and misleading. But though he was right in arguing that Pitt, Grenville, and Portland confused disturbances connected with high food prices and bread shortages with conscious and articulate political agitation, before he could hope to convince his fellow countrymen that he was other than a factious defeatist opportunist, the situation in Europe had to take a turn for the better in Foxite parlance, or for the worse in the vocabulary of most Englishmen. Here Fox was bitterly disappointed. He affirmed that peace was possible, but he was compelled to claim that the British government was primarily responsible for the continuation of hostilities; this meant that he had to pin too great a faith on the good intentions and political credibility of successive régimes in France. His understanding of the domestic situation was closely allied to the doctrines of party and the constitutional principles which he had formulated before the French revolution. His reading of the continental situation was also associated with his political expectations, and these in turn influenced his analysis of the war with France. During the war years Fox was courageous, foolhardy and tenacious—but he was never objective.

8 The War with Revolutionary France

Whatever Fox's beliefs about constitutional government in England, or his tortured sympathies with those he believed to be struggling for representative government in France, the outbreak of the war between Britain and France in February 1793 raised a new set of questions which were just as difficult to solve as old controversies about the nature of the revolution in France, and of an even greater political complexity. For Englishmen the war was a greater factor in defining their attitudes towards events in Paris than any concern with constitutional theory or political speculation. In destroying the whig opposition the war played a bigger part than any other comparable political issue, for it compelled men to stand forth as patriots in a struggle which seemed less a dispute about principles of government and more a fight for survival.

During the conflict between France and Prussia and Austria Fox's support had unhesitatingly been given to the French. The declaration of Pillnitz and the duke of Brunswick's manifesto were anathema to him; both represented naked intervention, typifying the reactionary fears which the birth of free government in France had roused among the traditional rulers of Europe. Fox wanted Britain to stay out of the war. He rejected any policy of alliance with the central powers and the prospect of Bourbon absolutism being restored by the efforts of Great Britain was abhorrent to him. Yet he could not be indifferent to the growing aggressiveness with which the French faced a hostile world, and provocations such as the edict of fraternity pained him deeply. He watched the situation decline with a sense of foreboding, and his early fears of the resumption of a type of warfare reminiscent of the wars of religion were fully confirmed and hideously realised. He saw the British government being dragged into the conflict and he knew not whether to condemn their folly or their criminality. During the months between the fall of the French monarchy and the execution of Louis XVI Fox's chief con-

cern was to urge the wisdom of negotiating with the effective rulers of
France, regardless of whether one approved of either their personalities
or their principles. His deepest condemnation was reserved for a policy
which would subordinate diplomacy to ideology. He believed that he was
advocating familiar and proven remedies in a deteriorating situation, and
he sought to argue his case in terms which would obviate the wider and
more bewildering controversy over the causes, principles and effects of
the French revolution. When many of those who supported a firm policy
towards the French based their arguments on ideology Fox strove to
remind men of the older concept of the balance of power, and the primacy
of recognisable diplomatic objectives, however tangled the web of circumstance and however frenzied the rage of passion and patriotism on all
sides.

A French invasion of Holland could well provoke a war between
Britain and France, but even here Fox reminded the commons that there
was a party in the Netherlands which was republican in outlook and
pro-French in sympathy, as the Dutch crisis of 1787 had demonstrated.
Such a war would not command the wholehearted support of Dutch
opinion, nor would it be wise to allow events to entice Britain into such
a war. Instead of condemning the French régime Fox asserted the
expediency of negotiating with the new French government. This was
the best means of averting the horrors of war. It was too simple to condemn the French: he remembered the way in which disgust and distaste
had been showered on the American leaders in the struggle against
England, but negotiation had finally taken place. He sympathised with
the plight of the French royal family and he was apprehensive about the
fate of the king; but he still pleaded for diplomatic relations to be preserved with the government of France. Nor did he deny the legitimate
fears which French aggrandisement roused in Britain. There were good
reasons for checking French aggression, but 'perhaps not to go to war
with them was to check their aggrandisement, for their cause upon the
continent was popular'. Negotiation might prevent the slide into war—
and to slide into war might well help the French. Since all traditional
governments had been stigmatised as their foes by the new rulers of
France, and since enlightened opinion throughout the continent detested
the principles expounded by the commanders of the Prussian and
Austrian armies, Fox believed that the French had gained a good deal
of popular support in Europe. It could not be assumed that an extension
of the war would favour the allies, and instead of being swept along
by a torrent of fear and prejudice the government had a primary duty to
discover the real motives and aims of the French. This could only be

done through negotiation: diplomacy was the means by which passion and tumult were to be curbed and tamed.

On 15 December 1792 Fox proposed that a minister should be sent to Paris to treat with the provisional government there. He was sensitive towards suggestions that this proposal condoned the violent means by which the monarchy had been overthrown, and he went out of his way to reassure the commons on this point.

> By his motion he did not mean to imply any approbation of the conduct of the existing French government, or of the proceedings that had led to the present state of things in France. His object was simply to declare and record his opinion, that it was the true policy of every nation to treat with the existing government of every other nation with which it had relative interests, without inquiring or regarding how that government was constituted or by what means those who exercised it came into power. This was not only the policy but frequently the practice. If we objected to the existing form of government in France, we had as strong objections to the form of government at Algiers; yet at Algiers we had a consul. If we abhorred the crimes committed in France, we equally abhorred the crimes committed in Morocco; yet to the court of Morocco we had sent a consul almost immediately after the commission of the crimes at which humanity shuddered.[1]

Whether one approved of the French régime or not was irrelevant to the conduct of diplomacy. It was undeniable that negotiations would have to be undertaken at some stage with the French government, and obviously such negotiations would have to be made with the existing administration. To refuse to treat would be to abandon the opportunity of saving Holland from the war, or of preserving the Dutch control of the Scheldt without a war. Fox was not worried by the technicalities of international etiquette: the important thing was to ensure that a negotiation took place. If the British people were to be plunged into war it was reasonable to ensure that they knew its real cause, and that a war would not depend on matters of mere form and ceremony. But Fox's motion was rejected without a division; despite his efforts to preserve a controlled foreign policy the tide was already flowing which would carry the nation into war. It was not that Pitt wanted war; as late as November Grenville was still emphasising that the government wanted to remain neutral and to avoid being drawn into the domestic quarrels in France. But it was one thing to desire neutrality and another to succeed in maintaining it.

Fox was careful to express in the most forceful terms his disgust at the humiliations inflicted upon the French royal family. His generous spirit was touched by the tragic spectacle of Louis XVI imprisoned like a common criminal and by the ominous signs of the likely final outcome of the proceedings which were arraigning the king as a traitor. Fox was in the unusual position of agreeing with Pitt. The proceedings against Louis XVI were unnecessary and unjust, and repugnant to feelings of common humanity. Fox thought it wrong to try individuals according to laws which were not in force at the time when the alleged crimes were said to have been committed. From this point of view the trial of Louis XVI violated every canon of natural justice. But English sympathy for the deposed monarch was a powerful emotion which made it more difficult to convince men of the reasonableness of negotiating with the new French régime, and Fox was sadly aware of the way in which the extremism of the French hindered those who were striving to avoid a war between Britain and France.

Fox believed that Pitt would be out of his mind to allow anything to draw Britain into a war with France. He was suspicious of the allies in whose company the country would have to fight, and he was distrustful of the way in which the British government would become embroiled in France's domestic quarrels. But he was prepared to admit the impossibility of keeping out of the war in all circumstances. Though he thought Pitt and Grenville were injudicious in their handling of affairs and insufficiently critical of the appeals addressed to them by French émigrés, he recognised that it would be difficult for Britain to stay out of the war if the situation on the continent deteriorated. In November 1792 he told Holland that it was impossible for a nation to say that in all circumstances it would not fight. But he clung to the hope that peace could be achieved with honour, despite his disdain for Pitt as 'a great bungler' in foreign policy. He did not take accusations of French aggression too seriously. Most of their conquests had been in the territories and dependencies of their avowed enemies, and he was as sensitive to the atrocities committed by the Prussians and Austrians as to those for which the French were responsible.

But Fox was also conscious of the way in which opinions about the internal state of France were intermingled with attitudes towards the foreign policy of the French republic. The execution of Louis XVI on 21 January 1793 threw this connexion into greater relief. English opinion was horrified, and since the new régime in Paris was now indelibly regicide the expulsion of French plenipotentiaries in London seemed a natural reaction. When the government sought parliamentary approval for the augmentation of the armed forces on 1 February (the date on which the French republic declared war on Britain) Fox tried to preserve the distinction between the way in which any country managed its own internal affairs and its relations with other states:

> He saw neither propriety nor wisdom in that house passing judgment on any act committed in another nation which had no direct reference to us. The general maxim of policy always was that the crimes perpetrated in one independent state were not cognisable by another. Need he remind the house of our former conduct in this respect? Had we not treated, had we not formed alliances with Portugal and with Spain, at the very time when those kingdoms were disgraced and polluted by the most shocking and barbarous acts of superstition and cruelty, of racks, torture, and burnings, under the abominable tyranny of the inquisition? Did we ever make those outrages against reason and humanity a pretext for war? ... Why, then, were the enormities of the French in their own country held up as a cause of war?[2]

The answer was that for many Englishmen the atrocities committed by the revolutionaries in Paris and the hostility which the French displayed towards the other countries of Europe seemed the natural and inevitable expression of those French ideas which constituted a threat to all traditional forms of government, and to the very foundations of civilised society. Once protestantism was firmly established in England the inquisition posed no threat to English institutions, however deeply men loathed it. But French ideas and French practice questioned the English constitution, and goaded working men into the dubious complexities of political agitation, and for many of Fox's opponents French aggression seemed the self-evident cause of all the woes afflicting the nations of Europe.

It was, therefore, imperative that Fox should refute the charge that the French were either primarily or uniquely responsible for the ills of Europe. He chose to emphasise the dangers to peace constituted by the Austro-Prussian alliance. This combination threatened the tranquillity of Europe and the liberties of mankind. Those who talked lightly of France as the chief aggressor should note the provocations of the declaration of Pillnitz, while if the king of Prussia had had grounds for claiming that he had suffered from French aggression he would have called on Britain for aid under the terms of the triple alliance. Furthermore, however detestable men might find the principles of the French revolution they ought to consider the principles represented by the central powers. Austria and Prussia had acted in concert in order to restore despotism; they had hoped to destroy constitutional government in France. No Englishman would ever approve of similar action being taken against his own country, and few Englishmen agreed with Burke's condonation of the duke of Brunswick's manifesto. But the country had stood by and contemplated its publication without alarm and without interference. Could it be that the nation saw no danger in the success of despotism, but that the moment fortune favoured the opposite cause fears became inflamed?

Passion and fury were the enemies of reason, and Fox argued that men's judgment was being blinded by the cunning exploitation of their passions. Nor were the usual explanations adequate for a resort to war. The danger to Holland, the edict of fraternity of 19 November, and the threat to European security from the progress of French arms, were put forward as grounds for war. Fox made great play with the failure of the Dutch to ask for help under the terms of the triple alliance; until such a request was made he denied that Britain was bound either by honour or the treaty to give military assistance to the Dutch. So far as the opening of the Scheldt was concerned, it was clear that the Dutch did not wish to make it a cause of war, and it would be wrong for Britain to force the Dutch into a war which they did not want. Fox regarded the notorious edict of fraternity as an insult, and the explanation given by the French was no adequate satisfaction, but he thought it worthwhile to point out that unsatisfactory as the French response had been it had nevertheless demonstrated that the French really wanted peace. The conduct of the British government he thought haughty and provocative. It was the highest arrogance to complain of an insult without deigning to state what reparation was required and Fox could not refrain from wondering whether the government's vagueness was intended to preclude, rather than to obtain, satisfaction. The British insistence on the withdrawal of French troops from the Austrian Netherlands seemed insolent and unrealistic. It ignored the fact that the presence of French soldiers in the Netherlands was the inevitable consequence of the war between France and Austria, and it was this conflict which British diplomacy ought to have been more committed originally to trying to prevent, and then to terminate as quickly as possible. Before going to war with France it was essential to tell the people—who would have to bear the cost of hostilities in blood and treasure—what objectives the government had in mind, the attainment of which would lead to an honourable peace.

Generalised appeals to the peace and tranquillity of Europe neither impressed nor convinced Fox. The British government had seen the partition of Poland without turning a hair, while the invasion of France had been greeted with marked indifference. It was therefore difficult to appear sincere in expostulating about the peace of Europe. The most sinister element in the confused situation was the recurrent suspicion that the British administration desired the restoration of despotism in France, but, because they were ashamed to admit that this was their real aim, they sought pretexts such as the navigation of the Scheldt and the invasion of the Austrian Netherlands. Though he thought 'the present state of government in France anything rather than an object of imitation' Fox maintained 'as a principle inviolable' that the government of every independent state was to be settled by those who had to live under it and not by foreign intervention.

The greatest danger to an intelligent diplomacy would be to fall into the folly of attempting to wage war against opinions. Opinions were not like commodities, the importation of which war could prevent. A war about principles in religion was as much a war about opinions as a war about principles in politics. The war would therefore be a reversion to an earlier and more savage type of struggle. Fox defined the justifiable grounds of war as 'insult, injury, and danger':

> For the first, satisfaction; for the second, reparation; for the third, security was the object. Each of these, too, was the proper object of negotiation, which ought ever to precede war, except in case of an attack actually commenced. How had we negotiated? Not in any public or efficient form, a mode which he suspected, and lamented, by his proposing it had been prevented.[3]

But events were already far beyond what it was in Fox's power to control. The French convention declared war on Britain on 1 February, and soon British troops were despatched to Flanders in the hope of giving aid to the Dutch and Austrians. Fox complained that the government had failed fully to use the resources of diplomacy in order to avert a conflict, but once the war had begun he had to shift his ground to the advisability of continuing to use every opportunity to limit the war by being willing to open negotiations even during the course of hostilities. Essentially Fox's approach was an old-fashioned one, for he was evoking the familiar eighteenth-century concern with wars for recognisable and attainable objectives, with war as an instrument of diplomacy, not a substitute for it. Fox made no secret of his conviction that the revolutionary war was reminiscent of the wars of religion, but he still hoped that the skills of eighteenth-century diplomacy would prove adequate to the new tests which he wished to lay upon them. Fox's critique depended on two assumptions: first, that the government had neglected to avail themselves of channels of communication which had been available to them before the outbreak of the war, and secondly, that the government's desire to restore the French monarchy prevented it from making the most of opportunities which existed of ending hostilities even after the war had broken out. Fox was assuming a continued willingness on the part of the French to negotiate, and he overlooked the impact of total war upon the mentality of France's new rulers. He thought that they were thinking in traditional terms of the necessary concessions which both sides would have to make in order to end the war without endangering the balance of power. He ignored the extent to which the revolutionaries rejected the restraints and formalities of conventional diplomacy, forgetting that men who were missionaries for a cause, and patriots striving against immense odds to save their country from foreign invasion and internal disruption, were not disposed to take the polite refinements of diplomatic practice very seriously. He exaggerated the extent to which the British government could influence events, forgetting that British policy was a series of responses to events in Europe. He confused what were often the bewildered reactions of baffled men with subtle and sinister conspiracies of a Machiavellian nature. His warning against the scale of the war did not lead him to appreciate the change which a war of opinions brought about in the conduct of war and in the practice of diplomacy.

Fox recognised that the war had become the most decisive single issue in determining the course of domestic British politics. It forced men to take sides in a way which disputes about the merits of the French revolution did not. But just as he had always interpreted the revolution in France too much in the light of British and American experience, so he made the mistake of drawing too many parallels with the situation created by the war of American independence. Once again the country was involved in a war of which he disapproved, and which he was determined to oppose, and just as defeat in war had brought down North, so the failure of Pitt's war policy might lead to the collapse of the government, with Fox and his friends being called in to end by negotiation the war which they had stigmatised as unnecessary, wasteful, and doomed to frustration. Those who treasured memories of the Rockingham ministry might yet play the role which Rockingham had played in 1782. It was tempting, and in the isolation in which Fox found himself in 1793 it was irresistible. Defeat would not only confirm Fox's original diagnosis, it would transform the political situation and bring him to power. Fox ignored the differences between the 1770s and the 1790s. The American war was, in the strictest sense, the outcome of policies advocated and applied by the British government. The French war was the result of events in France which Pitt had been powerless to control or even influence. Public opinion was virtually unanimous in favouring the French war, and defeat at the hands of the revolutionaries was thought to be synonymous with the breakdown of British society and the destruction of the English constitution. In a more immediate sense than the American war the struggle against the French republic was a struggle for the preservation of the British way of life. It was, therefore, much more difficult in the 1790s to prevent a consistent opposition to the war from being associated with a lack of patriotism, for the consequences of defeat seemed so unthinkable that men rallied round Pitt and the national cause. The American colonists could be seen as friends of the British constitution, but it was impossible to interpret French Jacobins in that light. The French were the enemies of English liberties and no amount of rhetoric could convince the majority of Englishmen that the ideas of 1789 were not synonymous with disorder, slaughter, and the destruction of civilised society. Thus, however eloquently Fox argued the case for a limited war for limited objectives, he was too commonly identified with pro-French sentiment and defeatism for many of his countrymen to follow the intricacies of his argument or the more sophisticated subtleties of his thought.

Nevertheless, Fox was able to make capital out of the contradictions on the government side. He knew that there was a marked division between those who followed Burke in interpreting the war primarily as a struggle between conflicting ideologies, and those like Pitt who took a more pragmatic standpoint. Between those who believed that French principles were to be rooted out in the interests of traditional forms of social order and government, and those who grounded their opposition to the French republic on specific cases of aggression for which the rulers of France were responsible, a great gulf was fixed. Fox realised that, though the government was chiefly motivated by the second type of response, it gained much popular support from those in the first category. Often Pitt appealed to one sort of sentiment while basing his conduct of policy on a more realistic reading of the situation. Fox was able to make great play with these paradoxes, though with little effect on divisions in the house of commons.

The main lines of the controversy became apparent during the debate on the king's message respecting the declaration of war by France on 12 February 1793. Fox drew attention to the difference between those who regarded France as 'a monster whose hand was against all nations', and who therefore felt that every nation's hand ought to be against France, and those who argued that the war was caused not by a general disapproval of the French but by specific aggressions which they had committed. It was unwise for the government to ignore the fundamental divergence which these viewpoints represented. If they did so they ran the risk of allowing a serious confusion to cloud the whole of their thinking, and to bedevil the whole of their policy.

So far the difference was great with respect to our immediate situation of being actually at war; and it was still greater when we came to inquire into our prospect of peace. If we were at war because France was a monster whose hand was against all nations, it must be *bellum internecinum*—a war of extermination; for nothing but unconditional submission could be adequate to the end for which the war was undertaken, and to that alone must we look for a safe or honourable peace. If, on the contrary, we were at war on account of a specific aggression, for that aggression atonement might be made, and the object being obtained, peace might be concluded.[4]

He hoped that few who were zealous for the prosecution of the war wished it to be a war of extermination, a war for extirpating French principles rather than circumscribing French power. But too often those who talked of the danger of French power claimed that the propagation of French ideas was a more immediate danger. In Fox's opinion this was a dangerous confusion. It was imperative for Britain to make it clear that she had not gone to war to effect a change in the internal government of France but to resist her power which was a threat to her allies and herself; once the power of France was confined within safe limits the way to peace would lie open.

Because of the incompetence of Pitt and his colleagues it was by no means clear that a demand for satisfaction in the cases of insult and aggression had been made with due definition and as definitely refused. Obscurity and confusion cloaked the government's handling of affairs; they had proposed nothing that would be accepted as satisfaction for an injury, just as they were notoriously vague about the real causes of the war. Fox reiterated his intention of pressing for 'a distinct and specific declaration of the causes of the war'. It was of the highest importance that both Britain and France should know the grounds of the conflict, for once this was achieved the duration of the war might be shortened. Fox criticised the government's refusal to allow Lord Gower to remain in Paris after the revolution of 10 August. No formal recognition of the new French government need have been implied if Gower had stayed on, but a channel of communication would have been kept open. He had no wish to condone the murder of Louis XVI but he denied that once that crime had been committed all negotiation with the French should cease. Even in the midst of war it was necessary to follow up any opportunity of initiating negotiations with the enemy. Fox was deeply committed to the view that diplomacy did not cease on the commencement of hostilities. War was a continuation of policy and diplomatic objectives ought to remain in the forefront of men's minds even when they were caught up in armed conflict. Fox despised the ministry for relying on the fortunes of war to provide them with a policy. Defeating the French would not solve the problems which were closely bound up with the response of the powers of Europe to the aggressions of the French republic. Once the war was over political problems would have to be faced, and here Fox believed that the influence of Burke and Windham would be powerful and baleful. He had no confidence in Pitt's ability to withstand such pressures; all the indications were that Pitt was allowing those who saw the struggle against France as a struggle for the principle of legitimacy too much weight in determining the conduct of the war. But despite Fox's eloquence, and the cogency of much of his argument, his resolution was rejected, the address which had been moved by Pitt being agreed to without a division.

On 18 February Fox returned to the attack, proposing a set of resolutions against the war with France. He repeated his distinction between the validity of the government of France and those acts committed by the French which extended their frontiers and offended British interests. Only the latter constituted a credible principle on which the war could be justified. But in examining alleged causes of provocation he maintained that they were all fit objects for negotiation, none of them constituting a cause for war until satisfaction had been explicitly demanded and refused. Fox did not believe that the ministers had actually followed the course of action which was to be expected from the professions they had continually made:

> He did not mean to charge them with adopting one principle for debate and another for action; but he thought they had suffered themselves to be imposed upon and misled by those who wished to go to war with France on account of her internal government, and therefore took all occasions of representing the French and utterly and irreconcilably hostile to this country. It was always fair to compare the conduct of men in any particular instance with their conduct on other occasions. If the rights of neutral nations were now loudly held forth; if the danger to be apprehended from the aggrandisement of any power was magnified as the just cause of this present war; and if, on looking to another quarter, we saw the rights of Poland, of a neutral and independent nation, openly trampled on ... for the aggrandisement of other powers, could we be blamed for suspecting that the pretended was not the real object of the present war?[5]

In drawing attention to the Polish catastrophe Fox was not suggesting that Britain should commit herself to a policy of defending free states throughout Europe. During the Orchakov crisis he had exploited Britain's impotence in eastern Europe as an argument for preserving a neutralist stance in the near east, and for pursuing a cautious rather than a provocative policy. He was concerned merely to throw into greater relief the dangers of replying on a moral justification for British policy; by talking in terms of general principle the apologists for the government were exposing themselves to effective counter-attack. British interests were a more secure guide in foreign policy than affirmations of general principle, however satisfying these might be to national self-esteem. Fox was eager to show that the government's policy secured no vital British interest; that in their judgment of events the administration had no thorough grasp of the realities of the international situation. He was able to move his ground of criticism in order to expose the inconsistencies underlying the ministerial case. But certain themes were constantly returned to, time and time again. The folly of intervening in the internal affairs of France, the foolishness of allying with those who wished to do so, the need to show a willingness to negotiate with the French over the opening of the Scheldt and the edict of fraternity even after hostilities had commenced, were the recurrent themes of Fox's oratory. He was conscious of the need to meet the accusation that he was being unrealistic in arguing the wisdom of attempting a negotiation with the French. The best means of approaching the issue of the territorial aggrandisement of France were far from obvious. Fox recognised acute problems here, for it involved the evacuation of conquered countries and firm undertakings that they should not be annexed to France. The extraordinarily complex question of the extent to which confidence could be shown in the French government was posed in an embarrassing fashion.

But confidence could not grow without the experience of diplomatic relations, and the French ought to be told what would be regarded as adequate satisfactions by the British government and what terms would procure some measure of conciliation between the two countries. Consequently Fox's resolutions contained the following chief points: that neither the honour nor the interest of Britain justified making war upon the French for the purpose of interfering in France's internal affairs; that the complaints made against the French government were not, in themselves, sufficiently strong to authorise a war without attempting to gain redress by negotiation; that the ministers had never adequately stated to the French the conditions upon which British neutrality might have been preserved; that the government had not attended to the rights of independent nations in the case of Poland; and (possibly most important of all) that

> it is the duty of his majesty's ministers ... to advise his majesty against entering into engagements which may prevent Great Britain from making a separate peace whenever the interests of his majesty and his people may render such a measure advisable, or which may countenance an opinion in Europe that his majesty is acting in concert with other powers for the unjustifiable purpose of compelling the people of France to submit to a form of government not approved by that nation.[6]

Fox's motion was defeated by 270 votes to 44; he failed to win over the disgruntled older whigs who were being driven by the inexorable pressure of events into looking more favourably upon the government, both for the maintenance of law and order at home and resistance to the spread of French power and French ideas abroad. Despite the persuasive attractiveness of Fox's case he was constrained by the fact that the French themselves had associated the diffusion of their ideals with the success of their armies; the ideas of the revolution were seen as potent inspiration for the French soldiers and as total justification for the French invasion of other countries. Conquest by France was synonymous with deliverance from senile rulers and antique systems of government. Fox was trying to fight a war of ideas with the weapons of traditional diplomacy; he overlooked the way in which the French had confused democratic political theory with the implementation of dictatorship at home and aggression abroad.

Fox hoped that early reverses in the field would lead to a speedy end to the war. He found it hard to allow for the intense hatred which so many MPs felt for the French and their ideas, and he assumed that disillusionment with Austria and Prussia might facilitate a negotiated peace. He thought that a negotiated settlement would confirm the establishment of a constitutional form of government in France. He was, therefore, all the more bewildered by the succession of governments in France and by the failure of disappointment with the war to bring about a prompt and just peace. There were reverses enough: the duke of York's campaign in the Low Countries was a dismal failure, while the Prussians soon preferred to leave the Austrians with the sole responsibility for defending the cause of monarchy in Europe.

Fox was compelled to lay the principal responsibility for the failure of negotiations at the British government's door: he could not concede that when the French were flushed with triumph abroad and terror at home they were hardly disposed to make a compromise peace. However vocal Fox was in criticising costly campaigns in the West Indies, efforts to aid rebellions in France against the republican government, and the uncertain return for massive subsidies to unreliable allies, he could not point to any clear solution of what had become an intractable deadlock. Britain was compelled to rely upon her allies for the conduct of the war in Europe; when they failed to defeat the French, when they were forced to accept humiliating peace terms because of their military incapacity, and when they preferred to compensate themselves in eastern Europe for the disappointment of their hopes in the west, there was little that the British government could do to redress the balance in the war on land. British supremacy at sea, and dearly bought West Indian islands highly prized by the commercial interest, were in themselves inadequate when it came to winning an honourable and credible peace, instead of denying victory to the French. The new order in France could not do business on the old terms, while Britain could not afford to accept French domination in the Low Countries or to ignore the need for some reasonable security against future French aggrandisement. Even when Pitt and his colleagues accepted the impossibility of a royalist restoration in France they were reluctant to admit the validity of a French government until there was some evidence that the régime had attained some measure of stability and permanence. Because one power was supreme at sea and the other on land there was no convenient diplomatic shortcut by which the stalemate could be resolved. The French believed themselves to be invincible on the continent, and they were insulted by British anxieties for securities for future good behaviour. The British believed it to be wrong to yield to the wish for peace without some satisfaction for the provocations which had played so great a part in bringing about the war. In the climate created by the events of the 1790s it was inevitable that conflicts of interest should be given ideological expression and justification; this made the conflicts all the more bitter and all the more recalcitrant. Fox's apologia for limited war and continuous negotiation was intellectually irrefutable. It was simply irrelevant to the realities of the situation.

Despite the fury with which he assailed Pitt Fox might well have acted in a very similar fashion had he been in office. His early enthusiasm for the establishment of a constitutional monarchy in France did not make him forgetful of British interests, and although he would undoubtedly have shown greater flair for the intricacies of negotiation than Lord Grenville, he would not have differed in his concern for the preservation of Holland as a free and sovereign state. Fox would have been more cautious in becoming caught up with the Austrians and Prussians but, once war broke out between Britain and France, like Pitt he would have had to make use of whatever allies were available. He would have been more forth-

372   *The War with Revolutionary France*

right in denying any intention of interfering in France's internal affairs but this would not of itself have kept England out of the war, since for the British government the problem was French intervention, both by subversion and military force, in the affairs of other countries. Once Britain became involved in the war, the ideological element in the struggle was bound to affect the conduct of policy. Just as the French hoped to exploit republican sympathies in Britain so their opponents were driven (with varying degrees of enthusiasm) to make use of royalist sentiment in France. Pitt did not see the war as primarily a conflict of ideologies, but once the fighting started it was impossible for him to ignore the ideological aspect in his appreciation of the overall situation. Fox hoped that some tolerable peace settlement could be achieved by the familiar processes of compromise, with territories and commercial privileges being exchanged in the light of national interests; but the French did not see the situation in those terms; as revolutionaries they believed their dominant position in Europe to be dependent on their military supremacy and the force of their ideas and the notion of a balance of power or of a diplomatic system was anathema to them. They feared any diminution of the overwhelming military predominance on which their régime was based; they saw no reason to defer to British sensibilities when these clearly involved making concessions far in excess of what it was in the power of the British to achieve by arms. France wanted recognition as the dominant power in the Low Countries and in western Europe; this was something the British government could not give. As long as the French insisted on a hegemony in Europe peace was impossible; as long as Britain demanded securities for her traditional interests peace was unthinkable. Both sides saw the price of peace as too costly and too risky, both in terms of power and pride. For as long as the appeal to arms was indecisive, despite all the frustrations of war, the appeal to arms would still be made. Fox seriously underestimated the arrogance of the French, just as he exaggerated the extent to which the British government was responsible for the continuation of the war. A common interest in peace was a necessary preliminary to a satisfactory negotiation and for most of the 1790s this common interest was lacking.

Fox also valued peace as the prelude to power. Throughout the early years of the war he could not forget the example of the fall of North, where military defeat had been the principal factor in bringing about a change of mood among MPs sufficiently powerful to bring down the ministry. But the reverses of the 1790s stiffened the resolve of Pitt and his followers, instead of weakening it, and the determination with which Pitt clung to power heightened Fox's anguish and deepened his sense of personal frustration. However admirable Fox's sentiments were, however subtle his arguments and resourceful his rhetoric, many MPs could not interpret Fox's criticisms of the war as anything other than further evidence of his insatiable appetite for power even if the price was national defeat. Fox's bitter memories of the way in which Pitt had outgeneralled him in 1784 and 1788 and his suspicions of the activities of Burke and his friends, drove him further into the extreme postures of opposition, with all the depressing futility that that entailed in the political circumstances of the time. Fox believed that his only chance of office lay in completely dissociating himself from the government; only then would he be able to exploit the defeat of the ministry's plans and the discrediting of their policies which would be the inevitable result of defeat in war. But stalemate did not produce the upsurge of pacific sentiment upon which Fox had relied, and when the defeat of Britains continental allies failed to bring down the government Fox had no alternative but to resort to one of the obsolescent tactics of eighteenth-century politics and secede from parliament (May 1797). His decision to do so, much though it was criticised at the time, made sense within the political context in which he was placed. He was no modern politician appealing to some national following. His horizons were limited by the house of commons and, so far as public opinion was concerned, by his constituency at Westminster. When the response to national emergency by the members of the commons was to rally round the king and Pitt, Fox recognised the defeat of all his hopes, the final exposure of the assumptions on which his parliamentary tactics had been based for four years. If he had been as mindful of the opinion of posterity as his Victorian admirers imagined him to have been he might have stayed at his post. But neither the plaudits of history, nor the interests of his constituents, could compensate him for the collapse of his political strategy. Once again he had miscalculated; once again he had allowed his experiences of political life to lure him into making false analogies and facile comparisons. Wishful thinking had blurred his perception. Now, alone, isolated, criticised even by those friends who remained faithful to him, and resigned to the almost perpetual presence of Pitt in Downing Street, Fox sought peace and fulfilment at St Anne's Hill.

Everything was against him: the political structure in which he had to work, the break-up of the old whig party, the intransigence of the French on whose good faith and pacific intentions he had depended, the obstinate belief of most backbenchers that there was no alternative to the war with France and that the preconditions for a just and lasting peace did not exist. However brilliant the speeches in the debates during the abortive negotiations of 1796 and 1797 Fox had little new to say. He pounced with his usual alacrity on confusions in the government's case; he decried the hesitancy and fumbling of Pitt and Grenville; he eloquently expounded yet again the virtues of a limited war and a negotiated peace. But there was little development in his thinking. He had expected that defeat on the continent would force the ministry humbly to beg the French for peace on virtually any terms, earning them the contempt of those MPs who had turned against them because of their incompetent handling of the war. But this did not happen: Pitt showed that he was willing to seek peace but that there were limits to the extent to which he was prepared to sacrifice vital British interests in the desire for a termination of the war. The house of commons, far from turning on Pitt seemed ever more faithful to him. Until the will of the house changed Fox knew that even the most virtuoso-style performance in the commons would have no effect on the course of events. However much there is to admire in his speeches in the mid-1790s—the wit, the feeling for words, the inventive exploitation of detail without losing the thread of his primary theme—they were devoid of the one quality which gave them value in Fox's eyes: the ability to change the mood of the commons and turn Pitt out of office.

Thus, for all Fox's advocacy of a formed and patriotic opposition in parliament, he had failed to give effect to the principles which he claimed to embrace so fervently. His political base was too constricted for his effort to have any chance of success. He knew how much he needed Portland and Fitzwilliam and the other aristocratic whigs; hence his bitterness when he found that they were being pressed to join Pitt. He knew, too, how distrusted he was by many members in the commons; only the justification of events could diminish this distrust. It was all the more dispiriting to feel that events had proved him right, and yet to see the majority of the house obdurate in its support of Pitt and the French war.

Against this background Fox's famous indiscretion—toasting 'our sovereign the people'—can be more properly appreciated for what it was: a wilful gesture by a weary and disappointed man. It was foolish; it was unlikely to commend Fox to true republicans while it was bound to exasperate and enrage his opponents. The king was furiously angry, striking Fox's name from the privy council in disgust and vindictive self-righteousness, and even Pitt talked of the seriousness of Fox's offence. But his enemies failed to see the desperation underlying Fox's action. Where they saw only perverse defiance and the encouragement of extremism and sedition there was really the futile obstinacy of a frustrated and dejected man. Far from indulging in a dangerous attempt to provoke disloyal sentiment Fox was keeping up his own spirits and trying to convey to his followers that he was not as downhearted as was in fact the case. He succeeded only in heightening George III's unrelenting distrust and in earning the dubious dignity of a pseudo-martyrdom. It all made Fox more sick than ever of the follies and hatreds of political life. He saw himself—after the event—as an injured prophet, whose warnings brought him no honour even when they were confirmed by events. He was an elderly, lonely politician, hated by his enemies, traduced by the public and misunderstood by his friends.

In circumstances such as these his moods fluctuated wildly and unpredictably. There were times when he lamented that the house of commons was very bad indeed, and that it seemed to like the violent measures of the government. He tried hard to believe that he had real popularity outside the house to make up for his unpopularity within the commons, and he swung in desperation from fondly seeing signs of significant revival among the opposition to gloomy confessions of total defeat. His chief complaint was that his supporters did not act in concert. It was not enough to convert old enemies or dubious moderates: a real effort had to be made to create sustained political cooperation as the prelude to effective parliamentary action. But Fox himself lacked the energy or the interest in organisation and political management to carry these generalisations into practice.

The most astonishing reconciliation during these years was that between Fox and Lansdowne. For many years they had been inveterate enemies; it had been Fox's bitter animosity which had driven Shelburne from office before his plans for administrative reform could be realised. Now a common dislike of the war drew them together. But Fox was aware of the limitations of their newly-found friendship. He confided to Holland that the circumstances of the time were the chief reasons for bringing Lansdowne and himself together. They counted for more than explanations, messages or communications. It was best to let the past die, to avoid re-opening old wounds by trying to explain away old antipathies. If the occasion for useful political collaboration arose Fox believed that he and Lansdowne were on sufficiently cordial terms to allow it to take place.

But his fate would really be settled by the way in which his foes responded to events: this was particularly galling, but inescapably true. The ministry could not make peace without considerable sacrifices and the differences of opinion within the government were so great that it would be unlikely for them to agree until necessity pushed them into conceding what sense—according to Fox—would have commended earlier. Fox knew that Pitt obstinately clung to his belief that, despite appearances, the economic state of France meant that the French could not carry on the war for much longer. He despised the optimism which sustained the minister's morale, but he admitted that the French were equally credulous in their expectation that England would soon be forced to make peace on almost any terms. In his own mind he thought French optimism better founded than Pitt's, but he was at a loss to foretell the future. His own prophecies had often been disproved by events; his own confidence had often been misplaced.

There were times when he dreamed of some public agitation which would make up for all the disappointments of parliamentary politics. By the end of 1797 he was talking of the good effects of more activity out-side the house of commons. If only the rest of the country had the good sense of Westminster! A successful campaign of petitioning would pro-duce one of two good effects. Either it would bring down Pitt, or it would prove that the unanimous will of the people could not prevail in the house of commons against the influence of the minister of the crown. This was harking back to the old tribulations and struggles of the 1770s and 1780s. Fox could not help seeing in every crisis some confirmation of his old diagnosis of the ills afflicting the body politic. He found it soothing to believe that what he had said many years before explained his current frustration and sorrow. But even when he took heart he quickly faltered amid depressing circumstances. In December 1797 he advised Holland to remember that in critical times the boldest and most sincere language was invariably the most prudent, only to go on to comment, 'if indeed there be any room for prudence in a situation so near absolute despair'.[7]

He was unmoved by invasion scares and panics. He refused to believe that unrest arising from shortage of bread was serious evidence of a threat to the stability of the country's institutions, and he despised the government for over-reacting to events, or, what he thought was much worse, for deliberately using falsely stimulated fears to carry through oppressive legislation. Despite his respect for the military prowess of the French he dismissed talk of a French invasion. His whiggish belief in the navy saved him from panic during the mutinies at Spithead and the Nore. He combined scepticism about the chances of defeating the French with a complacent refusal to defer to rumours implying that the French could successfully invade Britain. Such an invasion would be unwelcome, for he would then be forced to take part in a patriotic all-party government to resist the foreigner, which in practical terms could mean nothing but supporting Pitt. Believing that a negotiated peace made sense he attempted to impose his illusions on the world. However deeply he deplored the policies of the government he was less inclined to attend the house of commons than ever. In December 1799 he thought that the country was wholly without spirit, and without spirit there could be no hope of successfully resisting the ministry. Nor could he take comfort from what had happened in France; constitutional government had vanished, and whatever respect he had for the genius of Bonaparte he was unsympathetic to the form of government euphemistically described as a consulate. In Roman times consuls had been the agents of tyranny; the same was true in France. The ideals of 1789 had been betrayed, and yet he could not concede that Burke had been right. To do that would be to confess that his own political behaviour had been erroneous for a decade.

Wherever he looked he saw nothing but gloom and dejection. He wavered between unreal hope and black misery, but underlying his bursts of cheerfulness was a fundamental disdain for politics. Even when his friends told him of encouraging signs of public support he evaded taking part in any political activity. In January 1798 he had made his misgivings known to Lauderdale:

> I have no hope of any good, because I am convinced that nothing but our carrying everything as triumphantly as to give the appearance of something like unanimity can save us, and of this I see no prospect. Whether the object held out be reform or dismissal or both, I do not think material, but whatever it be, the less I appear publicly in it, not only the more pleasant it will be to me, but as I really think the better for the cause.[8]

Even when he was at his most perceptive he was riddled with defeatism; this was true both of his pronouncements on the war and of his relations with his political associates. He was justified in his continually repeated claims that the internal affairs of one country were no excuse for acts of aggression on the part of another. He pointed the finger of scorn at Pitt and Grenville when they were compelled to negotiate with the French, reminding the house that for his own part he had never thought that the form of government in France was relevant to negotiations for peace. He entertained his friends and infuriated his enemies by making fun of Pitt's allegation that the state of French finances made it impossible for the French to continue the war. He was even able to turn the mood of patriotic defiance to his own account when speaking in the commons on the conduct of the war on 10 May 1796: 'I hope, if ever we should be in the situation of the French, that we should not hesitate to expend the whole capital of the country rather than to have a constitution imposed upon us by a foreign enemy.' He was fond of reminding members that the surest way of making your foes obdurate in negotiation was to insult them before discussions commenced, and this, he claimed, had been the usual practice of the British government, which was too committed to the cause of the

Bourbons to be other than disrespectful towards the present rulers of France. The ministers would find that their efforts for peace were crowned with success only when they abandoned the sentiments which they entertained on the origins and objects of the war. It was best to make war upon France as a republic and to negotiate with France as a republic, without casting backward glances towards the exiled royal family. The ministry ought at least to be consistent, otherwise they would deserve their reputation for shabby double-dealing with the French royalists and republicans alike. He vowed that he could never take part in any administration until the principles on which the war had been waged, and the principles determining domestic policy during the same period, were renounced. No minister who commenced and carried on a war ever made an advantageous peace: if the present ministers wished to be the exceptions to the rule they would have to admit their past errors publicly.

All this was excellent debating: keen in argument, vivid in language, unfailingly scintillating in invective. But for most backbenchers the brilliance and the wit went for nothing when Fox reached his peroration; when they heard him state that Britain had failed in all the objects for which the war had been waged they gritted their teeth, and determined to see the matter out to a satisfactory conclusion, and while they conceded that it made sense to see if the French were willing to offer reasonable terms they had no wish to behave as if the country had been defeated. Despite all the difficulties the nation had encountered Britain was still defiant. When Malmesbury's attempt to secure a negotiated peace failed in December 1796 the commons were unimpressed by Fox's eagerness to crow, 'I told you so.' They were suspicious of Fox's association of foreign policy with domestic politics and even when he tried hard to refute the charge of defeatism Fox failed to carry conviction with the majority of MPs.

The right honourable gentleman has mentioned the breaking off the negotiation as 'a matter of disappointment, but not of despondency or despair'. I certainly am not one of those who despair of the country. I very well know that we are not yet at the end of our resources; but I am certain that we are every day approaching nearer to it. If we had peace at this moment, I have very little doubt but, with economy in every department, a due regard to the finances, and to the encouragement of the commerce and manufactures of the country we might still retrieve ourselves from our present difficulties: but if the war is to continue any length of time, God only knows what may be the dreadful consequences! Certain, however, it is that peace cannot be obtained by a perseverance in the present system. It must be changed. I am not one of those who wish to alter the constitution; I wish only to reform it; to restore the voice of the people to that rank in it which it is entitled to hold; to make the opinion of the minister nothing; to see that of the people everything. I am told, You wish for the removal of the present ministers. I for one certainly do. The country, in my opinion, cannot be saved without it. The people must choose. If there are those who love the constitution under which they were born, and not the defacings of it by the ministers, it is time for them to stand forward, to show themselves, and by constitutional means renovate that constitution which alone can save them and their prosperity from inevitable ruin.[9]

This was very much in line with the attitude which had proved so successful during the American war. The mistakes of the government in carrying on the war were represented as the natural consequences of an erroneous system of domestic politics. But however reasonable demands for the reform of parliament may have been, and however careful Fox was to assure his audience that renovation not innovation was the principle underlying his championship of reform, by mingling defence and domestic politics he inflamed the prejudices of the independent members upon whose sympathy he was counting for any significant shift of opinion with the house of commons. In any event, as has been noted, the assertion that the American war was the outcome of a plot against the constitution by the king and his ministers was without foundation, and to argue that the 'system' needed to be changed looked to many men as nothing more than confirmation of their darkest apprehensions about Fox: that he was, above everything else, eager to unseat Pitt, impose himself upon the king, and bring his friends into office as the first consequence of national humiliation. It would have been wiser for Fox to have limited himself to a discussion of the military and diplomatic aspects of the situation. He ought to have spoken more in sorrow than in anger, to have muted his shameless rejoicing in national frustration, and to have stood forth as an elder statesman, not a contender for power. To many men he seemed too indulgent to the French, too prone to condone their excesses, and too willing to palliate their territorial claims. If the chief political consequence of defeat was the installation of Fox in power, against the wishes of the king, this knowledge drove many men into hardening their hearts, and into supporting Pitt in his determination to fight on, whatever the prospects of victory, until a peace could be achieved which offered some real prospect of stability and security.

The theoretical attractions of Fox's case about the folly of intervention in the domestic concerns of other countries were overshadowed by the many changes of régime in France which made men dubious about the likelihood of any French government lasting for very long. There was always the nagging doubt that once the peace was signed the French would use the opportunity to build up their strength, especially at sea, for the resumption of hostilities at the first favourable moment. Many of his unassuming critics were wiser than Fox in realising that a régime pledged to revolution, and without roots in historical experience to carry it through desperate times, was at any time likely to toy with the idea of a vigorous foreign policy as a means of distracting attention from domestic disappointments. A revival of the idealism of the early years of the revolution could always reinvigorate French foreign policy at some unexpected juncture, while, whatever might be said about ideology and the rights of man, it was already possible to discern a continuity in foreign policy between the Bourbons and the revolutionaries who had succeeded them, despite the different vocabulary which was used to justify French aggrandisement.

The failure to build up an effective opposition to the war sprang from a lack of committed and widespread popular support for the Foxite cause. Men did not like the war; they hated its length, its cost, its disappointments and its bloodshed, but that did not mean that they were persuaded that the prime responsibility for the misery of a decade was the British government's. They did not share Fox's belief that the policy of making war against the French republic was a sign of the deliberate corruption of British institutions, and they had no wish to turn Pitt out of office to bring Fox in. If they wanted any change at the top they hankered for a more conservative figure than Pitt, some more conventional symbol of respectability, not a raffish debater with a too-obvious fondness for the French. Acquiescence was the principal explanation for the success of the government's measures directed against the British radicals, and this acquiescence boded ill for Fox. There was no equivalent for the dedicated parliamentary opposition to the policy of coercion in America, increasingly linked with respectable agitation directed against the government in the country.

The desertion of the Portland whigs deprived Fox of decisive political assets. Portland and his companions supplied the wealth, the organising ability, and the social prestige without which it was impossible to build up a really effective party in parliament. Argument, fluent rhetoric, dazzling oratory were not enough if Pitt was to be driven from office. Even the theoretical case for a formed opposition was still regarded with much distrust and considerable distaste, and nothing in Fox's conduct in opposition during the 1790s diminished these suspicions; if anything it heightened them.

Thus, however potent Fox's arguments against the war were for those Victorians who liked to imagine that Fox was temperamentally one of themselves, a Cobdenite before his time, they were politically sterile. Nor were they ahead of their time. Fox was not an apologist for internationalism. He was no pacifist, and certainly no visionary dedicated to an ideal such as a league of nations. He was not even committed to the doctrine of nationalism, while his liberalism was confined by the respect for the English constitution which was such an essential part of his reformist outlook. Although he advocated the reform of parliament he was preoccupied with the independence of the house of commons, the restriction of the influence of the crown, and the representation of interests, not mere numbers. He was a believer in eighteenth-century diplomatic expertise, an exponent of the balance of power, a believer in limited wars and a practitioner of the theory of permanent negotiation, even during hostilities. He was, if anything, prejudiced against the French in many ways, at least until the early 1790s, when he gave full vent to his distrust of Austria, Prussia, and Russia. His ideas about national character were often simple-minded and influenced by what he wanted to believe about any particular nation. He was not without vindictiveness, and he often put party before country. His words and deeds stemmed from the exigencies of the political situation, which he could neither direct nor control. Frustration was, therefore, a natural outcome, and his own secession from the house of commons demonstrated that he was too experienced a campaigner not to recognise the facts of the case. Stirring though his appeals for peace often were, his noble words were often inspired by less than noble calculations. Rather than a disappointed idealist he was a party politician who made decisive miscalculations—and lost.

9 *The Addington Ministry and Pitt's Final Years*

It was ironic that Pitt's grip on power should be weakened, not by the frustrations surrounding the French war, but by Irish affairs. Yet this is not as surprising as at first appears. For Pitt was always vulnerable to attack from the more conservative elements in his government, and so far as the rank and file in the house of commons were concerned they were more fond of ministers who were less interested in sophisticated schemes of financial reform and less prone to take up issues such as the emancipation of the catholics. Pitt's liberal record in the 1780s was held against him on all sides: by his radical critics, because they believed that he had deserted their cause, and by his reactionary foes, because they recalled his unreliability on certain key issues.

Fox remained in retirement during the Irish crisis. His sympathies lay with the more enlightened section of the Anglo-Irish ruling class. They had often worked together in the past. During the American war the English whigs had found Grattan and his friends valuable allies, and during the regency crisis the Irish had followed a Foxite line, which was favourable to the Prince of Wales and unhesitatingly anti-Pitt. This contributed to Pitt's later scepticism about the Dublin parliament and when the troubles of the 1790s came upon him it was natural that he should contemplate changing the constitutional relationship between the two countries. He had seen for himself how incapable the Irish were of keeping order in their own country, and he did not share the bitter anti-catholic feeling of many of the Irish protestants. But on Irish matters as on other issues Pitt was more enlightened than many members of his government, and this often produced tensions and confusions in Irish policy.

The uncertainties within the ministry contributed to the fiasco of Fitzwilliam's viceroyalty in 1795. Fitzwilliam, a known sympathiser with the catholics, was under the impression that he had been given

wider powers than was the case. Pitt was guilty of allowing the issue to
be blurred by indistinct instructions, and when Fitzwilliam outraged protestant sentiment by seemingly going beyond his instructions, in promising what looked like imminent catholic relief and in offending important
sections of governmental opinion in Dublin, there was little the government could do but recall Fitzwilliam in disgrace. He was made the
scapegoat for errors of judgment and hesitancies of policy which were not
his sole responsibility. He had been tactless and tragically he made the
prospects for reform less promising than formerly. The foes of any concession to the catholic Irish were put on their guard. Pitt himself was
under suspicion, and so deep-rooted was the determination of the protestant clique to retain its ascendancy that every ruse available to politicians of the time was ruthlessly exploited.

Fox had watched the course of events with mixed feelings. Despite
his breach with Fitzwilliam over the French revolution he could not
forget that they had been the closest of friends and the most devoted of
political companions. Fox favoured the catholic cause and he saw his
friend's humiliation as the outcome of deceit and treachery. He believed
that once again Pitt had shown his cold indifference to the finer points of
political conduct and his cruel disdain for humane feeling. He hoped that
Fitzwilliam might be reconciled with his old friends, but he was as
blind as most of his contemporaries about the state of affairs in Ireland.
Liberal as they were, sympathetic though they imagined themselves to
be with respect to the aspirations of the Irish catholics, they failed to grasp
the scope of Irish resentment against England. Although the Irish whigs
were willing to concede political rights to the Irish catholics they assumed
all too easily that the catholic masses would continue to accept the
leadership of the protestant ruling class. They were wholly in the dark
as to the bitterness among the presbyterians of Ulster, and although Fox
was horrified by the violence shown by both sides during the Irish
rising of 1798 he never fully appreciated the savagery with which the
contending factions confronted each other.

Fox was acutely sensitive to the threat which the disturbances in Ireland posed for Britain and although he liked to pour cold water on the
more extravagant fears of French invasion he knew that the Irish tragedy
raised great issues for the British government. He favoured catholic
emancipation, but he regarded the union of parliaments, with which
Pitt associated it, as a fraud, a cheat imposed upon the Irish by Pitt and a
violation of the constitutional relationship between the two countries.
Fox remembered that the Rockingham ministry had granted full legislative independence to the Dublin parliament. He fondly imagined that

this was one of the achievements of the whig opposition to the American war, and he believed that by conceding legislative independence he and his colleagues had prevented the situation in Ireland from becoming similar to that in America. In some ways this was true: by giving way to the Irish demands the Rockinghamites had averted a direct clash. They knew that the country was in no mood to face another constitutional crisis and rightly regarding Ireland as Britain's principal colony they made the best of things. What Fox tended to overlook was that the Dublin parliament was a corrupt assembly, representing a small proportion of the Irish people, and crudely determined to cling to every semblance of power and status, whatever the consequences. It was blithely unrealistic to imagine that there was any chance of carrying catholic emancipation without a union of parliaments. Without the precaution of merging the Irish parliament with the British it would be virtually impossible to persuade the majority of the English house of commons that granting full political rights to Irish catholics was not fraught with risk. There was the perennial difficulty of getting the Dublin parliament to show any liberality towards the catholic majority: however intense anti-popery was in England it was as nothing compared with the bitter intransigence with which the various Irish factions regarded each other. After the horrors of the rebellion of 1798, which had been bloody and brutal, and which would have been bloodier still had the north not been disarmed with merciless rigour by General Lake, it was possible for opponents of the catholic claims to argue that concession would have the appearance of a concession to violence, a reward for disloyalty and revolt. Pitt's failure to carry his own cabinet with him and his inability to move the king from his unflinching opposition to catholic emancipation, showed how difficult it was to persuade men of the wisdom or expediency of catholic relief even after the security of the union was assured. The means used to get the proposed union through in Dublin—bribery on an unprecedented scale—was utilised to discredit the union, even though many of those who did so had no viable political alternative. Had the union of parliaments been accompanied, as Pitt had intended, by commercial concessions and religious and political equality there was a faint chance that it might have succeeded. But union without emancipation came to be regarded as a betrayal by the catholic majority and the myth that Pitt was bent on deception from the start found many ready listeners.

The behaviour of Loughborough, the lord chancellor, in going down to Weymouth to warn George III of what was being discussed in the cabinet, and the manner in which the king's will prevailed, forcing out

16 'Parliamentary Reform – or Opposition Rats leaving the House they had undermined' *Cartoon by James Gillray, 28 May 1797*

17 'Introduction of Citizen Volpone and his Suite at Paris' *From a cartoon*

the minister who had served him so well for seventeen years, were reminders of how slowly old attitudes were changing. George III had installed Pitt in office; now he rid himself of him. Much though Fox rejoiced at Pitt's departure (he never showed any magnanimity towards the man who had defeated him in 1784) he did not approve of the means by which the king ejected Pitt from office. He had always hoped that some crisis would turn Pitt out, but he could take little comfort from the thought that George III's prejudices had played the most decisive role in his minister's fall. Fox gave Pitt no credit for sticking to his principles over the catholic issue. He wondered whether Pitt had seized the controversy over emancipation as a pretext for evading the responsibility of making peace upon terms which he had resisted for several years. This was doing Pitt an injustice. Fox underestimated both Pitt's fondness for place and his devotion to what he conceived to be his public duty. And the replacement of Pitt by Addington was disheartening. It marked the final exposure of those delusions which had sustained Fox throughout the disappointments of the war years. The fall of Pitt brought the Foxite whigs no nearer office. The will of the king seemed supreme; the people had not been consulted, and they accepted what had happened, either in stunned indifference or, if they were extreme protestants, with cheerful exultation. Pitt's cabinet had behaved in a way which showed how far men were from accepting those ideas of collective responsibility for which Fox had been pleading for twenty years. Fox believed that Pitt's departure made peace more likely, but he was divorced from the nerve centres of power, and as incapable of influencing events as ever.

Yet he had only himself to blame. Though it would be foolish to argue that a more active Fox would have been able to exploit Pitt's embarrassment more skilfully—Fox was himself committed to the catholic cause— the way in which the Irish union and the catholic emancipation crisis passed Fox by was the inevitable consequence of his secession from parliament. No matter how urgently his friends besought him to take the initiative he remained addicted to the homely ease of St Anne's Hill. Despite the depth of feeling underlying his response to the war and to Irish affairs he did not believe that it was worth his while to be more active in politics. He remained convinced that a more systematic opposition was the only method of procuring constitutional progress but he had lost all hope that he himself would be able to put his ideas into practice. His faith in what he could accomplish by opposition had been shattered. He lamented the union; he deplored the blindness of his contemporaries over the catholic issue; but he no longer believed that he could control events. In a mood of fatalistic resignation he relied upon circumstances proving him right, but he became indifferent as to whether this would bring him the political rewards for which he had longed so passionately and so desperately for so long. He was confused and uncertain of what to make of the situation. Early in 1801 he confided his misgivings to Lauderdale:

I am very anxious to hear your opinions. Upon the great point, how far all this business is or is not, on Pitt's part, a juggle, I do not expect that you at this distance can determine, when I, who am so much nearer the scene of action, cannot. Grey and the rest of our friends seem clear that it is no juggle but there are circumstances very difficult to account for, on their hypothesis. ... It is a great gulp to swallow, to believe that Addington himself should act without some understanding with Pitt. On the other hand ... it is certain that Lord Spencer and Canning are out of the secret. But juggle or no juggle what will be the consequences? This ministry cannot last, say our friends; so say not I, unless the public misfortunes should be such as would have equally forced out the others. The king's power is, as we know, great; and when exerted in conjunction with his ally the church, and therefore in the way and upon the points which he likes best, and into which he will enter with the greatest spirit, will not easily be foiled, and you may be sure that this ministry is one quite to his heart's content. But what ought to be the conduct of Grey and his friends? If Pitt, as is generally believed, means neither to move the catholic question nor to support it if moved by others, ought or ought not Grey or Ponsonby to bring it on? I say, yes; for if Pitt opposes it, as they say he will, it will tend more than anything both to disgrace him and to show the abject state both of the late ministers and of parliament in the strongest light, if a measure of importance to the welfare, and as Grenville has said to the safety of the empire, is to be waived because the king is said to have prejudices against it.[1]

When he had first heard rumours suggesting that Pitt was going to resign he had been more hopeful; initially he had thought that if Pitt's ministry was succeeded by one which was as unsuccessful then the opposition would have a wonderful chance of overturning the whole system. But these hopes were soon dashed, and Fox became more cautious and more defeatist in his expectations. By the beginning of January 1802 he was warning Holland about the difficulties of building up a new opposition, concluding with the lame assurance, 'Industry and youth can do much, and unless such a thing can be done no good can'.[2]

He was prepared to resume attendance at the house of commons to support Grey but he did so with little enthusiasm. He had ceased attending the commons because the proceedings of the late ministers had made parliamentary debates into a farce; he did not think that anything had happened seriously to change that situation. Those who had been content to be tools of the previous administration would be the dupes of the new ministry. His only wish was to aid the cause of peace. He wanted to add his voice to those pleading for a tactful approach to the armed neutrality of the north. Only peace and the catholic question could entice Fox into the commons. He was sick of politics. 'Do you think', he asked Lauderdale, 'they could have picked out any one fellow in the house of commons so sure to make a foolish figure in this new situation as Addington? I think not.'

The early days of the Addington ministry were unsettled by George III's illness. For a short time there were fears of another regency crisis or even of a fundamental upset in political arrangements. But soon it became clear that the king's illness was less serious than in 1788. However George III exploited his indisposition by blackmailing Pitt into confirming his undertaking not to raise the catholic question again during the king's lifetime, accusing his former minister of being responsible for his breakdown by bringing the catholic question forward. Fox saw these events with mixed feelings. He remembered bitterly the frustrations of 1788 and the high price which he had paid for his rashness on that occasion. It was with some relief that he told Grey there was no danger of a regency. He was glad that the king's health had improved, for he was indifferent as to the choice of first minister. Whether it was Pitt or Addington signified little.

His defeatism extended to the catholic question. Fitzwilliam was eager to raise the issue again and was doing his best to persuade Ponsonby and others to agree with him. Though Fox had originally hoped that the catholic controversy might be debated anew because this would embarrass Pitt he was now suspicious of falling into a trap. Perhaps Pitt hoped that the opposition whigs would raise the catholic question prematurely as the preliminary to inflicting further humiliations upon them. Despite his own convictions that the catholic cause was just and that those who wished to hold back on the concession of emancipation deserved little credit Fox now counselled patience and caution. He could not overlook the confused state of politics. Anything that might reunite Pitt's faithful supporters with his more wayward followers was to be avoided. It would not be sensible to court another confrontation with the king. After his illness there was a strong wave of sympathy for George III and Fox remembered that the king's stubborn opposition to catholic relief was another reminder of the way in which he shared the most fundamental of his subjects' prejudices. Fox was therefore ambivalent in his attitude towards the catholic controversy. He sympathised with Fitzwilliam and those who wished to forge ahead, but he was sceptical of the wisdom or expediency of putting pressure on his colleagues to commit themselves unreservedly to the catholic cause. Only four or five of the leading opposition whigs were prepared to support Fitzwilliam without reservation. Most of the whigs were increasingly sensitive to the dangers of being identified too closely or too exclusively with the catholic interest, and they were beginning to think that Addington might well be driven to try to broaden his administration by coming to terms with allies in the most improbable quarters. It was, therefore, best to let this issue rest.

Fox was relieved at this. He was reluctant to lose the reputation of being a supporter of catholic relief, but he never forgot that political tactics had to be brought into the reckoning and that naïve obstinacy on the emancipation issue was taking great risks without securing any commensurate advantages. He was trying hard to preserve his sense of the realities of politics without becoming too involved in political horse-trading, just as he sought to remain faithful to liberal ideas without allowing this to blind him to the harsh facts of political life. It was hard for him to know what to make of the political situation. There were persistent rumours of a deterioration in the king's health which Fox could not ignore. It was even claimed that George III had had a stroke, while others said that he had relapsed into complete madness. Fox therefore tried to avoid any hasty political commitments until the confusion cleared somewhat and it became easier to assess the balance of parliamentary forces with some degree of accuracy. Had he been as judicious in 1788 his career might have been different. This knowledge added only gall to his new maturity.

Fox therefore stuck to his decision to absent himself from the commons. He was much criticised for this by his friends. He seemed to be abandoning them when they needed him most and when the inspiration of his rhetoric could sustain their weary spirits. But Fox knew that he could not resolve the political situation in the way that many of his supporters hoped. Even when he did break his resolution to stay away from the house in order to attend the debate on the breakdown of the peace negotiations with Bonaparte on 3 February 1800 his parliamentary skill and brilliant speech had not brought new converts to the whig ranks. In the division they numbered only 64, although Fox's peroration had been in his most ironic and vivid style:

Where then, sir, is this war, which on every side is pregnant with such horrors, to be carried? Where is it to stop? Not till you establish the house of Bourbon! And this you cherish the hope of doing because you have had a successful campaign.... One campaign is successful to you—another to them; and in this way ... you may go on for ever; as, with such black incentives, I see no end to human misery. And all this without an intelligible motive—all this because you may gain a better peace a year or two hence? So that we are called upon to go on merely as a speculation—we must keep Bonaparte for some time longer at war, as a state of probation. Gracious God, sir! is war a state of probation? Is peace a rash system? Is it dangerous for nations to live in amity with each other? Is your vigilance, your policy, your common powers of observation, to be extinguished by putting an end to the horrors of war? Cannot this state of probation be as well undergone without adding to the catalogue of human sufferings? 'But we must *pause*!' What! Must the bowels of Great Britain be torn out—her best blood to be spilt—her treasure wasted—that you may make an experiment? Put yourselves—oh! that you would put yourselves in the field of battle, and learn to judge of the sort of horrors that you excite. In former wars a man might, at least, have some feeling, some interest that served to balance in his mind the impressions which a scene of carnage and of death must inflict. If a man had been present at the battle of Blenheim, for instance, and had inquired the motive of the battle, there was not a soldier engaged who could not have satisfied his curiosity, and even, perhaps, allayed his feelings—they were fighting to repress the uncontrolled ambition of a grand monarch. But if a man were present now at a field of slaughter, and were to inquire for what they were fighting: 'Fighting!' would be the answer; they are not fighting, they are *pausing*—This man is not expiring with agony—that man is not dead—he is only pausing! ... All that you see, sir, is nothing like fighting—there is no harm, nor cruelty, nor bloodshed in it whatever—it is nothing more than *a political pause*!—it is merely to try an experiment—to see whether Bonaparte will not behave himself better than heretofore; and in the meantime we have agreed to a pause, in pure friendship! And is this the way, sir, that you are to show yourselves the advocates of order? You take up a system calculated to uncivilise the world, to destroy order, to trample on religion, to stifle in the heart, not merely the generosity of noble sentiment, but the affections of social nature; and in the prosecution of this system you spread terror and devastation all around you.[3]

To many MPs all this seemed remote from the real decisions which the government had to make in dealing with the French. Until there were signs that the French were willing to make some compromise in the interests of peace there was no alternative but to continue the war, unless one was content to sue for peace on any terms and to pay any price. Fox seemed perverse and obtuse in refusing to contemplate the possibility that the real obstacle to a peace settlement might be arrogance on the French side of the negotiations. He recognised the mood of the house; he knew that Pitt had been right on 3 February in assuring the king of the satisfactory response of the majority of members to the debate. He therefore resumed the practice of absentee opposition, and even when he had misgivings about its efficacy there was little to tempt him to change his mind.

Fox began to think that only if there was a discernible measure of support for him outside the house of commons would he take his seat in the usual way and resume the leadership of the opposition in debate. Only the most decisive issues were likely to tempt him back: the chances of a negotiated peace, the possibility of significant reform, or an inquiry into the conduct of the king's ministers which promised to humiliate both Pitt and Addington and bring about a revolution in political alignments. In many ways Fox was not disposed to join any administration. He became ever more pessimistic about the future. So far as his own political ambitions were concerned he had only one: should the whigs be able to come in on the right terms he wished to be foreign secretary. He knew that he would never be head of a ministry, whatever happened to Addington or Pitt. He was compelled, nevertheless, to take notice of what men were saying when rumours suggested that the king's illness had taken a turn for the worse. There was talk of the earl of Moira becoming head of a new administration. Fox remained sceptical and indifferent. He doubted the trustworthiness of such speculation, just as he was embarrassingly aware of deficiences in the ranks of the whig opposition. He told Lauderdale that Grey and the duke of Norfolk were the only whigs whose judgment and sagacity could be relied upon. Moira was even more foolish than he had at first thought, while Sheridan was offending many of his colleagues and many important independents by his wounding speeches and cutting private sarcasms. Sheridan's victims often deserved their rebukes, but perhaps this made it all the harder for them to bear his witticisms. Grey was sensitive to anything savouring of a slight from Sheridan and Fox was constantly having to soothe his ruffled self-esteem. He had to pretend that Sheridan's speeches contained nothing of a personal nature directed against Grey. The whigs were falling into their old habit of quarrelling with each other more vigorously than they attacked their political foes. This was especially frustrating for Fox.

In the spring of 1801, however, he indulged himself in a bout of optimism about his political companions. On 1 April he wrote to Lauderdale in his most buoyant vein. Not even his low opinion of Tierney could make him depressed.

> Your old friend Landsdowne seems inclined to do everything that is right and in the pleasantest way. Sheridan too is in famous good humour. Tierney has been more out of the course than ever, but will be tractable enough if there is any prospect of success. By the way, he too seems to be more deficient in sense than I had thought. Grey is certainly improved, not only in speaking (in which he is very greatly so) but I think in everything.[4]

It was to Grey that Fox increasingly turned. The follies of Grey's youth and his impetuosity over the founding of the society of the Friends of the People were forgiven. Fox confided in Grey; he felt at ease with him, believing that the younger man appreciated his point of view in a way which few others—Holland excepted—did. When the Reverend Christopher Wyvill suggested that Grey had refused a place in the administration because Addington would not concede a moderate instalment of parliamentary reform, Fox appreciated the tribute to Grey's integrity even when he was compelled to deny the accuracy of the report. Grey had behaved honourably throughout the confusions of the catholic controversy, the fall of Pitt and the formation of the Addington ministry. Although he had conversed with a member of Addington's government it was going too far to suggest that some definite agreement was in the offing until Grey reiterated his fidelity to parliamentary reform. There was no hesitation on Fox's part in paying his own tribute to Grey's worth and character; he told Wyvill that while it would be improper for him to enter into any particulars there was no shadow of doubt in his mind that Grey had never acted, and could never act, inconsistently with his own honour and the good of his country, whether on the issue of parliamentary reform or on any other.

The peace of Amiens—that peace which everyone was glad of but no one was proud of—was welcome to Fox. It seemed like a lethargic and belated recognition that he had been right in arguing the case for a negotiated peace through so many harrowing and depressing years. He could not resist gloating over the discomfiture of those who had resisted his eloquence so stubbornly for so long. The peace was none the worse, in his opinion, for being so favourable to France. The French had yielded virtually none of their conquests, and the familiar Pittite plea for indemnity for the past and security for the future had withered into a partiality, so it seemed, for Ceylon and Trinidad. Even when some of his friends confessed that they feared that the peace was no more than a truce Fox was at first cheerfully confident. He hoped for a long peace. If his attitude during the 1790s was to be justified he could not accept that the peace was no more than a breathing space in which the two combatants would be able to prepare themselves for the resumption of the conflict. To do this would have been to go too far towards conceding the validity of Pitt's anxieties. The peace was popular, of that there could be no doubt, and Fox was unashamedly glad of it. But he could not refrain from making some caustic comments on the public who, having resisted his pleas for peace for so long, were now luxuriating in a peace which their own stupidity had delayed. Fox confided his thoughts to Maitland:

> The sense of humiliation in the government here will be entirely lost in the extreme popularity of the measure. I suspect there never was joy more universal and unfeigned, and this rascally people are quite over-joyed at receiving from ministers what, if they dared to ask it, could not have been refused them at almost any period of the war. Will the ministers have the impudence to say that there was any time (much less that when Bonaparte's offer was refused) when we might not have had terms as good? Bonaparte's triumph is now complete indeed, and since there is to be no political liberty in the world I really believe he is the fittest person to be the master.[5]

Fox obstinately denied that the situation in the war years had been much less simple and much more changeable than such an unsubtle interpretation suggested. He was compelled to be more generous to the French than the facts warranted, just as for too long he remained credulous about Bonaparte's actions and motives.

But it was good to enjoy the pleasures of peace again; to journey to old haunts, for too long denied to British holidaymakers by the exigencies of war. Fox was keen to cross the channel. He longed to go to Paris, and to appreciate for himself the changes which had been wrought since he had last been there in the remote years when the Bourbons had still ruled. Fox loved Paris; there he had first plunged into dissipation, there he had first appreciated the pleasures of painting and developed a taste for a foreign culture. In addition to these remembered joys he hoped to have the pleasure of meeting Bonaparte, the man regarded by many British mothers as an ogre and by many British politicians as a monster. Fox needed reassurance, too; at the back of his mind, despite his protestations, there lurked the repeated misgivings, shared by so many Englishmen, that the peace was but a pause (however welcome) in the protracted struggle against France. Fox was inclined to interpret British anxieties as a dangerous lack of faith, possibly even as evidence of double-dealing, which the French were fond of alleging was the chief characteristic of British diplomacy. But he wanted to be sure that the French were themselves sincere in their affirmations of peaceful intentions. His visit to Paris was more than a pleasure jaunt by an ageing politician and his middle-aged wife. It was necessary to confirm his own assumptions about the state of affairs in France, and most important of all the disposition and character of France's new ruler. It would have been more comforting for Fox if the French had remained faithful to constitutional monarchy or moderate republicanism, with men of impeccable propriety directing the destinies of a sober and temperate people. But it was too late to regret the passing of the old-style republicans. It was necessary to do one's best to appreciate the virtues of republicanism in its new guise of the consulate.

The other reason for going to Paris was to work on materials relevant to the history of the reigns of Charles II and James II on which Fox had been working during the years of secession from the house of commons. Because of his literary interests he was accompanied by his secretary, John Bernard Trotter, and Trotter published an account of his visit to France in the company of Fox and his wife. Trotter was by temperament something of a prig, and he constantly did his best to make Fox appear as respectable as possible. But his account is of value, nonetheless.

During the journey Fox passed much of his time reading novels. Fielding's *Joseph Andrews* was one chosen to pass the hours in the coach, Trotter reading it aloud. Fox was amused by the book; though he and his friends agreed that vulgarity was too prevalent in Fielding's novels they appreciated 'his faithful and admirable paintings from human nature'. Virgil was another author whose work was frequently read during the trip. Trotter had begun reading *The Aeneid* at St Anne's Hill before the party had left for the continent, and he continued his readings as opportunity allowed on the journey. Fox was as enthusiastic a Virgilian as ever. He gained great pleasure from sharing his opinion of favourite passages with Trotter, while Trotter, in return, dutifully recorded Fox's admiration for *The Aeneid* with the revealing comment that the tincture of melancholy which ran through the work was by no means displeasing to him.

At Ghent, Lille, and Antwerp Fox was received by the officers of each municipality; his holiday took on something of the splendours of a triumphal tour. Though he appreciated the signs that his pleas for peace had not gone unnoticed in France and the Low Countries he was not entirely happy at being the centre of so much public attention. It added to the strain of travelling, and he wanted to enjoy the country without the tiring and time-consuming necessity of official receptions. Besides he was conscious of how easy it would be for the ill-disposed to misrepresent his popularity in France and Belgium: it could be cited as further evidence that he was, after all, too fond of the French and not enough of a patriot. The weather was hot and humid, which added to the exhaustion brought about by the journey. But Fielding continued to divert the travellers from their discomforts and inconveniences. On leaving Brussels Trotter started reading *Tom Jones* again and soon everything else was forgotten. In his memoirs Trotter could not resist making some stuffy comments on the state of the modern novel, together with what Fox felt about contemporary fiction:

> Tom Jones is also with all his indiscretions on his head, far preferable to those much more dangerous personages in modern novels, whose voluptuous authors seem to conceive that libertine morality, clothed in eloquent language, are sure to gain approbation and support. Mr Fox was fond of novels, but not of any of this latter class. Their verbiage, and want of fidelity to nature, were sure to disgust him. I have read to him, at times, a great many, but none of this description. In the Arabian Nights entertainments he delighted much (and who would not?) for there was to be found a faithful and inimitable picture of Oriental manners and customs, as well as much ingenuity, fancy, and knowledge of human nature; but in the pages of sensuality, expanding itself in various shapes in the modern novel, he found no pleasure; and the irreligious passages gave him still less, as no man treated the sacred subject of religion with greater respect and forbearance than he did.[6]

Possibly this demure portrait of Fox owes more to Trotter's desire to win friends for his hero than to his historical accuracy. Trotter was conscious of Fox's reputation as a man indifferent to the conventions of respectable society. Though he was faithful to Elizabeth Armistead, and despite the fact that he had eventually married her, his reputation as something of an irreligious rake died hard. It was of course possible that in his middle age Fox was inclined to deplore the decline of literary standards, perhaps by comparing the great poets of the past with the minor figures of the present, but it is probable that he did so with less prudery and less smug complacency than Trotter implied.

One of the chief delights of Paris was the theatre. Fox greatly enjoyed the classical French tragedians and he took the opportunity to renew his acquaintance with them in performance while abroad. Racine was his favourite dramatist and one performance of *Phaedra* impressed him so much that he went to see it twice at the same theatre. But visits to the theatre were fraught with invasions of his privacy. On one occasion he was recognised by the audience; soon most people were looking towards his box, and a continual cry of 'Fox! Fox!' became audible. The audience rose, applauding him enthusiastically, but Fox seemed embarrassed and put out by the incident. At least that was how Trotter chose to explain his refusal to rise or to make any formal gesture of thanks or appreciation to those who were applauding him so cheerfully. He was bored with being regarded as some sort of exhibit or curiosity; like other men of affairs, when he went to the theatre he preferred to give his whole attention to the dramatic performance, instead of being a focal point of attention himself.

Entertaining and informative though Trotter's record of Fox's visit to Paris is its veracity may be questioned at times. The picture of a benign, modest, genteel and retiring Fox is a little overdrawn. When Trotter records the first occasion on which Fox saw Bonaparte he goes out of his way to make his effect. According to Trotter, when Bonaparte entered his box in the theatre the light from the stage fell upon his face 'so as to give an unfavourable and ghastly effect ... He was received with some applause but much inferior to that bestowed on Mr Fox.' This may have been the case; Fox was a novelty to Parisians, Bonaparte was not. But the slightly sinister portrait of Napoleon seems designed to appeal to English readers, just as the greater applause for Fox can be taken as an attempt to show that the French people were more peaceloving than the first consul and consequently more grateful for Fox's efforts on their behalf. It is all too convenient for the posthumous adulation of Fox as the man of peace.

There was no doubt that Fox was well received in Paris, nor was this limited to demonstrations of popular respect. Talleyrand was particularly polite and attentive; there was a tearful meeting with Lafayette; even the Abbé Sieyes had the honour of a visit. But the most dramatic event was the meeting with Bonaparte, suitably and piously overdramatised as it was by Trotter, who states that Bonaparte was a good deal flurried

and after indicating considerable emotion, very rapidly said—'Ah! Mr Fox! I have heard with pleasure of your arrival—I have desired much to see you—I have long admired in you the orator and friend of his country, who, in constantly raising his voice for peace, consulted that country's best interests—those of Europe—and that of the human race. The two great nations of Europe require peace; they have nothing to fear; they ought to understand and value one another. In you, Mr Fox, I see with much satisfaction, that great statesman who recommended peace, because there was no just object of war; who saw Europe desolated to no purpose, and who struggled for its relief.'[7]

Fox said little or nothing in reply. He always found complimentary addresses to himself as embarrassing as they were fulsome and he did not attempt to compete with Bonaparte in flattery. Perhaps Fox suspected that Bonaparte's remarks smacked somewhat of a prepared speech. A rather desultory and routine exchange of queries about Fox's tour closed the interview.

Fox thoroughly enjoyed his French holiday, and as well as his sightseeing and visits to the theatre he had worked a good many hours on the French papers for his history of the reigns of Charles II and James II. He enjoyed collecting the materials for his history (perhaps more than he enjoyed the actual writing of it) and although on one occasion his researches were halted because he had broken his spectacles he was pleased with what he found in the archives. His pleasure was clouded only by a lack of letters from Lord Holland. Fox admitted that he had himself been lethargic in writing but he excused himself by claiming that he had been waiting to hear from Holland first. When the correspondence was resumed on 21 November 1802 he told his nephew that he and Mrs Fox had had a smooth crossing from Calais, and that he was glad to be home: 'I have certainly seldom spent time pleasanter than at Paris, but yet never in my life felt such delight in returning home.'

The political prospects were as depressing as ever. The brief period of relief and congratulation over the peace of Amiens had already ended. Men were anxious about Bonaparte's intentions in Europe and the Mediterranean; a mood of resigned apprehension was general. Dissatisfaction with Addington was growing on all sides, despite Pitt's reluctance to take the lead in stirring up opposition to the administration. Men who had welcomed the peace now cast themselves in the role of prophets who had warned against it. Fox hoped that peace could be maintained; he tried to keep up his spirits by refusing to believe that the country could be panicked into another war against France. He did not believe that there was any widespread wish for war; much of the hysteria had been whipped up by the newspapers, which were all too often mistaken for public opinion. But he was sufficiently worried to start attending the house of commons again. He did so, not because he thought it probable that he would dissuade those who were set on a resumption of hostilities, but in order to help to keep up the morale of those in the commons who were striving desperately hard to keep the peace. He flattered himself with the thought that he might stiffen the ministers' resolve to resist those calling for a more bellicose policy. He had few illusions about what his enemies would say. 'I am told I shall be as much abused for pacific language now, as I was ten years ago, but as I am in parliament I must not blink such a question.'[8]

He found that the house was less antagonistic than he had anticipated. There were the usual taunts that he was an apologist for France and an agent of the first consul, but he thought that the members listened to him with more attention than had been the case since the Orchakov crisis. But he did not exaggerate the significance either of what he had said or of how the commons heard him out. He wrote to Holland in a sober mood.

> To say, as those inclined to flatter me will say, that I have done any-thing considerable for peace is more than is true; but it is true that by speaking a pacific language more decisively than others dared to do, and by that language being well received, I have been the means of showing that the real sentiments of the people are strongly for peace, and it is very important that this should be known.[9]

Fox thought that Pitt favoured a pacific policy and that he tended to be lenient towards Addington. But the more vociferous of Pitt's supporters, of whom Canning was the most demonstrative, were calling for Pitt's return, and this would have the effect, Fox thought, of forcing Pitt into committing himself more definitely either for or against the ministry or into making his virtual retirement from active politics all the more like a formal secession. Grenville was making a powerful impact on the lords as the most capable and relentless advocate of a tough anti-Bonaparte line, and Fox complained that there was so little governmental talent in the house of lords effectively to reply to Grenville's criticisms of the adminis-tration. The real danger to peace came from the weakness of the minis-try. Addington and his colleagues could easily be pushed into a more belligerent stance as the easiest way of averting charges that they were too feeble to deserve the confidence or even the patience of the house of commons.

In this situation Fox was compelled to give the ministry his support. He did so without any illusions as to the capacity of the ministers to cope with the problems pressing in on them from the continent. He was also bitterly conscious of the excesses of French policy. Deploring Bonaparte's conduct in Switzerland he could not see how Britain could act to check the aggression. He therefore exploited British weakness as an argument for doing nothing. This was dangerous, for it allowed the critics of the government to say that more should be done to strengthen the navy and to put the army in a state of readiness, while any confession that Britain could not act on the continent—however much she wished to do so—was hardly likely to moderate French demands and French actions. But Fox was not eager to join in the chorus of criticism so far as Bonaparte was concerned. Whatever his excesses in Switzerland he had good grounds for his anxieties elsewhere. Fox was sensitive about the technicalities of the quarrel over Malta; he knew that the French would be only too glad to point to the British failure to implement the terms of the Amiens agreement in order to extenuate their own behaviour towards their neighbours. Fox was loath to admit that the French were embarking on a policy of aggrandisement. He preferred to believe that they were simply overreacting to provocations which they should not have had to endure. Again and again he fell back on his belief that there was a universal wish for peace, that misunderstanding was the principal cause of Anglo-French hostility. He could not accept the possibility that either the British or French governments should ignore the desire of the peoples of both countries for peace. Even the growing detestation and distrust of Bonaparte in England was less of a menace than it at first appeared; Fox thought that much of it was hot air; the English liked to complain about foreign rulers, and Bonaparte was merely taking his turn with the rest.

But when Fox tried to reassure his friends his own deeper anxieties, which he would not have revealed to the public in any circumstances, came to the surface. There were no grounds for complacency, even if there was no need for panic. Both sides had done enough to allow the other to claim that there had been breaches of solemn undertakings and instances of bad faith. Distrust could lead to tragedy. It was, therefore, all the more necessary to support the ministry in their pacific policy. In public Fox wished to play down the seriousness of the crisis, believing that anything which stirred up public feeling would help the war party. He was therefore reluctant to organise pacific petitions; they would stimulate the other side to greater efforts and they would screw up emotion and heighten tension still further. Also, Fox was sceptical of their practicality. They would not, in themselves, persuade the ministers to defer to French demands if they were convinced that it was impolitic to do so, and all too often when the Foxites had sought to whip up public feeling on their side of the question their opponents had been better organised in ensuring that their supporters added their names to petitions and addresses.

But there was one rumour from France which disquieted Fox more than he cared to admit. It was said that Bonaparte intended to proclaim himself emperor of the French. Fox recognised that this would play into the hands of the anti-French party in London. It would be cited as proof of Bonaparte's ambition and aggressive spirit, and it would be deemed evidence that he was essentially illiberal, a warrior who harboured Caesar-like dreams of personal grandeur, not a selfless upholder of republican virtue and the rights of man. If Bonaparte destroyed the republic it would be a blow to those who had hoped that he would stabilise the régime in France without making too obvious a break with republican precedent. It was too much to hope that he would speedily restore free political institutions, but the consulate, however brutal the realities of power underlying it, still preserved a semblance of respect for the ideals of 1789. It would be impossible for English liberals to exonerate Bonaparte from the charges of being a Cromwell if he became emperor. Fox hoped that the rumours were false, but he could not brush them aside as if they were of no importance. 'I am not one of those', he confessed, 'who think that names signify nothing.'

As Britain was dragged into a renewal of the war Fox's spirits fell. He believed that the country was in the grip of a fate which was as relentless as his own harsh destiny. He knew that the situation was not fully parallel to that in 1793 but he felt equally powerless to avert a catastrophe he deplored. His compassion for the ministers withered as he became ever more aware of their incompetence. Addington's capacity was under attack, not only because of his supine foreign policy but also because men were beginning to doubt that he was managing the national finances efficiently. It was this aspect of policy which tempted Pitt to play a more active role in the opposition, and much as he longed for peace Fox ceased to concern himself with Addington's fate. His contempt for the administration was associated with long-standing fears and suspicious. If the ministry survived it seemed to him as if the immensity of the power and influence of the crown was proved beyond all reasonable doubt. Yet he was in a cruel predicament; if Addington fell it was virtually certain that he would be succeeded by Pitt, or by others who were even more committed to a warlike posture towards the French.

Not even the sad and mysterious affair of Colonel Despard enlivened politics. Most men thought Despard's execution justified, and although Fox would himself have recommended mercy he admitted himself to be virtually the only man in London who would have done so. If Fox is to be believed the affair produced little in the way of intense public interest. Apathy was the enemy Fox feared most, and apathy was what he felt himself most incapable of challenging. As usual he told Holland of his innermost feelings, writing on 23 February 1803:

> As to other politics, you know my complete despair of any real *good*; but the mischief of a war may perhaps be prevented, at least I hope so. The new opposition have been as dumb since Christmas as they were loquacious before, only Lord Grenville in the house of lords yesterday seems to have threatened a line of opposition, something more rational than his former one, I mean upon revenue and expenditure etc. In this I suppose he will be joined by Moira, and indeed so he would be by me, if I attended to general politics. Here am I then come to town for nothing; I am told however that something will soon come relative to the evacuation of Malta, in which case the new opposition must come forward or never. Pitt is ill with the gout at Walmer—I believe *really*, but half the world say *sham*. There seems to be a sort of deadness in the house of commons, worse than even in the worst times in the house of lords.[10]

It was hard for Fox to grasp the full scale of French intransigence. He believed that peace was possible, whatever provocations were offered by Bonaparte. He came to regard Addington and his colleagues as fools and knaves, men lacking in conviction and deficient in the resolution and skill necessary to give effect to those principles which they knew to be right. Fox was compelled to charge the British government with the chief responsibility for the renewal of the war. He thought that it was the height of folly to push Bonaparte into war because he was offered no alternative to abject humiliation. Yet Fox had also hoped that if war came it would be possible to believe that the British cause was just. Because of what he considered the government's lethargy in making necessary concessions, he could not accept that the war was justified or the British cause a righteous one. The truth was that he was reluctant to face the genuine clashes of interest which were driving Britain and France towards a renewal of the conflict.

Neither had been defeated in the previous hostilities; neither could concede that there was any overriding necessity to defer to the other's point of view. The French saw Britain as an obstinate foe, seeking to exploit every ruse to thwart the legitimate aspirations of France on the mainland of Europe. The British believed that the French were wedded to a policy of indefinite expansion, trampling on the rights of the other nations of Europe, especially the smaller ones, and seeking to challenge longstanding British interests in the Mediterranean and the near east. There was no way of resolving this clash of ambitions other than armed conflict. Until one side or the other had been unambiguously defeated it was impossible for either to give way to their opponent's demands. After a century of strife the two countries were not disposed to concede anything to the old enemy, whatever the ideologies of the time suggested. The British were worried precisely because the French republic had shown itself so prone to follow policies which were the logical extension of those pursued by Louis XIV, although the theoretical justifications given for these policies were different from those propounded by the Sun King. For all the talk of the rights of man and of natural frontiers the policy of the French from 1792 was all too reminiscent of that which had brought France and Britain into conflict during the reigns of William III and Anne. The British faced the apparently insuperable problem that however superior they were at sea they could not hope to inflict any decisive reverse upon the French until they had effective and powerful allies on the continent. The French were compelled to accept the fact that no matter how often they defeated British and allied armies on land until the naval supremacy of Britain had been destroyed or broken for long enough for a successful invasion of the British Isles to be mounted no decisive outcome of the struggle was likely. To someone brought up, like Fox, in the traditional eighteenth-century style of diplomacy it seemed advisable to accept the deadlock which was inherent in the balance of power, and to turn deadlock into creative negotiation by the intelligent exploitation of skilful diplomacy. But this ignored the new passions injected into the conflict by the French revolution and the whole pattern of events since 1789. It was no longer possible for a régime which claimed to represent the mass of the people and the general will of the French nation (as well as invoking ideals which were held to be of universal validity) to settle for the compromise solutions of traditional diplomacy. Fox never fully appreciated the extent to which the internal upheaval in France had transformed the context in which international relations had to be conducted.

He was similarly obstinate in his fondness for seeing the influence of the crown as the source of all domestic political ills. He clung desperately to the hope that once again an unsuccessful war would transform British politics in a way which would enable him to enter office in much the same way as Rockingham had succeeded North in 1782. He had learned nothing from his experiences during the revolutionary war: he seemed obsessed with the early 1780s whenever he sought to draw on his political experiences to try to discern the murky future. In March 1803 this well-worn and jaded theme ran through one of his letters to Holland:

> If there is war, I have a kind of second sight of very unexpected jumbles in parties here; and I will not say a probability, but a possibility of junctions of a very important nature; if anything of the sort can be of importance in the present state of the constitution. Your supposition that Addington's strength may be owing not wholly to the power of the crown, but to the division of parties, may be plausible to one at a distance, but if you were here you would clearly see the contrary. You ask whether if Pitt had appeared, and for war, he would have succeeded? My answer is, not the smallest chance *against* the ministers: nay, if I and all our friends had joined him, we should have made altogether a very small minority. No, the king's minister, be he who he may, is in peace at least all powerful; whether or not, in case of war, the universal apprehension of mischief from the weakness of these men, if such apprehension was supported by junctions of different parties, could do anything, may be more of a question; but even in that case (a case, by the way, very improbable to happen) I think the crown, in earnest, would beat all. The only chance the other way would be if, in addition to all the rest, the prince of Wales was to declare himself; but whether even that declaration (which considering the present circumstances of the king's age and health would be very important indeed) would be decisive I have great doubts.[11]

To this had the bold dreams of a formed and systematic parliamentary opposition shrunk. Despite the disillusionments of two decades Fox had been forced to fall back on the dubious possibility that George IV would transform the situation on succeeding his father. The confusion of Fox's thinking, his aloofness from the day-to-day business of politics, and his tendency to persuade himself that events were following a predestined course which no exertion on his part could change, all combined to render his leadership purposeless and fitful. He hoped that a decisive shift of public opinion would take place if the resumption of the war should lead to new reversals, and he suspected that if Addington fell political alignments might be drastically altered; yet when Holland suggested that divisions among Addington's opponents were the chief reasons for his survival in office, Fox dismissed his nephew's comment as the wishful thinking of a man who was remote from the circumstances which he was attempting to explain.

But Fox also knew that any realignment of political groupings which might follow the collapse of the Addington ministry would not be that for which he hoped. There was always the chance that the war party would claim that Addington's weakness emphasised the need for a more vigorous prosecution of the war, rather than its abandonment. Nor could Fox forget his distrust of Pitt. He remained reluctant to serve under Pitt, whatever the conditions in which this possibility was discussed, while although Grenville was sound on the catholic question and on the necessity of pruning government expenditure he was even more committed to a stern anti-French line than Pitt was. In other words, a new junction of parties in a fashion similar to that of 1782 was unlikely. But Fox still allowed his memories of the American war and its aftermath to cloud his judgment. He stubbornly saw the events of 1782 as establishing the only possible model for conduct in the event of the government going out of office as a result of general dissatisfaction with its handling of the war. He forgot that, however deep-seated the popular desire for peace was, most men were convinced that the principal responsibility for the resumption of the war lay with the French and that only a fight to the finish would settle matters for the future. This had not been the case during the American war; although opinion had been divided (and support for North's government remained more powerful and more consistent than Fox had ever liked to admit) there had never been virtual unanimity that a fight to the finish was the only way of bringing about an acceptable solution. The British government had not ignored the possibility of a negotiated settlement, even if it usually mishandled its attempts to achieve one. Many of those who had supported the taxation of the colonists wished to come to terms with the Americans, if only to free the country to concentrate on settling old scores with France. Nor had there been any equivalent in the 1790s to Yorktown: an occasion when even the most faithful of government supporters had been compelled to recognise the inescapable fact of a decisive defeat. No matter how frustrating British reverses were, no matter how often her continental allies were broken by the French military machine, there had never been a time in the war against the French republic when defeat was accepted as final. Because so many of his political calculations and hopes depended on such an eventuality there was much in the contemporary view of Fox as a defeatist, placing too gloomy an interpretation on events for reasons of political self-interest.

So, as the Addington ministry shuffled into war, and as Bonaparte cheerfully faced renewed hostilities with absolute confidence in his star and the superlative qualities of the French army, Fox became more oppressed by futility and depression. The opposition to Addington was still divided into Pittites, Grenvillites and Foxites, with Pitt himself behaving more independently than his disciples. Fox knew how difficult a union with his former foes would be, and yet without a better organised opposition Addington would be able to stagger on. There was also the problem of Charles Grey's growing tendency to linger on his Northumbrian estates, preferring the joys of his home to the strains of politics. Because of his wife's recurring pregnancies he was able to plead domestic duty in extenuation of his political laziness. Fox was not the man to carry the burden of routine parliamentary opposition: for this he thought Grey better fitted. So, in addition to his other woes, he frequently pleaded with Grey to come to town in order to help to thwart the war party.

It was one thing to talk persuasively of a realignment of parties; it was another to carry it into effect. The political activists were too scarred by long-standing feuds to find it easy to work together against Addington, particularly since their reasons for being dissatisfied with the king's ministers were startlingly different. Nor was Fox eager to collaborate with Pitt. He preferred to damn him with faint praise, to see signs of failing powers, and to comfort himself for the way in which Pitt had frustrated his own career by delighting in what he regarded as Pitt's lonely sojourn in the political wilderness. But even when he rejoiced at Pitt's isolation he could not rid himself of the fear that Pitt was about to spring some surprise on the unsuspecting public which would transform the political situation out of all recognition. He saw Canning and Grenville carrying into effect some of his own ideas on the organisation of a parliamentary opposition, but he still suspected both of them intensely. Windham he dismissed as an absurdity, and even an old friend like Fitzwilliam could not escape the lash. 'Fitzwilliam, to whom I need not tell you how every motive of affection draws me nearer than to all men else, may possibly, when he has got the war he so longed for, get out of Burke's altitudes into the regions of common sense.'[12]

He wrote at great length to Grey on a number of occasions, telling him of his feelings about possible associates, whether these were old enemies or familiar friends. But the principal drift of this correspondence was to assure Grey that he did not think a coalition likely on anything like the right terms. Fox was becoming increasingly sceptical about the possibility of entering any new cabinet.

Do not imagine I see any prospect, by any junction whatever, of forming such a government as *you*, much less *I*, could be a member of. I see no such prospect, but if there is war apprehensions from the imbecility of the present men will be very great, and may lead to new scenes; and if our reliquiae could be kept together, if it were only Russells and Cavendishes and a few more, with you at the head of them, not only would it give me great satisfaction, but it might be a foundation for better things at some future period. Only consider what changes one event might produce; and in the jumbles what would ensue, how very advantageous to the public it would be that among the various knots and factions that would be formed, there would be one at least attached to the principles of liberty. When I am in this train of thinking, I sometimes feel that there are strong political duties incumbent both upon you and myself. ... As to my great object of keeping something together, I am willing to hope that if we hit upon a proper language and system at the outset of the war, it may be compassed to sufficient degree without any constant attendance either on your part or on mine afterwards.[13]

He yearned to throw the government out, but he shrank from the hard work which this entailed. He blamed Addington and the rest of his cabinet more than Bonaparte for the deterioration in Anglo-French relations, and he despised Addington as a devious bungler, but if turning out Addington meant preparing the way for Pitt or Grenville or Canning and their friends he shrank from encompassing Addington's downfall because the consequences were more than he could contemplate with equanimity. He tried to think of ways in which a pacific policy could be forced on Addington without the opposition whigs being committed to supporting his ministry in general, but his dissatisfaction with Addington's handling of the national finances goaded him into criticising the administration, despite his horror of doing anything to bring the pro-war faction into power. Fox scribbled letter after letter to Grey, speculating on the possibilities which might be opened up to them in various eventualities. He wanted Grey to be more active in leading the opposition, but he himself shrank from providing effective leadership. If he chose to give priority to the preservation of peace he would be forced to give some general measure of support to Addington's administration, otherwise, because of Addington's weakness, a more bellicose note would be struck in British foreign policy. Fox was distressed by the knowledge

that Addington lacked the temperament and the convictions to make him
a strong and powerful advocate of a peaceful policy. At any moment,
so it seemed to Fox, Addington would capitulate to those who were urging him to be more intransigent in his dealings with the French. The
consequence of all this was that the whig opposition had no real influence in the debates leading up to the resumption of the war. They lacked
cogency in policy and decisiveness in leadership. Far from taking up a
credible political stance Fox merely yearned for peace, striving desperately to persuade himself that it was possible to preserve it without trans-
lating his feelings into a practicable political approach to the problems
posed by Bonaparte's intransigence and Addington's weakness. Another
letter to Grey, written in March 1803, further reveals the confusions
which rendered Fox politically impotent at this period:

> What I meant was not a support of Addington's ministry (which must
> depend on further circumstances) but a support of Addington's *ac-
> commodation* with France—if he should make one; and the case, I
> suppose, in which such support would, in my judgment, be so very
> becoming to us, and in some degree useful to the public, is that
> of a smart opposition being made, not to him in *general*, but to the
> particular *convention* or *act* by which these impending discussions
> shall be terminated, and in consequence of which the armament shall
> cease. You think this would not be the plan of the Grenvilles ... and if
> it is not I agree with all you say. Whether or not it will be their mode
> of attack I know not.... But probably their determination will be
> influenced by events not yet known, and at any rate it is not in our
> power to direct it. All this is in the case of peace.... It is material that
> the well-wishers to peace in the public at large should have some
> authority beyond that of the ministers to support and confirm them
> in their opinions. In the event, too, of future opposition, it is surely
> of importance that a great body of those who form it should have the
> reputation of being friends to peace.... If one is to attend, it would
> certainly be a great relief to one's mind to allow oneself to abuse
> Addington's pompous nonsense as it deserves.... As to union of parties
> in case of war it is very difficult indeed; but, if decidedly called for, not
> perhaps altogether impossible. In that case, however, I should feel
> myself obliged to intreat your consideration of what you seem to have
> determined in regard to yourself. I have not the slightest doubt ...
> of the sincerity of your determination; only consider that the circum-
> stances of this world are so variable, that an irrevocable resolution
> is almost a synonymous term for a foolish one. I have a strong opinion

that, if there is war, you are the only, literally the only, man capable of conducting it. I lay aside all personal prejudices—but I think it completely demonstrated that Pitt, with all his great talents, is wholly unfit for it—indeed he seems so conscious of it himself, that he leaves the whole management, in such cases, to others. Lord Melville, who, by the way, is now talked of, besides being now old, seems to be the worst hand that ever was employed. Lord Grenville is an able man, but not, I think, for such a purpose; and Lauderdale, with all his incredible activity, would be less fit for such a task than any other. . . . You will see we shall go to war, and be in the wrong in the opinion of all Europe.[14]

Fox's pessimism deepened as the drift to war continued. He preferred that the whole of Europe should support France, rather than Britain risking a war with the solitary support of Austria. It would be virtually impossible effectively to aid Austria alone, and in addition to the immense cost he feared that the Austrians would be unreliable allies. Although it was generally believed that a resumption of hostilities would bring back Pitt as first minister, Fox was sceptical that this would be the outcome of a declaration of war. But the evil of war was so great that he was almost indifferent to what he regarded as the lesser evil of Pitt's return to office. There was much speculation about a union of all men of talent, whatever their previous disagreements, in order to depose Addington and set up a powerful ministry on a really broad basis, but Fox was still hesitant about becoming involved in negotiations with Pitt. Old feuds and old hatreds died hard. He could never lose the suspicion that Pitt would merely deceive the whigs, abandoning them when he had established his own grip on power. Fox warned Grey of the need for caution. 'I do not think you will suspect me of being partial to the Doctor', he wrote on 16 April 1803, 'but if we should have anything like the power of turning the scale, it is surely worth thinking of, whether we should, either by action or inaction, be instrumental in restoring Pitt and the old ministry.'[15]

Fox admitted that nothing could be more favourable to Addington than the continued disunity of his critics. He had now come round to perceiving the sense underlying Holland's earlier comments on the reasons for Addington's continuation in office. But whereas at one time the prospect of a change of ministry, regardless of its immediate consequences, would have had him on tiptoe for any chance of seizing a means of returning to power, he was now torn by a fondness for the lazy domestic life, which had been his for so long, an obstinate aversion to any alliance with Pitt, and a sentimental desire to install some of his friends in office whatever happened to himself. In some moods he longed for the status of an elder statesman, seeking respect and influence rather than power and responsibility; in others he fell back on his antipathy to Pitt and the king, feeling that he would be foolish to accept a post in any administration committed to the French war and dominated by men with whom he had little in common. There were times when he hoped that if no alternative to the Addington ministry could be created, the war would be feebly prosecuted, with a greater chance of a change of ministry when it came being a concession to the advocates of a negotiated peace.

Not even the tactless publication of Sebastiani's report convinced Fox that there was any foundation to fears of French aggression. He regarded Sebastiani's report as impertinent and its publication as a mistake, but he could not regard it as a serious reason for going to war. He did not think that anything new had been revealed with respect to Bonaparte's interest in Egypt, and he was reluctant to believe that Bonaparte had treated Lord Whitworth, the British ambassador in Paris, with the insolent vulgarity which had so offended British sensibilities. But it was no surprise to Fox when the war was resumed in May 1803.

His opinion of Addington and his colleagues was even lower than previously. He believed them incapable of making peace and incapable of waging war. He resolved to face the prospects of a French invasion coolly. He did not think that the French would really attempt an invasion of England, but he recognised that the way in which the invasion had been spoken of in France made any decision not to attempt it an admission of failure. Could Bonaparte afford to take this risk? Fox could not see the French evading the British fleet with a sufficient armament for a successful invasion. But if the French did succeed in real strength he admitted that the situation would then become more gloomy. With feeble military leadership and a general lack of preparedness—a deficiency which various defence schemes had succeeded only in emphasising all the more—it was difficult to see how the French could be foiled, if they either defeated or evaded the royal navy. But Fox could not concede that the French would gain a decisive supremacy at sea.

The summer of 1803 was dogged by invasion scares. New rumours of a change of government were also rife, and Fox was constantly trying to sort out his own ideas and sound out opinion among his friends. The prince of Wales was toying with the idea of promoting a new opposition, based on a union of Spencer, Windham and the Grenvilles, on the one hand, and Fox and his friends, on the other. The prince was hostile to Pitt, and the attraction of replacing Addington with a stronger ministry, in which Pitt had no place, was tempting. Fox was cautious. He was now too weary and too experienced to rise gleefully to the first suggestion of a new fusion of opposition groups. He prevailed upon the prince to accept the need for care and restraint. It was impossible to do very much at once. The only thing that made sense was to wait upon events, while refraining from saying or doing anything that would make junctions of the sort which the prince desired more impracticable or more unlikely than they already were. The ministers were becoming more universally despised every day, but though there was talk of a rising groundswell calling for Pitt's return Fox was sceptical that this was the case. Pitt was not at his best. Although he had refused to play any energetic or systematic part in opposition to Addington, despite the pleas of his friends, his speeches in the commons had not been particularly impressive if they were meant as bids for non-party support. The confusion that characterised politics in the first months of the Napoleonic war was made all the more complicated by the behaviour of Sheridan, who took it into his head to court Addington and other ministers, possibly with the notion that a negotiation with the ministry was a surer path to office than any far-fetched talk of a renovated opposition. If Addington was under pressure he would be only too pleased to broaden his ministry in order to stave off trouble. But since the prince of Wales was averse to the ministers of the day it was not easy for the opposition whigs to do business with them.

Yet the feebleness of Addington's government meant that speculation about its future continued throughout the summer and into the autumn. Fox was very much on the side of waiting upon events. He had seen many realignments in his time and he was conscious of the disastrous consequences of any ill-judged or premature switching of allegiances. On 19 October he told Grey of his misgivings in a long and discursive letter.

The prince's doing nothing is, in some views, of great consequence; for, whatever opinion may be generally entertained of his steadiness, still his name, and interference, would have great effect in smoothing difficulties and facilitating junctions. An apparent reversionary prospect goes a good way with many, and, most of all, with that numerous class of persons who are never easy without something that is like royal favour. Whether, without such a *smoother*, the difficulties, which you are as well aware of as I, can be got over, is very doubtful: but parliament meets the 22nd of next month, and something must be determined. . . . You seem to state four plans to choose out of. 1st. Support of ministers—which, however, you term impossible. For you and me I am sure it is—because to hold out to the country that *they* have deserved well of it, or can administer it well, would be a base falsehood on our part. 2nd. To attack present and past conjointly. The *best* thing that can be said of this mode is, that it would be throwing away our time ineffectually, and sacrificing our cause for nothing; but, in reality, it would be worse, as such a conduct would in good measure tend to strengthen the court. 3rd. To act in a manner that may lead to the forming of a party against the *court*, composed of the old and new opposition. 4th. To do nothing.[16]

Fox thought that the real choice lay between the two last propositions, but he was inclined to cast the responsibility for deciding which of the two plans should be followed on to Grey. His own inclination was to do nothing. Life would be much pleasanter if that were the case, but he was conscious of falling into the temptation of yielding to private ease rather than performing his public duties, freely admitting to Grey that it was best to be on one's guard lest one should take the easy way out. The difficulty about uniting the old and new oppositions against the court was that it would be virtually impossible to resolve the problem presented by Pitt. In Fox's view there was little chance of Pitt committing himself to a systematic parliamentary opposition. Pitt would have to unsay much to be convincing in such a guise. Furthermore, Fox had something more in mind than building up a united opposition against the ministry of the day. By an opposition against the court he meant its leaders would have to pledge themselves to act consistently and in concert, whether in office or in opposition, and that they would have to regard their primary loyalty as being owed to the head of the ministry and to each other, and not the crown, should they be successful in driving Addington out. A greater measure of collective responsibility would have to be practised within the cabinet, and there was to be no deferring to the royal will, as Fox believed had happened too frequently during Pitt's long ministry. If a new style coalition came into office it would do so, not because of the king's choice, but because of the dominant preferences in the house of commons. Without these safeguards—and however platitudinous they seem today they represented a remarkable set of constitutional innovations in Fox's time—there was no prospect of replacing the ministers, representative in Fox's view of a discredited pattern of constitutionalism, with a new set of men committed not only to seeking peace with France and some moderate measure of reform at home, but also to accepting new conventions in the way in which they worked together in government. Such an arrangement would make sense of the years spent in opposition since the fall of the

Fox-North coalition, and Fox could claim that this would prove a final justification of the constitutional ideas which he had been advocating for so many years. The problem was that these ideas were not fully understood even within the Foxite group itself. Nor were all of Fox's supporters parliamentary reformers. The party of peace was riddled with as many contradictions as the party of patriotism.

Fox began to look with some confidence towards Grenville and Windham. They were unpopular, and some of the opposition whigs found it hard to forgive them for old squabbles, but Fox believed that they were men of their word, however stiff and obstinate they might be. They were the only members of the opposition to Addington with whom he would be able to collaborate. If they once acted together he believed that Grenville would honour his obligations. For Canning and the other Pittites Fox harboured only suspicion and distrust.

By December Fox believed that Pitt was bitterly opposed to Addington and the administration. It was said that in private conversation with his friends Pitt had denounced the government vehemently. Fox began to think that at last Pitt was appreciating some of the inconsistencies of his situation. But although Pitt was out of favour with George III Fox thought that he still hankered for some evidence of royal approval. Fox was uncertain and confused. He thought one thing one day and something quite different the next. While feeling himself still committed, for example, to the catholic cause he yet recognised the impossibility of achieving anything in the field of catholic relief. He confessed to Grey that he did not know what to do.

January saw renewed scurries and negotiations. With every week Addington's stock fell, but it was impossible to agree on the sort of ministry which was to take his place. Grenville, Spencer, Windham, Carlisle, and Fitzwilliam were all eager for a united opposition, on a comprehensive basis, to be set up, and by now Fox was convinced of the sincerity of those advocating such a step. But Pitt remained the subject of contention and perplexity. He explained to Grenville his objections to belonging to a formed opposition, and in consequence all political connexions between Pitt and Grenville were severed. It was agreed, therefore, that no consideration was to be taken of Pitt in negotiations with other interested parties, except that if a change of ministry took place Pitt might be approached on an individual basis. Fox suspected that Pitt was standing aloof from any schemes to bring down Addington to make himself the most acceptable person to succeed him. Here the rift between Pitt and Fox became apparent again. It went back to the early 1780s and it represented the gulf which separated Fox and his ideas of concerted opposition and party government from Pitt with his more conventional assumptions about the dangers of party and the necessity for ministers to represent the national, not a party, interest. On 27 January 1804 Fox wrote to his old friend Fitzpatrick, telling him of the approach which had been made to Grenville, and of the plan to attack the government's proposals relating to the Volunteers. He also commented on Pitt's refusal to join the formed opposition. Fox was eager to press ahead, despite the complications caused by Pitt's aloofness: 'Pitt may return to power, and after having proposed terms in vain to some of the opposition, may put himself at the head of the present administration, or one like it, and this is admitted to be an objection to the plan.'[17] Fox did not feel as strongly as Thomas Grenville did on this matter, but he admitted that many others would share Grenville's anxieties.

It was, therefore, inevitable that what Fox called 'sliding' into a junction of parties was adopted, despite the disadvantages of allowing many men to think of Pitt as playing a more decisive role in the attack on Addington than was the case. Fox appreciated the skill with which his old adversary was keeping all his options open, but as criticism of Addington mounted in the house of commons, he consoled himself with the thought that the majority of MPs would soon be of the opposition's way of thinking and that this made sophisticated speculations about Pitt irrelevant to the main task facing the whigs. Circumstances were dragging Pitt the opposition's way, too, despite the fact that he supported the critics of the ministry in some things but not in others. Like Fox he did not always know his own mind. As Fox put it to Lauderdale, 'his temper makes him more and more in opposition, whatever his intentions may be'. There was the perennial doubt as to whether or not Pitt would play fair, but Fox was beginning to think that Pitt's interests were synonymous with those of the opposition and that this would settle the issue. The Grenvilles were as steady and honourable as it was possible to be; every time Fox met Lord Grenville the more he was impressed by him. His integrity was unquestionable and Fox was glad to note that Grenville was 'a very direct man'.

By the spring of 1804 Fox's growing confidence in his new allies made him willing, if necessary, to serve with Pitt in a broadly-based ministry, although he rejected the notion of serving under him. He remained sceptical about coming to any arrangement with Pitt, for Pitt was insisting that he should not be treated on a footing of equality with other contenders for office. As it happened, whatever Pitt's hesitations about systematic opposition, he pressed Fox's claim to a place in the government after Addington's fall, only to be thwarted by George III's obstinacy. Cold and reserved though Pitt was he was not as indifferent to the calls of honour as Fox imagined. Fox never grasped the depth of Pitt's commitments to attitudes which he himself thought outmoded. He forgot the intensity of Pitt's filial piety and the strength of his devotion to what he considered were his father's political ideals.

Fox was approached by Lord Grenville about catholic emancipation and the likelihood of forming a government without running foul of the divisions of opinion which still divided the various opposition factions on the subject of catholic relief. Fox assured Grenville that if a ministry was formed on the basis of giving a substantial measure of relief to catholics, and admitting them to their full share in the government of the country, he thought some consideration ought to be given to the king's prejudices, at least to the extent of contemplating some delay, particularly when it was remembered that the king was in poor health (he had another bout of illness in 1804). Fox wanted to carry a measure of catholic relief, but he saw that it would be foolish to jeopardise the chances of forming an other-wise united ministry by insisting too rigidly on immediate catholic emanci-pation. Like most other politicians Fox was now convinced that George III did not have long to live. It seemed sensible to get into office, assuming that this was possible once Addington was defeated, agree on a measure of relief, but to respect the king's obstinacy for as long as he lived, with the resolve of putting the reform into effect whenever the king died, or, pos-sibly, whenever his illness incapacitated him to the extent that a regency was established. Fox was critical of Pitt in 1801 over the catholic issue, and he never gave a formal promise never to raise the issue during George III's lifetime, but his attitude in 1804, and later when he came into office on the death of Pitt, amounted to a decision not to provoke the king's wrath by prematurely raising the matter of catholic relief. He was, never-theless, uneasy on the subject, as his letter of 20 April 1804 to Grenville makes clear:

What I said, I meant to say in perfect confidence, and not to go further than us two. But upon recollection I fear you must have understood that it might be repeated to Mr Pitt. What I should wish to have said to him is, that the inclination of my mind is to think catholic emancipa-tion absolutely necessary; but that I am willing to consider of the pos-sibility of temporising, whenever by a *full* knowledge of *all* the circumstances with which such temporising is proposed to be accom-panied, I shall be enabled to give that question a fair consideration. The concomitant circumstances must indeed be very favourable to induce me to think even delay admissible in this business. You will observe that there is nothing in this answer inconsistent with what I said to you in confidence, but it is something different, and the difference appears to me to be not immaterial.[18]

Fox was prepared to admit that even during a regency circumstances might justify some delay; if, for example, the regent were to think that a discussion of catholic relief would retard his father's recovery; this would be enough to justify delay in the minds of all reasonable men. But Fox wondered whether it would be right, in current circumstances, for Grenville to yield the very point on which he had resigned three years earlier. This ran the risk of making it appear that he had cravenly deferred to the king's prejudices, possibly for the most dubious reasons. He might be suspected of making a crude bargain for personal advancement. By entering the ministry it might transpire that Grenville had made it more difficult for himself to resist the king's will on the issue at a later stage with any chance of success. Fox thought that he was in a different position; he had not resigned on the catholic issue, and it would not be possible for men to accuse him of using the catholic question as one of the pawns in the political game. But he could see that there were some arguments against taking office at all, unless the catholic question was settled unequivocally.

> Now, on the other side, if you were to stand out on the emancipation, in which of course I should join you, and if Mr Pitt, without any of us, should form an administration, giving up the point, is it not evident that you would stand upon the highest ground possible? that you would gain much in character with all the men of right and honourable feelings, and all this, considering the state of the king's health and mind, by a very small sacrifice? If Pitt would think the same it would be best of all, but of that I have no hope; and if I had, I have no degree of intercourse with him which would justify my speaking to him as I do to you.[19]

Possibly Fox was considering whether the chances of George III surviving much longer were minimal anyway, and that therefore, with the support of the prince of Wales to count on, there was no need to make any concessions on the catholic issue. It might be one way of isolating Pitt, for if a really comprehensive ministry were formed, it would stay in office even if George III died, while a weak Pitt ministry would soon founder if George IV ascended the throne within a short space of time, Fox and his friends being brought in by the normal workings of the reversionary interest, and free from the embarrassments of having had to work with Pitt or of having given undertakings on the emancipation issue to George III. Perhaps calculations of this type were going through Fox's mind. It was strange that after conceding the expediency of some delay on the catholic issue that he should hedge this concession round with more qualifications within twenty-four hours. At the same time, Fox had not withdrawn his former undertaking. A tacit concession was agreeable to him; what he wished to avoid was a formal promise of the sort which George III had dragged out of an unhappy Pitt. But fundamental to Fox's thinking was his distrust of Pitt, the fear that just as he had been outwitted in 1784 so he might be outwitted in 1804.

On 29 April 1804 Addington resigned. His majority in the commons had fallen to 52, with both Pitt and Fox voting against the government on a motion which Fox had proposed criticising the government's defence policy. George III sent for Pitt and a protracted struggle now took place over the question of Fox's place in the new administration. There is no doubt that Pitt wished to form a government with the broadest possible support in the house of commons. He wanted Fox as foreign secretary, Grenville as lord president, Fitzwilliam as home secretary and Grey as secretary at war. But George III was adamant in turning his face against Fox. He recalled the old trials and tribulations of the prince of Wales' youth and the far-off days of the American war, but he also remembered Fox's ill-judged toast to our sovereign the people and the necessity to strike his name off the list of privy councillors. The king expressed his astonishment that Pitt should think it proper even to put forward Fox for consideration. Furthermore, the king made it clear to Pitt that the catholic question was to remain closed. It was one thing to bring the respectable friends of catholic belief into the ministry, providing they respected their sovereign's wishes, but it was another to impose Fox upon the king. Pitt hoped that despite George III's veto on Fox his friends would serve and that the Grenvilles would come into the administration. Fox urged his friends to take office without him; the king's hatred was nothing new, but it was insurmountable and perhaps he could render more help outside the ministry rather than in it. Possibly Fox was in some ways reluctant to take up the burdens of office after so many years; possibly he was relieved at having an excuse which allowed him to avoid serving under Pitt, without shouldering the obloquy of having wilfully jeopardised the chances of a patriotic ministry being set up. Nor could he forget that there was still the catholic issue lurking in the background, or that if after entering the ministry the Grenvilles and other opposition whigs found Pitt an unsatisfactory chief there would be political advantages if he had remained independent of any link with the administration.

There were, therefore, powerful personal and political reasons for acquiescing in the king's decision. As an individual, giving support to a government containing many of his closest friends, Fox could achieve much. Perhaps he would be able to influence Pitt towards the acceptance of a more collective and less personal style in government. But it was not to be. Grey and Grenville and all of Fox's friends refused to be drawn into an administration without Fox; they declined Pitt's invitation, just as they rejected Fox's advice. There was still sufficient distrust of Pitt among them to make it hard for them to join him without Fox as a safeguard and a companion. It was to Fox that they looked for inspiration, if not for day-to-day leadership. Grenville tried to make a virtue out of necessity, condemning a government formed on 'a principle of exclusion'. Pitt was compelled to soldier on with his own friends and various members of the Addington administration, including, for a while, the Doctor himself. Pitt regretted that he had not been able to carry Fox into the government, but he could not respect what he regarded as Grenville's mulish obstinacy and selfish lack of cooperation: 'I will teach that proud man, that in the service, and with the confidence of the king, I can do without him, though I think my health such that it may cost me my life.' He braced himself to the tasks ahead, but he knew how weak his ministry was and how exposed it would be to attack.

For the whole of its brief life Pitt's second ministry was bedevilled by internal weaknesses. The frustrations of the war were paralleled by political confusions. Pitt remained disposed towards bringing Fox into his administration; he knew that this was the best means of substantially strengthening his government, especially after the resignation of Addington in July 1805. But he could not move the king. George III suggested sending for members of the opposition without Fox; Pitt replied that it would be wrong for them to listen to such proposals and that even if they did he regarded their acceptance as useless without the presence of Fox. Pitt argued the case for some time. He told the king that he thought Fox's speech in the commons of 20 June 'a most noble one', stating that 'the man who could make it was the fittest to be applied to for advice'. The king admitted that Addington had acted like a fool (George III never approved of those who behaved like deserters), but he was convinced that Fox himself had a personal aversion to him, and that they would never be able to cooperate. The king used delaying tactics, advising Pitt to patch up the ministry as well as he could for the present. But it is a striking sign of the potential strength of the monarch in the early nineteenth century that George III's distaste for Fox should be so effective in excluding him from office, even when Pitt was convinced of the necessity and the wisdom of bringing Fox in.

Fox was sceptical about rumours that Pitt had gained the king's consent to a broadened ministry without any stipulated exclusions. He was resigned to the king's hostility and he continued to doubt Pitt's genuineness. He thought that Pitt was capable of winning a reputation for magnanimity by pretending to negotiate, while remaining obdurate and essentially ill-disposed all along. It was commonly said that Pitt wished to bring six members of the opposition into his cabinet: Grenville, Spencer, Windham, Moira, Grey and Fox. But Fox could not see how this was to be reconciled with either the prejudices of the king, or Pitt's own determination to remain at the treasury, and to retain Hawkesbury and Castlereagh as secretaries of state. The opposition were especially antagonistic towards Castlereagh and it was widely known that his appointment was especially dear to Pitt. Fox thought that Pitt would lose credit by insisting on Castlereagh staying on, as well as by jeopardising any chance of a national ministry by clinging to his own situation. But Fox was frequently baffled by the reports which his friends avidly passed on to him. On 12 July 1805 he told Lauderdale of his anxieties about the political future:

Concerning the state of politics here, accounts differ so from day to day that it is quite useless to write about them.... I *now* think ... that Pitt will not make any proposal to opposition, but, on the other hand, I have good reason to think he mentioned to the king his intention of making what *he* (Pitt) thought a very ample one, and he obtained the king's consent. What to make of this I cannot tell. I know that nothing ought to be consented to unless he will consider the present ministry as annihilated in all its parts and consult about forming a new one. He will not, I think, bring his mind to this, and yet his weakness since the defection of the Doctor is extreme; however that is his affair. The only thing that could hurt us would be an apparently fair offer on his part, when, though we might be justified in refusing, we might not be able to make the public see it in the same light. On the other hand, I think I see every disposition in the Addingtonians to join heartily against him, and if they have as good a cause as they pretend, they will be pretty strong. The house of commons is evidently divided into four parties, nearly upon a loose calculation, as follows:

Supporters of the chancellor of the exchequer for the time being	180
Opposition	150
Pitt	60
Addington	60
	450

There are, besides, several members who vote whimsically or ... from fear of constituents ... and many ... who never or very seldom attend. ... What is clearest of all is, that Pitt is very low and does not seem to have any notion of what plan he can follow to raise himself.[20]

As Pitt's second ministry struggled on, buffeted by the shocks of Napoleonic victories abroad, and political desertions at home, Fox came to be more attracted to the formation of a coalition ministry, not as the agent by which a joint government could be formed with Pitt, but as the means by which Pitt was to be cast out of office. It would be 1783 in reverse. Fox's distrust of Pitt was so deeply embedded in his nature that nothing could move him to anything other than rejoicing at the minister's discomfiture.

The idea of a comprehensive ministry had been inspired by the thought of a ministry of all the talents to wage the war more effectively. With the defeats and disappointments afflicting the third coalition against France, Fox, ever mindful of the example of the American war, began to feel that at last the chance of forming a ministry to negotiate a peace was a real probability. He believed that Pitt was in a weaker state than North had been on the eve of Yorktown, and as his own warnings about the dangers of relying on the Austrians and Russians to fight the land battles against Napoleon came to be borne out as allied indolence and lethargy were savagely vanquished by Napoleonic brilliance, he turned his thoughts more and more to the ministry which would succeed Pitt, spurning any understanding with him as futile and irrelevant. Suddenly the prospect seemed full of promise. A long and certain tenure of political power, and the comforting realisation of hopes which had been jealously harboured and regularly frustrated for fifteen years and more, seemed on the brink of becoming part of the hard fact of politics. His spirits were high. He tried to persuade Grey to leave his Northumbrian home for the rigours of political campaigning in London. The opposition was stronger than it had been at any time since the desertion of Portland and Fitzwilliam and their friends in 1794. Fox became alert to every piece of news. His lethargy and indifference to negotiation were cast aside, and he prepared himself for the final battle against Pitt.

For Pitt the outlook was dismal. Everything was conspiring against him. Although his invasion schemes had been thwarted Napoleon turned against the Austrians in impatient disgust with his admirals' inability to carry his grandiose strategy into effect. He marched east in the hope of smashing the Austrians before the Russians could make their presence felt. There was little to brighten the military situation. Even Nelson had been exhausting his energies in a series of wild-goose chases, desperately trying to locate the French fleet once it had escaped from the close blockade. In October Napoleon struck the Austrians with a speed which surprised them completely. Outmanoeuvred, Mack surrendered at Ulm, and although October also saw the victory of Trafalgar public spirits were as depressed by Nelson's death as they were uplifted by his greatest triumph. The full significance of the battle was not at first appreciated. It did more than save England from invasion, for that danger had already receded. It was a great demonstration of a strategy which was as aggressive in conception as Nelson's new tactics. Pitt had hoped to use sea power to bring aid to his allies, and to shift the decisive sphere of operations to the Mediterranean where British naval power would more effectively help Austria and Russia. But hardly had the good news of Trafalgar arrived when the catastrophe of Austerlitz wrecked the third coalition. Even Pitt's fortitude quailed under the stresses of the hour. His friends talked of the Austerlitz look and his frail health visibly broke. Some ministers thought it only a matter of time before Pitt would be driven either to make a more generous offer to the opposition or to retire from the position of first minister.

Fox had mixed feelings on hearing of Trafalgar. He told Holland that it was 'a great event' and that 'by its solid as well as brilliant advantages, far more than compensates for the temporary succour which it will certainly afford to Pitt in his distress'. He was very sorry for 'poor Nelson'. Although he believed that his conduct at Naples had been atrocious he thought that at bottom he was a good man: 'it is hard he should not enjoy (and no man would have enjoyed it more) the popularity and glory of this last business'.[21] As for Ulm Fox blamed Pitt for the débâcle, for he held him responsible for urging the Austrians to attack before they were ready, and without waiting for the Russian armies. Austerlitz confirmed Fox's conviction that nothing could be done about Napoleon's command of the continent and that an attempt would have to be made to come to terms with him.

The news of Pitt's illness led to further political speculation. Fox had heard that he was unwell but only on 17 December did he learn that anything serious was apprehended. Reports were circulating that Pitt was gravely ill with gout in the stomach. Fox was reluctant to credit these rumours, though he admitted that Pitt had had stomach disorders before. If Pitt died Fox thought that another Addington ministry was the most likely outcome, 'peace of Amiens and all'.

During Pitt's last illness there were further rumours that he had resigned, and these Fox was thoroughly sceptical about. He was so suspicious of anything emanating from Pitt that he wanted to be sure of the factual basis of any report before believing it. He thought Pitt capable of stooping to any trick to deceive his opponents and retain office. Even if he were dying his chief thought would be to keep his place until the end. Fox warned his friends not to react too quickly to any proposal that they join the government or form an administration. He urged Holland to do all in his power to prevent their friends from coming in until they were sure of being 'quite and entirely masters'. Taking anything short of complete power would be 'worse than anything that has yet happened'.

Yet when the news of Pitt's death on 23 January 1806 came Fox was deeply upset. Possibly because he had been unconvinced of the seriousness of Pitt's illness the news distressed him all the more. Though he rejoiced at the prospect of a new government and the hope of peace he deplored the fact that death, rather than political defeat, had removed Pitt. It was, Fox confessed, a poor way of getting rid of his enemy. Something distinctive had vanished from the political scene. Fox thought that the debates in the commons would never be the same again, and he talked wistfully of pairing off with Pitt. What he had in mind was retirement, but, as one contemporary remarked, he was soon to pair off with Pitt in a final and ultimate sense.

In the commons he preferred his public duty to the indulgence of private emotion or the expression of unctuous sentiment. He could not agree with a motion calling for the public funeral of William Pitt, 'that excellent statesman'. Fox was ill at ease. He strove to avoid the accusation that he was lacking in magnanimity, that he was taking a cheap political advantage of the dead, and that he was seeking to exploit a national tragedy for narrow political purposes. Many men thought that he was pursuing a vendetta to the grave and beyond it. But Fox felt that the wording of the motion was wrong and inappropriate. To agree to it would make his conduct throughout the war years and during his long rivalry with Pitt seem like that of a hypocrite. If he honestly thought Pitt an excellent statesman why had he opposed him for so many years? He could not, even in the interests of public propriety or of respect for his dead opponent, pay an insincere tribute or allow his name to be associated with a motion which itself smacked too much of partisanship. Fox's situation was unenviable. Whatever he did, he laid himself open to abuse. Either he would be accused of selfish vindictiveness or he would be denounced as a consummate hypocrite. His embarrassment led to his making a speech which all too clearly exposed his confused and uncertain feelings. He conceded that Pitt had many fine qualities; he cited his disinterestedness and his refusal to exploit his public situation for private profit. But he could not consider

Pitt an excellent statesman when he recalled the parlous state in which the country found itself and which was the consequence of the policies which Pitt had endorsed and followed. Nor was there any real parallel with the case of Pitt's father. During his great ministry Chatham had reduced the power of our greatest enemy to its lowest ebb. The same could not be said of his son's administration, despite his skill in managing the nation's finances. Indeed, Fox went so far as to claim that Pitt was responsible for the persistence of a sinister system of government which had been marked throughout the whole of the reign of George III:

> I always thought, and do still think, than an unfortunate system of government has pervaded the whole of the present reign; and I firmly believe that system to have been the cause of all the disasters and disappointments which the country has experienced, almost uniformly throughout the whole course of it. Being of this opinion, how can I conscientiously say that he who followed this system was 'an excellent statesman'? ... Thinking as I do of the disastrous effect of that system, which I before stated to have prevailed throughout the present reign, I cannot but accuse the late minister of having, I will not say criminally, for the expression might sound, in some ears, too harsh, but, most unfortunately, lent his brilliant talents and commanding eloquence to the support of it. In having done so, and with the knowledge he must have had of it, I esteem him the more culpable, as without that splendour of mental endowment, which enabled him to throw a veil over the hideous deformity of the system alluded to, I am fully persuaded that it could not have resisted the attacks made upon it, and consequently could not have existed, and spread its baneful influence, half so long.[22]

There was a certain inevitability about the speech. Its language and its sentiment echoed old feuds and remote quarrels. It called to mind the bitter wrangles of the American war, and all the harsh accusations which the Rockinghamites had cast at George III and North. Fox had begun his speech by referring to party. He claimed that on such an occasion he was above party feelings, and that if he wished to gratify either private ambition or party interests he would have found it to his advantage to speak for the motion; but he could not resist defending party, describing it as the best mode of 'effectually carrying into execution those measures which ... are the best calculated to promote the public prosperity and happiness'. When a man was convinced that his opinion, if acted upon, would be of benefit to the country, and that the only chance of having them acted upon was to act in connexion with a party, then party was justified as being of service to the public.

Fox had not changed his ideas since the early 1780s. Just as he had defended a more collective idea of the cabinet, a formed opposition, and the efficacy of party whether in government or out of it, Pitt had been the spokesman for the more traditional point of view, which emphasised that ministers were the servants of the crown, that their first loyalty was owed to the king, and that it was wrong for any group of men to impose either themselves or their policies upon the king. It was fitting that in the last speech which he made in direct criticism of his old adversary Fox should refer, not only to the conduct of the war against France, but also to older and in some ways more fundamental controversies. Possibly Fox could have been more tactful in the manner in which he refrained from supporting the official resolution; possibly his charges that the same system which had governed the country in the years of North still governed it were doubly unfortunate, for they were not only factually inaccurate, they also antagonised independent opinion, to which Pitt had always been more sensitive than Fox. For the historian, if not for his contemporaries, there is at least a satisfying consistency in Fox's obdurate and misleading assertion that Pitt had been as much a tool of the king as North. The roots of their hostility went back to the years following the Rockingham ministry. Even the controversy over the French revolution and the war owed much of its intensity to remembered bitterness and distrust going back to those years when Pitt had so deftly and so ruthlessly outgeneralled Fox in their scramble for power. At the end, when the commons were debating the most seemly means of honouring Pitt's corpse, Fox recurred, with unalloyed passion to their old differences over the nature of the constitution and the conventions by which it was given life. Fox cannot be blamed for refusing to call Pitt 'an excellent statesman'; but the specific charges which he used to justify his refusal confirmed the way in which over a period of twenty years his constitutional ideas, and his understanding of the years dominated by the struggle with George III over the American colonies and the influence of the crown, had changed not at all. Fox has long had a reputation for magnanimity, for a unique generosity of spirit, with historians; but there was little in his speech concerning Pitt's public funeral to qualify him for such a reputation. Although it was easy to understand the unique pressures which were on him at the time, and the difficulty with which he faced trying to convey his hesitations to a largely unsympathetic audience, he could have explained himself with less embarrassment had he not raised issues of such long-standing bitterness and ill-understood complexity.

Once Pitt was dead his government could not continue. Despite his private feelings George III was compelled to accept the Foxites and Gren-villites as the only alternative to political chaos. When Grenville told the king that he must consult Fox on receiving an invitation to form a ministry George III replied that he had thought that this must be the case, and that he had meant it to be so when asking Grenville to head the new administration. Towards Fox himself the king was remarkably affable, despite their long enmity and the fact that only two years earlier the king had adamantly refused to have Fox as foreign secretary. But their first meeting under the new arrangements was not without awkwardness. The king broke the ice by saying that he had little thought that he and Fox would ever meet again under such circumstances, but that he had no desire to look back to old grievances, and that he would never remind Fox of them. Fox replied that he hoped that his deeds, not merely his words, would commend him to his majesty. It would be false to suggest that George III suddenly lost his suspicion of Fox, but he acknowledged that Fox always treated him 'frankly and yet respectfully, as it became a sub-ject to behave'. His manner, the king afterwards recalled, 'contrasted remarkably with that of another of the whig ministers, who, when he came into office walked up to me in the way I should have expected from Bonaparte after the battle of Austerlitz'.[23] Years later Lord John Russell was told by the duchess of Gloucester, the king's daughter, that her father had deeply regretted Fox's death, lamenting that the country could not afford to lose such a man, and confessing sadly, 'I never thought I should have regretted the death of Mr Fox as much as I do'. There may be some uncertainty about the depth of feeling underlying an old man's confiden-ces, and possibly Hobhouse was exaggerating when he told Grey that during the ministry of all the talents George III had liked Fox and no one else; but the king had a tendency to come round to ministers who behaved well in office, and he had nothing to complain of in Fox's conduct. On the catholic question Fox behaved with appropriate restraint, and as foreign secretary Fox disciplined himself as he had done years before. The king thought that Fox's efforts for peace were bound to be thwarted by the arrogance and obstinacy of Napoleon, but he did not find anything per-sonally offensive in Fox's conduct of negotiations. George III had a high regard for the proprieties of public life, and he therefore found it possible to thaw, if not to warm, to his old opponent.

Yet, despite the reassuring attitude of the king, Fox's last months in office were a saddening experience. In many ways he found himself just as much a prisoner of circumstances as Pitt had been, and he was unable to turn his longing for peace into a negotiated settlement. Fox had always been an advocate of a limited war and a negotiated peace. But however attractive his principles were, it was impossible for him to win the final satisfaction of bringing the war to an honourable conclusion. Despite the abolition of the slave trade Fox's last spell at the foreign office was disillusioning and disheartening. After so many years of political escapism he had to grapple with cruel realities which called for more than rhetoric to restore peace and sanity to a ravaged Europe.

10 The Last Endeavour

Lord Grenville headed a powerful and able administration. Fox at the foreign office, Grey at the admiralty, Fitzwilliam as president of the council, Erskine as lord chancellor, and Sheridan as treasurer of the navy: the wounds of the 1790s had been largely healed, and Fox and his friends could be pardoned for assuming that their tenure of office was assured. If they could not contemplate as long a ministry as that headed by their late rival from 1783 onwards, they had the comfort of knowing that the prince of Wales was their patron, so that when the king died they could expect the familiar reversionary interest to work in their favour. If they could get a decent peace they could look forward to a long and stable ministry, and a good peace would gain them not merely the plaudits of a grateful people but a gratified sense of having been right throughout the long years of war.

But behind this promising facade there were weaknesses. Grenville was morose and gloomy; the return to power brought him no joy. He complained of the burdens of office and he believed the prospects for peace were poor. Looking back on his own experiences at the foreign office in the 1790s he was less sanguine than many of his colleagues about the chances of pulling off an acceptable peace. George III was suspicious of the French. He regarded them as an immoral and unprincipled nation, and he was inclined to think his ministers (or the more pacific of them) naïvely optimistic. Although Fox was eager to try for a peace settlement the pace was initially made by the Russians, and it would seem that throughout the negotiations the French were toying with the British envoys, rather than seriously attempting to devise a just peace treaty. Certainly the French were arrogant in their approach to the peace feelers, interpreting the negotiation in terms of recognition for their dominant military position on the continent, rather than the patient resolution of diplomatic problems and the softening of clashes of interest in order to restore the polity of Europe.

Hopes rose because of Fox's chivalry in warning Napoleon of a con-

spiracy intended to carry out his assassination. A malcontent called Ger-
villiere approached Fox with the suggestion that the best way of bringing
peace to Europe was to murder Napoleon. Fox was appalled at the suggestion, violating as it did every convention of civilised diplomacy. He
ordered the arrest of the would-be assassin and warned Talleyrand,
Napoleon's foreign minister, of what was afoot. Talleyrand replied
warmly, even fulsomely, while Napoleon was full of compliments on the
'principles and honour which have always distinguished Mr Fox'. Possibly Fox thought that this exchange of courtesies, and the proof of his
own high-mindedness, would assist negotiations. It helped to give the
impression that he and Napoleon were on terms of personal rapport,
especially when judged in connexion with exaggerated versions of their
meeting during Fox's visit to Paris during the truce of Amiens. But the
actual conduct of negotiations was dismal and depressing. For Fox it was
a particularly frustrating experience; he was unfortunate both in his
choice of representatives and in the circumstances surrounding the behaviour of the Russians, who at one stage appeared to be eager for peace
on almost any terms.

Napoleon had shocked civilised opinion throughout Europe by keeping
as prisoners those British tourists who had been stranded in France when
the war was resumed. Most civilised countries would have permitted these
civilians to return home, but Napoleon made them the victims of his displeasure. Among the better-off of these internees was Lord Yarmouth, a
nobleman of dubious reputation, with an astonishing capacity for im-
bibing alcohol, and a marked deficiency in anything savouring of tact or
restraint. He was hardly the sort of man to choose for a diplomatic mission
of exceptional delicacy, but the French decided to use him as a pawn in the
power struggle, sending him to England as a sort of emissary, and clearly
expecting that the British government would send him back to Paris as
their accredited representative. Yarmouth was an oaf, but he was on
friendly terms with Talleyrand and perhaps he had cheerfully used the
situation to feather his own nest. There were suggestions that he was
laying in stores of brandy in the hope of a successful termination to the
peace negotiations, and instead of stringently guarding British interests
he was exceptionally receptive to suggestions which Talleyrand cleverly
put into his head about extravagant plans for the compensation of Britain's
allies in the most unlikely places, such as the Ottoman empire, Africa or
Cuba, as the price of what might look dangerously like their betrayal.

The French were not interested in a gentlemanly peace settlement or the
skilful balance of diplomatic forces. Napoleon's empire was entering its
most arrogant and bombastic phase, and although Talleyrand deplored

and distrusted the voracious demands and excessive ambitions of his master he could do nothing to moderate them. So, as Yarmouth plied his trade in a state of baffled bewilderment and occasionally alcoholic amazement, it became apparent that there was little chance of a settlement. Napoleon was wholly indifferent to the claims which Britain's allies had upon her loyalty. He ignored their interests, and whenever there were signs of a reluctance to submit to his wishes he used the tactics of a bully, instructing his negotiators to talk of new armies and more vindictive annexations. Grenville felt that he had been through it all before. He was reminded of the negotiations of 1796 and 1797, and throughout the peace talks he showed a more unyielding front than Fox—the same attitude which Fox had so bitterly denounced ten years before.

Fox had to learn a harsh and painful lesson. Eventually he saw through the deceits and duplicities of the French, but he was especially outraged by the lack of scruple which Napoleon had shown. 'The manner in which the French fly from their word ... disheartens me. ... They are playing a false game; and in that case it would be very imprudent to make any concessions which ... could be thought inconsistent with our honour, or could furnish our allies with a plausible pretence for suspecting, reproaching or deserting us.'[1] Napoleon's refusal to discuss the question of the slave trade until issues of greater importance were settled keenly disappointed Fox, who was hoping that an international agreement could be reached to stamp out the traffic. It also made him feel that the French emperor was deaf to any entreaties except to those which were related to the naked realities of national advantage. The knowledge that the Russians were engaging in fits and starts in independent negotiations with the French added a further complication to a series of diplomatic exchanges which had been dogged by confusions and misunderstandings from the start. And all the while Fox's health was failing. Despite what the doctors advised he stuck to his post as long as he could, perhaps because he still believed that he could achieve more than the more formal and severe Grenville. Yet it was Fox, not Grenville, who was guilty of clinging to illusions during the negotiations; Grenville had lost his years before, and his part in the negotiations of 1806 was marked by a greater diplomatic professionalism than that displayed by Fox.

At the same time Fox was realising the error of allowing Yarmouth to act as the principal British envoy. He was a man totally devoid of any of the skills of a diplomatist, and Grenville's choice of Lauderdale as an additional negotiator was scarcely more fortunate. Had Fox not been ill his nephew, Lord Holland, would probably have been sent to Paris, but it was felt that his place was beside Fox. Lauderdale was clumsy and tact-

less; he found it difficult to communicate with his French opposite numbers, whether in their own language or his native tongue, and he had no
appreciation of the finer sophistications of diplomacy. He and Yarmouth
were an ill-assorted pair, more inclined to quarrel than to agree about the
best means of discharging their responsibilities. Fox had hoped that the
French would negotiate on the basis of each side keeping the territories it
held, but he realised that Napoleon had plans which rendered this impossible. Although it is often said that if Fox had lived the chances for
peace would have been greater it is difficult to see any evidence to substantiate this assertion, which was originally put out by the French themselves, for their own convenience, after Fox had died. A few words of
dubious tribute from Napoleon hardly justify the conclusion that Fox's
death robbed the country of a just and popular peace. Fox himself was
disillusioned before his death, and even while the negotiations had been
thought promising there was much hesitation among the English government about rushing into peace on any terms. If the French were supreme
on land the British were supreme at sea, and this statement was itself a
reminder that too much could be given up for the sake of a treaty. Men
remembered Amiens, and regretted it, yet it had been popular at the time.
However difficult it was to see how the struggle against Napoleon could
be carried on if Russia made peace it was nevertheless felt that it would be
foolish to give up the advantages which had been gained at sea without
securing some real concessions from the French in return. When it became
clear that the Russians were not going to make a separate peace, and when
the French attitude was one of mingled arrogance and deception, the
British thought it better to wait and see how the war developed between
Russia and France and whether or not war broke out between Prussia
and France before committing the decisive and humiliating step of accepting Napoleon's harsh peace terms.

Yet the personal tragedy for Fox was very real. Like others he had
thought of a peace as in some ways magically depriving Napoleon of his
greatest asset, his ability to wage total war with overwhelming speed and
success, and if he had successfully negotiated a peace it would have
crowned his career, justifying his past and guaranteeing his future. But
despite the intensity with which he yearned for peace there were principles
which he was not prepared to abandon. He could not betray Britain's
allies and yield to every French demand merely to end the war. As the
negotiations dragged on his attitude stiffened. Alerted by French duplicity and the extremism of Napoleon's demands he was taking a tougher
line when illness forced him to hand over the conduct of affairs to Grenville. Much as Fox believed in the principle of carrying on negotiations

even in time of war he did not think that this condoned the senseless exchange of insincere promises, linked with suggestions of new aggressions and innuendos of further annexations. The sad truth was that as long as Napoleon was confident of his ability to defeat any of his European enemies in the field, whether singly or in alliance, he was not disposed to moderate his demands in any way. With each victory he piled on the necessity for new territories with which to augment his empire, reward his marshals or his family, and establish new spheres of influence where, in the guise of semi-independent confederations, he could set up a convenient ring of puppet states. Talleyrand perceived that the diplomacy of extremism would overreach itself, but few could see how French power could be defeated in war or contained in negotiation.

The English view that unless the conditions for a satisfactory peace existed there was no alternative but to carry on the war, as long as some possibility of doing so was available, was regarded as another instance of mulish English obstinacy. But, though at first it could be mistaken for a crude neglect of diplomacy, it was eventually justified by events. Whether Fox would have embraced this attitude had he lived is questionable, to say the least. It was an attitude which Grenville was fully committed to, and for which he had been harshly criticised by Fox in the past. Fox would probably have always advocated taking any opportunity for negotiation in the hope of coming to terms with the enemy, but after the failure of the Yarmouth-Lauderdale negotiation he would have been tougher and less open in his attitude, more suspicious of French demands, more mistrustful of their good faith, and more cautious about committing himself to any optimistic assumptions in his dealings with Napoleon. Fox found it costly to forgive treachery. Anything savouring of the sophistical exercise of Machiavellian expertise offended him. He thought honesty indispensable to any successful diplomacy, even when this entailed admitting a direct clash of interests between the parties. His dislike for Shelburne and his bitterness towards Pitt stemmed from his conviction that he had been the victim of dubious political subtlety. Possibly he would have retained a similar distrust for Napoleon after 1806; even the resourceful and courteous Talleyrand, who carried the elegance of the *ancien régime* into the parvenu emperor's court, had shown himself capable of the shabbiest tricks. The sheer effrontery of Napoleon's pretensions was something which a man schooled, as Fox was, in traditional eighteenth-century diplomacy, with its fondness for understatement and the art of the possible, found it almost impossible to appreciate. It was depressing to realise that the French emperor did not accept the familiar rules of the game, and that he was indifferent—even contemptuous—of the civilising

notion of a concert of European nations, and the idea that however legitimate it was to jockey for a position of advantage within the diplomatic
framework, it was unthinkable to throw the whole balance of the international mechanism out of order by making outrageous and extravagant
demands. With every victory Napoleon's arrogance became more inflamed, and much as Fox longed for an end to the war he recognised that
this virtually ruled out the chances of anything like an intelligent settlement.

But if Fox's attempt at negotiating a peace was a failure his short spell in
office was blessed by one achievement, the abolition of the slave trade. It
was appropriate that he should be a member of the administration which
made abolition possible. He had been a faithful and consistent supporter
of the principle of abolition, when many powerful voices had contented
themselves with propounding controlling the trade, and he had hoped that
even Napoleon would respond to the British initiative for effective international action to outlaw the trade. Opinion in Britain had gradually
moved forward to favour outright abolition. The division between the
gradualist and the immediate abolitionist now meant much less than it had
twenty years before. As Fox stated in his speech in the house of commons
on 10 June 1806, the fact that the gradualists had once wanted to fix on
1800 as the date for final abolition seemed to have made them abolitionists
too. Six years had passed since that date; the time for action had surely
arrived.

This was more than a skilful debating point. It was a fitting gesture of
conciliation and cooperation; in the Indian summer of his political career
Fox was more concerned to heal old feuds than to rend them afresh. He
wanted the abolition of the slave trade to be carried with the minimum of
bitterness, and in the midst of disappointment over the peace negotiations
with France, it was heartening to feel that the cause of liberty was being
forwarded in one area of human conduct, on the initiative of the country
which was claiming to be defending freedom. The speech on the slave
trade was not, strictly speaking, Fox's last in the house of commons; he
made several appearances in the house afterwards and spoke briefly on a
handful of occasions. But it was his last major pronouncement and when
the struggles of the past were remembered it was a fitting culmination
to a lifetime's endeavour to root out a contemporary abuse. Fox's humanitarianism was seen at its best over the slave trade. Here he was immune
from any charge of political calculation or self-seeking, and it was one
issue on which his generous spirit was able to escape from the trammels
of controversy and the stifling pressures of office. So much of his final
spell in office was overshadowed by his failure to procure peace with

France that it was a happy break in the clouds to find, at long last, that the commons had accepted the wisdom and the expediency of abolishing the traffic in human lives.

But there were other worries which soon distressed Fox, his wife, and their friends. Even before Pitt had died Fox had been unwell, and he had suspected that his usually robust health was giving way. He began to rise later in the morning, and after dinner he came into the habit of taking a rest. His friends saw a change in his appearance with concern and then with consternation. There were times when Fox confided that he wondered whether he had long to live. In December 1805 he was confined to his bed for several days, his legs swelling in a disturbing fashion. For many years he had rarely called in a doctor, priding himself on his ability to prescribe his own medicines. He shared the contemporary belief in laxatives and purgatives. Rhubarb and vegetable decoctions were his favourite medicines, and he once told Trotter that the best purgative was 'fruit with thin skins, currants, raspberries'. But soon he found it necessary to call in a doctor; despite his anxieties about his health he did not realise at first that he was suffering from dropsy. His slowness in recognising his disease helped to aggravate it.

Nevertheless the bustle and excitement of forming a new administration, the novelty of office after so long an interval, and the prospect of terminating the war made him forget his physical ailments. He shrugged off his weakness as a distraction from more important activities. Perhaps he hoped that by throwing himself unrestrainedly into his new duties he would recover his old vigour. Only his friends knew of his private discomforts and worries. To some of them he confessed his innermost fears. 'Pitt', he said, 'has died in January, perhaps I may go off in June.' Probably he said it half in jest, a weary humour pervading the remark, but those who heard it recalled it when his illness took a serious turn, and they saw in it the prescience of a dying man.

In the early months of 1806 Fox lost his appetite, suffered from persistent attacks of exhaustion, and watched his legs swell once more. But in May he threw off his tiredness and recovered much of his former energy. A doctor saw little cause for anxiety in what Fox told him of his symptoms. The recovery was brief; by the end of June he was ill again, and this time there was no disguising the seriousness of his situation. Dropsy was diagnosed and when all medicines failed the physicians resorted to the painful operation of tapping. On 7 August about five gallons of water were taken from Fox, and one contemporary account of Fox's final illness gave plenty of circumstantial detail:

The water followed the stab with great violence; it was very fetid and discoloured, and as it were a mass of blood, which, on being exposed to the air coagulated within half an hour. The weakness immediately consequent was such as to excite a general alarm that he could not long survive it. He was for a long time speechless, and this at a moment when the newspapers of the day announced 'that he was in most excellent spirits'.... In spirits indeed! He was prostrate on the bed, and with scarcely any appearance of life. His eye was half-closed, and the light of life, as it were, extinguished.[2]

For four days he was critically ill, but there was then some improvement. He appeared to gain both strength and spirit. He entertained a few friends at breakfast and showed something of his old enthusiasm for conversation. But he never lost a mood of deeper seriousness. One discussion of plans for Christmas led Fox to affirm his belief in the immortality of the soul; when he went on to say that he would know the facts of the matter by Christmas Mrs Fox broke down, but Fox reassured her, 'I am happy and full of confidence, I may say of certainty'.

Throughout his last illness Fox behaved with great courage and stoical fortitude. He faced death calmly, and what was perhaps more testing he endured the pain and discomfort of illness without complaint. Tapping brought only temporary relief; the swelling returned. On 22 and 23 August Fox could not pass urine and on 25 August his doctors told him that another tapping operation was necessary. Fox consented, and in the hope of mollifying his wish to be taken if possible to his favourite house at St Anne's Hill he was moved to Chiswick on 27 August. But his condition was too poorly for him to complete the journey. He was tapped again, and his general debility compelled the doctors to defer completing the tapping from Sunday to Wednesday. For two days there was slight improvement, but after that nothing could disguise the deterioration in Fox's condition. He had no illusions. When he was told that he might not live another twenty-four hours he replied, 'God's will be done! I have lived long enough, and shall die happy.'

On Friday 12 September he was so weak that Mrs Fox expected every moment to be the last. He did his best to comfort his wife and friends, telling them that death was in the course of nature, that he died happy, that there was no cause for despair and that he pitied them for their grief and sorrow. But by the afternoon of Saturday 13 September it was impossible to make out what he was saying, and when Mrs Fox tried to grasp what he was trying to tell her he could only comment, 'It don't signify my dearest, dearest Liz'. At three o'clock in the afternoon he looked slowly round the room, gazed steadily and lovingly at Lord Holland and Mrs Fox, and then closed his eyes. At twenty minutes to six he died.

On 10 October he was buried in Westminster Abbey, and Elizabeth Fox saw her angel carried to his last worldly home.

Fox's private life and public career mirrored the assumptions and indulgences of his age and his political outlook and behaviour can be understood only in eighteenth-century terms. Despite the legend of Fox as a liberal he was essentially a man of his time. His advocacy of parliamentary reform sprang from traditional beliefs and conventional ideas about mixed government and a balanced constitution. His attitude towards democracy was ambivalent even when he spoke on behalf of household suffrage in 1797; for most of his life he rejected the principles of democracy. Victorian apologists presented him as the darling of the radicals, but he was a man of the people only in a very restricted sense and by the end of his career radicals such as Cobbett were dubious of Fox's reformist credentials. To many advanced democrats he was too fond of defending the privileges of the house of commons and the need to preserve the balance of the constitution. Furthermore, despite all his efforts for peace, his last spell in office demonstrated beyond all reasonable doubt that he was capable of making the usual compromises involved in parliamentary politics, compromises which emphasized the extent to which he was committed to the traditional system. He was willing to damp down demands for catholic relief, and by the time the ministry of all the talents was formed his advocacy of parliamentary reform amounted to little more than the repetition of familiar platitudes, with very little indication that he wished to press the matter on his more reluctant colleagues. The coalition with the Grenvillites invoked memories of the coalition with North, at least so far as popular radicals were concerned, for the staunch opposition of the Grenvillites to parliamentary reform was as well known as their obdurate hostility towards Napoleon. The spectacle of Fox speaking in the commons in support of a bill permitting Lord Grenville to retain a sinecure office as well as being first lord of the treasury was one which roused radical anger, and which inspired suspicions that Fox was no more than an opportunist after all. Men still remembered his defence of civil liberties in the dark days of the revolutionary war, but radicals were aware that, whatever his virtues, he was not one of themselves. Nor had he ever claimed to be. He occasionally supported extra-parliamentary agitation, but he believed that the crucial stage for political activity was the house of commons, and in this assumption he never wavered.

Throughout his life he believed in political and religious liberty, but he understood these conceptions in traditional contexts, with the revolution settlement of 1689 as the foundation for all his thinking and his practice. In so far as his history of the reign of James II had a serious purpose, it was to vindicate the whig revolution, and to try to draw out the lessons of history as a proof of the justice and liberality of whig ideals. He worked hard at his history, but although he collected much material he found it hard to shape it satisfactorily; he was a debater, not a writer, and as a serious exercise the book was a failure. Just as his political ideas were essentially those which the eighteenth-century took for granted, so he spoke to precise political situations, allowing the practicalities of political activity and the complexities of negotiation to direct his thoughts; his ideology was an afterthought, a comment on his actions, rather than a considered and cogent doctrine of political beliefs. He always affirmed that abstract speculation was repugnant to him and that he had little taste for it, and on this issue his judgment was sound.

His innovations in constitutional theory, therefore, were the results of the stresses and strains of politics, not the reasoned solutions of an intellectual trying to formulate a new political system. He advocated party, because it seemed to hold out the promise of checking the influence of the crown. He supported a greater degree of collective responsibility within the cabinet, and a larger say by the members of the cabinet in the choice of a head of ministry, because these suggestions seemed to be the most efficacious means of outwitting and defeating George III. He defended a formed parliamentary opposition because this appeared to be one way of procuring a complete change of ministry and a surer hold on power. Yet he had no wish to democratise English politics or to diminish the independence of ministers and the dominant role of the house of commons. To subordinate the commons to the electorate was abhorrent to him, and to the end of his life parliamentary reform was much more a matter of redistribution and purification than of broad extensions of the franchise. He always claimed that he was seriously interested in the preservation of the truly aristocratic element in English government, despite the way in which his critics denounced him as a democrat, and he was sincere in making this assertion.

In practical politics he did much to familiarise the younger whigs with the practice of party, but it was characteristic that he was less interested in the daily routine of organisation than in the struggle within the house of commons. Broad and general principles appealed to him more than the cultivation of relevant sectional groups, yet modern historians have stressed the significance of organisation in the development of party, correcting, so they believe, the traditional emphasis on ideology—that traditional type of historiography which laid too much weight on Burke's definition of party and Fox's advocacy of a formed opposition. Whenever circumstances called for it Fox dropped his new theories for old-fashioned practice. His dependence on the prince of Wales and the reversionary interest had disastrous effects on the opposition during the regency crisis of 1788, and possibly he was so eager to come to an agreement with Grenville during Pitt's second ministry that he can be accused of giving much more to his conservative allies than his previous attitudes ought to have warranted. In any event, Fox's whig party was more like a group of friends than a formal political organisation. Its efficacy depended on trust, the sort of unthinking confidence which springs from intimacy and affection. This was one reason why the break-up over the French revolution and the French war was so agonising. But it would be false to see too much identity of viewpoint among Fox, Burke, Portland and Fitzwilliam even before the French storm broke. The truth of the matter was that on one set of issues they were in agreement: the American controversy and the alleged dangers to the constitution from the influence of the crown. On parliamentary reform, catholic relief, and law and order there had always been a definite divergence of attitudes. It was therefore natural that when Fox sought to demonstrate the consistency of his career he should refer to the struggle against the policy of coercion in America, and to the primary urgency of confining the influence of the crown. This theme, more than any other, recurred throughout most of his career. But it was one which was becoming more irrelevant as time went on, and it had always depended on assertion, rather than argument, even in its heyday, for research has emphatically exposed the inaccuracy of the accusations which were directed against George III as a sinister intriguing figure, bent on the corruption of the house of commons.

Fox did not understand the French revolution. He saw it too much as a reflection of the English and American revolutions and this led him to make many false analogies between wholly different situations. Yet it is worth noting that one of his chief justifications of the French revolution was that it was a good stout blow at the influence of the crown, a comment which reveals both the extent of his ignorance and the agility with which he applied the wrong criteria in assessing the French situation. His devotion to liberty was real enough, but it was vague and generalised, and his desire to take comfort in the French situation for the disappointments of domestic politics led him sadly astray. Where he was at his best during the revolutionary war he was at his most traditional. His defence of limited war and the theory of permanent negotiation, even during hostilities, was a superb statement, in circumstances of great political difficulty, of the conventional eighteenth-century notion of the nature and functions of diplomacy. It was unfortunate that the ideological element in the French war rendered the traditional standards of judgment inopportune. The excruciating experience of 1806 was a tardy but tragic lesson.

Thus Fox was deficient in his understanding of the French revolution, just as previously he had had no answer to the constitutional issues raised by the American dispute, whatever the political merits of the policies which he advocated in the commons. For too long Fox was credited with an insight into events in France, apparently to the discomfiture of Pitt. But Fox's attitude towards the French changed with each piece of news which came over from Paris, and though he always claimed that the principles of 1789 were those of 1689, he never forgave the French for being unworthy practitioners of the faith they claimed to hold. The exigencies of English politics—far more than French ideals or events in Paris—determined Fox's response to the crisis of the 1790s. He drew false parallels with the American war, and paid the penalty of political frustration. There was a personal, even a perverse, element in his behaviour, almost a determination to oppose Pitt whatever the consequences. Fitzwilliam had commented on this aspect of Fox's conduct in 1792: 'I have seen Charles Fox ... I by no means like him.' And there was a mulish obstinacy in Fox's response to a situation which called for the most subtle political craft if it was to be surmounted without serious consequences for the whig party. It contributed little to swear that there was no motion or address which Pitt might introduce which he would not divide the house of commons upon. Fox was dominated by memories of 1783, and he could not accept the necessity of serving under Pitt, whatever he said about his willingness to serve with him. He ignored the generosity with which Pitt was prepared to treat the whigs, if they joined the administration. If antagonism to the influence of the crown was the most persistent of Fox's political attitudes, a distrust of Pitt, and an inability to forget or forgive Pitt's triumph in 1783-4, kept it company. Perhaps this, more than anything else, helped to explain Fox's failure in the 1790s to discriminate between various aspects of government policy, leading him to take up a much less subtle stance than the much abused Sheridan over such matters as recruitment to the navy and the defence of the realm.

In economic and financial matters Fox was hopelessly out of date. He had little interest in commercial problems, and he had no sympathy for Pitt's preoccupation with them. His attitude to Pitt's customs reforms, and to his attempt to introduce free trade with Ireland, was obscurantist and wilfully partisan, while his denunciation of the Eden treaty with France allowed Pitt adroitly to reveal his ignorance and prejudice. In this important aspect of government Fox was not only not ahead of his time, but positively behind it. In fiscal and commercial policy it was Pitt who looked ahead to the age of Peel and Gladstone, not Fox.

Yet, fanciful though the mythology propagated at Holland House was, it was accurate in three significant ways. It projected Fox as an advocate of peace, a supporter of parliamentary reform, and a defender of civil and religious liberties. However seriously Fox's record must be criticised, and however much the traditional element in his thinking must be emphasized, these causes did mark a significant measure of continuity between the party of Fox and the party of Grey. It is appropriate that historians have so convincingly shown the importance of conservative objectives and traditional concepts in explaining the motivation of the whigs at the time of the passing of the first reform bill. Although Fox was able to mute any of these themes whenever the needs of practical politics demanded it, they do give a certain cogency to his career. Far from being justified as a prophet of liberalism or nationalism, far from standing forth as the first exponent of some sort of Cobdenite internationalism, Fox really represents one aspect of the great tradition of English whiggery. Far from anticipating the future he represents the culmination of an important tradition in English political development. His faults and his strengths are those of a whig, and the true meaning of his ideas and the most convincing explanation of his behaviour can be ascertained only in the context of late eighteenth-century politics, when the house of commons still retained its independence of both crown and people, and when popular movements were no more than ancillary to the rivalries engendered by parliamentary circumstances. Party for Fox meant a parliamentary group, not a national movement, and opposition was a means of gaining greater consistency of support in the commons, not a vehicle for a radical programme or a revolutionary creed.

The greatest irony of all was that Fox's gifts suited him for office. He needed the routine and the responsibilities of office to discipline his waywardness and to compel him to cast off his innate tendency to indolence. The tragedy was that because of several crucial misjudgments—and the obstinacy with which he refused to recognise that he had made grave errors in assessing the political balance of forces—he spent most of his career in opposition. Had he accepted the need to serve under Pitt, had he been prepared to admit his own share of responsibility for the frustrations of his public life, then he might well have proved what may reasonably be suspected, that he had it in him to be a great foreign secretary,

438   *The Last Endeavour*

the disappointments of the 1806 negotiations notwithstanding. The further irony is that had he been in office in 1789 he would, in all probability, have followed the same policy as Pitt: neutrality. And like Pitt, despite his reluctance to become involved in the ideological turmoil inspired by Burke, he would have found himself ineluctably dragged into the conflict, at the expense of his desire for peace and reform. For Fox, even the tributes earned by his defence of civil liberties in the revolutionary war, would have been cheerfully exchanged for the trials and opportunities of power. He was no nineteenth-century visionary; he was an eighteenth-century whig, whose great gifts were vitiated by grave mistakes at decisive moments, and whose private qualities could not compensate for the disastrous eruption of immaturity at times of crisis and tension. He would willingly have given up all the plaudits of Victorian apologists for five years at the foreign office, but he could never confess his own part in bringing about his discomfiture. The tragic frustration of his life, the sense of greatness dissipated and tremendous potentialities unrealised, reflected his own deficiencies of character. He paid a high price for folly and misjudgment, for impatience and restless ambition. His career is a demonstration of the truth that the most brilliant and most versatile talents are no guarantee of success in politics, and a reminder that no amount of posthumous adulation can compensate for frustration and failure. Fox's career illuminates the nooks and crannies of eighteenth-century politics, revealing the interplay between ideas and realities, and demonstrating the close inter-relationship between the political conventions of an age and the way in which they influence the attempts of gifted and fallible mortals to breathe life into the traditions and practices of a particular mode of political behaviour.

References

Abbreviations used in References

Add. MSS   Additional Manuscripts, British Museum (Fox Papers and Holland House Papers)

Speeches   *Speeches of the Right Honourable Charles James Fox in the House of Commons* 6 volumes, London 1815

M&C   *Memorials and Correspondence of Charles James Fox,* edited by Lord John Russell, London 1853-7

PH   *Parliamentary History* (ed. Cobbett)

1 *The Young Tory (pages 9-53)*

1 John Drinkwater, *Charles James Fox* (1928) 335-6
2 Lord John Russell, *The Life and Times of Charles James Fox* (1859-66) I 18
3 Edward Lascelles, *The Life of Charles James Fox* (1936) 19
4 M&C I 22
5 M&C I 41
6 Add. MSS 47580 f3
7 Add. MSS 47580 f4
8 M&C I 54
9 Speeches I 4
10 Speeches I 5-6
11 M&C I 85
12 Speeches I 18-19
13 Speeches I 13-14
14 Speeches I 14

2 *The Champion of America (pages 54-127)*

1 C. Grant Robertson *Select Statutes, Cases, and Documents 1660-1832* (1925) 245
2 *Correspondence of Edmund Burke* (ed. L. Sutherland 1960) II 516
3 Speeches I 17

4 Speeches I 28
5 Speeches I 42
6 M&C I 140
7 M&C I 143
8 Speeches I 93-4
9 M&C I 147
10 M&C I 169
11 *Correspondence of Edmund Burke* III (ed. G. Guttridge 1961) 384
12 Ibid.
13 M&C I 169-70
14 M&C 171
15 M&C 200
16 Speeches I 237
17 M&C I 207-8
18 M&C I 210
19 M&C I 216
20 The fullest text of Fox's speech on this occasion is *The Speech of the Hon. Charles James Fox delivered at Westminster on Wednesday February 2 1780* (London n.d.)
21 Speeches I 227-8
22 Speeches I 245
23 *Correspondence of Edmund Burke* IV (ed. J. A. Woods 1963) 282-3
24 Speeches I 413-5
25 Speeches I 397-8
26 M&C I 268
27 Speeches I 427
28 Speeches I 428
29 Add. MSS 47570 f170
30 Add. MSS 47570 f175
31 15 January 1797 Add. MSS 47569 f73
32 Add. MSS 47570 f187

3 *The Breach with Shelburne (pages 128-159)*

1 M&C I 315-6
2 28 April 1782 M&C I 316
3 Add. MSS 47559 f19
4 Add. MSS 47559 f22
5 M&C I 352
6 M&C I 355
7 M&C I 368-9
8 M&C I 370
9 M&C I 379
10 M&C I 399
11 M&C I 407

12 M&C I 410
13 M&C I 412
14 Speeches II 60-7
15 Speeches II 75
16 Speeches II 82-3
17 Speeches II 83
18 PH XXIII 191
19 M&C I 460-1

4 *The Coalition with North (pages 160-188)*

1 Speeches II 122-3
2 Speeches II 123
3 February 22 1783; M&C II 20
4 M&C II 114
5 M&C II 115
6 M&C II 116-7
7 Speeches II 197
8 M&C II 218
9 M&C II 219-20
10 *The Works of Edmund Burke* (Bohn edition 1882) II 246-7
11 Speeches II 238
12 Speeches II 257
13 Speeches II 258
14 M&C II 220-21

5 *The Triumph of William Pitt (pages 189-213)*

1 Speeches II 278
2 Speeches II 345
3 Speeches II 346
4 Speeches II 346
5 Speeches II 352
6 Add. MSS 47561 f64
7 Speeches II 417
8 Speeches II 419
9 *Anecdotes of the Life of Richard Watson, Bishop of Llandaff* (1817) 128
10 M&C II 269
11 PH XXIV 928

6 *The Peacetime Opposition (pages 214-292)*

1 Add. MSS 47561 ff81-2
2 M&C II 278-83
3 Prince of Wales to Fox 11 December 1785, M&C II 283-4

4 Speeches III 147-51
5 Speeches III 78
6 Add. MSS 47570 f171
7 M&C II 273
8 Speeches III 254-5
9 Speeches III 258
10 Add. MSS 47568 ff235-7
11 Speeches III 273
12 Speeches III 278
13 Speeches III 317
14 Speeches IV 3
15 Speeches IV 4
16 Speeches IV 5
17 Speeches IV 7
18 Speeches IV 10
19 Speeches IV 57
20 Speeches IV 15
21 Speeches IV 16
22 M&C II 362
23 Add. MSS 47570 f182
24 Speeches III 331
25 Speeches III 333
26 Speeches III 336
27 Speeches III 337
28 Speeches IV 89
29 Speeches IV 90
30 Lord Campbell, *Lives of the Lord Chancellors of England* (1846) VI 199-200
31 PH XXVII 704-5
32 PH XXVII 706
33 PH XXVII 709-10
34 *Memoirs of the Courts and Cabinets of George III* (ed. Buckingham) (1853) II 64
35 PH XXVII 718-9
36 Add. MSS 47570 ff180-1
37 Lord Campbell, *op. cit.* VI 206
38 *Grey Papers* (Prior's Kitchen, Durham) Box 70
39 PH XXVII 1034
40 Speeches IV 174
41 Speeches IV 176
42 Speeches IV 178
43 Speeches IV 195-6
44 Speeches IV 198-9
45 Speeches IV 279

7 *The impact of the French Revolution* (*pages 293-357*)

1 Speeches IV 34
2 Speeches IV 51-2
3 Speeches IV 53
4 Speeches IV 221
5 Speeches IV 228
6 Speeches IV 230-31
7 Speeches IV 232
8 Speeches IV 235-6
9 Speeches IV 296
10 Speeches IV 297
11 Speeches IV 264-5
12 Speeches IV 440
13 Northampton Record Office Box 44 No. 9, ff1-5; printed in F. O'Gorman, *The Whig Party and the French Revolution* (1967) 80
14 Add. MSS 47571 f11
15 Add. MSS 47571 f13
16 Add. MSS 47571 ff113-4
17 Add. MSS 47571 f116
18 Add. MSS 47570 f191
19 Add. MSS 47571 ff18-19
20 Add. MSS 47580 f145
21 Add. MSS 47571 f28-9
22 Add. MSS 47571 ff42-3
23 Add. MSS 47571 f144
24 Add. MSS 47572 f82
25 M&C III 257-8
26 M&C III 259
27 M&C II 262
28 Speeches IV 446
29 Speeches IV 461
30 Speeches V 2-3
31 Russell, *Life and Times of Charles James Fox* II 322
32 Speeches V 7-10
33 Speeches V 211
34 Speeches V 282; 17 May 1794
35 Speeches V 289
36 M&C III 63 4
37 Add. MSS 47571 ff106-7
38 Add. MSS 47571 f143
39 Add. MSS 47571 f144

8 *The War with Revolutionary France (pages 358-381)*

1 Speeches IV 474
2 Speeches V 18
3 Speeches V 24
4 Speeches V 28
5 Speeches V 39-40
6 Speeches V 45-6
7 Add. MSS 47572 ff199-200
8 Add. MSS 47564 f28
9 *Speeches of Charles James Fox During the French Revolution* (ed. Cooper Willis, 1924) 379

9 *The Addington Ministry and Pitt's Final Years (pages 382-424)*

1 Fox to Lauderdale 19 February 1801 Add. MSS 47564 ff81-2
2 Add. MSS 47574 f174
3 *Speeches of Charles James Fox During the French Revolution* 414
4 Add. MSS 47564 f95
5 Add. MSS 47564 f108
6 J. B. Trotter, *Memoirs of the Latter Years of the Right Honourable Charles James Fox* (1811) 161
7 Trotter *op. cit* 267
8 Fox to Holland 21 November 1802, Add. MSS 47574 f203
9 Fox to Holland 19 December 1802, Add. MSS 47574 f224
10 Add. MSS 47575 f23
11 Add. MSS 47575 f29
12 Fox to Grey 12 March 1803, M&C III 399
13 Fox to Grey 12 March 1803, M&C III 399-400
14 M&C III 405-7
15 M&C III 410
16 M&C III 428-9
17 M&C IV 19
18 M&C IV 46
19 Add. MSS 47565 ff128-9
20 M&C IV 99
21 Fox to Holland 7 November 1805, M&C IV 121
22 Drinkwater *op. cit.* 378-9
23 H. Twiss, *Public and Private Life of Lord Chancellor Eldon* (1844) I 510

10 *The Last Endeavour (pages 425-438)*

1 Drinkwater *op. cit* 362
2 *Circumstantial Details of the Long Illness and Last Moments of the Right Honourable Charles James Fox* (1806) 67

Bibliographical Note

The chief sources for any study of Charles James Fox's career are the Fox Papers and the Holland House Papers now deposited in the British Museum. Substantial selections from Fox's manuscripts appeared in Lord John Russell, *Memorials and Correspondence of Charles James Fox*, 4 volumes, London 1853-7, and in the same author's *The Life and Times of Charles James Fox*, 3 volumes, London 1859-66, but the editing is arbitrary and sometimes defective. Among older studies of Fox, R. Fell, *Memoirs of the Public Life of the Late Right Honourable Charles James Fox*, London 1808, and J. B. Trotter, *Memoirs of the Latter Years of the Right Honourable Charles James Fox*, London 1811, contain useful information, much of it of an anecdotal character. G. O. Trevelyan, *The Early History of Charles James Fox*, London 1881, is a justly famous book, which is still worth reading despite its emphatic whig bias. J. L. Hammond, *Charles James Fox: a Political Study*, London 1903, is very dated in both approach and content. J. Drinkwater, *Charles James Fox*, London 1928, is a neglected and under-rated book. E. Lascelles, *The Life of Charles James Fox*, Oxford 1936, is a sympathetic account, but it cannot compete in vigour and style with C. Hobhouse, *Fox*, 2nd edition London 1947, which remains the classic among the older lives; although essentially pre-Namierite it is by no means a simple-minded whig version of Fox's career. L. Reid, *Charles James Fox: a Man for the People*, London 1969, is of particular interest because of the author's expert treatment of Fox as an orator and public speaker. Fox's speeches are happily available in *Speeches of the Right Honourable Charles James Fox in the House of Commons*, 6 volumes, London 1815, while his speeches during the war years are published in volume No. 759 of the Everyman Library series.

To make suggestions concerning general reading in the period covered by Fox's public life is to embark on a daunting task: the reader can easily be overcome by the sheer volume of material available. But the following books indicate the main lines of approach to a highly complex era. R. J. White, *The Age of George III*, London 1968, provides a lucid, elegant and thoughtful introduction to the period as a whole, in which shrewd comment is skilfully mingled with narrative and analysis. Among modern text books three are of particular merit: D. Marshall, *Eighteenth-Century England*, London 1966; J.

Steven Watson, *The Reign of George III*, Oxford 1960; and A. Briggs, *The Age of Improvement*, London 1959. The classic account of the constitutional aspects involved in the political conflicts of the reign is R. Pares, *King George III and the Politicians*, Oxford 1964. Sir Lewis Namier's books are indispensable to any serious student of the eighteenth century: *The Structure of Politics at the Accession of George III*, 2nd edition, London 1957; *England in the Age of the American Revolution*, 2nd edition, London 1957; *Crossroads of Power*, London 1962. For politics during the earlier years of George III's reign the following are recommended: G. Rudé, *Wilkes and Liberty*, Oxford 1962; I. R. Christie, *Wilkes, Wyvill and Reform*, London 1962; J. Brooke, *The Chatham Administration*, London 1956; H. Butterfield, *George III, Lord North and the People*, London 1949; S. Maccoby, *English Radicalism 1762-1785*, London 1955; B. Donoughue, *British Politics and the American Revolution*, London 1964; P. Mackesy, *The War for America*, London 1964; I. R. Christie, *The End of North's Ministry*, London 1958. For the later period the following studies are the most useful: J. Cannon, *The Fox-North Coalition*, Cambridge 1969; J. Ehrman, *The Younger Pitt: the Years of Acclaim*, London 1969; D. G. Barnes, *George III and William Pitt 1783-1806*, Stanford 1939; J. W. Derry, *The Regency Crisis and the Whigs*, Cambridge 1963; F. O'Gorman, *The Whig Party and the French Revolution*, London 1967; P. A. Brown, *The French Revolution in English History*, 2nd edition, London 1963; G. S. Veitch, *The Genesis of Parliamentary Reform*, 2nd edition, London 1963; A. Bryant, *Years of Endurance*, London 1942, and *Years of Victory*, London 1944. L. B. Mitchell, *Charles James Fox and the Disintegration of the Whig Party*, Oxford 1971, appeared after this book was completed. This bibliographical summary makes no claim to either comprehensiveness or finality, but those who wish to follow up reading this study of Fox by reading more widely in the period for themselves will find the principal themes of historical interpretation indicated in the books recommended.

Index

Grenville, William Wyndham—cont. with, 411-7; forms ministry, 425; and negotiations of 1806, 427-8
Grey, Charles, 126, 263, 266, 273, 296, 332, 351, 386, 387, 390, 391, 404, 405, 407, 409, 410, 417, 437; forms Friends of the People, 312, 318
Guilford Courthouse, battle of, 109, 111

Habeas corpus, suspension of, 74, 345, 349
Hammond, J. L., 41
Hanoverians, 24, 55, 58, 248
Hardwicke's marriage act, 35-7
Hardy, Thomas, 346
Harris, Sir James, *see* Malmesbury, Lord
Hastings, Warren, 252-3, 293, 296
Hawkesbury, Lord, 417
Henry VI, King, 19, 144, 261, 270
Herefordshire, 94
Hertford College, Oxford, 16
Holland, Lady, *see* Fox, Lady Caroline
Holland House, 13, 437
Holland, Lord, 48, 50, 52, 320, 323, 327, 352, 355, 376, 391, 396, 400, 401, 419, 427, 433
Homer, 14
Hood, Admiral Lord, 205-7, 209
Horace, 14
Horne Tooke, John, 45, 346
Howe, Sir William, 72
Huntingdonshire, 94

Ilchester, earl of, 11
India, 70, 170, 175-83, 190, 191, 194, 252-3
India bills, *see* East India bills
Ireland, 93, 97, 138-42, 170, 228-34, 275, 383-4

Jacobins, 315, 323, 324, 346, 353, 366
Jacobitism, 23, 39, 78, 244

James II, King, 10, 63, 183, 393, 396, 434
Jebb, Dr John, 94, 99, 104
Joseph II, emperor, 279

Keppel, Admiral, 93, 130, 173
Kew, 276
Kingsgate, 52

Lafayette, 134, 323, 395
Lake, General, 384
Lansdowne, marquis of, *see* Shelburne, earl of
Larochefoucault, 323
Lauderdale, Lord, 377, 386, 390, 412, 427-9
Leeds, duke of, 279-80, 328, 330
Leicester House, 27
Lennox, Lady Caroline, *see* Fox, Lady Caroline
Lennox, Lady Sarah, 12
Leopold II, Emperor, 279
Lexington, battle of, 65
Lincoln, Lord, 106-7
Liverpool, 205, 252
London Corresponding Society, 345
Loughborough, Lord, 31, 33, 168, 172, 262-3, 267, 329-30, 332, 384
Louis XIV, King, 326, 257, 401
Louis XVI, King, 235-6, 257, 283, 303, 310; execution of, 325, 358, 361, 367
Lowther, Sir James, 143
Luther, Martin, 344
Luttrell, Colonel, 31, 33
Lyons, 18

Macartney, Sir George, 17-18
Mack, General, 419
Mackintosh, Sir James, 120, 121, 312
Mahrattas, 156-7, 190
Maitland, Lord, 392
Malmesbury, 106
Malmesbury, Lord, 235, 255, 378
Malta, 398, 400
Manchester, 231, 232